Money, Markets, and Monarchies

Framed by a critical analysis of global capitalism, this book examines how the six states of the Gulf Cooperation Council are powerfully shaping the political economy of the wider Middle East. Through unprecedented and fine-grained empirical research – encompassing sectors such as agribusiness, real estate, finance, retail, telecommunications, and urban utilities – Adam Hanieh lays out the pivotal role of the Gulf in the affairs of other Arab states. This vital but little recognised feature of the Middle East's political economy is essential to understanding contemporary regional dynamics, not least of which is the emergence of significant internal tensions within the Gulf itself.

Bringing fresh insights and a novel interdisciplinary approach to debates across political economy, critical geography, and Middle East studies, this book fills an important gap in how we understand the region and its place in the global order.

ADAM HANIEH is a Reader in Development Studies at the School of Oriental and African Studies (SOAS), University of London. He holds a PhD in political science from York University, Canada, and his research examines the political economy of the Middle East, with a particular focus on the states of the Gulf Cooperation Council. His recent books include *Capitalism and Class in the Gulf Arab States* (2011), *Lineages of Revolt: Issues of Contemporary Capitalism in the Middle East* (2013), and (co-edited with Abdulhadi Khalaf and Omar AlShehabi) *Transit States: Labour, Migration and Citizenship in the Gulf* (2014).

The Global Middle East

The Global Middle East series seeks to broaden and deconstruct the geographical boundaries of the 'Middle East' as a concept to include North Africa, Central and South Asia, and diaspora communities in Western Europe and North America. The series features fresh scholarship that employs theoretically rigorous and innovative methodological frameworks resonating across relevant disciplines in the humanities and the social sciences. In particular, the general editors welcome approaches that focus on mobility, the erosion of nation-state structures, travelling ideas and theories, transcendental techno-politics, the decentralisation of grand narratives, and the dislocation of ideologies inspired by popular movements. The series will also consider translations of works by authors in these regions whose ideas are salient to global scholarly trends but have yet to be introduced to the Anglophone academy.

Other books in the series:

1. *Transnationalism in Iranian Political Thought: The Life and Times of Ahmad Fardid*, Ali Mirsepassi
2. *Psycho-nationalism: Global Thought, Iranian Imaginations*, Arshin Adib-Moghaddam
3. *Iranian Cosmopolitanism: A Cinematic History*, Golbarg Rekabtalaei

Money, Markets, and Monarchies

The Gulf Cooperation Council and the Political Economy of the Contemporary Middle East

Adam Hanieh

School of Oriental and African Studies, University of London

CAMBRIDGE
UNIVERSITY PRESS

University Printing House, Cambridge CB2 8BS, United Kingdom

One Liberty Plaza, 20th Floor, New York, NY 10006, USA

477 Williamstown Road, Port Melbourne, VIC 3207, Australia

314–321, 3rd Floor, Plot 3, Splendor Forum, Jasola District Centre, New Delhi – 110025, India

79 Anson Road, #06–04/06, Singapore 079906

Cambridge University Press is part of the University of Cambridge.

It furthers the University's mission by disseminating knowledge in the pursuit of education, learning, and research at the highest international levels of excellence.

www.cambridge.org
Information on this title: www.cambridge.org/9781108429146
DOI: 10.1017/9781108614443

First published 2018

Printed and bound in Great Britain by Clays Ltd, Elcograf S.p.A.

A catalogue record for this publication is available from the British Library.

Library of Congress Cataloging-in-Publication Data
Names: Hanieh, Adam, 1972- author.
Title: Money, markets, and monarchies : the gulf cooperation council and the political economy of the contemporary middle east / Adam Hanieh, School of Oriental and African Studies, University of London.
Description: 1 Edition. | New York : Cambridge University Press, 2018. | Series: The global Middle East ; 4 | Includes bibliographical references and index.
Identifiers: LCCN 2018010109| ISBN 9781108429146 (Hardback) | ISBN 9781108453158 (Paperback)
Subjects: LCSH: Gulf Cooperation Council. | Persian Gulf Region–Economic integration. | Persian Gulf Region–Economic policy. | Arab cooperation. | Persian Gulf Region–Politics and government–21st century. | BISAC: POLITICAL SCIENCE / Government / International.
Classification: LCC HC415.3 .H365 2018 | DDC 337.1/536–dc23
LC record available at https://lccn.loc.gov/2018010109

ISBN 978-1-108-42914-6 Hardback
ISBN 978-1-108-45315-8 Paperback

Contents

List of Figures — *page* vi
List of Tables — vii
Acknowledgements — ix

1 Framing the Gulf: Space, Scale, and the Global — 1
2 Gulf Financial Surpluses and the International Order — 29
3 Boundaries of State and Capital: Mapping the Gulf's Business Conglomerates — 63
4 From Farm to Shelf: Gulf Agro-Commodity Circuits and the Middle East — 112
5 The Arab Built Environment, Accumulation, and the Gulf — 146
6 Spaces of Financialisation in the Middle East — 174
7 Visions of Capital: The GCC and the 'New Normal' — 199
8 Future Paths and Political Ends — 237

References — 270
Index — 295

Figures

2.1 Foreign reserves: Gulf, China, and Japan (as percentage of total global reserves) *page* 37
2.2 GCC holdings of US Treasury securities, 1974–2015, billions of dollars 41
2.3 GCC net position vis-à-vis the United Kingdom 44
3.1 Sites of accumulation in the Gulf 65
6.1 Financial assets as percentage of total assets for 22 non-financial companies 181

Tables

2.1 Gulf holdings of US long-term securities as a proportion of Chinese and Japanese holdings *page* 42
2.2 UK net external position vis-à-vis GCC states 45
2.3 Value of cross-border mergers and acquisitions and number of deals, 2000–2016, selected countries/regions 50
2.4 Share of world merchandise import value, selected years 53
2.5 Share of World Commercial Services import value, selected years 57
3.1 Gulf capital and Saudi Arabia's eight largest non-SABIC petrochemical firms 70
3.2 GCC raw steel, cement, and related products 74
3.3 Construction and contracting firms 78
3.4 Leading GCC real estate developers 83
3.5 Retail and distribution of consumer commodities 91
3.6 Gulf banking systems and interlocking directorships 104
4.1 Share of country food exports destined for GCC 131
4.2 GCC market share of top three agro-commodity exports for selected countries 132
4.3 GCC involvement in Egyptian agribusiness 136
5.1 Large-scale real estate projects in selected countries, 2008–2017 153
5.2 Listed real estate firms 157
5.3 Country breakdown of power, water, and transport projects 163
5.4 Telecom operators in selected Arab countries, 2017 166
6.1 Selected indicators of financialisation 179
6.2 M&A investments by origin in selected country financial sectors, 2006–2015 187
6.3 GCC-related banks in Arab banking systems 187

7.1 PPPs and privatisation planned or under way 213
7.2 New fiscal measures in the GCC 226
7.3 Change in reported profits of listed firms 231
8.1 IFI engagement with selected Arab countries (2012–2017), loan values, and policy targets 257

Acknowledgements

The motivations for this book lie in my interest in processes of class and state formation across the six Gulf Arab monarchies: Saudi Arabia, the United Arab Emirates, Kuwait, Qatar, Oman, and Bahrain. In some of my earlier work I had begun to tentatively explore the connection between these states and the political economy of the wider Middle East, but it was the massive wave of social protest that erupted in December 2010 that led me to attempt a more systematic conceptualisation of these intra-regional connections. Since that time, the Gulf states have emerged as chief protagonists in the political trajectories of the Middle East; at the same time, the spiralling conflicts across the entire area seem to mark a profound setback to the hopes, dreams, and aspirations that first brought millions onto the streets a few short years ago. All of this confirms the importance of seeing the past in the present. I have tried to keep a sense of these temporalities broadly in view – with the hope that the book may say something useful about how a better future might be reached.

Writing a book can appear as an intensely solitary experience, but I firmly believe that any intellectual endeavour is always a collective project – pushed forward in dialogue with a wide range of diverse interactions, conversations, and debates. I am extremely privileged to work in the Department of Development Studies at the School of Oriental and African Studies (SOAS), where colleagues and students continue to make teaching and research such a pleasure. Many wonderful friends have discussed and debated the ideas in this book, helping in innumerable ways during the writing process and my trips to the region: Ala Jaradat, Alberto Toscano, Alessandra Mezzadri, Ali Cantay, Alfredo Saad-Filho, Ayed Abueqtaish, Brenna Bhandar, Burcu Erciyes, Catherine Cook, Christian Henderson, Dae-oup Chang, Gilbert Achcar, Greg Albo, Hanan Elmasu, Hazem Jamjoum, Laleh Khalili Leandro Vergara-Camus, Lori Allen, Mandy Turner, Mayssun Sukharieh, Mazen Masri, Mostafa Henaway, Nimer Sultany, Omar Shehabi, Paolo Novak, Paula Hevia, Parvathi Raman, Rashmi Varma, Robert Knox, Ryvka Barnard, Sahar Francis, Subir Sinha, Tieneke Dykstra, Yang-Ji Lee. I am particularly indebted to Dale Tomich, Jeffrey Webber, Rafeef Ziadah, Thomas Marois, and Tony Norfield, all of whom generously gave their time to read and critique various parts of the manuscript. I have learnt a lot from all these exchanges – and continued to be inspired by their individual work as scholars across numerous disciplines.

I am also grateful to the *Global Middle East* series editors, Arshin Adib-Moghaddam and Ali Mirsepassi, as well as Maria Marsh and Abigail Walkington at Cambridge University Press, who first showed support for this book and patiently steered it from its initial conception. The continued love given to me by my extended families in Adelaide and Athens – and their understanding of my prolonged absences and preoccupations – has kept me going throughout the entire writing process. Finally, I owe the greatest thanks to Rafeef Ziadah, whose intellectual inspiration and deep friendship made this book possible.

1 Framing the Gulf

Space, Scale, and the Global

Late in the evening of 31 August 2016, a 500-strong delegation of Saudi business leaders and government officials touched down in Tokyo, Japan. Arriving on 13 planes, the visit was led by Saudi Arabia's then-Deputy Crown Prince, Mohammed bin Salman al-Saud, who was scheduled to meet Japanese billionaire Masayoshi Son a few days later. Initially, the trip garnered little attention beyond scant coverage in the Saudi press. Its results, however, were to leave financial commentators worldwide stunned. The two men agreed to establish a $100 billion private equity venture, the SoftBank Vision Fund (SVF), pledging to invest in emerging technologies in order to realise 'a world where humans, devices and the internet are more closely integrated' (Primack 2016). The scale of the fund surpassed anything that the private equity (PE) business had ever seen. It would be the largest fund in history – vastly exceeding the past record of $21.6 billion raised by the PE behemoth Blackstone Group in 2006 – and worth more than all the money raised by the entire US venture capital industry over the preceding 30 months.

The record-breaking nature of this deal is one sign of the role that Saudi Arabia, along with five other members of the Gulf Cooperation Council (GCC)[1] – the United Arab Emirates, Kuwait, Qatar, Oman, and Bahrain – now play in global financial markets. Backed by large surpluses accruing from more than a decade of rising oil prices, Gulf investors, both state and private, have come to control a global asset base worth several trillion dollars. Ranging from banking, industry, technology, and real estate across Western Europe and North America, through to farmland, retail chains, and manufacturing plants in some of the poorest places on the planet, Gulf investments are encountered in virtually all countries and economic sectors. Many well-known international firms – Credit Suisse, Deutsche Bank,

[1] Throughout this book I avoid any claims over a national identity for the Gulf, reflected in the long-standing official disputes over nomenclature such as 'Persian' or 'Arabian' Gulf – I will simply refer to the region as 'the Gulf' and use terms such as Gulf Arab states or Gulf Cooperation Council (GCC) where appropriate.

Barclays, Volkswagen, Glencore, P&O, British Airways, Sainsbury's, and Twitter, to name just a few – now count Gulf investors as major shareholders or controlling owners. London property icons such as Camden Market, Canary Wharf, Harrods, the Shard, New Scotland Yard, and the London Stock Exchange are fully or partially owned by Gulf investors – even the US embassy in the United Kingdom pays rent to a Gulf landlord. And through a little-known acquisition that took place in 2014, a Gulf-based firm became joint owners of HC-One, now the largest operator of nursing and residential homes in the United Kingdom. Moreover, it is not only traditional business activities that have been targeted in this buying spree – some of Europe's most prominent football teams are controlled by individuals and firms based in the Gulf, or emblazon logos of Gulf firms on their uniforms and stadiums (Barcelona, Arsenal, Manchester City, Bayern Munich, and Paris Saint-Germain). Almost a decade ago, investments such as these led the global consultancy firm McKinsey to describe the Gulf as one of the 'new powerbrokers' in the global economy. Since that time, the oil price has crashed and much of the world economy remains mired in stagnation – nonetheless, as the SVF deal indicates, Gulf investments appear to continue apace. Indeed, in 2016, the net value of cross-border mergers and acquisitions made by firms based in the UAE, Saudi Arabia, and Qatar ranked twelfth in the world, coming in just behind net purchases from the United Kingdom (UNCTAD 2017, p. 231).

These cross-border capital flows form just one part of the Gulf's interaction with the global economy. There are, of course, other sides to this relationship. Most importantly are the Gulf's vast reserves of oil and natural gas, which remain critical to transport and industrial production across the planet. By 2014, the Gulf Arab states were responsible for nearly one-quarter of global crude oil and natural gas liquids production, a level that had risen from around one-fifth in 2000.[2] Over the same time frame, the Gulf's share of world exports of these commodities had grown from 27.6% to 32.5%. The circulation of such resources through global production chains – as energy or feedstock for other industries – has made the region, and by association the wider Middle East, a pivotal focus of global politics ever since the transition to an oil-centred world economy in the early twentieth century (Bromley 1991; Vitalis 2007; Hanieh 2011a; Mitchell 2011). They remain essential to understanding contemporary patterns of global capitalism – China's emergence as a major economic power, for instance, is heavily dependent upon oil from the Gulf, which now supplies around one-third of the country's total crude imports.

[2] Figures from International Energy Agency Database.

But the Gulf's involvement in international trade patterns cannot be reduced simply to its oil and gas exports. Today, the Gulf plays an increasingly central role in the worldwide circulation of *all* commodities. Gulf-based firms and the region's aviation and maritime industries are frequently described as 'global super-connectors' – transit routes that link different zones of the world market and integrate production and consumption across the planet. This is true for people as well as for goods. The Gulf now boasts the busiest airport in the world for international passengers – Dubai International Airport, which surpassed London's Heathrow Airport in 2015 (Ulrichsen 2016, p. 151) – as well as Dubai's Jebel Ali, the fourth largest container port in the world. The speed of the region's integration into global trade and supply chains – often lauded in business magazines as evidence for the foresight and outward-oriented vision of the Gulf's rulers – is held up as an exemplary model for other developing countries to follow. Indeed, many of the buzzwords that define the corpus of trade and logistics policymaking today – 'intermodal transport hubs', 'logistics cities', 'integrated free trade zones', and the like – find their preeminent examples in the Gulf.

As the Gulf extends itself globally it has likewise deepened connections to its immediate neighbourhood. Over the last two decades, the Gulf monarchies have taken a distinctive and highly consequential role in the affairs of most Arab countries. As later chapters will show in some detail, capital flows from the Gulf now encompass and dominate key economic sectors across the Middle East – reshaping patterns of ownership and control, and pivoting the centre of gravity of Arab capitalism increasingly around a Gulf axis. From 2003 to 2015, the Gulf was responsible for a remarkable 42.5% of total new (so-called greenfield) foreign direct investment (FDI) across 10 non-Gulf Arab states.[3] Mergers and acquisitions (M&A) figures further illustrate these trends. From 2010 to 2015, European, Gulf, and North American investors spent just over 20 billion euros on M&A in the Arab world – the Gulf's share of this was 45%.[4] At the same time as these economic linkages with the Middle East have

[3] Figures from country information reports, *Arab Investment and Export Credit Guarantee Corporation*, www.iaigc.net/ (in Arabic). Jordan, Egypt, Lebanon, Tunisia, Libya, Iraq, Morocco, Syria, Palestine, and Algeria. As Chapter 2 will show, this does not mean that Gulf investments went *primarily* to the Middle East region (the United States and Europe remained the principal focus). Relatively, however, the Gulf's weight within regional accumulation circuits grew in comparison to historical patterns and other foreign investment sources.

[4] Investment from the European Union (EU) (28), North America, and the GCC, going to Algeria, Egypt, Jordan, Lebanon, Morocco, Palestine, Syria, and Tunisia. Calculated from Zephyr M&A database. Figures include only confirmed M&A deals with known values.

intensified, so has the Gulf's political weight in the region. From the devastating wars in Yemen and Syria to the new governments that have emerged following the Arab uprisings of 2011, the Gulf states are now pivotal to the course of political processes across all Arab countries. The Gulf's political and economic interests increasingly superintend the regional system – one marked by massive polarisation of wealth and power, alongside unprecedented levels of violence, conflict, and mass displacement. Most strikingly, the struggle to contain and direct these regional trajectories has precipitated sharpening tensions between the various Gulf states themselves – and with other regional powers (most notably Iran). These patterns not only hold serious implications for the 'big' issues of Arab politics and economics; they also intensely mould the lived, day-to-day reality of social life for much of the Middle East's population.

All of this suggests that we can learn something about global capitalism and its spatio-temporal dynamics from the vantage point of the Gulf. Yet much contemporary writing on the global economy tends to marginalise the position of the Gulf, either ignoring it completely or viewing it simply as a source of oil or a protagonist in conflict.[5] As a result, the considerable flows of capital, commodities, and labour – both from and through the Gulf – are largely invisible in narratives around the making of the global. This partly reflects a more general geographical blind spot of political economy scholarship, which, as David McNally observes, typically focuses 'on a number of capitalistically developed nations – the US, Germany and Japan – and treat[s] the world-economy as largely an aggregate of these parts' (McNally 2009, p. 43). But even attempts to more fully integrate the role of 'emerging' markets into a global frame usually overlook the Gulf – the concept of 'BRICS', for example, terminologically excludes the Gulf, despite the region's striking parallels with these other rising powers.

One of the goals of this book is to address such theoretical and geographical gaps in approaches to the global. I seek to ask what we can learn about global processes from the perspective of the Gulf Arab states. In investigating this question, I will particularly emphasise the concurrent reworking of the broader Middle East – a regional shift that has been closely implicated in the Gulf's global trajectories. In doing so, I hope to show that approaching the world market in a top-down fashion – simply by focusing on what is going on in its 'commanding heights' – omits something very important about how the world works. Our

[5] Two recent exceptions to this are Chesnais (2016) and Norfield (2016), both of which will be drawn upon in the pages that follow.

understanding of the global must look beyond simply the additive interaction of individual national states – it needs to also incorporate an appreciation of how the *regional* itself is being reshaped as part of the making of the global. This is not only a matter of adding yet another case study to our understanding of global processes; it is about seeing the global *in and through* its relation to the Gulf, viewing the whole as more than just an aggregate sum of supposedly lesser or greater parts. By better understanding the relation between the global and the Gulf – including, most centrally, what this means for the Gulf's wider regional neighbourhood – we reveal something qualitatively new about the whole itself.

For evident reasons, scholarship on the Gulf itself has generally shown a much greater concern with the region's interaction with the global than the more general political economy literature. The Gulf, of course, has been bound up in global processes for many centuries. Situated along important trade routes connecting India, Europe, and East Africa, the region materialised within a complex network of overlapping land and maritime interests that involved British, French, Ottoman, and Persian powers. From the seventeenth century onwards, British colonialism emerged dominant among these respective empires. Utilising a combination of military force and diplomatic treaty-making with individual rulers – hence the name Trucial States given to the sheikhdoms of Southern Arabia – British colonial rule came to rest upon a political apparatus of agents situated across various Gulf port towns (Fattah 1997; Zahlan 1998; Fuccaro 2014). These coastal settlements not only constituted political and administrative centres for British colonialism and the lucrative pearl industry, but also bridged 'cultural and economic exchange between sedentary, agricultural, nomadic and maritime populations', serving as 'the hub of a dynamic regional and cross-regional maritime economy' (Fuccaro 2010, p. 20). The path-breaking research of Nelida Fuccaro has especially emphasised the globally constructed nature of the Gulf at this time, understanding 'the gulf littoral as the site of interconnections between different imperial systems … and as the nodes of different political and strategic frontlines, which demarcated larger areas of imperial influence' (Fuccaro 2014, p. 29). Notions of hybridity and cosmopolitanism are frequently deployed to describe these early Gulf societies – with their large immigrant diasporas, highly mobile workforces, and peripatetic merchants that linked transnational networks across the Gulf, India, and East Africa (Keshavarzian 2016).

By and large, this historical writing has consciously challenged periodisations of the Gulf that posit an overly sharp disjuncture between pre- and post-oil eras, showing instead a deliberate sensitivity to the complicated interplay of global, regional, and local dynamics that were to shape the Gulf's emergence. This approach contrasts with many popular conceptions of the contemporary Gulf, which tend to identify oil and the region's integration into global capitalism as marking a qualitative break with a so-called traditional past. Such binary antimonies, as Ahmed Kanna points out in a recent provocative intervention, accord well with the self-image projected by Gulf rulers, eager to present their models of development as exemplary crystallisations of the 'telos of urban modernity' (Kanna 2016, p. 109). By embracing the imperatives of globalisation, the Gulf not only represents what *should be*; it also stands starkly counterposed to 'the chaos and misery' afflicting other Arab states (p. 106) – an ever-present warning of what a rejection of the global potentially heralds.

Underlying this dominant view of globalisation is an instrumentalisation and reification of the global as a modernising force that exists 'out there', a process that arises externally, encounters the region in some form of pristine and undisturbed state, and then acts to irrevocably change it. Such inside/outside dichotomies ultimately rest upon an ontological division of the global and local as two separate spheres – interconnected, but discrete and spatially distinct. This ontological separation has encouraged a pervasive methodological nationalism in much work on the Gulf (and, indeed, on the Middle East more widely) – an assumption 'of the nation-state as the self-evident container of political, cultural, and economic relations' (Goswami 2002, p. 794). By viewing the global as a process or force existing external to the local, the nation-state is posited as a self-contained and discrete repository of social relations, with analytical attention drawn to the supposedly determinate factors operating inside national borders and the ways that these may shape patterns of interaction with an externally imagined outside. From this methodological starting point, much of the literature on the contemporary Gulf has traditionally sought explanations for the Gulf's developmental trajectory in various supposedly 'unique' internal characteristics: the institutional structures mediating the deployment of oil rents, Islam, authoritarian political regimes, tribal legacies, and the like. Consequently, the Gulf – as two insightful scholars of the region comment – is often treated as a kind of 'constructed exceptionalism' (Thiollet and Vignal 2016, p. 4), singularly distinct from not only other spaces 'in the Arab world, but also in the wider space of economic, cultural and political globalization' (p. 3).

In recent years, this dichotomous view of the local and the global has been challenged by a new generation of work that attempts to theorise the Gulf as a constitutive element to broader patterns of global processes and transnational flows – not apart from, or in reaction to, an externally posited outside. Scholars working on the region have begun to explore how the Gulf exists as a formative part of the global, examining such issues as the position of the GCC in the changing architecture of international power relations and global governance (Ulrichsen 2016; Vignal 2016), the place of Gulf port cities and logistical infrastructure in the circulation of global commodities (Ramos 2010; Cowen 2014; Khalili 2017; Ziadah 2017), the ways in which such global relations are embodied in development models and forms of Gulf urbanism (Kanna 2011; Menoret 2014; Kamrava 2016), and the historical and contemporary significance of transnational flows of labour and diasporas, which have created different kinds of non-state-centric networks between the Gulf, the Indian Ocean, Africa, and elsewhere (Gardner 2010; Alpers 2014; Khalaf et al. 2014; Hopper 2015; Bishara 2016). These and other works embody a common rejection of any exceptionalising frameworks, and also point to the importance of placing an analysis of class, capitalism, and social power upfront in our understanding of the region. As Rosie Bsheer has noted in a detailed survey of recent academic work on the Gulf, we must take seriously the fact that 'the authoritarian regimes of the [Arabian] peninsula were not formed outside class politics and global economic processes. On the contrary, class formation and dominant capitalist orientations were as instrumental to the production and maintenance of power in the [Arabian] peninsula as they were – and are – in states elsewhere' (Bsheer 2017).

This study is intended as a contribution to this emerging body of literature on the Gulf in two distinct ways. *First*, I endeavour to explore the co-constitution of the Gulf's political economy with that of the global. I argue (in Chapter 2) that the flows of Gulf financial surpluses are an essential component to understanding the concrete form of the contemporary world economy – a structure marked by persistent levels of overaccumulation, continued predominance of US and European capital, but the emergence of new centres of accumulation and political rivalries emanating from China, East Asia, and elsewhere. This uneven and hierarchical global structure, moreover, shapes the nature of capital accumulation and class formation in the Gulf itself, as I demonstrate in Chapter 3. *Second*, alongside a focus on this global-Gulf relation, I seek to integrate the Middle East as a whole into this analysis, arguing that the Gulf's location within the global has been articulated through shifting patterns of accumulation in the wider region. This is a critically important theme to the following chapters, which I will investigate through a detailed mapping of major economic activities in the Middle East – including agriculture and agribusiness; real estate development; urban infrastructure such as power, water, transport, and telecommunications; and banking and finance (Chapters 4–6). These interweaving spatial relations between the global, Gulf, and regional political economies help us understand why – as one astute observer notes – the Middle East's 'centers of economic, commercial, diplomatic and political gravity' have increasingly shifted away from the Levant and North Africa towards the Gulf (Kamrava 2016, p. 43). Moreover, they are crucial to unpacking the implications and potential trajectories – which, at this moment, remain open-ended – of the severe crises currently cascading through the Middle East (Chapters 7 and 8).

But before exploring these themes further, it is first necessary to clarify some essential analytical concepts. In the following section, I turn to the general theoretical puzzle, which is how to understand the interaction of different parts of the global political economy in a way that recognises *both* the distinct geographical spaces in which accumulation occurs and, at the same time, the unity of these spaces as part of a single whole. Answering this question involves grappling with a range of important conceptual debates: the nature of space in contemporary capitalism, the question of how objects of analysis (and concepts) relate to one another at an ontological level, and the interaction of the 'parts' and the 'totality'. These questions are critical to understanding the overall logic and argument of later chapters. Following this discussion, I will return to the specificities of the Gulf – providing a brief sketch of the six Gulf monarchies and their social structures, and then setting out in more detail the basic topics and chapter outline covered throughout the book.

1.1 Spaces of Neoliberal Capitalism

Much of the discussion in this book focuses on the near 30-year timeframe stretching from the early 1990s to the current day – a period marked by a major reworking of global production, trade, and financial networks that has become known as globalisation. A defining feature of these decades was the emergence of globally constituted value chains linking production of commodities in low-wage and poorly regulated zones outside the advanced capitalist core, the transport of these goods across increasingly complex logistical networks, and their final sale in markets centred upon the United States and Western Europe (Harvey 2005; McNally 2009). A whole set of political and social developments provided the backdrop for this reconstitution of the world market: the devastating debt crisis that hit many countries in the South during the 1980s and the subsequent rolling out of structural adjustment programmes; the collapse of the Soviet Union and the opening up of China as a platform for low-wage production (Bellamy Foster and McChesney 2012); the emergence of new technologies, logistical infrastructures, and modes of disciplining labour all aimed at speeding up the circulation of goods and information across the globe (Cowen 2014); the unprecedented explosion of financial instruments that knit together and commensurate prices across different commodities, spaces, and times (Coe et al. 2014); and, in an overarching sense, changing social behaviours, norms, and modes of governance that reflect the deep-seated generalisation of market discipline throughout all spheres of life (Langley 2008; Dardot and Laval 2013).

Enabling all of these changes has been the reorientation of economic and social policy around the core precepts of neoliberalism (Duménil and Lévy 2004; Harvey 2005; Dardot and Laval 2013). With its intellectual origins drawing eclectically on neoclassical and Austrian economic thought, neoliberalism emerged as a dominant policy framework in response to the deep crisis of profitability and overaccumulation that hit all major capitalist economies in the 1970s. Incrementally embraced by policymakers throughout the 1980s, the basic assumptions of neoliberalism have held almost universal sway since that time. This new stage of capitalism represented, above all, a '*material structure of social, economic and political reproduction* underpinned by financialization' (Fine and Saad-Filho 2016, p. 686; emphasis in original) – the latter term referring to 'the increasing role of globalised finance in ever more areas of economic and social life' (p. 687). Through policies such as privatisation, market deregulation, and cutbacks to social spending, neoliberalism aims at a fundamental reshaping of social relations in favour of capital – embedding financial imperatives throughout all aspects of human activity (Albo 2008). But precisely because it exposes so much more of daily social life to the turbulence of market dynamics and the metric of financial profitability, neoliberalism needs to be understood as an ongoing process with no fixed terminus. In the struggle to overcome impediments to capital accumulation, new barriers are inevitably thrown up. In this manner, neoliberalism is much more than a simple set of static policy prescriptions; intrinsically generative of instability and crisis, it works through these moments of disjuncture, incorporating them into itself in a permanent attempt to surpass the (always temporary) limits to accumulation.

One aspect to these limits is spatial, and here the link between neoliberalism and the recent forms of the global economy is immanent. Marx noted that the 'world market' is given in the very concept of capital; capitalism always acts to 'tear down every spatial barrier to intercourse, i.e., to exchange, and conquer the whole earth for its market ... [as capital develops] the more does it strive simultaneously for an even greater extension of the market' (Marx 1973, p. 539). In this sense, while there is much that is new about the neoliberal era, it also sits in a continuum with earlier periods of capitalist history. Most significant to my analysis is the ongoing *internationalisation of capital* – a process that stretches back across the twentieth century, and that has seen the progressive development of complex, interlocking commodity chains arrayed across the globe and dominated by a handful of massive conglomerates; these globally oriented firms now conceptualise their field of accumulation at a scale much wider than those provided by their home markets – from the production of raw materials to the sourcing of inputs, research and development (R&D), assembly, transport, marketing, financing, and retail. A primary impetus of neoliberalism has been about bringing down the spatio-temporal barriers to this geographical expansion, creating a world market in the image presupposed by capital. Today, the production of a typical commodity involves labour and material inputs from across the globe. The place where a given commodity is eventually sold is very likely not the same place as where it is produced. The largest capitalist firms consider their production and marketing decisions from the perspective of a global marketplace, not only from within their own national borders. These processes indicate that the world market has become the horizon of capital, the space where the commodity is 'conceptualized, produced, and realized' as Christian Palloix noted presciently in the 1970s (1977, p. 20).

But the reality of capitalism as 'a social system driven by the encompassing accumulative imperatives of a world market' (Albo 2012, p. 86) does not mean that place and space have dissolved into a transnational ether. The term 'globalisation' captured something about the immense expansion of global capital flows and the closely associated changes of technological infrastructures, cultural forms, and institutional structures, but accumulation always requires a 'momentary fixity in order to appropriate labour power and use nature in the production and realisation of surplus value' (Munoz Martinez and Marois 2014, p. 1104). This tension between the mobility and fixity of capital is mediated through the historically specific political jurisdictions demarcated by states and a multiplicity of variegated spatial arrangements and bordering regimes. As one geographer noted in a riposte to the often breathless rhetoric that surrounded the concept of globalisation in its early days: 'while capital expands its geographical reach and breaks through all manner of geographical barriers, new boundaries are created while older ones are broken down or become more porous' (Swyngedouw 2004, p. 30). Numerous scholars have pointed to the normative implications of erasing such spatial differences from view, making 'processes of de-territorialisation and re-territorialisation . . . equally a-spatial or a-geographical and, as such, profoundly disempowering' (Swyngedouw 2004, p. 30). We certainly have a world market, but it is one that continues to generate and forge spatial differentiation; barriers, borders, and boundaries remain an ever-present feature of the global (Novak 2017).

The Scale Question

Nonetheless, precisely how to theorise the new spatial arrangements produced by neoliberal globalisation has been a highly contested question. Much of the initial debate around this question (particularly in the critical political economy literature) focused upon understanding the changes to the roles and capacities of national states concomitant with these global processes. Some scholars argued that the erosion of national boundaries under globalisation was pointing towards the 'supersession of the nation-state as the organizing principle of capitalism, and with it, of the inter-state system as the institutional framework of capitalist development' (Robinson 2002, p. 212). In this new deterritorialised order, capital sought 'a smooth space defined by uncoded flows, flexibility, continual modulation, and tendential equalization' – this 'immanence of capital' conflicted with modern forms of sovereignty and was leading to the decline of nation-states (Hardt and Negri 2000, p. 327). In contrast to this purported overcoming of the national, an alternative perspective emphasised the continuing salience of national states as institutional mediators of global processes – as capital internationalised so did state functions (Poulantzas 1974; Bryan 1987; Cox 1987; Panitch and Gindin 2003). Within this latter approach, the precise nature of the forms of rivalry and interdependence existing between states remained a subject of intense debate – polarising between positions that emphasised the role of the United States as the architect of globalisation itself, interpenetrating national social and class formations, and binding other national state apparatuses to a US-led system (Meiksins Wood 2003; Panitch and Gindin 2003; 2012), or, alternatively, a global order in which the United States sought to offset its decline in the context of interstate competition and potential conflict (Harvey 2005; Arrighi 2009; Callinicos 2009).

Alongside these attempts to grapple with the relation between the global and the national, a further body of literature – largely originating in critical geography debates – stressed much more the multiple, variegated nature of spaces of accumulation through the contemporary period. Against a certain tendency to take for granted national rivalries and the national/global division as the main spatial fissures under theoretical dispute, this literature attempted to relativise space itself, arguing that capitalism was marked by a continued transformation of multiple 'temporal and spatial horizons ... interconnected in proliferating networks and flows of money, information, commodities and people' (Swyngedouw 2004, p. 31). Such a view implied there were no '"natural" geographical units within which capitalism's historical trajectory develops' (Harvey 2000, p. 57) but rather 'ever-changing forms of territorial or geographical organisation and ... territorially shifting forms of governance' (Swyngedouw 2004, p. 32). For this reason, it would no longer do to single out the national state as 'the pre-eminent locus for the crystallisation and resolution of these tensions and conflicts' (Swyngedouw 2004, p. 32). While the nation-state remained essential to how the world market functioned, it was necessary to develop a more complete picture of the various spatial forms that underpin global processes.

Much of this critical geography literature drew inspiration from the work of Henri Lefebvre, a French philosopher and urban theorist writing from the vantage point of mid-twentieth-century Paris. Lefebvre produced a voluminous series of path-breaking work on the nature of space and capitalism, in which he argued that we need to move away from a conception of space as something static, natural or pregiven – a set of fixed lines that are distributed on the map. Instead, Lefebvre emphasised that capitalism depended upon the continuous production of specific, historically conditioned sets of sociospatial organisation. This 'production of space' gave a spatial form to the concrete structure of social life, generating an ever-present tendency towards the reworking of space itself. Most important for the themes of this book, he linked this to processes of class formation, noting that the 'the mode of existence of social relationships' was necessarily spatial, and that 'social relations of production have a social existence to the extent that they have a spatial existence; they project themselves into a space, becoming inscribed there, and in the process producing that space itself' (Lefebvre 1991, p. 130).

Lefebvre's notion that space is socially produced has proved hugely influential in the recent interrogation of capitalism's multiple forms of spatiality. One reflection of this can be seen in the idea of *scale* – a term that will be employed centrally in my analysis of the Gulf and the wider Middle East. Starting from the recognition that capital accumulation is always territorialised in particular ways, the concept of scale denotes the various forms of sociospatial layers that are subsequently produced as part of 'fixing' this process (Lefebvre 1991; Brenner 2005; Smith 2008). Scale exists as a 'hierarchical scaffolding of nested territorial units stretching from the global, the supranational, and the national downwards to the regional, the metropolitan, the urban, the local, and the body' (Brenner 2005, p. 9). These scales emerge as different instantiations of the production of space, through which flows of capital and other social resources are territorialised, regulated, and contested. The key point is that scales are not neutral or fixed; rather, as an embodiment of the production of space, they are constantly shifting in reaction to – and contestation with – changing forms of human social relations.[6]

The notion of scale is a profoundly useful one that can tell us much about the workings of globalisation. Most relevant for our purposes is the way in which it points to the need to move beyond methodologically nationalist perspectives that take for granted the fixity of the national scale as a natural vantage point from which to understand social phenomena. Greater sensitivity to the ways in which capitalism necessarily operates throughout *all* scales – and, as part of this, incessantly produces new scalar configurations – also helps us overcome a certain analytical narrowing of vision typically associated with binary models of spatial differentiation, e.g. centre/periphery, urban/rural, North/South, First/Third World. This does not mean a flattening of space or inattention to divergence and unevenness – rather, it points to how spatial polarisation is intrinsically generated by, and cascades through, a multiplicity of variegated scales.

Much of the writing on scale as it relates to globalisation focuses on the ways in which the expansion and changing nature of the global economy is deeply entwined with a 'rescaling' of state functions and capacities (Brenner 2005). The spatiality of capitalism, in other words, is characterised by a 'perpetual reworking of the geographies of capital circulation and accumulation' (Swyngedouw 1997a, p. 68) that shifts the ways in which different scales are hierarchised within the global system. Seen in this manner, globalisation is not 'a mono-directional implosion of global forces into sub-global realms'; rather, it involves 'a reconfiguration and re-territorialization of superimposed spatial scales' in which the relations existing between them should not 'be conceived as one that obtains

[6] From this perspective, Marston highlights three key features of the scale literature that encompass its role as both a heuristic device and a proposition about the nature of our lived spatial reality (Marston 2000, pp. 221–222). The first of these is that scale is something that emerges through social praxis; it is a product of human interaction and should not be understood simply in the sense of pregiven boundaries, or distinct levels, that separate different geographic units from one another. Second, scale has a tangible *effect* – it shapes subsequent human action, both at a rhetorical level and materially. Third, precisely because of these rhetorical and material consequences, the lived reality of scale is contested by different actors and becomes a major pivot around social action. This last point has been a key preoccupation of the scale literature, with numerous scholars examining how social movements attempt to – or are compelled to – 'jump' scale in order to leverage access to social and power resources that may be constraining their operation at another scale (or, alternatively, to block such access to other actors). In this manner, scales are 'materially real frames of social action' that operate to both hold back and enable human praxis (Smith 2003, p. 228).

among mutually exclusive levels of analysis or forces' (Neil Brenner, cited in Marston 2000, p. 227). As such, processes of globalisation have not so much superseded the national scale – as some of the critical political economy literature noted above tends to argue – but rather the form of the national has changed as part of a wider shifting of scale relations, intensifying the roles of sub- and supranational scales (Brenner 1999, p. 52). States adopt, for example, decentralisation and new governance strategies, in which certain core functions or services are devolved to subnational scales (e.g. municipalities or cities); through this rescaling, competitive tendencies are heightened between subnational scales over access to potential resources, financial flows, tax-raising abilities, and the like. Decentralisation does not herald the demise of the national scale, but rather accentuates the power of the central state through the reworking of scalar relations within its domain (Peck 2001; Swyngedouw 2005). Alternatively, state functions may be 'uploaded' to higher scales, subsequently shaping processes occurring at the national scale (Greece's negotiations with the European Union through the summer of 2013 provides a perfect illustration of the implications of such rescaling). Examples such as these show how the relations of power inscribed within processes of globalisation can be 'altered through the differential restructuring of state responsibilities and capacities' (Leitner and Miller 2006, p. 120) – the focus becomes, as Jamie Peck puts it, not how the national state has 'become "less" powerful ... but how it has become *differently* powerful' (Peck 2001, p. 447; emphasis in original).

Internal Relations and the Totality

Given the fact that scales are mutually forming and intersecting, how should we precisely understand the relations between scales and their constitution vis-à-vis the global? In the context of the Gulf and the wider Middle East, later chapters will trace the mutual co-constitution of different scales in the region – the urban scale of cities and the built environment, the national scale of various Gulf states, the pan-GCC scale, the regional (Middle East) scale, and so forth – as a part of the formation of the global scale itself. *In doing so, I focus on the social relations involved in the production and circulation of commodities and capital as the core lens through which to examine this relationality of scales.* In this sense, I am departing somewhat from much of the scale literature, which often emphasises social action or institutional activity as the key articulation between scales. While certainly not disputing the significance of institutional or political relationships – indeed, throughout my analysis I will look at these factors in some detail – I aim to move away from some of the dominant neo-Weberian assumptions of the literature (even though these frequently go unstated) that treat institutional factors and their interactions as autonomous from capitalist social relations; in contrast, following Derek Sayer, I posit institutions as social forms that emerge through the production and reproduction of society itself (Sayer 1987, pp. 96–111). This should not be read as saying that institutions are derivative, second-order, or in any way unimportant. Rather, precisely because one of my aims is to utilise scalar concepts to better understand processes of class formation in the Middle East, it is necessary to trace the actual dynamics involved in the accumulation of capital and the social relations that form around these. These class relations are too often ignored in the literature, and in this respect I hope to return to the key point made by Lefebvre in the passage cited earlier: 'the social relations of production have a social existence to the extent that they have a spatial existence; they project themselves into a space, becoming inscribed there, and in the process producing that space itself'.

In regards to these cross-scalar interlockings of social relations, my approach will draw upon the rich philosophical literature developed around the concept of 'internal relations', best exemplified in the work of the philosopher Bertell Ollman. According to this perspective, the relations existing between objects (and concepts) should not be considered external to the objects themselves but as part of what actually constitutes them. Any object under study needs to be seen as 'relations, containing in themselves, as integral elements of what they are, those parts with which we tend to see them externally tied' (Ollman 2003, p. 25). Objects, in other words, are not self-contained, preexisting, independent, or autonomous things that affect one another through their external impact (like billiard balls might bump into one another on a pool table). Instead, objects are actually made up *through* the relations they hold with one another. These relationships do not exist 'outside' these objects but are intrinsic to their very nature. As these relations change, so do the things themselves. The analytic method thus focuses on exploring the manifold relations that exist between things and the movement of these relations over time, rather than considering objects of study as discrete building blocks that can be compared or contrasted but remain understood, in an ontological sense, as existing a priori or separate from one another.

This approach provides a very useful lens for understanding the mutually conditioned interaction of social relations across scales. When we think about the urban, national, regional, or global scales, for example, we need to avoid reifying these as distinct or separate levels that interact in an external fashion; the relations between these scales are instead understood to be jointly formed and co-constituted. The challenge is to examine these relations and the ways that they evolve over time, rather than considering space as made up of discrete, bounded layers. Likewise, when we think about 'class' we need to explore the ways that processes of class formation are internally related to those of scale formation. Precisely because the production of scale takes place through 'capital circulation and accumulation' (Swyngedouw 1997a), it necessarily involves the imbrication of different sets of social relations – and thus classes – across scales, confounding any conception of class as a set of self-enclosed social relations circumscribed, or contained, a priori within the national scale. For this reason, as we shall see in later discussions, when we think about class formation in a particular country – e.g. in Egypt – we need to examine the ways that class formation at other spatial scales is interiorised within the making of class at the national scale. There *is* an Egyptian capitalist class, but it is wrong to think of it as solely 'Egyptian'.

Given this conception of internal relations, how do the relations existing between the variegated (internally related) scales that striate the world connect to a conception of the 'the global'? Here my approach emphasises the notion of the *totality*, the whole, which arises through the interaction of its parts. This whole, however, should not be seen as a simple aggregate of individual bits, in which 'the sum of all the small-scale parts produces the large-scale total' (Howitt 1993, p. 36). Rather, the totality emerges as something more than its parts, a 'structural, evolving, self-forming whole' (Kosik 1976, p. 18), in the words of Czech philosopher Karel Kosik, which is made up of parts that *only exist* in their relations with other parts and – through these relations – the totality itself.[7] Kosik points out that such an approach 'implies that every

[7] I owe many thanks here to the historian Dale Tomich, who first pointed me to Kosik's work and whose own body of scholarship draws directly on the same approach. Tomich has developed over a number of decades a thought-provoking account of colonial slavery in the sugar-producing island of Martinique, and its interaction with the evolution of global capitalism through the sixteenth century. What is distinctive about Tomich's work – and sets it apart from much other recent work on slavery and capitalism – is his attempt to explicitly theorise the nature (and origins) of the capitalist world market, the interconnectedness of different forms of labour within this, and – most significantly for this book – the ways in which we can conceptualise the mutual formation of multiple spatial zones within the 'global'. Theoretically, Tomich's approach uses Kosik to develop a particular conception of the interaction between the parts and the whole (of which the local and global can be seen as one instance). Fundamentally, Tomich conceives of slave labour 'as part of the organization of social labour on a world scale. Slave relations are not treated as existing separate from or prior to the world market and division of labour. Instead they constitute a specific form of commodity production that is related to other such forms through the world market and world-scale processes of integration and division of social labor' (Tomich 2016, p. 7). In other words, we must be very careful to avoid setting up the 'local' (Martinique) and the 'global' (the world economy) as two distinct, separate spheres whose interaction is conceptualised as external. Martinique was

phenomenon can be conceived as a moment of a whole ... this interconnectedness and mediatedness of the parts and the whole also signifies that isolated facts are abstractions, artificially uprooted moments of a whole which become concrete and true only when set in the respective whole' (p. 22). In this manner, cognition of any fact (such as the nature of a particular scale) involves situating bits of empirical reality in their constantly shifting relation to one another – 'all concepts *move with respect to one another*, and mutually illuminate one another' (p. 23; emphasis in original). Through this mutual illumination, the totality forms as a historically developed structure that determines the 'objective content and meaning of all its elements and parts' (p. 29).

Crucially important to this conception of totality is the need to avoid hypostatising the whole as a reality above or separate from its parts – the whole does not exist independently of its elements, but is constantly coming into being through their interactions. Put another way, we must be careful of turning the whole (e.g. the global scale) into an a priori entity that is severed from the mutual internal relations of its parts (e.g. other scales), sitting above them like some form of deus ex machina. In contrast, the interaction of the parts is the means through which the 'whole form[s] itself as a whole' (p. 22).[8] As Dale Tomich, who draws upon a similar framework in his highly perceptive work on slavery and capitalism, notes: 'The whole is understood as being formed and reformed by the changing interactions among its constituent elements. Each particular element derives its analytical significance through its relation to the totality ... Each contains, encompasses and expresses the totality of world-economy while the totality expresses, unifies, and gives order to the relations among the particulars' (Tomich 2016, pp. 30–31).

Such an approach helps us avoid a conception of the movement of the whole as some kind of 'teleological Hegelian monster slouching inexorably towards an appalling totalitarian "totality" that imposes uniformity on heterogeneity' – to quote a recent insightful contribution by Gillian Hart (Hart 2016, p. 2). Instead, we gain a view of various regions

not a 'local particularism' that was created by French colonialism as an outside force; rather, both spaces – Martinique and the world economy – constitute 'a unified, structured, contradictorily evolving whole' (p. 5).

[8] This is a very useful insight of Kosik's, as it allows us to see the process of the whole's emergence (its coming into being) as part of its contemporary essence – 'the genesis and development of totality are components of its very determination' (p. 29). In this manner, the ever-present flux of temporality is captured as part of the dynamic of the totality itself. Historical antecedents matter – not only in the sense of path dependency, preconditions, or context – but as ongoing parts of the concrete totality as it actually exists in the present.

throughout the world economy as 'connected yet distinctively different nodes in globally interconnected historical geographies – and as sites in the production of global processes in specific spatio-historical conjunctures, rather than as just recipients of them' (Hart 2016, p. 3). From this perspective, scales emerge as particular (spatial) instantiations of global processes that they themselves help constitute – they are produced by, and simultaneously produce, the global itself. There is no reductive or a priori causality implied here; each scale exists simultaneously and each conditions one another (Tomich 2016, p. 9). It is the internal relations between these scales that must be more fully interrogated in order to better understand the motion of either the whole or any of its constituent parts. Such an approach puts an emphasis on processes, practices, and interconnections, rather than on the supposedly bounded, pregiven and discrete spatial units through which we are accustomed to viewing the world. Of course, categories such as nation, city, or region are essential to any analysis, but they are better viewed as 'vantage points from which to try to begin to grasp the coming together and interconnections of what (at least initially) appear as key processes' (Hart 2016, p. 19). This 'vantage point' approach to both the ontology and epistemology of scale is precisely what I seek to replicate in various chapters.

1.2 Introducing the Gulf Monarchies

The themes of scale, internal relations, and the totality constitute the major theoretical axis around which my overall argument will proceed. Prior to setting out the basic outline of this argument, however, we must briefly summarise the main characteristics of the six Gulf monarchies – Saudi Arabia, Kuwait, Qatar, United Arab Emirates (UAE), Bahrain, and Oman – that together form the geographical focus of my analysis. I should emphasise at the outset that this book is not intended as a comprehensive account of the political economy of any individual Gulf state nor, indeed, of the Gulf as a whole. Nonetheless, it is important to sketch some of the main commonalities of Gulf societies, their historically conditioned paths of development, and the differences that mark them out from one another. In doing so, I hope to flag some of the specificities of class and state in the Gulf that will become apparent in later discussions.

The Gulf monarchies are all located on the strategically significant Arabian Peninsula and have long been entangled with the regional ambitions of foreign powers. Dominated by ruling families who have held power since the pre-oil period, leadership succession in these states is effectively hereditary, although competition between different royal lineages has led to numerous coups and widespread factional intrigues (most notably in Saudi Arabia and Qatar, where ruling families are very large and divided). Elected legislatures exist in only two Gulf states – Bahrain (*majlis al-nuwab*) and Kuwait (*majlis al-umma*) – but voting rights are restricted to a small portion of the resident population and the rulers in both states have the power to dissolve the parliament. The kings, princes, emirs, and sheikhs that sit atop each of the Gulf states control the political apparatus and a very large share of economic wealth – they are central actors in the story that follows. There are important variations, however, in how these monarchies came to power, and the relationships they have forged with other social groups.

Saudi Arabia, the most populous and wealthiest Gulf state, was formed in 1932 under the leadership of Abd al-Aziz ibn Abd al-Rahman Al Saud, known simply (in the West) as Ibn Saud. Like much of the Middle East, the modern Saudi state has its origins in the struggle over the fragmenting Ottoman Empire that intensified after the First World War. Ibn Saud emerged as the head of the country with the favoured support of the British, who were looking to secure allies in a region strategically vital to their wider colonial interests.[9] In addition to British backing, Ibn Saud's rise to power depended critically on two local social forces. The first were the *mutawwa'a*, religious educators located in the central area of the country known as Najd (the birthplace of Ibn Saud). The *mutawwa'a* supplied ideological legitimacy and a disciplining force that guaranteed Ibn Saud 'the political submission of the Arabian population under the guise of submission to God' (Al-Rasheed 2010, p. 54). Alongside the *mutawwa'a* were the *ikhwan*, a religious-military force drawn from sedentarised tribes who provided the physical coercion to ensure Al-Saud rule. This configuration of early state formation is important for the contemporary period as it cemented a long-standing alliance between the ruling family and a religious elite who drew their beliefs from an austere version of Islam known as Wahhabism. Once in power, Ibn Saud consciously sought the support of prominent merchant families and other elites – many of whom we shall encounter in later chapters – drawing upon their wealth to finance military campaigns and incorporating them into the nascent Saudi state bureaucracy (Al-Rasheed 2010, p. 86). He often built these intraelite alliances through the strategic use of marriage, and today

[9] Madawi Al-Rasheed points out that British support to Ibn Saud was marked by its personalism. Indeed, a 1927 treaty signed between the British and Ibn Saud is almost unique in that it was agreed with an individual and not a state. The treaty conferred independence to 'the dominions of his Majesty the King of the Hejaz and of Nejd and its Dependencies' – a forerunner of what would later become Saudi Arabia (Al-Rasheed 2010, p. 46).

the Al-Saud dynasty is split across a variety of family lines originating from the many offspring of Ibn Saud.[10] As a result, the size of the ruling family is very large – by some estimates upwards of 10,000 people – with various groupings and factional divisions marking Al-Saud internal politics.

Qatar's powerful ruling family, the Al-Thani, also trace their origins to Najd, from where they departed to Qatar in the mid-eighteenth century. Similar to Saudi Arabia, there are numerous factional divisions within the Al-Thani linked to the descendants of Jassim bin Mohammed Al Thani, the country's founder, and, as a result, leadership transitions have typically occurred through intrafamily coups. Indeed, Qatar's current ruler, Tamim bin Hamad Al Thani, is the only emir since the country's independence in 1971 who did not come to power through a forced abdication. Despite fractious internal power struggles, the Al-Thani are marked by their very deep hold over Qatar's political and economic structures. The reasons for this have much to do with the weakness of other potential contenders for power. Unlike Saudi Arabia, for example, where the Wahhabi doctrine was uniquely fused with the rise of the Al-Saud, Al-Thani rule emerged independently from religious institutions (Kamrava 2009, p. 410).[11] Similarly, Qatar's merchant class was relatively weak due to the country's small size and comparative lack of trading networks in the pre-oil period; in the eighteenth and nineteenth centuries, much of the merchant class migrated to neighbouring areas in the Gulf in search of economic opportunities in pearling and trade, leaving the Al-Thani behind (Crystal 1995).[12] As a result, the descendants of different branches of the Al-Thani make up large proportion of the country's (already very small) citizen population. The Al-Thani's deep-seated penetration of both political and economic structures has led to a tight interlacing of capital accumulation with the institutions of the state. Consequently, as we shall see at numerous points later, Qatar's biggest conglomerates tend to be closely linked to the Al-Thani, with members of the ruling family controlling these institutions and sitting on their boards.

[10] The most important of these lineages are the descendants of the so-called Sudairi Seven, the seven sons of Ibn Saud by his favoured wife, Hussa Sudairi. Saudi Arabia's current king is from the Sudairi branch of the ruling family.

[11] This does not mean that Islam is not important to Al-Thani rule – indeed, as we shall see in Chapter 8, religion has formed a vital component to Qatar's projection of regional influence.

[12] By some estimates, the Al-Thani made up half of the indigenous population of Qatar in 1900.

The historical relationship between the ruling family and the merchant class is also important in the case of Kuwait. During the pre-oil period of the eighteenth to early twentieth centuries, Kuwait formed a major crossroads for intraregional trade, pearling, and ship building. Due to these economic activities, a prosperous merchant class emerged that held considerable strength vis-à-vis the ruling Al-Sabah family, with the latter depending heavily on duties that they imposed on trade and other merchant activities (Crystal 1995; Fattah 1997). Partly as a result of this intraelite balance of power, Kuwait today possesses a much more restive citizen population and an influential business class whose origins can be traced to these early merchant families. In the post-oil era these business elites have come to rely significantly upon their linkages to the state (as I shall show later in some detail), but they still retain a relative independence from the ruling family. One of the consequences of this is the frequent recurrence of political disputes between Kuwait's parliament – where business elites wield substantial influence – and the Al-Sabah.

The UAE is unique among the Gulf states in that it consists of a federated structure of seven different emirates, each controlled by a different ruling family. This structure gives a much more decentralised character to UAE politics, with individual emirates pursuing their own development strategies through separate state institutions. Despite this decentralised structure, there is a sharp hierarchy of political and economic power between the various emirates. The country as a whole is politically dominated by Abu Dhabi, where the Al-Nahyan family have held power since the eighteenth century (supported, as in other areas of the Gulf at that time, by British colonialism). Most of the UAE's hydrocarbon reserves – and the seat of federal government – are located in Abu Dhabi. Abu Dhabi's neighbour, Dubai, is the second major emirate within the country and is controlled by the Al-Maktoum family. With highly developed logistics and port infrastructure, and a heavy focus on real estate and finance-driven growth, Dubai will take a prominent role in my overall narrative. The other five emirates – Sharjah, Ras Al Khaimeh, Umm al-Quwain, Fujairah, and Ajman – are much weaker relative to Abu Dhabi and Dubai.

Bahrain also has a distinctive social structure within the Gulf. Its small size and lack of hydrocarbon reserves (sharing only a single oil field provided to it by Saudi Arabia) have led the country's ruling Al-Khalifa monarchy to pursue an economic strategy largely based upon offshore banking and finance. This role became particularly apparent in the 1970s and 1980s, when, following the Civil War in Lebanon, the archipelago took over the historic position of Beirut as an intermediary for capital flows between the Middle East and Western countries. Bahrain's relative lack of petrodollar revenue, and the concentration of financial wealth in the hands of the Al Khalifa and their allied business elites, has meant the political and economic marginalisation of much of Bahraini citizenry. As a result, the country's political history has been punctuated by several large-scale uprisings against the monarchy, the most recent of which occurred as part of the region-wide revolts of 2010–2011. Moreover, many of Bahrain's poorest citizens identify as Shi'a Muslims, while the Al-Khalifa – as with all ruling dynasties in the Gulf – are Sunni. Such sectarian differences have been instrumentalised by the Al-Khalifa as a means to justify state repression, often with reference to neighbouring Iran's alleged meddling in Bahraini politics.[13] These sectarian dynamics are accentuated by the fact that the Al-Khalifa depend heavily upon Saudi Arabian patronage for their continued survival (powerfully demonstrated by the Saudi-led military intervention in the country during the 2011 uprisings). The country's particularly tight economic, political, and military relationship with Saudi Arabia will form a recurring theme throughout the pages that follow.

The last of the six Gulf states is Oman, strategically located at the juncture of the Indian Ocean and the Straits of Hormuz, a critical waterway through which 20% of the world's oil supplies pass. Oman is the only country in the Gulf where political power is concentrated in the hands of a single individual, Sultan Qaboos, who has neither children nor brothers. Qaboos has been the longest serving Arab ruler since he ousted his father through a bloodless coup in 1970; since then, all the most important governmental roles – including prime minister, head of the armed forces, chair of the central bank, and minister of both foreign affairs and finance – have been in his hands. Despite this highly personalised system, Omani business elites are intimately connected to Qaboos and have greatly benefitted from positions in the state and their access to a share of oil revenue; indeed, as Marc Valeri has shown in his authoritative work on Omani politics and society, Qaboos has relied much more on such elites as a social base of power than he has on the Al-Busaidi dynasty from which he comes (Valeri 2009). As with Bahrain, Oman has relatively fewer hydrocarbon reserves and a smaller economy than other Gulf states, and its large (and rapidly growing) youth population has

[13] This should not be taken to mean that the Sunni/Shi'a split is the most appropriate lens through which to understand Bahraini society. There are numerous wealthy Shi'a business elites in Bahrain, who confound a simple conflation of Bahrain's poor with Shi'ism. Other identities also exist within Bahrain, some of which are associated with the different national origins from which citizens trace their descent. Politically, much of the Bahraini opposition has emphasised a non-sectarian position (including through the 2011 uprisings).

been hard hit by a lack of economic opportunities. Consequently, Oman also saw the emergence of protest movements through 2011, most notably in towns such as Sohar and Salalah where development strategies have led to high levels of inequality and marginalisation. These social tensions will become important in later chapters as we examine the Gulf's policy response to recent economic difficulties.

Despite these different trajectories of state formation, there are numerous commonalities to the Gulf states. First, due largely to their role as the world's most important source of hydrocarbons, the Gulf monarchies have been sharply connected to the rise of the United States as the major global power in the period following the Second World War. The formation of the Gulf Cooperation Council (GCC) in 1981 is a powerful symbol of this imperial relationship – with the United States encouraging the six monarchies to draw closer together within a regional integration project that would be overseen by US military and political protection (Hanieh 2011a). Today, the GCC remains a principal host in the Middle East of US military facilities and personnel, from where wars and interventions in other neighbouring regions are coordinated. In this manner, the extension of US power in the Middle East has both been facilitated by and acted to reinforce the position of the Gulf's ruling families. The GCC remains one of the three central poles on which US policy in the Middle East has historically rested (the others being Israel and a range of Arab client states) – this idiosyncratic position within the architecture of US power gives the bloc, as a whole, a character distinct from other neighbouring states in the Gulf and Arabian Peninsula (such as Iraq, Iran, or Yemen).

Another critical commonality to the GCC is its overwhelming reliance on a temporary migrant labour force that is almost universally denied any route to citizenship and lacks virtually all political and social rights. These migrant workers constitute more than half of the labour force in every GCC state – in some countries, such as Qatar, Kuwait, and the UAE, the actual proportion exceeds 80%. The presence – and marginalised status – of these migrant workers needs to be seen as elemental to how the citizen–ruler bond is constituted in the Gulf (Longva 2000; Khalaf 2014). If we agree, following Sandro Mezzadra, that 'citizenship emerge[s] as an abstract legal and political framework' involving the 'disruption of multiple "concrete" belongings' (2012), then the creation of a singular national identity in each of the GCC states was partly borne out of the privileges associated with citizenship status – privileges that depend ultimately (both materially and mentally) on a simultaneous exclusion and denial of rights for most of the Gulf's labour force. Although my analysis will be principally focused on capital in the Gulf, it is imperative to keep the presence of migrant workers (and the related construction of citizenship) in view. Migrant workers are not only essential to how capital accumulation in the Gulf takes place; their precarious status is critical to understanding what happens in the Gulf during moments of crisis.

All of this should not be taken to mean that the GCC is a homogenous whole. There are considerable and long-standing tensions between the Gulf Arab states themselves (as the 2017 dispute between Saudi Arabia/UAE and Qatar so palpably demonstrated). One of my goals in the pages that follow is to draw out these differences, situating them within the context of the coherent whole that the GCC project represents. Specifically, I will show that the hierarchies of the GCC project revolve around a Saudi/UAE axis, which has come to form the main core of capital accumulation in the Gulf. Not only is this reflected in the predominance of Saudi and UAE conglomerates throughout the circuits I examine in the coming chapters, but also, perhaps even more significantly, it is shown in how the Saudi/UAE axis acts to mediate the relation between the GCC and other scales. In this sense, we need to simultaneously keep in mind the commonalities shared by all the Gulf countries within the GCC – as well as the hierarchies and internal differentiation that continue to mark how this scale is constituted.

1.3 The Argument in a Nutshell

This book is about the spatiality of capital accumulation in the contemporary Gulf, its relation to the global, and implications for the wider Middle East. The key object of inquiry through which this relational tracing proceeds is Gulf capital – what I have referred to in earlier work as *khaleeji* capital, a capitalist class made up of large conglomerates that dominates the political economy of all the GCC states. Echoing the historical patterns of state formation I have just outlined, this class is closely connected to ruling families in the Gulf states, although it also consists of private Gulf capitalists controlling large holding companies that stretch across all moments of accumulation. The connection between state and capital is thus understood as an internal relation – state institutions in the Gulf are a social form through which the power of this class is expressed in relation to the rest of society, the wider region, and the global (Sayer 1987; Ollman 2003). In this sense, one of the key points I will repeatedly emphasise is the need to reject any sharp conceptual antimony between capital and state – the line between these two categories is not a 'perimeter of an intrinsic entity, which can be thought of as a free-standing object or actor'; rather, 'it is a line drawn internally, *within* the network of institutional mechanisms through which a certain social and political order is maintained' (Mitchell 1991, p. 90; emphasis in original).

This conception of the state as a social form of class power should not lead us to overlook the very real contradictions and competitive tendencies that exist within (and between) the state, ruling families, and capitalist conglomerates. Such tensions are always immanent to capitalism, but in the Gulf they take on particular significance precisely because of the importance of the state to capital accumulation. We shall frequently encounter examples where access to highly lucrative contracts and other business opportunities is dependent upon privileged connections with certain individuals in the ruling family. As a result – particularly in countries such as Saudi Arabia that possess very large ruling families composed of different factions, lineages, and interests – capitalist elites can quickly fall out of favour following shifts in the balance of power within the state itself. There is thus a constant jostling of alliances and royal intrigue that marks how the internal relation of capital and the state concretely exists in the Gulf.

Utilising this theoretical framing, the development of Gulf capital is examined here in its relational sense to a variety of spatial scales. I am interested in asking how capital accumulation in the Gulf is connected to other spaces of accumulation, and how these spatial relations shape Gulf capital's own formation as well as the political economy of the wider region. I begin by tracing how Gulf capitalism has emerged over recent decades alongside the making of the global political economy. Chapter 2 examines this relationship through the lens of the Gulf's financial surpluses and their role in contemporary capitalism. These capital flows take place within a world system structured by persistent rivalries between different national states, economic blocs, and emerging powers – all of which simultaneously share joint interests as component parts of a common whole. Gulf capitalism has developed within this complex and contradictory structure. I explore this positioning from two particular vantage points: first, Gulf capital flows into various international markets, and, second, the Gulf's role as a consumer of both goods and services within global capitalism. In examining these two interrelated aspects to Gulf capitalism's position in the global totality, I aim to probe the ways in which Gulf capitalism contributes to forming the hierarchal world economy that has materialised over the last two decades. Through this analysis, I also assess how the Gulf's particular insertion into the world economy stands in relation to other geographies of capital accumulation – including Japan, China, and so-called emerging markets such as Brazil, Russia, and India.

Having established this relationship between Gulf and the wider world market, Chapter 3 turns to the other side of this internal relation – the contemporary features of capitalism in the Gulf itself. In particular, I focus on the structure and forms of accumulation of the large conglomerates that make up the Gulf's capitalist class. In developing this analysis, I explore three essential sites of accumulation: industry, the built environment, and financial markets. Each of these sites starkly exemplifies the manner in which the accumulation of Gulf capital is enmeshed in the reworking of space, criss-crossed and drawn together over variety of scales, including the global, national, pan-GCC, and urban. The chapter examines the structure of the conglomerates that dominate these particular sites, the relation these business groups hold with the state and international capital, and their propensity to internationalise beyond domestic borders.

Chapters 4–6 retain a focus on scalar processes of accumulation, but broaden this to explore the interlocking of social relations in the Gulf with those throughout the wider Middle East. Attention is placed, in other words, on the evolving internal relations between Gulf capitalism and the regional scale. Chapter 4 looks at the circulation of food and agro-commodities. I first outline changes in the way that Gulf food systems are inserted into global agricultural markets, particularly following the intensification of 'food security' strategies in the Gulf following the 2008 global price rise for key agro-commodities. These strategies have propelled the outward expansion of Gulf capital into global agriculture. Focusing on Saudi Arabia and the UAE, I examine two sides to these internationalisation processes: first, the so-called land grabs that have seen Gulf firms and state institutions purchase or lease land around the world, and, second, the extension of Gulf agribusiness interests across all parts of the agricultural value chain. Of particular interest here is the way that these value chains have become inextricably linked to the control and operation of logistics infrastructures, such that agribusiness firms are increasingly diversifying into transportation, warehousing, ports, and other sectors that underpin the circulation of food commodities. The second part of the chapter places these trends in the context of the Middle East. I show that Gulf agro-circuits have become a main pole around which agricultural production in the wider region pivots. Although there is notable regional variation in how this occurs, several of the key Arab agricultural producers have seen their export markets reorient dramatically around the GCC. The Gulf, moreover, has become much more than a market for Arab agricultural products. Paralleling the internationalisation of Gulf agro-firms at a global scale, Gulf capital has become powerfully embedded in the production and circulation of food in neighbouring Arab states. I examine this process in some detail for the case of Egypt, one of the most important Arab agricultural producers and a major reference point for food security debates at a global level.

Chapter 5 explores the intertwining of capital accumulation across the urban and regional scales in the Middle East. Empirically, the focus is on the countries of North Africa and the Levant – particularly Egypt, Jordan, Lebanon, Morocco, Tunisia, and Palestine – where neoliberal urban development models have taken centre-stage as part of wider economic reform processes. I show that the characteristics of urban development in these countries have increasingly been drawn into the accumulation circuits of Gulf capitalism, as Gulf conglomerates internationalise through the regional scale. To demonstrate this argument, I examine two particular moments of accumulation at the urban scale: (1) the production and development of commercial and residential real estate and (2) private sector provision of infrastructure elements, focusing on power, water, and transport and telecommunications. In choosing these two moments, I attempt to go beyond a tendency in the literature to single out the specificities of one or another feature of the Arab built environment – typically, housing, mega-projects, tourism, or infrastructure – at the expense of the whole. The aim is to draw these within an integrated unity, and ask how accumulation takes place – and who benefits from this – through all these variegated moments.

Chapter 6 returns to the theme of finance to place the development of the regional financial circuit in the context of Gulf capitalism. Beginning with an examination of financial sectors across major Arab countries, I show that the global features of financialisation identified in the critical political economy literature are also extant in the region, despite variation and specificity. This is important to note, as the region tends to be ignored in the wider scholarly work on finance. The chapter then turns to asking how a spatial lens that takes into account the relations between Gulf capitalism, the regional, and the national scales alters our view of financialisation as a process characteristic of contemporary capitalism. Through an examination of Gulf capital's role in the regional financial circuit, I show that financialisation processes embody not only the increased weight of financial markets in individual Arab states, but a rescaling of accumulation marked by the imbrication of *all* scales within regionally articulated circuits dominated by Gulf finance capital.

In Chapter 7, I come back to the GCC scale itself, asking what the oil price decline that began in mid-2014 might mean for the forms of development of Gulf capital and social structures in the Gulf. I look particularly at the policy goals embodied in a set of 'Vision' strategies promulgated by all Gulf states in the wake of the oil price decline – examining what they imply for Gulf citizens, the region's migrant labour workforce, and the fortunes of the large Gulf conglomerates. As part of this analysis I draw out a major point about the nature of 'crisis' itself. I show that conjunctures such as these – marked by shrinking oil revenue, budgetary pressures, and severe economic downturn – are being seized by the Gulf monarchies as an opportunity, a chance to rework class and state structures in a manner that deepens and extends preexisting trajectories. In understanding how this 'crisis as opportunity' actually works – and whose interests it ultimately serves – it is necessary to carefully differentiate social structures and the forms of class power extant in the Gulf.

Finally, Chapter 8 extends this critical assessment of crisis to the numerous political and military conflicts currently wracking the Middle East. The chapter looks at the contradictions and tensions embodied in this period, which has been largely shaped through the evolution of the Arab uprisings that shook the region so forcefully from 2010 onwards. I examine both the internal contradictions between individual GCC states (notably the rift between Qatar and other GCC countries) and the Gulf's political engagement in the wider region, including the rivalries and shifting alliances with regional powers such as Iran and Israel; interventions in Syria, Yemen, and other Arab states; and the relationship of the Gulf to major international actors in the Middle East. I situate these political trajectories within the processes of capital accumulation mapped throughout earlier chapters, bringing the political and economic spheres – with all their frictions and antagonisms – into closer analytical alignment and allowing us to assess what this might mean for the future of the Middle East itself.

2 Gulf Financial Surpluses and the International Order

The past three decades have seen fundamental and deep-reaching changes to the geography of global production and the international division of labour. At the centre of these shifts is, of course, the rise of China – the new 'workshop of the world' (Gao 2012) – where a spectacular increase in both foreign investment flows and direct commercial relationships with Chinese firms has sought to take advantage of the country's large supplies of cheap labour.[1] China itself sits at the core of a wider East Asian regional production system, with a dense network of intraregional flows of commodities and finance mediating the production of goods that are then exported further afield (Chang 2016). This 'continent of labour', to employ Dae-oup Chang's evocative phrase, has pivoted much of the world's commodity production around an East Asian axis – shifting the historical patterning of manufacturing and trade flows that had characterised the world economy throughout most of the twentieth century.

For the Gulf, these new realignments have had immense implications. Workshops need more than labour and machines – they also require energy and raw materials – and here the Gulf's hydrocarbon exports have been indispensable to the rise of the East. By 2014, two Gulf countries – Qatar and Oman – provided just over 25% of all China's liquefied natural gas imports, the second largest proportion from any country in the world (just behind Australia).[2] At the same time, one-third of China's crude oil imports came from the GCC, with Saudi Arabia supplying the largest amount (around 16%), followed by Oman (10%) and the UAE (4%).[3]

[1] By 2014, China was the world's largest recipient of foreign direct investment (FDI) inflows and ranked second in the world for FDI stock. Most of these FDI flows have taken the form of wholly foreign-owned enterprises (WFOEs), which have represented more than 75% of total real FDI since 2008 (Davies 2013, p. 14).

[2] Figures for 2015. BP Statistical Review of World Energy, June 2016, p. 28.

[3] When oil exports from Iraq and Iran are included in such figures, the Middle East as a whole meets around one-half of all China's oil import needs. Remarkably, 75% of all Middle East oil exports were flowing towards Asia by 2014. These are trends that look set to continue and deepen – the International Energy Agency predicts that China's imports

Beyond basic hydrocarbons, the GCC has also been an essential source of downstream petrochemicals destined for Asian manufacturing facilities. The GCC's share of global petrochemical capacity doubled between 2000 and 2014 – the second highest rate of growth of any region in the world – with nearly two-thirds of Gulf petrochemical exports now going to Asia (GPCA 2015, p. 97).[4] Alongside the Gulf's crude oil and gas exports, such commodities have been foundational to the contemporary structure of the world market – without this supply, and the GCC's ability to meet growing demand for hydrocarbons, the rise of China and the new spatial distribution of capitalist production would have taken radically different forms (if it had been possible at all).

Historically, the immense significance of such Gulf hydrocarbon exports to the making of global capitalism (and their connection to imperial domination of the Middle East) is well recognised and has been extensively debated and discussed in the literature (Vitalis 2007; Hanieh 2011a; Mitchell 2011; Jones 2012). What has received much less attention, however, is a closely linked corollary to these oil and gas exports: the large amount of surplus capital that has accrued in the Gulf, which is then deployed and recirculated through major centres of the world economy. Over the past several decades, growing international demand for the Gulf's hydrocarbons – accentuated by a near continuous 15-year increase in the price of oil from 2000 to mid-2014[5] – has brought a massive expansion in

of Middle East oil will double again by 2035, and that 90% of Middle East oil exports will be directed to Asia by that time.

[4] Given the fact that China is located in a regional system, much of its petrochemical imports are sourced at an intraregional level, including Korea, Singapore, and Japan. But for 2015, around 9% of the value of China's hydrocarbon-based plastics imports and 14% of its organic chemicals came from the Gulf, figures that exceeded those from any other non-Asian country. In some specific commodities, the Gulf took the largest global share of all exports to China – these include polymers of ethylene (29% of total import value), polymers of propylene (22%), ethylene glycol (57%), acyclic alcohols (42%), and high-density polyethylene (40%). Figures calculated by author from Comtrade database.

[5] From an average monthly price of around $40/barrel in 2000, global oil prices saw a sustained rise through the new millennium, eventually peaking at more than $150/barrel by mid-2008. A short downturn then occurred following the global economic crash of 2008, but oil prices resumed their upward trend from January 2009, reaching more than $120 in April 2011. Despite considerable global economic uncertainty as a result of the Eurozone sovereign debt crisis that intensified in 2012, oil continued to hover in a band around $100 until mid-2014. Since that time, prices have fallen back to levels seen at the beginning of the millennium. East Asian demand was not the only reason for the increase in oil prices – various authors have put forward other explanations for this rise, including speculation, where investment funds bet on a trend rise in energy prices through the futures markets – but with more hydrocarbons being sold at a seemingly ever-increasing price, the resultant outcome was a very large expansion in the quantities of capital amassing in the Gulf. In Chapter 7, I will examine the impact of the recent oil price downturn on the Gulf.

the quantities of such surplus capital held by the Gulf. A conservative estimate puts the collective value of disposable wealth and foreign assets of GCC governments, sovereign wealth funds, private Gulf firms, and individuals at well over US$6 trillion by 2016, a level that has swollen greatly since the early 2000s (see later discussion). How these long-standing Gulf surpluses move through the world market is formative to the global system; in turn, the resulting totality helps order and structure the Gulf's place within it. A mapping of the various routes, markets, and geographic spaces that mediate these flows can help illuminate this critical relation between the Gulf and the global.

My goals here are to explore these pools of Gulf surplus capital – unpacking who holds them, where they go, and what they do. I will argue that the levels and directionality of these long-standing Gulf surpluses are formative to a global system marked by three key characteristics. *First*, this is a global system that continues to be dominated by US financial institutions and markets, where the US dollar plays the role of global reserve currency, and in which the United States runs persistent current account deficits that are funded through the inflow of surpluses from the rest of the world. *Second*, despite this continued dominance, there has been a relative attenuation in the position of the United States over the past few decades. The liberalisation of markets and the shift in global commodity production has led to the emergence of new centres of capital accumulation, most notably in East Asia. *Third*, particularly since the economic crash of 2008–2009, global capitalism is today typified by sluggish growth rates, overcapacity in many sectors, low investment levels in real activities, and slowing demand for goods and services. There are considerable levels of variability in how these weaknesses play out across different parts of the world market, but this is leading to heightened competition over markets and spheres of influence.

In this chapter, I analyse the place of GCC financial surpluses within such a global structure. In doing so, I begin by briefly outlining the importance of contemporary finance and the historical role that Gulf cross-border capital flows have played in sustaining the spatial unevenness of production and consumption under neoliberal capitalism. I then turn to assessing the relative size of Gulf surpluses, their magnitude over time, and the various actors in the region that hold and deploy this wealth. The chapter then moves to an empirical analysis of two principal routes through which Gulf surpluses form part of the wider world economy. The first consists of direct flows into global financial markets, of which three in particular are highlighted: (1) US debt and capital markets, including treasuries, corporate bonds and stocks; (2) the international banking system, especially banks located in the United Kingdom; and

(3) foreign direct investment, including cross-border mergers and acquisitions made by Gulf-based companies, sovereign wealth funds, or wealthy individuals. By tracking these flows, we reveal the considerable importance of Gulf financial surpluses to both the historical development and the contemporary structure of global capitalism.

Second, the chapter considers a more indirect path through which Gulf surpluses flow through the international economy: the Gulf's consumption of goods and services sold to it by the rest of the world. In this respect, I examine the Gulf's relative weight in world imports, the linkages with different parts of the world economy that have emerged around this trade, and the specific types of imports that have been connected to the forms of development witnessed in the Gulf over the past two decades. One particularly significant feature that emerges through this analysis is the centrality of the Gulf's built environment – as a market for both goods (machinery and transport equipment) and services (engineering and construction). Later discussions will pick up this theme from a different vantage point – the role of the built environment as a critical site for capital accumulation and class formation in the Gulf. In addition to these types of conventional imports, another commodity of a special type examined later is military hardware – a sector for which the Gulf stands out as a major source of global demand. Taken together, the Gulf's role as a market for all of these goods and services represents another route through which the region's surpluses are recirculated to different geographical areas.

My analysis of these different kinds of financial flows focuses in particular on the Gulf's relationship with the core global markets – North America, Western Europe, and East Asia – while also assessing the relative weight of the Gulf in these processes vis-à-vis other geographical zones and the so-called emerging markets. In this sense, I am attempting to capture one aspect of the interaction between the different parts that produce the totality. Naturally, there is considerable overlap between each of these financial circuits and there are major limitations to available data on some of these flows. But, in their broad outline, they provide a revealing insight into the important (and changing) role that Gulf surpluses continue to have on contemporary capitalism. Obviously, I do not mean to suggest that the Gulf is somehow the central component of global capitalism or the main pivot around which global fault lines now turn – but the issue is not only one of rank importance; rather, if we take seriously the conjecture that the whole and its parts are co-constitutive, then we can learn a lot about the specificities of both the Gulf and the global through examining how these financial surpluses are deployed. Moreover, these relations are essential to understanding my subsequent arguments – providing the global context for a more fine-grained analysis of the Gulf and Middle East.

2.1 Financial Markets, Neoliberal Globalisation, and the Gulf

Finance is the nerve centre of modern capitalism. Without it, the kinds of changes to the world market seen throughout the last quarter of the twentieth century would have been impossible. Financial instruments, for example, were indispensable to the widening global reach of large international firms from the 1960s onwards – allowing cross-border investment through equity purchases or other types of acquisitions; helping to manage risks associated with fluctuations in interest rates, currencies, and commodity prices across different geographical spaces; and enabling firms to stabilise overseas financing costs through a variety of long-term debt markets (Panitch and Konings 2008; Subasat 2016). According to the McKinsey Global Institute, the value of world financial assets – including equities, private and government debt securities, and financial deposits – grew at compound annual average rate of 9% between 1990 and 2007, reaching a remarkable 359% of world GDP at the end of that period (Chesnais 2016, p. 38). Today, the growth rates for the financial sector far outpace the anaemic levels found in industry or trade, and have provided highly lucrative opportunities for speculation as well as a substitute for investment in productive activities (Roberts 2016; Shaikh 2016). With all aspects of social life and daily reproduction embroiled in financial markets, the decisions and behaviours of firms, governments, households, and individuals are increasingly determined by – and respond to – the imperatives of financial processes.

Historically, the Gulf's role in the genesis and subsequent trajectories of this global financial structure has been substantial. An early illustration of this was the consolidation of the so-called Euromarkets – financial markets that emerged in Europe through the late 1950s and 1960s, which lay outside the jurisdiction of national regulatory systems and were largely exempt from taxation and other domestic financial restrictions. London became the key international centre for Euromarket operations, allowing banks and companies to deal in deposits and bonds that were denominated in currencies different from their domestic markets (Gibson 1989; Norfield 2016). Following the nationalisation of Gulf oil companies in the 1970s and the large increase in oil prices that ensued (see Mitchell 2011, ch. 7),[6] Gulf capital deposits in North American and European banks operating in these Euromarkets reached very high levels. These flows of Gulf surpluses, popularly known as 'petrodollar

[6] Mitchell provides a rich analysis of this period, arguing that it was deeply foundational to the emergence of a new 'technology of rule', in which governance increasingly became elaborated through the concept of the market.

recycling', greatly increased the capacity of international banks to lend to multinational firms, governments, and other borrowers (Mandel 1975; Hanieh 2011a). The lightly regulated Euromarkets became a key institutional element to the growing weight of finance within global capitalism, allowing companies to borrow widely (often at a lower cost than in domestic markets), and thereby underpinning the internationalisation of production that began to gain ground from the 1970s onwards. They spurred the further development of other 'offshore' financial zones in the world market such as the Cayman Islands, where banks could conduct dealings in the Euromarkets from loosely regulated locations. These new markets were also pivotal to how the 'Third World' debt crisis unfolded through the 1980s, with cash-strapped countries in the South forced to borrow recycled petrodollars through Euromarkets, thereby becoming tightly enmeshed in debt relations to international financial institutions (Hanieh 2011a, pp. 40–56). Today, the power of the City of London and the dominance of US and European banks in the global financial system are the direct legacy of these markets (Norfield 2016).

Gulf financial flows, moreover, were also highly consequential to the emergence and consolidation of the United States as the dominant global power through the second half of the twentieth century. By agreeing to invest oil revenues in US Treasury securities, equities, and stocks – coupled with the denomination of the price of oil in US dollars – the surpluses of Gulf countries helped cement the preeminent status of the US dollar as 'world money' (Spiro 1999; Cooper 2011). In return, the Gulf monarchies received unconditional military and political support from the world's most powerful state. This four-decade arrangement was first codified through a secret deal negotiated between the Nixon administration and the Saudi government in June 1974, which committed the United States to 'buy oil from Saudi Arabia and provide the kingdom military aid and equipment. In return, the Saudis would plough billions of their petrodollar revenue back into Treasuries and finance America's spending' (Wong 2016). Diplomatic cables released in 2016 from the US National Archives revealed that this agreement was designed to remain hidden from public view, with the United States devising a system that allowed Saudi Arabia to bypass the usual process for buying Treasuries in order to conceal their involvement in the US government debt market (Wong 2016). With high levels of global demand for dollars the United States could issue its currency with relative lack of worry around inflation or devaluation and, in this manner, was able to spend more abroad than it actually earned, while avoiding the balance of payments problems that constrained the spending policies of other countries. US banks and financial institutions also became the main source for international companies and governments seeking to borrow – dollar centrality thus reinforced the size and weight of Anglo-American financial markets within the wider world market (Gowan 1999; Rude 2005; Panitch and Gindin 2012). The dollar's position as 'world money' also added a further weapon to the US government's power over other states, with the possibility of being cut off from the US banking system constituting an ever-present reminder of the American force behind global hierarchies.

More recently, flows of Gulf financial surpluses have been critical to supporting the sharp imbalances characterising the global economy over the past two decades – specifically, an international system where consumption remains mostly concentrated in the world's wealthiest countries, while production has shifted perceptibly away from the advanced core. At the beginning of the millennium, North America and Europe were responsible for around two-thirds of the value of all world imports (see later discussion), and by 2005, the World Bank was to note that the wealthiest 10% of the global population accounted for 59% of global consumption (World Bank 2008, p. 4). These levels of consumption, however, coincided with the sustained period of job outsourcing and stagnation of domestic wages that accompanied the emergence of neoliberal globalisation. For the United States in particular, the maintenance of these rising consumption levels thus came to depend heavily upon the provision of cheap credit. Numerous analyses confirm the rising inequality of US incomes during the 1990s and 2000s, which was ultimately offset by rapidly increasing household indebtedness that allowed consumption spending to continue apace (Palley 2002; Brown 2008; Setterfield 2013). The extension of credit to US consumers – facilitated primarily through housing mortgages and other forms of lending such as credit cards, 'zero-down' financing, student loans, and so forth – not only provided real effective demand, but also reinforced a wider ideological perception that growth in financial markets was essential to maintaining standards of living. Moreover, the various asset bubbles and financial income streams associated with this extension of credit – e.g. mortgage-backed securities – provided a highly lucrative avenue for speculation in an environment of overaccumulation and declining profitability of investment in production (Roberts 2016; Shaikh 2016).

But most importantly for the purposes of our story, this entire edifice necessarily rested upon the recirculation of global surpluses into US financial markets. Those countries that accumulated capital surpluses – principally China, Japan, and the Gulf monarchies – used them to purchase US financial instruments, and thereby supported continued growth of American consumption. Various financial bubbles, such as stock markets in the 1990s and US housing markets through to 2007, encouraged these flows of surplus capital from exporting countries, and were thus 'inextricably linked to the explosion of consumer debt in the United States' (Ivanova 2012, p. 65). Moreover, foreign capital purchases of US Treasury securities helped keep yields on key Treasury bonds low, and thus depressed the levels of mortgage rates linked to these securities (Ivanova 2012, p. 65). The financialisation of everyday life, in other words, was powerfully connected to the global imbalances associated with the internationalisation of capitalist production.

The crisis that emerged in US financial markets in 2008–2009 revealed the fragility and underlying tensions of a structure that rested upon such profound global imbalances. This 'Great Recession' saw the collapse of several prominent US financial institutions, a massive slump in world trade, and the emergence of a debt crisis through the Eurozone – it was the longest and deepest contraction in global output since the 1929–1932 Depression (Roberts 2016, p. 66). Although China was initially able to redirect some of its surpluses into domestic spending on infrastructure and thereby support exports from commodity producers across Latin America, Africa, and the Asia Pacific, global growth rates and investment levels remained at historical lows in the years following 2009 (Zhu and Kotz 2011; Roberts 2016, pp. 117–119). Nonetheless, despite the ongoing slump – or, perhaps better put, *as a result of it* – Gulf capital flows remain highly significant to the new environment of low growth, high debt, and stagnating investment levels. The remainder of this chapter analyses these flows empirically and conceptually, situating them within the Gulf's relationship to the wider world market before, during, and after this most recent crisis.

2.2 How Much and with Whom? Levels of Surplus Capital in the GCC

Any assessment of the volume and directionality of Gulf capital flows needs to contend with a variety of overlapping actors. These include state institutions – such as central banks, specialised investment bodies, and sovereign wealth funds – that hold revenues from hydrocarbon sales and invest these in various assets throughout the world. But beyond the state, it is also important to consider the wealth of the large business conglomerates and private individuals who play such an important role in the Gulf's economies. In examining the relative size of financial surpluses held by both these public and private entities – however problematic such a dichotomy might be in the case of the Gulf – we are also faced with

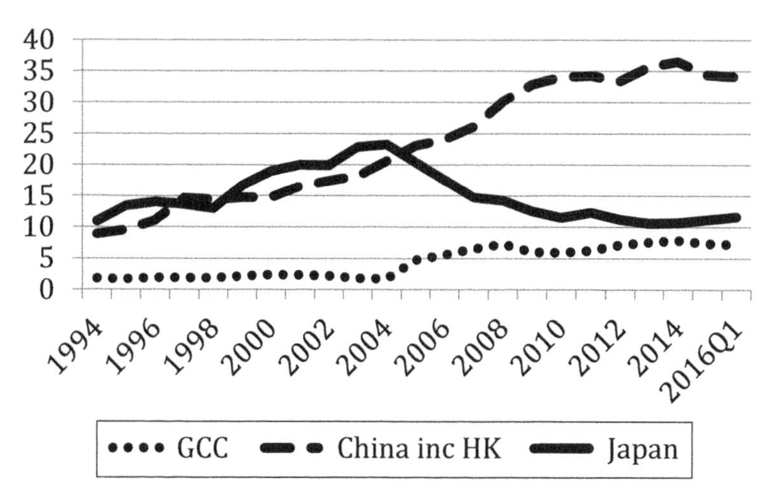

Figure 2.1 Foreign reserves: Gulf, China, and Japan (as percentage of total global reserves). Calculated from IMF International Financial Statistics.

many limitations in data availability and reliability, as well as deliberate attempts to conceal the volume of wealth and the uses to which it is put.

With these caveats in mind, we can begin with official holdings. Data from the International Monetary Fund indicate that foreign reserves held by GCC states stood at just over US$763 billion by the end of first quarter 2016. While this figure had fallen from a peak of US$920 billion in June 2014, it was nonetheless nearly 50% higher than in 2007, just prior to the global financial crisis. How does this compare with other countries with large reserve holdings? One broad indicator of these patterns is shown by the size of a country's foreign reserves as a proportion of total global reserves. Figure 2.1 displays this ratio for three of the largest holders of foreign reserves in the world – China (including Hong Kong), Japan, and the GCC. Two features of these international reserve data stand out. First, they confirm the very large imbalances that have emerged within the global economy over the past decade; remarkably, more than half of the world's total reserves are located in just China, Japan, and the GCC, a ratio that has increased from around one-fifth during the mid-1990s.

Second, there has been a noticeable shift in the relative weight of these three geographical areas over the two-decade period shown in the figure. From 1994 to 2004, Japan's reserves generally surpassed those of China and were the highest in the world, reaching 23.3% in 2004 compared with China's 20.6%. During the same time frame, the GCC's reserves fluctuated within a narrow band of 1.8%–2.4% of total global reserves. From 2004 onwards, however, the GCC's proportion increased around five-fold, while Japan's contribution halved. By the end of the first quarter of 2016, China held 34.1% of world reserves, Japan 11.7%, and the GCC 7.4%. These patterns may change in a scenario of prolonged low oil prices (see Chapter 7), but it is noteworthy that the data for the most recent two years do not indicate any substantial decrease in the GCC's weight globally, and, for the time being, it is clear that the GCC's official reserves make it one of the three core geographical zones of financial surplus within the global economy.

These figures, however, give a very incomplete picture of the levels of surplus capital in the GCC, as they do not include all foreign assets held by the Gulf's enormous sovereign wealth funds (SWFs) and other investment bodies.[7] In 2016, it was estimated that GCC SWFs accounted for a prodigious 37% of the world's total SWF assets under management (Townsend 2016). According to the US-based Sovereign Wealth Fund Institute, the total value of foreign assets held by the six largest GCC SWFs stood at US$2.5 trillion in 2016 – the region's largest fund, the Abu Dhabi Investment Authority (ADIA), held an estimated US$792 billion of this total and ranked second in the world behind Norway's Global Pension Fund.[8] To put this in historical perspective, in 2007, just prior to the global economic crisis, the McKinsey Global Institute (MGI) estimated that *all* GCC SWFs held a combined total of around US$1.5 trillion in assets (McKinsey Global Institute (MGI) 2008, pp. 12–13). In other words, the amount of assets held by SWFs in the GCC has increased by more than two-thirds over the last decade. Back in 2008, these levels led MGI to describe GCC SWFs as part of one of the four 'new powerbrokers' in the global economy; alongside Asian governments, hedge funds, and private equity firms, they reflected a 'dispersion of financial power away from traditional institutions in Western developed economies and toward new players and other parts of the world' (MGI 2008, p. 5). Today, there can be little doubt that the influence of these institutions on the global economy has greatly increased.

[7] These issues have raised a series of conceptual debates within the International Monetary Fund (IMF) on how best to measure reserve assets (see IMF 2007).

[8] These six are the Abu Dhabi Investment Authority (ADIA) at $792 billion, the Saudi Arabia Monetary Authority ($598 billion), Kuwait Investment Authority ($592 billion), Qatar Investment Authority ($256 billion), the Saudi Arabia's Public Investment Fund ($160 billion), and the Abu Dhabi Investment Council ($110 billion).

In addition to GCC governments and SWFs, it is also necessary to include levels of private wealth circulating within the Gulf as part of any assessment of how Gulf capitalism interacts with global accumulation. Within the GCC, it is estimated that privately held wealth grew by 17.5% each year from 2010 to 2014, with the total dollar amount doubling from US$1.1 trillion to US$2.2 trillion over this period (Strategy& 2015, p. 3). This trillion-dollar increase in GCC private wealth – which, it should be noted, does not include 'illiquid' assets such as real estate or business equity or collectable items such as artwork – was largely driven by booming stock markets and rising oil prices.[9] Importantly, the absolute number of Gulf families considered 'wealthy' also increased over this period, and is now believed to include up to 1.6 million households across the GCC (Strategy& 2015, p. 7). Of this figure, around 5,000 Gulf families are estimated to hold more than $500 million per household in liquid assets; with their combined total assets exceeding $700 billion, these households collectively constitute a second ADIA in the region (Strategy& 2015, p. 8). One striking confirmation of these trends is the Gulf's proportion of 'millionaire households'. According to a 2014 report by the Boston Consulting Group, countries from the GCC occupied 6 of the top 12 spots for the proportion of millionaire households at a global level in 2013; tiny Qatar ranked number one in the world with 17.5% of households holding at least a $1 million in wealth (up from 14.3% of households in 2012) (Boston Consulting Group (BCG) 2014). Very importantly, as I shall discuss in Chapter 7, this private wealth has continued to grow despite the recent oil price downturn, and thus remains a very substantial determinant of Gulf investment levels globally.

All of these figures need to be treated with some caution – the precise holdings of SWFs (or their geographical distribution) are often not disclosed, and estimates of private wealth do not give a clear indication of the split between foreign and domestic assets. Foreshadowing a theme that will be returned to later, there are also frequently blurred boundaries between SWFs and the investment vehicles that are privately owned by the Gulf's ruling families, making it difficult to discern ultimate ownership of assets.[10] There are undoubtedly large levels of capital held by Gulf companies and private individuals (particularly those from the

[9] Just less than 75% of this private wealth resides in Saudi Arabia and the UAE. See Strategy& (2015, pp. 4–9) for full discussion of these figures.

[10] Kristian Coates Ulrichsen discusses numerous examples of such blurred lines between SWFs and ruling family investment vehicles. Qatar's 2008 stake in Barclays Bank, for example, was split between the Qatar Investment Authority and another fund, Challenger, which was privately owned by then prime minister and head of the Qatar Investment Authority Sheikh Hamad bin Jassim Al Thani (Ulrichsen 2016, p. 119).

ruling families) held in offshore accounts with little transparency; indeed, the 2016 leaking of 11.5 million files from the Panama-based law firm Mossack Fonseca, the so-called Panama Papers, revealed a sizable number of GCC companies and individuals with offshore holdings that would likely not be recorded in the figures given earlier. Nonetheless, despite these limitations, by any conservative estimate the level of wealth held in the GCC certainly reaches into the many trillions of dollars.

2.3 GCC Surpluses and Global Financial Markets

Having established the rough magnitude of these figures, it is now possible to turn to a more concrete assessment of how this capital intersects with the broader trends of the global economy previously outlined. First, following historical patterns, Gulf financial surpluses have continued to be invested in US Treasuries and other types of US long-term securities. One set of data enabling us to partially capture how these patterns have evolved over recent years are the US government Treasury International Capital (TIC) statistics, which give monthly information on foreign purchases of US securities (including government and corporate debt). For most of its history – due to the secret deal noted earlier that kept Saudi holdings of US debt confidential – TIC data did not provide a detailed breakdown of holdings by individual GCC countries. In May 2016, however, following a Freedom of Information request from Bloomberg News, the US Treasury released a detailed breakdown of oil exporter holdings.[11] Using this new reclassification of the data, Figure 2.2 shows the total GCC holdings of US Treasury securities from 1974 to 2015. Closely following the Gulf's trend line shown in Figure 2.1, GCC holdings were relatively stable through the 1980s to early 2000s, and then underwent an extraordinary increase from 2004 onwards, with the value of these holdings increasing at an annual average rate of 29% from 2004 to 2015.

This TIC data need to be viewed with some uncertainty, and they are widely believed to significantly understate the level of Gulf capital flows into US Treasuries. The main reason for this is that the data do not reveal purchases made on behalf of a foreign investor through a third-country broker or custodian. Due to the desire for anonymity, much global investment takes place through such channels – hence the

[11] Interestingly, the impetus for this Freedom of Information request was a threat by Saudi Arabia to liquidate its treasury holdings in response to bipartisan moves to allow the Kingdom to be held responsible for the September 11 attacks. The subsequent debate confirmed the importance of Saudi holdings – although did little to clarify their actual magnitude.

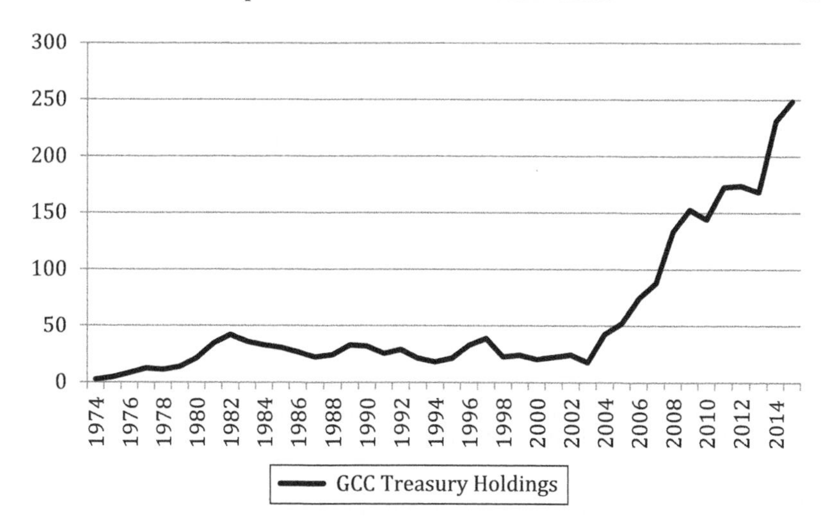

Figure 2.2 GCC holdings of US Treasury securities, 1974–2015, billions of dollars.
Source: US government Treasury International Capital (TIC) statistics.

extremely high proportion of US securities held by offshore financial centres such as in the Cayman Islands and other loosely regulated financial markets like the United Kingdom and Luxembourg. It is reckoned that a large proportion of Middle East investment in the United States is routed through such centres – in particular the City of London (see later discussion) – and some analysts put the real figure of Gulf investments at more than double that revealed by TIC (Wong 2016).[12]

With these provisos in mind, it is possible to use the TIC data to assess the relative weight of Gulf financial flows into US long-term securities at a global level. Leaving aside offshore financial centres for the reasons mentioned, China and Japan are by far the most important sources of foreign holdings of US securities in the world. In this context, Table 2.1 shows the holdings of GCC states[13] for various categories of US long-term securities

[12] For earlier discussions of these measurement issues, see Setser and Ziemba (2009).

[13] Despite the May 2016 release, historical TIC data do not provide a breakdown of the types of securities held by individual GCC countries – instead including them within a category of 'Asian oil exporters' (Bahrain, Iran, Iraq, Kuwait, Oman, Qatar, Saudi Arabia, and the UAE). However, it is safe to assume that the vast majority of holdings within this category are actually held by GCC countries, and because the following analysis is focused on looking at the more detailed breakdown of holdings (Treasuries, agency debt, US corporate bonds and stocks), this category of Asian oil exporters is used as a proxy for the GCC.

Table 2.1 *Gulf holdings of US long-term securities as a proportion of Chinese and Japanese holdings*

	Total US long-term securities	US Treasuries	US agency bonds	US corporate and other bonds	US stocks
2011	11.1	6.1	2.8	11.7	43.5
2012	11.2	5.9	2.5	10.2	40.6
2013	13.3	6.4	3.4	13.1	47.0
2014	14.7	7.7	3.1	15.7	45.8
2015	15.3	9.6	3.5	16.6	40.3
2016	15.1	9.6	3.8	15.9	43.4

Figures calculated by author from TIC data, yearly totals indicate monthly averages. Data run from September 2011 to March 2016.

as a proportion of total Chinese and Japanese (C&J) holdings from 2011 to 2016. Over this period, the table illustrates a notable increase in the Gulf's proportion of total C&J holdings in all categories except for US stocks, where the Gulf's proportion has remained essentially static (after a temporary sharp rise in 2013). Significantly, however, in this category of US stocks, the Gulf holds a very high proportion relative to C&J total holdings (43% in 2016). Indeed, according to the March 2016 TIC data, the GCC holdings of US corporate stocks was the seventh highest in the world, behind the Cayman Islands, United Kingdom, Canada, Luxembourg, Japan, and Switzerland; once again, the prevalence of offshore centres in this list further highlights the significance of the Gulf to US foreign holdings.

These data confirm that the Gulf has been one of the major sources of foreign capital inflows into the United States (alongside China, Japan, and offshore financial centres) throughout the period leading up to and immediately following the 2008–2009 crisis. Relative to Chinese and Japanese lending to the United States, the weight of the GCC within this structure has increased over this time frame. In this respect, flows of surplus capital to the United States from the Gulf remain a vital element to a global structure typified by persistently large current account deficits in the United States and large fiscal imbalances throughout other parts of the world market.

But the global financial system needs to be understood beyond simply US markets. While the United States remains the predominant power within global finance, the system as a whole needs to be viewed more akin to a web that incorporates a variety of financial markets within a deeply interconnected and hierarchical structure. One of the most important nodes within this web – whose long-standing linkages to the United States was closely connected to the development of the Euromarkets noted earlier – is the United Kingdom. The presence of international and UK banks operating through the City of London, in particular, has been a central feature of how the global financial system has operated for many decades. In this respect, the linkages between Gulf capital and UK financial markets are an important part of understanding how GCC financial surpluses reinforce the broader tendencies of global capitalism.

International Banks and the City of London

The need to move beyond a US-centric frame becomes evident when considering the distribution of GCC financial surpluses through the international banking system. According to the Bank of International Settlements, international banks held liabilities worth just over US$500 billion to the GCC in the last quarter of 2015. The vast majority of these liabilities are loans and deposits made by GCC banks or GCC non-bank firms to international banks (they are described as liabilities because they are essentially debts that international banks have to the GCC).[14] There is no reliable detailed breakdown of how these liabilities are ultimately distributed geographically – not least because of the presence of offshore financial centres – but it is evident from UK data that UK-based banks have held a very significant proportion of the GCC's global banking deposits since the late 1970s. By the end of 2015, GCC deposits in UK banks stood at around $160 billion, around one-third of the total liabilities of the international banking system to the GCC, and a figure considerably higher than liabilities of US banks vis-à-vis the GCC.[15]

The work of Tony Norfield (2016) – whose pioneering analysis of the City of London traces the emergence of the United Kingdom as a core centre of global finance in the post-war period – provides a useful framework through which to analyse the role of Gulf financial surpluses in this regard. Norfield argues that we need to take seriously the position of the United Kingdom as an imperialist power with its own global interests, separate from – but closely linked to – those of the United States. A key part of how these interests work is the position of the City of London as the world's largest international banking centre, and a major site for global currency deals and derivatives trading. Through the City's financial markets and institutions, which have their origins in the

[14] Loans of international banks to the GCC, by contrast, are considered as assets of these banks because they represent a claim on a GCC entity.

[15] By the end of 2015, US banks and financial firms held liabilities of US$119 billion to all 'Asian oil exporting countries', a category that includes, but is larger than, the GCC countries (see earlier discussion). There is no available individual breakdown for the GCC. Data from US Treasury Statistics, http://ticdata.treasury.gov/Publish/lb_46612.txt.

Euromarkets noted earlier, the United Kingdom is able to act as a 'broker for global capitalism, taking a cut from deals that account for more than two-fifths of all foreign exchange transactions in the world economy' (Norfield 2016, p. 194). In addition, the City is a key node in a global web of financial markets (both 'onshore' and 'offshore'), intermediating capital flows from around the world that are then redirected into funding the balance of payments of richer countries (notably the United States) (Norfield 2016, p. 208).

Within his account of the United Kingdom's position at a global level, Norfield discusses the significance of Gulf financial flows – particularly from Saudi Arabia – to the evolution of London finance. Data provided by Norfield demonstrate that UK net borrowing from Saudi Arabia reached US$71 billion by the end of 2014, at a time when UK net bank borrowing at a global scale was US$341 billion. These UK liabilities represented Saudi deposits in UK banks minus UK-based bank loans to Saudi Arabia – they are, in effect, net loans made by Saudi Arabia to the UK banking system.

It is possible to extend Norfield's analysis to provide a more detailed look at the role of the GCC as a whole within the UK financial system. Figure 2.3 shows the quarterly levels of GCC deposits and loans vis-à-vis the UK banking system from 1986 to March 2016. It reveals that from

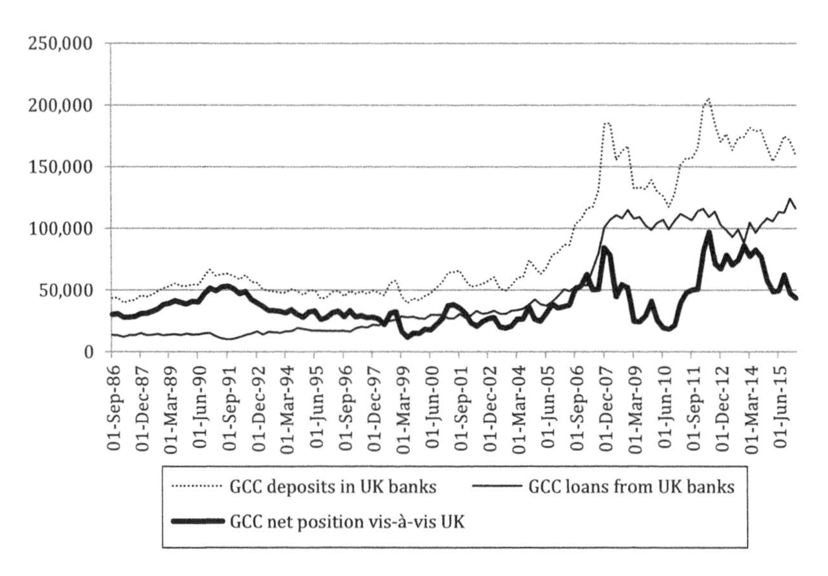

Figure 2.3 GCC net position vis-à-vis the United Kingdom.
Source: UK Office for National Statistics, www.ons.gov.uk/.

Table 2.2 *UK net external position vis-à-vis GCC states (US$bn)*

	UK net external position vis-à-vis the world	Of which:					
		Saudi Arabia	Kuwait	UAE	Qatar	Oman	Bahrain
2000	−119.0	−16.9	−3.3	−7.6	−0.9	−1.0	3.1
2003	−324.9	−11.9	−2.5	−8.6	−0.7	−1.4	4.5
2006	−513.0	−43.4	−6.4	−8.9	0.4	−2.0	7.0
2009	−756.3	−63.9	−7.6	4.8	9.9	0.4	15.9
2012	−491.2	−82.7	−13.1	22.2	3.3	−1.4	4.7
2015	−246.0	−78.4	−14.4	27.7	14.9	−0.2	3.2

Source: UK Office for National Statistics, www.ons.gov.uk/.

1986 to the early 2000s, the GCC was a net lender to the United Kingdom, although the amount of deposits remained relatively stable through this time. From 2003 onwards, however, there was a very large increase in both deposits of GCC funds in UK banks and the Gulf's borrowing from the United Kingdom – both trends related to the rapidly growing Gulf financial surpluses, on one side, and the prodigious building boom that has taken place across the GCC since the early 2000s, on the other (see Chapter 3). Most significantly, the GCC's net position vis-à-vis the United Kingdom has widened considerably through the 2000s, albeit with fluctuations.[16]

Table 2.2 breaks these data down further, showing the United Kingdom's net external position globally for various years, and its position vis-à-vis the six different GCC states. It indicates that the United Kingdom has consistently been a net borrower from the rest of the world, confirming similar data from Norfield, who notes that the 'persistent [UK] deficit grew dramatically in the 2000s, peaking around 2007 at more than $800bn, before the onset of the latest financial crisis' (2016, p. 208). As part of this overall deficit, however, there has been very large net UK borrowing from the GCC, particularly Saudi Arabia and Kuwait. Interestingly, the UAE and Qatar were also net lenders to the United Kingdom in the early 2000s, but this has turned to a net borrowing position in

[16] It should be noted that these figures represent aggregate flows from different companies and institutions. It may be the case that one group of firms put more funds into the United Kingdom, while another tends to borrow more. It is not possible to differentiate between these sources from publicly available information.

recent years – likely connected to the very high levels of real estate and infrastructure construction in both countries that has been partly funded through borrowing from international banks.

Beyond the precise numbers, what does the relationship between UK banks and the GCC imply for the wider global financial system and the position of the United Kingdom within this? First, as with all banking transactions, loans and deposits made between UK-based banks and the GCC attract small margins and commissions, which reinforces the bottom line of financial institutions operating in the United Kingdom. In this respect, the GCC is part of a wider global pattern, through which London's position as a centre for global finance operates in a mutually reinforcing relationship with the power of the world's largest banks. Gulf capital flows bolster both sides of this relationship, and are significant to this structure given the fact that such a large proportion of the GCC's banking deposits are placed within the United Kingdom.

But perhaps even more consequential than the individual profits of banks and the general importance this accords to the United Kingdom, GCC deposits constitute a major enabling factor for why UK financial markets can play the particular role within the global system that they do – a role that sees the United Kingdom as a large net borrower from areas such as the GCC and, simultaneously, a net lender of these funds to other key financial centres of the global economy like the United States (see Norfield 2016). In this manner, by acting as a transmission belt that reroutes the world's savings into the core zones of the world economy, the City of London reinforces and reproduces the strength of US dollar–based financial markets; within this structure, the GCC's centrality is indicated by its position as one of the world's largest net lenders to the United Kingdom (alongside offshore financial centres). Taken as a whole, these patterns provide another insight into how Gulf capital flows bolster the financial mechanisms underpinning neoliberal globalisation – specifically, persistently large US current account deficits that reflect the global production and consumption patterns characterising the latest phase of internationalisation.

In assessing these trends, however, it is important to consider that the relative proportion of GCC surpluses that flow into the international banking system (such as banks headquartered in the United Kingdom) has likely declined through the 2000s.[17] On one side, this is partially

[17] According to the Bank of International Settlements, the proportion of liabilities held by international banks to the GCC in 2007 was about half what it was in the 1990s (Sturm, Strasky, Adolf, and Peschel 2008, p. 43).

explained by the growing share (described earlier) that instead went to the US long-term securities; but in order to more fully capture the role of Gulf financial flows in the global economy, it is necessary to turn to a third form through which these surpluses are incorporated into the world market: foreign direct investments by Gulf companies, SWFs, or wealthy individuals.

Foreign Direct Investment

Discussion of foreign direct investment (FDI) by GCC-based entities hit global headlines following the economic crisis that erupted in 2007. Through the ensuing collapse, as fears of further downturn cast a spotlight on company balance sheets, many large corporations turned towards the GCC as a potential source of capital. GCC investors subsequently took high-profile positions in some of the world's biggest companies and brands, including financial institutions such as Credit Suisse, Barclays, Deutsche Bank, and Citigroup;[18] car manufacturers Daimler and Volkswagen;[19] UK-based firms including P&O, the London Stock Exchange Group, Travelodge Hotels, Canary Wharf, and British Airways;[20] mining and natural resource companies such as Glencore and the Spanish oil company CEPSA;[21] Italy's largest airline, Alitalia;[22] and the leading Formula One and automotive technology firm, McLaren

[18] For Credit Suisse, the two largest shareholders (including purchase rights) were the Saudi Olayan Group (10%) and Qatar Holding (10%) as of November 2017; one-third of shares in Barclays Bank were owned by investors from the Gulf in 2007, although that proportion has since dropped; the Qatari royal family was the largest shareholder in Deutsche Bank until May 2017, when it was overtaken by a Chinese group. Saudi prince and businessman Waleed bin Talal is the largest individual investor in Citigroup.

[19] The largest individual shareholder in Daimler is the Kuwait Investment Authority, while the third largest shareholding in Volkswagen (16.7% as of July 2016) is held by a Qatari SWF.

[20] P&O was bought by Dubai World in 2006, creating the third largest ports operator in the world. UAE and Qatari firms became the two largest shareholders of the London Stock Exchange following investments in 2007. In the same year, Travelodge was bought by Dubai International Capital, which imposed a 'calamitous high-debt financing structure' and later sold it on to two US-based hedge funds (www.theguardian.com/business/nils-pratley-on-finance/2012/sep/04/travelodge-buyout-pain-dubai-nils-pratley). The Qatar Investment Authority owns Canary Wharf, and Qatar Airways is the largest shareholder of British Airways, with around 12% as of May 2016.

[21] The biggest shareholder in Glencore, one of the largest mining companies in the world, is the Qatar Investment Authority (www.cityam.com/239750/glencores-biggest-shareholder-reduces-stake-in-embattled-miner), while CEPSA – the fourth largest industrial company in Spain – was bought by an Abu Dhabi firm in 2009.

[22] Owned by the UAE's Etihad Airways.

Group[23] – even the social media company Twitter now counts a Saudi billionaire as its second largest shareholder.[24]

Of course, these high-profile deals should not be taken to mean that Gulf investments now exceed cross-border flows originating from the advanced capitalist states. Although there has been a slight shift away from North America and the EU as the major origin of FDI over recent decades, flows of FDI continue to predominantly come from European countries (33% of all global FDI outflows between 2009 and 2015), North America (27%), China (13%, including Hong Kong),[25] and Japan (7.8%).[26] Likewise, the stocks of accumulated foreign investment remain concentrated in these core zones of the world market. North America and Europe, in other words, continue to be both the source and destination for the majority of cross-border capital flows in the contemporary period.

Nonetheless, within this overall structure of the world market, the magnitude of Gulf FDI flows has grown notably over the past decade and a half. Between 2000 and 2015, the GCC's global share of FDI outflows tripled, reaching 1.6%, a level that exceeded the whole of South Asia (including India), the entirety of Africa, and sitting at about the same as those of all South American countries combined.[27] For so-called greenfield investments – new cross-border investments that are built from scratch – the Gulf has been particularly prominent. Indeed, from 2009 to 2015, four GCC states – the UAE, Qatar, Saudi Arabia, and Kuwait – ranked within the top 40 of all countries in the world for total greenfield FDI, with UAE placed at number 10, ahead of India, Hong Kong, Switzerland, and the Netherlands. During this period, the total value of greenfield FDI investments made by the GCC was fourth highest of all regions in the world – behind the EU, North America, and East Asia. Remarkably, the GCC was responsible for 4.5% of the entire world's greenfield investments – a level comparable to China (4.7% of the world total), and surpassing Korea, Spain, Hong Kong,

[23] McLaren Group is 50% owned by Bahrain's SWF Mumtalakat. A French-Saudi businessman Mansour Ojjeh owns another 25% of the company (http://news.sky.com/story/ousting-dennis-risks-deals-worth-163160m-mclaren-bosses-warn-10658644).

[24] www.bbc.co.uk/newsbeat/article/34474798/meet-twitters-second-biggest-shareholder-saudi-prince-alwaleed-bin-talal.

[25] The figures for China and Hong Kong are 6.8% and 6.2%, respectively.

[26] Data from UNCTAD.

[27] Figures calculated by the author from UNCTAD World Investment Report, 2016, annex table 02. It should be noted that these figures do not capture the scale of GCC portfolio investments (i.e. under 10% of total equity value). Such portfolio flows from the GCC are likely much higher (partly because they help conceal the identity of the investor). I am grateful to Tony Norfield for pointing this out to me.

Canada, and all individual European countries except for Germany, the United Kingdom, and France.

These broad trends (drawn from UNCTAD data) provide a suggestive illustration of how Gulf financial flows have become a significant component of the global control of capital. But as aggregate figures, they do not differentiate where these investments take place or the levels of FDI that might be occurring internal to particular regions as opposed to those that occur between the region and the rest of the world (e.g. UK investment in France would be counted as part of the total EU FDI). Reported figures for FDI often also measure the value of *announced* deals – they thus do not necessarily indicate that the investment actually took place. At a more systematic level, therefore, how can we understand flows of Gulf financial surpluses into different areas of the world market, and how does the Gulf compare with the other prominent so-called emerging markets, popularly known as the BRICS?

Table 2.3 presents a partial analysis of these trends, through examining cross-border merger and acquisition (M&A) data for eight key regions and countries between 2000 and 2016. M&A differs from greenfield investment as it measures the changing ownership of existing corporate entities and not newly built up assets; it is, nonetheless, an important component of total FDI (UNCTAD estimated in 2016 that M&A deals made up just over 40% of the value of global FDI in 2015) (UNCTAD 2016, p. x). Due to the fact that these figures are based on individual deals that are confirmed to have taken place, and in which the nationality of the investor and seller is known, they also enable us to track approximate levels of cross-border purchases within, and from, specific locations (ignoring, once again, the not-insignificant investments from offshore zones).[28]

These data provide a revealing insight into the nature of the world market hierarchies described earlier. First, the table confirms that corporate mergers and acquisitions remain fully centred upon two core regions – North America and the European Union. More than 85% of both the entire value and number of M&A deals across the geographical areas displayed in Table 2.3 involved acquisitions by North American or European firms. North America and Europe also constituted the principal geographical target for these deals (80% of total deal value and 70% of the number of deals). Japan, viewed for many years as the third key pole of a triadic global economy, now sits in a much weaker position.

[28] The one important proviso for these data is that, for a small minority of deals, the actual value of the transaction is unknown. The precise values should thus be taken as indicative, although their relative magnitude can be considered broadly accurate.

Table 2.3 *Value of cross-border mergers and acquisitions (in euro bn) and number of deals (in parentheses), 2000–2016, selected countries/regions*

To From	North America	EU	Japan	GCC	China	India	Russia	Brazil	Total
North America		1,418 (23,804)	94.5 (1,434)	15.0 (204)	73.9 (2,625)	49.1 (2,257)	25.4 (414)	51.4 (1,122)	1,727.3 (31,860)
EU	1,780 (12,544)		75.7 (816)	9.5 (363)	64.5 (1,543)	63.3 (1,637)	159.6 (1,924)	132.0 (1,239)	2,284.6 (20,066)
Japan	146.9 (1,052)	77.8 (811)		3.4 (36)	24.3 (949)	9.5 (316)	0.2 (41)	8.7 (80)	270.8 (3,285)
GCC	39.1 (215)	110.1 (547)	n.a. (4)		8.8 (19)	4.9 (116)	0.1 (5)	1.6 (10)	164.6 (916)
China	35.9 (439)	54.5 (443)	0.3 (37)	0.01 (9)		2.17 (23)	10.8 (21)	13.2 (25)	116.9 (997)
India	17.8 (519)	11.0 (600)	0.06 (12)	0.6 (76)	0.5 (40)		2.8 (8)	1.0 (23)	33.76 (1,278)
Russia	13.5 (146)	40.4 (839)	0.02 (4)	n.a. (4)	2.4 (17)	4.7 (12)		0.06 (9)	61.03 (1,031)
Brazil	5.8 (94)	28.4 (100)	1.1 (3)	0.2 (4)	0.6 (7)	n.a. (1)	0.01 (2)		36.11 (211)
Total	2,040 (15,009)	1,740.2 (27,144)	171.7 (2,310)	28.71 (696)	175 (5,200)	133.67 (4,362)	198.91 (2,415)	207.96 (2,508)	4,695.1 (59,644)

Note: In order to avoid double counting, deals involving multiple partners have been attributed to the country/region in which the primary acquirer is based. Deal value is not always available, so amounts should be taken as indicative only. Purchases made through offshore financial centres located outside one of the identified regions have not been included (e.g. the Cayman Islands). Figures from Zephyr M&A database. Data show value of M&A deals in billion euros (number of M&A deals). EU is EU-28; North America is United States and Canada. China does not include Hong Kong.

At the same time, the data also point to the substantial weight of the GCC in financial flows to Europe and North America, relative to other countries outside the advanced core. The value of M&A deals involving Gulf capital in the areas shown vastly surpassed Chinese, Indian, Russian, and Brazilian investments and came close to reaching that of Japan. Of the countries listed, more than half the value of all non-North American/European M&A targeting the EU came from the GCC during this period. Although the same figure for the US/Canada market was much less (17.7%), GCC-led purchases of North American companies still exceeded the value of those from China, Brazil, Russia, or India. These figures should not be taken to imply that GCC M&A is greater than that of the so-called BRICS at the global level – indeed, UNCTAD statistics show that from 2000 to 2015, total GCC M&A purchases globally were around one-third that of Brazil, Russia, China, and India combined (still a striking figure given the weight of these four countries in the global economy).[29] Rather, the lopsided nature of these figures suggests that M&A from the latter four countries have principally targeted their own regional neighbourhoods or other developing countries, while GCC capital flows are much more oriented towards the advanced capitalist core.[30] Nonetheless, these trends raise interesting questions around theoretical limitations of the BRICS concept as it is commonly formulated – given the Gulf's preponderance in cross-border investment flows, an argument could certainly be made that the GCC deserves consideration for inclusion in this category.

Returning to the theoretical framing outlined in Chapter 1, we can see how this aspect of the Gulf's interaction with other parts of the world economy – a relation expressed through the mediation of financial flows – has been an important constitutive element to how the global whole looks from the vantage point of the early twenty-first century. The different routes of Gulf financial flows examined in this section – US debt and other markets, the international banking system, and cross-border investment flows – confirm the ongoing centrality of the Gulf to the structure of global finance. Alongside Chinese and Japanese surpluses, the recycling of Gulf foreign reserves has helped to support the US balance of payments and the particular position of US power within the global

[29] Calculated by the author from UNCTAD (2016, annex table 10). Moreover, from 2012 to 2015, the combined value of M&A purchases from Brazil, Russia, and India stood at only two-thirds that of the GCC.

[30] UNCTAD notes, for example: '14 per cent of Brazil's outward FDI stock in 2014 was in Latin America, 35 per cent of Indian outward FDI stock is in Asia, and ... [s]eventy-five per cent of Chinese FDI stock abroad is invested in Asian developing economies' (UNCTAD 2016, p. 12).

economy. This role has become even more important following the financial crisis of 2008–2009 and its continuing global reverberations. At the same time, GCC financial flows are pivotal to how other aspects of global finance are currently constituted – from the position of centres such as London to the ownership and control of corporate structures throughout all areas of the world market. Although the relative weight of the GCC within all these processes has increased, future trajectories will critically depend on the path of global oil prices and the domestic fiscal needs of the GCC states – questions that I will return to in later chapters.

2.4 The GCC as a Market

A further crucial element to the GCC's relationship with other parts of the global whole is through its purchase of the world's goods and services – a more indirect means by which financial surpluses are recirculated into international markets. In this regard, the Gulf stands out as one of the world's fastest growing sources of global demand over the past two decades – its share of world imports increasing at a much faster rate than most other zones of the world economy. This aspect of the Gulf's integration into global capitalism is closely related to the forms of inter-capitalist competition that have developed around access to this market (particularly in the context of generalised global stagnation); it has also significantly shaped the nature of capitalist class formation in the Gulf.

Beginning with the global trends, Table 2.4 shows the Gulf's share of world merchandise imports (by value) from 2000 to 2015, in comparison to the EU, North America, Japan, China, India, Russia, and Brazil. Taken together, these eight areas accounted for more than three-quarters of all global merchandise imports in 2015 – a stark indication of the patterns of uneven development that have characterised the development of the world market over recent decades. The EU and North America remain the principal markets within this structure, accounting for 30%–50% of all world imports in 2015 (the precise figure depends on whether internal EU trade is counted in the global total). Nonetheless, despite this unevenness, a relative shift away from North America/EU is also clearly evident, with both blocs seeing a decline of around seven percentage points each in their share of world imports since 2000. Similarly, Japan has also experienced a relative drop in its importance as a global market over this period, with its share of world imports falling at the fastest rate of all countries/regions shown in the table.

In contrast, the share of other markets outside the EU, North America, and Japan has increased very considerably over this period – from a total of around 10% of global imports in 2000 to more than 20% in 2015.

Table 2.4 *Share of world merchandise import value, selected years*

	2000	2003	2006	2009	2012	2015	Growth in share of world imports, 2000–2015 (%)
EU (28) (including internal trade)*	38.5 (13.6)	41.0 (13.4)	39.1 (13.8)	37.6 (13.5)	31.8 (12.3)	31.8 (11.4)	−17.4 (−16.0)
North America	25.0	21.9	20.4	17.0	17.1	18.8	−24.8
China including Hong Kong	6.5	8.2	9.0	10.6	12.7	13.4	105.2
Japan	5.6	4.9	4.6	4.3	4.7	3.9	−31.3
GCC	1.3	1.6	1.8	2.5	2.6	2.9	130.9
India	0.8	0.9	1.4	2.0	2.6	2.3	205.9
Russia	0.7	1.0	1.3	1.5	1.8	1.2	74.0
Brazil	0.9	0.6	0.8	1.0	1.2	1.1	22.6

Source: WTO Statistics.

* Figures in parentheses indicate the EU's external trade, i.e. excluding those imports that occur within the European Union.

China clearly stands out in this respect – a phenomenon related to the more general trends I discussed at the beginning of this chapter – but the very rapid increase in the GCC's share of world imports is also apparent. Over the period shown, the rate of growth of the Gulf's market share has been second only to India, which it now also exceeds in absolute terms – a striking trend given that India's population is more than 25 times that of the Gulf. With almost 3% of the world market, the GCC also holds a greater import share of the world total than Russia or Brazil, and if present trends continue, will soon surpass Japan.

What are these imports, and where do they come from? In value terms, most of the GCC's merchandise imports originate from the EU, China, and the United States – in 2015, these three sources accounted for more than one-half of all Gulf imports from the world (EU 2016, p. 8). The European share of this is high and growing, making up 27.8% of the Gulf's total imports in 2015 (up from 23.5% in 2012) (EU 2013, p. 9; EU 2016, p. 8). Reflecting the recent growth in sectors such as construction, industry, transport, and logistics, a large part of world exports to the GCC are machinery and transport equipment, reaching around one-half of all European and US exports to the region, and around one-third of Chinese exports (by value in 2015).[31] Indeed, the Gulf represents a major market for this particular type of high value-added export: in 2015, 7.3% of Europe's global exports of machinery and transport went to the Gulf (up from 5.7% in 2012). Similarly, for the United States, 4.8% of its world exports of machinery and transport equipment were destined for the GCC in 2015, an increase from only 1.5% in 2000.[32] The Gulf's share of Chinese exports of this type has also doubled between 2000 and 2015, reaching just over 2% by the end of this period. The import of this equipment is closely connected to patterns of class formation in the Gulf, as well as the centrality of the built environment to accumulation in the region. In this sense, we can see the other side to the GCC's internal relation to the world economy: patterns of capital accumulation (and class formation) in the Gulf are both shaped by – and act to shape – their forms of interaction with other parts of the global totality.

Another aspect to this mutual conditioning of the GCC and the global can be seen in the import of basic consumer commodities such as food, clothing, and other household goods. This import trade is a key site for capital accumulation in the Gulf, which Chapter 3 will demonstrate in

[31] For China, a higher proportion is made up of other manufactured items such as clothing and footwear.

[32] Figures calculated by the author from the UN Comtrade website.

some detail. As with much of the rest of the world, everyday basic consumer imports tend to originate from China, India, or the rest of South Asia; China, for example, supplies more than half of all clothing imports to the GCC, and India is the largest source of staple foods such as rice. But alongside these everyday necessities, the Gulf is also a significant global market for luxury goods and international brands, with demand in this area driven by tourism and the Gulf's extremely high proportion of wealthy individuals. One astonishing case is that of Qatar, where it has been estimated that each citizen spends on average US $4,000 per month on luxury products (Walker 2016). The marketing and distribution of these luxury goods have been closely linked to the specific forms of urban development seen in the Gulf – particularly the ubiquitous mega-malls and shopping centres of the Gulf that are now expanding across the Middle East.

It is important, however, to disaggregate the role of different GCC states vis-à-vis this import trade. The two principal entry points for imports are the UAE and Saudi Arabia, which together account for around three-quarters of the value of the world's exports to the Gulf. In turn, these two states are major exporters to other Gulf countries. Taken together, the sum of UAE and Saudi exports to other Gulf states exceeds that from any other individual country; in 2014, UAE/Saudi exports ranged from around 14% of Kuwait and Qatar's total imports to 36% and 47% for Oman and Bahrain, respectively. A notable aspect of this intra-GCC trade is the UAE's role as a 're-exporter', by which it imports goods from the rest of the world and then sends them on to other Gulf states without processing. In 2015, the UAE was the largest exporter to Oman and the third largest to Kuwait, Qatar and Bahrain – around 70% of all UAE exports to these four countries were re-exports that had been previously imported from the rest of the world. I will draw this point out further in subsequent discussions; at the moment it suffices to note that the GCC regional integration project is a partial expression of how the pan-GCC scale increasingly mediates the relation between the national (i.e. individual Gulf state) and the global – further illustration of the importance of carefully delineating the interaction of different scales as part of understanding the character of the whole.

Commercial Services

Perhaps even more notable than the Gulf's position as a market for global merchandise exports is its role in commercial services trade. The prodigious growth in 'mega-projects' and other forms of urban development across the GCC has been accompanied by a demand for various forms of imported services – including transportation, telecommunications, insurance, wholesale trade, marketing, construction, engineering, and legal services. Particularly noteworthy in the case of the Gulf are transport and logistics; these sectors have been critical to consolidating the position of the region within the world market, accelerating the turnover time of commodity trade and enabling the Gulf's deeper integration into the global accumulation circuits that stretch from East to West (Cowen 2014). Such shifts are reflected in the rapid growth of the Gulf's air and maritime infrastructure, which holds significant implications for both forms of urban development and the GCC's position within regional circulatory routes (Ziadah 2017).

Given these trends, Table 2.5 shows the share of world commercial services for the same geographical areas listed in Table 2.4, along with the subsector of transport services (detailed breakdown of data for other types of services is not available). Similar to the patterns of global merchandise trade, it is clear that the EU and North America have historically been the major sources of global demand for commercial services, although this has undergone a relative change in recent years with the emergence of China as a third key pole in this aspect of global trade. China's growth in this respect has been substantial – with its share of the world market for imported services growing much more rapidly than its share of merchandise imports.

Likewise, the Gulf's global position has also increased significantly. In 2015, four GCC states were among the top 25 individual country importers of commercial services globally in value terms (the UAE, Saudi Arabia, Qatar, and Kuwait) (WTO 2016).[33] Taken as a whole, the GCC constituted 4.0% of the world's imports of commercial services in 2015 (Table 2.5). This share was the fourth highest in the world – behind the EU, United States, and China. With the exception of China, the growth in GCC market share has exceeded that of all regions/countries shown in Table 2.5. Within this, the transport component of commercial services is of particular note. For this sector, the GCC market share has grown faster than any other region in Table 2.5, and is now approaching levels found in China and North America.

In addition to transport, another critically important sector of demand for services in the Gulf is the provision of construction and related engineering services. The GCC is one of the most important markets in the world for this sector, due to the massive building boom over the last decade associated with new infrastructure, shopping malls, and other

[33] This top 25 list excludes intra-EU imports.

Table 2.5 *Share of World Commercial Services import value, selected years; world total includes EU internal trade; transport is a component of commercial services*

		2005	2007	2009	2011	2013	2015	Growth in world share (%)
EU (28) (excluding internal trade)*	Commercial services	n.a.	n.a.	43.2 (17.6)	39.3 (15.8)	38.3 (15.6)	37.2 (15.9)	−13.8 (−9.7)
	Transport	n.a.	n.a.	34.9 (15.4)	31.2 (14.0)	30.1 (13.6)	30.0 (13.1)	−14.1 (−14.9)
North America	Commercial services	14.5	13.5	13.7	12.9	12.6	12.9	−11.0
	Transport	14.5	12.0	10.9	10.6	10.8	11.9	−18.0
China including Hong Kong	Commercial services	3.3	5.9	6.1	7.7	8.8	11.7	252.6
	Transport	4.2	6.4	7.1	8.8	9.5	8.6	104.7
Japan	Commercial services	5.5	4.7	4.6	4.2	3.7	3.8	−31.2
	Transport	5.9	5.4	4.8	4.4	4.0	3.8	−36.6
GCC	Commercial services	2.2	3.1	3.2	3.7	3.7	4.0	84.3
	Transport	3.2	4.4	5.5	6.4	6.8	7.7	141.0
India	Commercial services	1.9	2.1	2.4	3.0	2.7	2.7	42.4
	Transport	3.1	3.5	4.3	5.2	4.8	4.8	56.3
Brazil	Commercial services	0.9	1.0	1.3	1.7	1.8	1.5	74.2
	Transport	0.7	0.9	1.0	1.2	1.3	1.0	30.9
Russia	Commercial services	1.6	1.8	1.8	2.1	2.7	1.9	19.6
	Transport	0.7	1.0	1.1	1.4	1.5	1.1	44.7

Source: Calculated by author from WTO Time Series Statistical database (http://stat.wto.org/).

* Figures in parentheses exclude internal EU trade.

housing and commercial real estate projects. There is no single statistical source for figures related to construction services, but a rough estimate drawn from figures from the WTO and UNCTAD indicates that GCC imports of these services reached around 25% of the world's total in 2014.[34] This proportion is far in excess of any country in the world – including China, Russia, and Japan, the other three main markets for construction services globally.

These imports of services provide a further conduit through which the Gulf is integrated into global circuits of accumulation. For the world's largest providers of commercial services – including transport, engineering and contracting, logistics, legal, and financial firms – contracts won in the Gulf have formed a vital source of revenue over the past decade. This is particularly relevant in the context of stagnating demand for these services in other parts of the world market since the crash of 2008–2009 (with the exception of China), as the figures in Table 2.5 illustrate. I will return to these trends in later chapters, where I explore the nature of capital accumulation through these types of services, and place them in the context of wider urban development patterns throughout the Middle East.

Military Imports

A further crucial route for the recirculation of GCC surpluses into the international economy is through the import of military hardware. Historically, this has been an important part of the Gulf's relationship with Western states. As Timothy Mitchell notes, in contrast to other commodities bought by the Gulf, 'weapons ... could be purchased to be stored up rather than used, and came with their own forms of justification' (2011, p. 156). Moreover, their technical sophistication and high expense provided a very compact means through which to recycle petrodollars to Western producers, and levels of consumption were not limited by any practical capacity to consume (Mitchell 2011, p. 156). For these reasons, high military expenditure has long been a characteristic of state spending in the Gulf – from 1985 to 1990, for example, the annual value of Saudi military imports accounted for between 28% and 39% of

[34] Figure calculated by the author using the 2014 UNCTAD Comtrade data for construction services, which provides details for 98 countries including China, Russia, India, the United States, United Kingdom, and most other European states. Apart from Saudi Arabia and Kuwait, however, Comtrade data on construction services imports are not available for the other GCC states. I have extracted the information for Bahrain, UAE, Qatar, and Oman from the World Trade Organization (WTO) database (http://i-tip.wto.org/services/ChartResults.aspx), added these figures to the Comtrade data, and calculated the relative share.

the country's total imports (Hanieh 2011a, p. 77). In the most recent period, largely due to the Gulf's regional rivalries with Iran and the Saudi war against Yemen (see Chapter 8), this military expenditure has exploded in size. Today, the GCC has become the largest market for weapons in the world.

According to the SIPRI Arms and Military Expenditure Programme, nearly 20% of world military imports went to the GCC in 2015, with Saudi Arabia and the UAE ranking, respectively, as the first and fifth largest importers globally. Taken together, Saudi Arabia and the UAE were responsible for 80% of all GCC's military imports in 2015, although Qatar, Kuwait, and Oman also ranked among the world's top 40 importing countries. The GCC's share of the global market has more than doubled since 2011, with only India rivalling it in import levels – between 2011 and 2015 India was the destination for around 14.1% of the world's weapons imports, a level just below that of the GCC over the same period (14.4%).

But unlike India and other major weapons importers such as China, who tend to rely heavily on Russian-produced arms, the majority of the Gulf's weapons are purchased from the United States, United Kingdom, and – to a lesser degree – France. Between 2011 and 2015, more than three-quarters of GCC imports came from these three countries, with the United States alone responsible for 53% of total weapons sold to the Gulf. It is difficult, however, to determine with any precision the amounts of money involved in this form of commodity export, as individual country reporting is unreliable and the standard trade data used in Tables 2.4 and 2.5 do not appear to record all military imports or distinguish between dual use items. SIPRI uses its own value indicator that attempts to measure the production costs of weapons – thus enabling longitudinal comparison of volumes of military transfers – but it does not reflect the actual financial amounts of completed deals.

Nonetheless, some general indications are available of the scale of this trade in the cases of the United Kingdom and United States. According to official statistics from the UK Ministry of Defence, total global export orders for defence equipment and services between 2007 and 2014 were valued at £59.6 billion (Ministry of Defence, Finance and Economics Bulletin – Trade, Industry and Contracts, 2015, table 9). While this figure is not broken down by precise geographical destination of sales, a high proportion can be attributed to the GCC. Indeed, the Ministry of Defence notes that certain 'boom' years in UK military exports were associated with particularly large orders from the Gulf – in 2007, for example, a £4.4 billion order for Typhoon aircraft by Saudi Arabia and sales of naval patrol vessels to Oman saw UK total export orders to rise to £9.7 billion for that year. From 2005 to 2014, 61% of all UK defence exports went to the Middle East, equivalent to £42.1 billion – the majority of which can likely be attributed to the GCC states (UK Defence & Security Export Statistics, 14 July 2015, charts 7 and 8). According to the Campaign against the Arms Trade, more than one-third of all UK military export licences issued between 2008 and the end of 2015 were for sales to the GCC.[35]

In the case of the United States, a total of $250 billion worth of arms transfer agreements were made worldwide by US suppliers between 2007 and 2014 (Theohary 2015, table 1, p. 23); of this figure, more than one-third (equivalent to $87 billion) were made with GCC states (table 11). If we exclude from this figure agreements with Europe and countries such as Canada, Japan, Australia, and New Zealand, then GCC states made up nearly one-half (48.2%) of all US suppliers' agreements (Theohary 2015, table 9, p. 35) – a striking indication of how important the Gulf is to US military production. Of course, not all agreements turn into actual deliveries, but even here the GCC proportion of US military exports remains high, making up 21% of all US arms deliveries to the world between 2007 to 2014 ($23.6 billion) and 31% of its deliveries to developing countries (Theohary 2015, table 11, p. 37).

In both the US and UK cases, the contracts associated with these sales have frequently generated controversy around allegations of bribery and payments made to 'middle men' acting on behalf of Gulf decision makers who then take large sums for agreeing to the purchase. In this manner, military sales not only represent another route through which Gulf petrodollars are recirculated to the large US and Western European companies that produce these weapons; they also reinforce the ways in which GCC ruling families and other elites use the state apparatus itself as a conduit of accumulation (Hanieh 2011a, p. 77). Moreover, these mutually beneficial commercial relations are a critical element to sustaining the long-standing political and strategic alliances that exist between the GCC and Western states.[36] Toby Jones has observed that 'oil and war [are] increasingly interconnected in the Middle East' and that this

[35] Calculated by the author from the Campaign against Arms Trade, UK Arms Export Licences (www.caat.org.uk/resources/export-licences).

[36] In 2014, a revealing indication of these linkages between military sales, corporate corruption, and strategic interests came from the UK Ministry of Defence following a Freedom of Information request concerning allegations of bribery by a UK-based firm operating in Saudi Arabia. The UK firm – a subsidiary of Airbus, the European defence manufacturer – allegedly provided gifts to Saudi officials and made payments to a Cayman Islands bank account in order to secure a £1.5 billion military contract. In response to the Freedom of Information request, the Ministry of Defence argued that disclosure of the details of the contract would damage the relationship between the United Kingdom and Saudi Arabia, which was a 'key component of the UK's strategic

connection is becoming 'seemingly permanent' (Jones 2012, p. 209). The implications of this relationship for the region have become even more acutely felt over the most recent period – an issue that I shall come back to in Chapter 8.

2.5 Conclusion

The enormous levels of wealth accruing in the Gulf over recent decades are essential to the contours of the international order. Most importantly, direct flows of Gulf surpluses into the global financial system continue to buttress the particular position of the United States within the forms of internationalisation that mark the last 20 years of contemporary capitalism. The expansion of US productive capital to low-wage regions such as China, which exists in such an organic and mutually reinforcing relationship with the financialisation of US capitalism, rests in numerous important ways on how Gulf surpluses are deployed. The Gulf is not exceptional in this respect – but along with Chinese and Japanese surpluses, it stands as one of the three principal pillars to this specific aspect of global finance. Distinct, however, from Asian countries and most other parts of the export-oriented periphery is the Gulf's particular historically determined relationship with Western states – characterised by an apparently indissoluble political and military alliance that rests ultimately on US global hegemony. This strategic relationship with the core of power in the world system gives the Gulf a unique place within global capitalism.

More broadly, the GCC's insertion into the systemic architecture of international financial markets – through other essential nodes such as the UK – has been a formative element to the wider hierarchies of global finance. The location of the Gulf itself within these hierarchies has also perceptibly shifted, alongside the internationalisation of its own capital. Today, the GCC's position within the ownership and control of capital worldwide is noteworthy and growing – albeit remaining much smaller in comparison to the leading Western states. Given these trends, any notion of emerging poles of accumulation or a potential recalibration of the

relationship in the region ... [that is] underpinned by defence cooperation going back around 50 years' (Information Commissioners Office, Freedom of Information Act 2000 (FOIA) Decision notice, Reference: FS50538627, 25 September 2014, p. 5). Moreover, the Ministry of Defence contended that Saudi Arabia held a 'different cultural perspective' on such matters, which would likely lead it to be 'highly critical' of the UK government if the latter did not 'use its powers to protect what the KSA [Kingdom of Saudi Arabia] considers as important and strategic commercial interests' (p. 5).

balance of power within the world market needs to fully consider the place of the Gulf within this.

Moreover, in a global political economy marked by persistent overaccumulation and overcapacity, the Gulf stands out as a particularly resilient source of demand whose weight in global consumption has been increasing. The Gulf's role as a market partly arises from how it is inserted into global circuits of accumulation – the particular emphasis on logistical and transport infrastructure, for example, is largely a result of its essential position in supplying the hydrocarbons necessary to feed a global economy centred upon Asian production. At the same time, however, the pools of surplus capital accumulating in the Gulf – which are, ultimately, also an outgrowth of the region's particular insertion into global capitalism – have produced their own distinct dynamics with important implications for the Gulf's position as a global market and its own forms of development. One such example is the feverish search for profit by these pools of capital, materialised in the extravagant building schemes that so typify the Gulf's urban landscape and that are now expanding across the Middle East. Taken together, these tendencies are manifest in the particular character of the Gulf's imports – including those of heavy machinery, engineering and transport equipment, and a range of associated commercial services. Alongside the enormous scale of weapon sales, these imports of both goods and services provide another route by which the Gulf's financial surpluses recirculate throughout the world market.

Running through the complex web of capital flows that link the Gulf and the global is a key conclusion: as one element of a global totality, the incorporation of the Gulf's financial surpluses into global capitalism is a constitutive element to the hierarchies of the world market and the particular characteristics of neoliberal globalisation; simultaneously, forms of capitalism in the Gulf can be understood as an expression of these same processes. A deeper understanding of this mutually constitutive relationship necessitates a closer exploration of how Gulf capital has developed within these global dynamics, and the ways in which such a 'global Gulf' acts to shape – and is shaped by – a reworking of accumulation across the wider Middle East.

3 Boundaries of State and Capital

Mapping the Gulf's Business Conglomerates

Saudi businessman Salah Abdullah Kamel likes to portray himself as a self-made man. Reminiscing about his pious and humble upbringing during the 1940s, Kamel relates how his early business acumen developed at age six or seven.[1] Born into a family of *mutawwifeen* – guides for Muslim pilgrims to Mecca – he would earn a bit of money on the side through selling his mother's chickpea soup *(balila)* as well as polished sheep bones as toys for his friends. Later, while at school in Jeddah, Kamel would purchase scouting equipment from Iraq, which he would market at a profit to his schoolmates. From these and other early entrepreneurial beginnings, Kamel would go on to become the fifth richest man in Saudi Arabia in 2017 (Forbes 2017) with an individual net worth estimated at US$2.7 billion, mostly earned through his massive holding company, the Dallah Al Baraka Group. Today, Kamel's business interests include ownership of an influential satellite network, Arab Radio and Television (ART) with the biggest movie library in the Arab world,[2] as well as the Middle East's largest Islamic bank, Al Baraka Banking Group. In addition to media and finance, he is active across construction and contracting, real estate, healthcare, agribusiness, telecommunications, and trade – even holding a 12% stake in the Belgian chocolate maker Godiva, for which he is the exclusive distributor across the Middle East, North Africa, Turkey, India, and Pakistan. Outside business, Kamel has also starred in his own TV programme, *Al-Suq* (The Market), where – in an Arabic-language echo of Donald Trump's *The Apprentice* – he mentors promising young businesspeople across the region.

[1] Amr Elissy, interview with Salah Kamal on Egyptian TV programme, 'ana' ('I'), 26 August 2010 (www.youtube.com/watch?v=qEYkMvtU198) (in Arabic).

[2] Kamel's interest in satellite TV was reportedly inspired by Rupert Murdoch's entry into Pay TV in Britain. He was a partner in the first Arab satellite TV station, MBC, and after selling his interest in 1994 to two brothers-in-law of then-Saudi ruler, King Fahd, went on to launch ART (Sakr 2001, p. 78).

Of course, the real story of Kamel's rise to fame and fortune has much more to do with lucrative connections to the Saudi state rather than any apocryphal rags-to-riches tale he might like to recount (Galal 2016). But beyond the historical details, Kamel and his Dallah Al Baraka group epitomise a wider feature of the Gulf's political economy – the powerful role of large, privately owned, business conglomerates whose activities stretch across a diverse range of economic sectors. Numerous examples of such conglomerates can be found across the Gulf – the Al Kharafi, Al Rajhi, Al Shaya, Ghurair, and so forth, whose names have become synonymous with wealth and economic influence. Commonly, firms such as these are controlled by single families drawn from older Gulf merchant classes or by descendants who have divided company control across the generations. In some instances, individuals or a group of unrelated investors may hold majority ownership. The growth of these firms is closely bound up with the way the Gulf has formed within the making of the global, it thus constitutes the other side of the Gulf/global internal relation analysed in the previous chapter. As I foreshadowed at numerous points in that earlier discussion, viewing the GCC scale as a site of 'the production of global processes in specific spatio-historical conjunctures' (Hart 2016, p. 3) means that patterns of class formation in the Gulf – embodied so vividly in the activities of individuals such as Kamel – can be understood as an instantiation of global processes.[3]

Taken as a whole, the accumulation and expansion of these Gulf conglomerates – both within and across borders – is a core theme of this book. This chapter provides a preliminary analysis of such firms at the scale of the GCC itself – unpacking their ownership structures, forms of accumulation, and linkages to state and international capital. In approaching this analysis, I focus on three key sites of capital accumulation in the Gulf: (1) industry, (2) the built environment, and (3) financial markets (see Figure 3.1). These three sites are not the only types of business activities in the Gulf, but together they capture the principal ways in which the production and circulation of commodities and capital takes place in the region. The three sites involve different types of firms and institutional structures, which are mutually connected through the interchange of capital and commodities. The largest Gulf conglomerates are active across all three sites, organised through holding companies that involve a

[3] This does not mean that class in the Gulf is simply a passive reflection (or recipient) of a reified global totality existing independently from its parts – to emphasise once again a key argument of Kosik, Tomich, and others – but, rather, that class formation in the Gulf should be viewed as one of the constituent parts *of* the global, formed in mutually conditioned interaction with it.

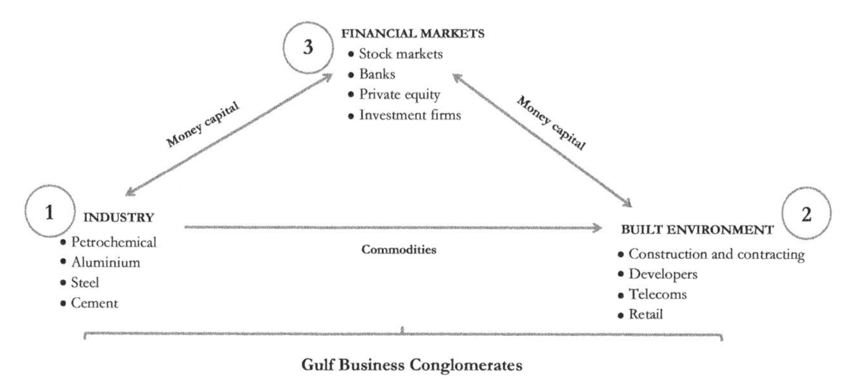

Figure 3.1 Sites of accumulation in the Gulf.

dense – and often opaque – network of subsidiaries and interlocking directorships. State investment funds and international businesses are tightly enmeshed in all of these firms; together, they help buttress the position of Gulf capital throughout the entire circuit of capital.

Industry, the first of these sites, spans a range of different manufacturing activities, four of which I survey later: petrochemicals, aluminium, steel, and cement. Manufacture of these commodities is highly energy intensive and also relies heavily upon feedstock from the crude hydrocarbon industry. The growth of the petrochemical and aluminium industries, in particular, is closely related to the global processes discussed earlier. In tracing these manufacturing activities across the GCC, I look at the relative weight of various Gulf states in producing these industrial commodities, as well as the different ownership patterns of firms that dominate these industries today. The aim is to situate these manufacturing activities as an important moment of accumulation for the large Gulf conglomerates.

The commodities produced in these manufacturing industries circulate in their material form through the second major site shown on the right of Figure 3.1: the urban built environment. The rapid transformation of the Gulf city space over the last two decades is a striking feature of the region's development – one that has been indispensable to the growth of Gulf capital. I analyse four different types of activities situated within the built environment, each of which is firmly bound up with capital accumulation: (1) construction and contracting companies (i.e. the actual building of physical space), (2) real estate development (the marketing and development of large real estate projects), (3) telecommunications (an essential part of urban infrastructure, which increasingly drives the actual form of urban planning), and (4) the import and retailing of consumer commodities (i.e. the distribution of day-to-day goods that underpin daily consumption). These four activities span both the physical creation of the built environment and the reproduction of social life in these urban spaces; they will later reappear in important ways as we examine how accumulation of Gulf capital has come to envelop the wider Middle East.

The final site of accumulation I look at is that of financial markets and their related institutions. Finance is critical to the principal arguments of subsequent chapters, connecting flows of capital across various economic sectors and geographical spaces. For both industry and the built environment, financial markets have been an essential place for Gulf firms to draw upon wider pools of surplus capital (through, for example, listing on equity markets), as well as borrowing money for further expansion (debt markets). In this chapter, I investigate the ways in which these markets have evolved in the Gulf during recent years, and their centrality to the broader development of Gulf firms. In particular, I draw out the decisive role of Gulf banks in shaping the operation of financial markets, unpacking the ownership structures of these banks and their interlocking relationships with other capitalist firms in the Gulf.

There are two overarching goals to my analysis of these interconnected sites of accumulation. The first of these is to explicitly identify many of the major firms and conglomerates that make up the Gulf capitalist class. To this end, the chapter contains a substantial amount of concrete, empirical detail, drawn from a study of several hundred market-leading firms, stock market data, and discussions with business leaders in the Gulf. This may appear in places as unnecessarily intricate, but I firmly believe that such ownership structures are critical to understanding how power works in the Gulf and wider Middle East, and that scholarly work on the region does not pay sufficient attention to them. I urge readers – particularly those who may be less familiar with the complexities of the Gulf business world – to keep a mental note of the key firms and conglomerates that recur throughout this discussion. They are essential actors in the story of later chapters.

My second aim is to introduce a key theoretical issue that will also reappear frequently: the relationship between the Gulf state and private capital. I will argue in this and later chapters that we should avoid an overly sharp conceptual division between the state and ruling family, on one side, and private business elites, on the other. Against such a dichotomous reading, I propose that we need to reformulate the concept of 'private' Gulf capital – the business conglomerates focused upon later – as one actually *inclusive* of state elites and ruling families. Numerous examples will show how ruling families operate across these varied business sectors in a personal capacity, while private sector conglomerates are often represented in the state apparatus itself. In this manner, it makes little sense to view the state and private capital as existing independently or autonomously from one another.

In a related manner, hydrocarbon exports and the huge levels of surplus capital in the GCC – both of which are largely routed through the state – play a critical role in fostering the development of this capitalist class. Throughout each of the three sites of accumulation discussed later, I shall provide various illustrations of this relationship, including joint investments of private companies with state-owned entities, privileged access to state-funded contracts and the supply of resources such as land, partial listing of state firms on stock markets, and interlocking directorships linking state and private companies. From this perspective, rather than seeing the state as a competitor, obstacle, or hindrance to private capital accumulation and 'free markets' – a view expressed in much Weberian and 'rentier state' approaches to the Gulf (and Middle East) – we should view the state as an institutional form that articulates and intermediates the power and interests of the capitalist class itself (again, a class that must be understood as inclusive of – but broader than – the ruling families). The Gulf state is – as in all capitalist societies – a *class state*, not a neutral or parasitic institution severed from the social relations of production and accumulation or one that 'crowds out' the private sector.

But to underline a key point raised in Chapter 1, this class character of the state does not mean that there are no contradictions or rivalries between and within different business interests, the state apparatus, or ruling families. Indeed, precisely *because* the relation between class and state is an internal one – i.e. part of what constitutes the nature of capital itself – the ways in which individual conglomerates concretely relate to the state apparatus and the balance of power within the ruling family are critical determinants of business success. Who you know matters. The internality of state power and capital accumulation means that political alliances can be a quick route to fantastic riches – or a misjudged path to marginalisation and financial collapse. A proper understanding of this state–class relation will be essential as we move forward in tracing the influence of Gulf capital on the wider political economy of the region.

3.1 Site of Accumulation 1: Industrial Activities

Unsurprisingly – given the Gulf's weight in global oil and gas markets – industrial activities in the GCC have historically been closely linked to the production and circulation of hydrocarbons. In the upstream sector of crude exploration and extraction, large state-owned oil firms have held absolute dominance since the nationalisation of oil and gas resources in the 1970s.[4] Due to this predominance of national oil firms, private Gulf companies have been largely excluded from direct participation in crude oil and gas production. Instead, their activities have consolidated in other industrial activities that depend upon the primary raw materials produced in the oil and gas sector – namely, hydrocarbon feedstock and cheap energy. These raw materials are essential inputs to the production of a variety of other commodities, and the Gulf's access to plentiful supplies of oil and gas has thus given the region a relative global advantage across a range of manufacturing industries.

A primary example of such downstream sectors is petrochemical production. As noted in Chapter 2, the Gulf's petrochemical exports have increased greatly in the post-2000 period alongside the rise of East Asian production networks. Utilising both its relatively cheap energy and the derivatives of oil and gas that form raw inputs for petrochemical products,[5] the Gulf's petrochemical capacity grew at 9.5% per annum between 2000 and 2014, the second highest rate in the world, only exceeded by China itself (13.8% annually) (GPCA 2015, p. 68). Between 2009 and 2012, the GCC's volume of chemical exports expanded by a striking 20% each year – one of the highest rates of growth in the world – with the total value of this trade increasing by more than 175% from 2009 to 2014 (GPCA 2015, p. 81).

Large state-owned firms – often subsidiaries of national oil companies – have been the major players in the Gulf's petrochemical industry since the 1970s. The most important of these is the Saudi Basic Industries Corporation (SABIC), which is the fourth largest publicly listed chemicals company in the world – just behind Dow Chemicals – and the biggest company listed on any Middle East stock exchange (Forbes 2017). SABIC has 65 manufacturing plants spread across the Middle East, Asia, Europe, and the Americas, from which it produces basic

[4] In Saudi Arabia, for example, the state-owned Saudi Aramco controls all the country's oil resources, and is responsible for around one in every nine barrels of oil produced globally. Similarly, in Kuwait, the Kuwait Oil Company took over the upstream hydrocarbon sector in 1975, with a constitutional provision banning foreign companies from ownership of Kuwait's oil. In other GCC states, foreign oil and gas corporations continue to have some presence – typically through minority holdings in joint ventures or through service contracts – but state-owned firms play the major role in extraction and production. In turn, these state-owned oil companies control a large number of subsidiaries across all moments of the hydrocarbon circuit – exploration, drilling, marketing, refining, and distribution.

[5] The most common raw materials for Gulf petrochemical manufacturing are naphtha, derived from oil refining, and gases such as ethane, propane, and butane produced from natural gas liquids.

chemicals, polymers, plastics, fertiliser feedstock (such as urea and phosphates), and metals. For many of these products – including ethylene, methanol, granular urea, and engineering plastics – the company ranks among the leading producers worldwide. Through its exports of these products, SABIC has constituted a vital substrate to the rise of East Asian industry and manufacturing.[6] SABIC's operations are also highly internationalised – reaching fourteenth in the world in UNCTAD's 2017 measure of transnationality for the largest non-financial, state-owned multinational firms (UNCTAD 2017, p. 33).[7] Ranked according to the proportion of workforce employed overseas, SABIC comes in at number three in the world.

Despite the fact that 70% of SABIC's shares are held by the Saudi government's Public Investment Fund, the company nonetheless forms an important bridge to the accumulation of private Gulf capital. First, the company's listing on the Saudi stock market in 1983 saw 25% of the company privatised, but these shares were made available only to Saudi and other GCC investors. Throughout this and following chapters, we shall repeatedly encounter examples of such state-controlled firms that have been partially listed on Gulf stock markets; effectively, these listings allow private capital (through minority stock ownership) access to a share of the revenue stream earned by state firms (in this case, hydrocarbon exports). SABIC's board of directors partially reflects these links – with prominent business leaders sitting alongside members of the Saudi ruling family and other state officials.[8]

A second route by which SABIC has facilitated the development of private capital is through the company's extensive network of subsidiaries and affiliates. This network, which numbers more than 80 different firms spread across the world, is marked by interlocking ownership ties with numerous major private sector Saudi capitalist groups.[9] Through such

[6] For ethylene – a basic chemical that forms the feedstock for much global industry – SABIC holds the second largest global capacity in the world, with production ranking third in 2016 (behind the United States and China). The company is also the world's third-largest producer of polyethylene and polypropylene, and the world's largest producer of mono-ethylene glycol, methyl tertiary-butyl ether, granular urea, polycarbonate, polyphenylene, and polyether imide.

[7] UNCTAD's 'Transnational Index' is calculated as the unweighted average of the following three ratios: foreign assets to total assets, foreign sales to total sales, and foreign employment to total employment.

[8] SABIC's board of directors, for example, includes members of the Al-Issa family, who have interests in finance, agribusiness, real estate, and other industrial firms.

[9] One example of this is the Arabian Industrial Fibers Company (AIFC), which is 48% owned by SABIC. Private owners of AIFC include Khaled Saleh Abdulrahman Al Shathry (the 93rd richest Arab in the world according to Forbes), as well as the Al Ghosaibi and Ali Reza Groups (see Table 3.1).

Table 3.1 *Gulf capital and Saudi Arabia's eight largest non-SABIC petrochemical firms*

Firm	Major conglomerate ownership
SIPCHEM	Zamil Group, Al Rajhi Group, Olayan Group
Sahara	Zamil Group
Farabi Petrochemicals	Al Rajhi Group
Safra	Ali Reza Group
Alujain	Ali Reza Group
National Petrochemicals	Ali Reza Group
National Industrialisation Company (Tasnee)	Kingdom Holding Group
Nama Petrochemicals	Al Gosaibi Group

Source: Saudi Arabia stock exchange data and company reports.

joint investments and various production arrangements, SABIC has given a major boost to private petrochemical manufacturing – in the production of plastics, for example, the OECD estimates that 800 private Saudi firms have emerged as a result of links with SABIC (OECD 2013, p. 40). Today, as Table 3.1 indicates for the eight largest petrochemical firms in Saudi Arabia (excluding SABIC), a number of the Kingdom's most prominent conglomerates are involved in this kind of manufacturing activity. All of these petrochemical firms manufacture chemical products from feedstocks supplied by state-owned oil and gas firms, and are directly supported by Saudi state investments (including social insurance and public pension funds).

Much like Salah Kamel's Dallah Al Baraka Group, the conglomerates listed in Table 3.1 are all privately owned and highly diversified companies, involved in a wide range of other activities including construction, finance, and retail. Most can trace their origins to Saudi merchant families that emerged in the pre-oil era, and who subsequently grew to prominence through fostering close relationships with successive Saudi monarchs and the Saudi state. We shall encounter these same firms – and others like them – many times. Their involvement in the petrochemical industry is important to highlight, not only because of the lucrative earnings that come through the production and export of basic chemicals, but because it reveals one way in which forms of capital accumulation – and thus Saudi class formation – have been co-constituted by Saudi Arabia's relationship to the global whole.

While Saudi Arabia remains the regional leader in the petrochemical sector with more than two-thirds of the Gulf's production capacity

(GPCA 2015, p. 73), other GCC states have also established firms that manufacture chemicals either directly or through their subsidiaries and affiliates.[10] The largest of these firms are typically state-owned but – much like SABIC – the petrochemical companies they control are sometimes listed on Gulf stock markets or have minority investments from private Gulf capital. Through such linkages, large private conglomerates are directly involved with the processing and export of Gulf hydrocarbons – and, in a few cases, have even partnered with state-owned Gulf petrochemical firms to invest in petrochemical sites across Europe and North America.[11] These are critical trends to watch over coming years – increased private capital involvement in petrochemicals (and even upstream hydrocarbon production) is a major objective of the Gulf's policy response to the recent oil price decline (see Chapter 7), and is likely to play an important role in the future growth of the Gulf's biggest firms.

Aluminium, Steel, and Cement

Alongside petrochemical production, three additional major manufacturing sectors in the GCC are aluminium, steel, and cement. Each of these industries is highly energy intensive – with electricity representing between 20% and 40% of total production costs – and they have thus benefitted from the region's abundant and relatively cheap oil and gas resources (compared with other global suppliers). Private Gulf conglomerates play a prominent role in each of these industries, particularly through the manufacture of downstream value-added commodities that are essential to construction and real estate activities. As with petrochemical production, state involvement has been a critical enabling factor to the development of these industries.

Once again reflective of the global patterns noted previously, the Gulf's aluminium industry has expanded at a very rapid pace over the recent

[10] These firms include Qatar Petroleum, the Kuwaiti Petrochemical Industries Company, the Bahrain Petroleum Co., the Oman Oil Co., and the Abu Dhabi National Oil Co.

[11] Kuwait's Equate Petrochemical Company provides a good illustration of this. The firm is majority held by the Kuwaiti government-owned Petrochemical Industries Company and the US giant Dow Chemicals (each with a 42.5% share), but two smaller private Kuwaiti petrochemical firms own the remaining 15% of the company's shares. Through such ownership, Kuwaiti conglomerates such as the Babtain, Al Ghanim, and Al Kharafi groups hold stakes in petrochemical sites located across Europe and North America. The company continues to expand: in 2015 Equate was the world's second-largest producer of the important industrial material ethylene glycol, and in 2016, it became the first Kuwaiti petrochemical company to establish an industrial complex in the United States and the first Middle East firm to utilise US shale gas as a feedstock (www.equate.com/en/This-EQUATE.html).

period; with more than 9% of the world's primary aluminium production, the Gulf ranked as the second largest producer in the world behind China in 2016 (up from 6% and number five in the world in 2010) (World Aluminium n.d.). This remarkable growth is reflected in the size of the Gulf's aluminium smelters – by 2013, three of the 10 largest aluminium smelters in the world were located in the GCC (Nagraj 2013), including the world's largest, lowest cost, fully integrated aluminium facility – Saudi Arabia's Ma'aden Aluminium. The UAE's Emirates Global Aluminium – formed in 2013 following a cross-emirate merger between Dubai Aluminium (Dubal) and Abu Dhabi's Emirates Aluminium (Emal) – is also noteworthy as the world's fourth biggest producer of the metal. Unlike other aluminium producers at a global level, the GCC is the only region with projected growing surpluses, and around 60% of its total production is exported to different parts of the world (Attar 2014, p. 20).

The six primary aluminium smelters in the GCC are state-owned (some through joint ventures with international firms).[12] But much like the relationship between upstream hydrocarbon extraction and petrochemicals, private Gulf capital interlocks with these state-owned firms through downstream manufacturing of aluminium products such as cables, rods, wires, extrusions, and aluminium powder. According to the Gulf Aluminium Council, there are more than 30 large firms involved in these types of manufacturing activities across the GCC, the vast majority of which are controlled by one of the large Gulf business groups. The materials produced by these firms flow into domestic construction and are also exported across the globe.

Similarly, the production of steel and cement is heavily reliant upon cheap energy and also forms an important moment of accumulation for the domestic capitalist class. Saudi Arabia and the UAE dominate the steel and cement industries across the Gulf – these two countries were responsible for around two-thirds of GCC steel production in 2015, and are the second and fourth largest producers in the Middle East as a whole (WSA 2016, p. 2).[13] For cement production, 48 of the 61 firms found across the GCC are located in Saudi Arabia and the UAE (Cemnet n.d.).

[12] These six smelters are owned by five GCC-based firms: Ma'aden (Saudi Arabian Mining Company and Alcoa), Emirates Global Aluminium (EGA, Investment Corporation of Dubai and Mubadala Development Company), ALBA (SABIC, Bahrain Mumtalakat Holding Company), Sohar Aluminium Company (Oman Oil Company, Rio Tinto Alcan, and the Abu Dhabi National Energy Company), and QATALUM (Qatar Petroleum and Norsk Hydro). Of these, only Bahrain's ALBA is publicly listed, although Abu Dhabi has announced plans for an IPO of EGA (see Chapter 7).

[13] Iran is the region's largest producer, while Egypt is number three. In 2015, Saudi Arabia and the UAE consumed around one-third of all steel used in the Middle East (including Iran) (WSA 2016, pp. 80–81).

Despite the relatively large number of firms active in both these industries, there is a high concentration of production among a few producers – in cement, for example, the top three firms in Saudi Arabia and the UAE held 42% and 50%, respectively, of total domestic capacity in 2014 (Riyad Capital 2015, p. 1; Saunders 2015, p. 56).

Table 3.2 provides the ownership breakdown of 58 of the biggest GCC firms involved in steel, cement, and related manufacturing. A mix of state institutions and domestic private capital tends to control upstream production of these commodities (raw steel and cement). For downstream manufacture of products such as prefabricated buildings, steel towers, concrete blocks, and other structures, large privately owned conglomerates are overwhelmingly dominant. There is considerable overlap of firms involved in both the steel and cement industries, and many of these same conglomerates will be found in the other sectors discussed later.

The products of all the manufacturing industries discussed in this section – petrochemicals, aluminium, steel, and cement – form a vital input into the construction of residential housing, shopping malls, infrastructure, and the like. In this manner, the largely domestic supply of these basic building materials not only constitutes an important source of direct profit for the large conglomerates listed in Tables 3.1 and 3.2; they are also an essential precursor to the second site of accumulation detailed in Figure 3.1, the transformation of the built environment.

3.2 Site of Accumulation 2: Built Environment

In recent years, a number of thought-provoking interventions have unpacked the ideological and discursive elements that characterise standard conceptualisations of the Gulf's urban form. This work has pointed to the ways in which much of the discussion around cities in the Gulf – whether emanating from official state bodies, journalists, or scholars – tends to occlude the particular relations of power that both shape and become embodied within the city itself. In its dominant framing, the Gulf city is treated as representative of a forward-looking, modern cosmopolitanism – one that sits in sharp distinction to the urban life found throughout the rest of the Arab world, where unruly, violent, and chaotic scenes play out on city streets (Kanna 2016, pp. 104–106). Juxtaposed in this way with the rest of the region, the urban scale acts as an emblematic site for the Gulf's projection of power – one that is often steeped in an avowed reclamation of Islamic architectural heritage and tradition (Elsheshtawy 2008a) while firmly drawing upon Western styles, knowledge, and practice (Mahgoub 2008; Ramos 2011; Kanna 2016). By treating the 'city' – and the more general categories of 'urban' and 'urban

Table 3.2 *GCC raw steel, cement, and related products*

Sector	Largest firms	Related conglomerate ownership
Raw steel	Hadeed Steel (Saudi)	SABIC (Saudi)
	Al-Ittefaq Steel (Saudi)	Al Tuwairqi Group (Saudi)
	Rajhi Steel (Saudi)	Al Rajhi Group (Saudi)
	Solb Steel (Saudi)	Al Jedaie Group, Saudi Pan Kingdom Holding Company, Qatar Steel
	Emirates Steel (UAE)	UAE Government
	Zamil Steel (Saudi Arabia)	Zamil Group (Saudi)
	Qatar Steel (Qatar)	Industries Qatar (majority government owned)
	Star Steel (UAE)	Al Ghurair Group (UAE)
	Conares (UAE)	Joint venture between Indian and Filipino investors
	Hamriyah Steel (UAE)	Russian-UAE joint venture
	Bahrain Steel (Bahrain)	Al Kharafi Group (Kuwait), Qatar Steel, GCC governments (through the Gulf Investment Corporation)
Steel products	Sabhan Steel Company (Kuwait)	Al Kharafi Group (Kuwait)
	Kirby Building Systems (Kuwait)	Al Ghanim Group (Kuwait)
	Steel Products Company (Saudi Arabia)	Olayan Group (Saudi)
	Al Rashed Building Materials (Saudi)	Al Rashed Group (Saudi)
	Al-Yamamah Steel Industries	Al Muhaidib Group (Saudi) and Al Rashed Group (Saudi)
	Masdar Building Materials (Saudi)	Al Muhaidib Group (Saudi)
	Binladen Industrial Company	Binladen Group (Saudi)
	National Metal Construction (Qatar)	Al Mana Group (Qatar)
	Engineering Building Materials Company (Qatar)	Al Mana Group (Qatar)
	Al Fara'a Steel Structures (UAE)	Al Fara'a Group (UAE)
	Al Ghurair Iron & Steel (UAE)	Al Ghurair Group (UAE)
	Al Jaber Steel Products (UAE)	Al Jaber Group (UAE)
	Al Jaber Iron & Steel Foundry (UAE)	Al Jaber Group (UAE)
	Modern Steel Mills (Oman)	Zubair Group (Oman) and Omani government

Table 3.2 (*cont.*)

Sector	Largest firms	Related conglomerate ownership
Cement	Saudi Cement (Saudi Arabia)	Al Rajhi Group and government funds
	Yamamah Cement (Saudi Arabia)	Prince Sultan Bin Mohammed Bin Saud Al Kabeer Al Saud (private capacity)
	Southern Cement (Saudi Arabia)	Government owned
	Arkan (UAE)	Government funds, Al Fahim Group (UAE), Bin Darwish Group (UAE)
	Union Cement (UAE)	Emirates of Abu Dhabi and Ras Al Khaimi, Sheikh Khalid Abdullah Mohammed Salem Al Qassimi (in a private capacity)
	Gulf Cement (UAE)	Ras Al Khaimi government, Abdulaziz Hamad AlWanyis (Saudi)
	Kuwait Cement (Kuwait)	Kuwait Investment Authority, Al Kharafi Group (through National Industries Group Holding), Al-Rashed Industrial Trading and Contracting Company
	Oman Cement Company (Oman)	Government owned
	Qatar National Cement Company (Qatar)	Government owned
	Hilal Cement (Kuwait)	Boodai Group (Kuwait), Suez Cement (Egyptian-based firm owned by French, Moroccan, and Saudi capital)
	United Cement Company (Bahrain)	Saudi Cement, Bahraini government funds, Olayan Group (Saudi)
Cement and concrete products	National Concrete Company (Bahrain)	AlMoayyed Group (Bahrain)
	RDB-ELSEIF (Saudi)	El Seif Group (Saudi)
	Saudi Readymix Concrete	Al Turki Group (Saudi)
	Bina Advanced Concrete Products Company	Al Muhaidib Group (Saudi)
	Bina Ready-Mix Concrete Products	Al Muhaidib Group (Saudi)
	Construction Products Holding	Bin Laden Group (Saudi)
	Binladen Concrete Solutions (Saudi)	Bin Laden Group (Saudi)
	Rabiah and Nassar Precast Concrete factory (Saudi)	Zamil Group (Saudi)
	Alamiah Building Company (Kuwait)	Al Kharafi Group (Kuwait)

Table 3.2 (*cont.*)

Sector	Largest firms	Related conglomerate ownership
	Kuwaiti British Readymix (Kuwait)	Al Kharafi Group (Kuwait)
	National Industries Company (Kuwait)	Al Kharafi Group (Kuwait); Kuwait government funds
	United Gulf Cement (Qatar)	Al Misnad Group (Qatar)
	Gulf Concrete Products (Qatar)	Al Mana Group (Qatar)
	Khalid & Hamad Ready Mix Concrete Company	Al Mana Group (Qatar)
	Star Line Blocks Factory (Qatar)	Al Mana Group (Qatar)
	Xtramix Concrete Solutions (UAE)	Al Jaber Group (UAE)
	Al Ghurair Readymix (UAE)	Al Ghurair Group (UAE)
	Al Ghurair Masonry (UAE)	Al Ghurair Group (UAE)
	Al Naboodah Ready Mix Concrete (UAE)	Al Naboodah Group (UAE)
	Al Fara'a Precast Factory (UAE)	Al Fara'a Group (UAE)
	Unibeton ReadyMix (UAE)	Al Fara'a Group (UAE)
	Galfar Aspire Readymix (Oman)	Galfar Group (Oman)

Source: *International Cement Review*, stock market data, and company websites.

space' – as self-evident, non-political objects of technocratic intervention, standard approaches to the Gulf's urban transformation function as part of a broader 'politics of legitimation', helping to bolster local elites and their claims on power (Kanna 2016, p. 115).

But beyond these discursive aspects, a less explored feature to the Gulf's dramatic urban transformation has been the ways in which the urban scale operates as a key site of capitalist class formation (Buckley and Hanieh 2014). In what follows, I will show how Gulf business conglomerates have been the pivotal actors in driving urban change, benefitting in multiple ways from the transformation of the built environment. Similar to the manufacturing and industrial activities discussed earlier, Gulf capital's involvement across this site has been strongly supported and encouraged by the Gulf state. Moreover, firms that are privately owned by Gulf ruling families have played a leading role in many of these activities.

The significance of the built environment to the accumulation of Gulf capital can first be seen in the actual construction of physical space, represented by construction and contracting work. According to industry sources, the budget for contracting and construction projects in the GCC totalled more than US$4.5 trillion between 2000 and July 2016, with the value of awarded contracts amounting to $1.65 trillion.[14] To put this huge project market in perspective, the GCC was responsible for around 75% (by value) of all contracts awarded across the entire Middle East between 2000 and mid-2016.[15] Within the GCC, the two most important markets are Saudi Arabia and the UAE, which made up 40% and 29%, respectively, of the value of all projects awarded since 2000. Although there has been a notable decline in the level of these projects since oil prices began to fall in mid-2014 (see Chapter 7), the Gulf remains a core focus of the project market worldwide.

These projects cut across a range of different sectors, the largest of which is real estate construction (35.7% of total contract value between 2000 and 2016). Private Gulf-based firms take the vast majority of work in this sector, and, consequently, construction is a major business activity for virtually all of the large conglomerates. Table 3.3 lists 16 of the most significant GCC-owned construction companies, alongside their ownership patterns, the value of their projects won from 2000 to 2016, and their degree of regional expansion. As would be expected given the distribution of construction projects across the Gulf, the dominant firms in this sector are concentrated in the UAE and Saudi Arabia, with the former accounting for more than half of all real estate projects in the Gulf as of late 2015 (Al Masah Capital 2015, p. 8). In many cases, these firms are owned or controlled by prominent business families who entered construction in the early days of the Gulf states' industrial and urban development, and have since expanded from basic contracting tasks to more complex engineering and design work.[16] Significantly, the firms

[14] These are projects that are either ongoing or completed (they do not include projects in the planning stage). Figures from the MEED Project database.

[15] All Arab countries along with Turkey and Iran.

[16] It is important to note that the opportunities presented by these types of contracting activities have not been restricted to Gulf capital alone. Some of today's most important Arab firms built their initial businesses through the same kinds of work – particularly those Arab communities linked to diaspora and refugee groups, such as the Palestinian and Lebanese, who had been dispersed through the region as a result of war and conflict. In some cases, prominent individuals associated with these firms have been granted Gulf citizenship (such as the Lebanese Hariri family) – a rare occurrence for foreigners in the Gulf. In this manner, the Gulf forms a core zone of accumulation for other regional capitalist classes. This phenomenon is an extremely salient feature of the contemporary period, especially given the crises that have wracked the Middle East from 2011 onwards, and will be returned to in some depth in later chapters.

Table 3.3 *Construction and contracting firms*

Company	Total contract Value in the GCC (2000–2016)	Ownership, corporate activities, and regional expansion
Saudi Bin Laden (Saudi)	34.2	Controlled by the Bin Laden family, who are also active in food distribution; telecommunications; manufacture of marble, concrete, and other building materials; port development; healthcare management; television commercials; hotels; and finance. The company has subsidiaries in Qatar, Kuwait, and the UAE.
Arabtec Construction (UAE)	19.7	Owned by Arabtec Holding, a company in which the Dubai government holds the largest share (36%) via various investment vehicles. Arabtec Construction and its controlling parent have subsidiaries in Qatar, Saudi Arabia, Bahrain, Syria, Jordan, Kuwait, Egypt, and the Palestinian Territories.
Saudi Oger (Saudi)	12.5	Controlled by the Lebanese/Saudi Hariri family, a powerful business group involved in finance, media, telecommunications, power generation, and numerous other sectors. Saudi Oger has subsidiaries in Abu Dhabi, Dubai, Jordan, Morocco, and Lebanon.
Al Jaber Group (UAE)	11.9	Controlled by the family of UAE businessman Obaid Khalifa Jaber Al Murri, the group is active in manufacture of building materials, shipping, transport, and logistics. Al Jaber has subsidiaries and projects in Saudi Arabia, Kuwait, Qatar, and Oman.
Al Futtaim Group (UAE)	11.2	Controlled by the Abdullah Majed Al Futtaim family, the group is also active in automobile and truck distribution, manufacture of building materials, private equity and asset management, insurance, logistics, import and distribution of retail commodities, ownership of schools, advertising, and corporate computer services. In addition to the UAE, it operates across Egypt, Qatar, Saudi Arabia, and Pakistan.

Table 3.3 (*cont.*)

Company	Total contract Value in the GCC (2000–2016)	Ownership, corporate activities, and regional expansion
El Seif (Saudi Arabia)	8.1	Controlled by the El Seif family, who are also active in automobile distribution, manufacture and distribution of building materials such as concrete, waste management, hospital ownership, operation of district cooling plants, security, travel, power, utilities, and environmental management. The company has branches in UAE, Qatar, and Lebanon.
Al Kharafi Construction Company (Kuwait)	4.7	Controlled by the large Kuwaiti conglomerate Mohammed Abdulmohsin Al-Kharafi & Sons Company, one of the Middle East's largest food producers and distributors, and also involved in restaurants and hotels, manufacturing, and finance (see Chapter 4). Al Kharafi has subsidiaries and affiliates operating in the real estate sector in Egypt, UAE, Lebanon, and Syria.
Al-Arrab Contracting (Saudi Arabia)	4.2	Fully owned by the Al Rajhi family, a large conglomerate involved in a wide range of sectors such as food distribution, manufacturing, banking, power, and utilities. Al Arrab has a subsidiary in the UAE, while its parent conglomerate is active across the region.
Al Fara'a General Contracting (UAE)	3.4	The company is controlled by the Al Fara'a Group, which is also involved in concrete manufacture (with distribution to Saudi Arabia and Qatar and offices in India, Turkey, Oman, Kazakhstan, and South Korea); supply of aluminium, glass, and steel; distribution of paints; and interior design. It has operations in Qatar and Saudi Arabia.
Commodore Group (UAE)	3.1	Majority ownership by a member of Dubai's ruling family, the group is involved in production of building materials, concrete blocks, wooden products, and lights. Operates sister companies in Turkey, Morocco, Lebanon, and Iran.

Table 3.3 (*cont.*)

Company	Total contract Value in the GCC (2000–2016)	Ownership, corporate activities, and regional expansion
Al Hamad (Qatar)	3.0	Owned by the Al Mana Group, and also involved in manufacture of concrete; distribution of wood, steel, and safety equipment; and production of aluminium extrusions, tanks, and glass. Has subsidiaries in Bahrain, UAE, Kuwait, and Qatar.
ETA Ascon (UAE)	2.4	Fully owned by the Al Ghurair Group, the company distributes food products; manufactures escalators, elevators, and steel; operates a university; and supplies services such as security, cleaning, insurance, and automobile repair and maintenance. Operates subsidiaries in Bahrain and Jordan.
Naboodah Construction Company (UAE)	2.3	Fully owned by the Al Naboodah family, the group also manufactures concrete; distributes construction equipment, cars, and furniture; and provides travel agency and freight forwarding services. Operates subsidiaries in Qatar, Oman, and Saudi Arabia.
Al Muhaidib Contracting Company (Saudi Arabia)	1.3	Fully owned by Abdulkadir Al Muhaidib and Sons, a group involved in food production, water and power, production of building materials, and finance. The construction business is focused on Saudi Arabia.
Galfar Engineering and Contracting (Oman)	1.2	Largest shareholder is Omani businessman Salim Alaraimi, along with other investors. The company is involved in transportation and manufacture of concrete and asphalt. Has subsidiaries and affiliates in India, Kuwait, and Libya and a branch in Saudi Arabia.
Combined Group Contracting (Kuwait)	1.1	Controlled by Syrian and Kuwaiti investors, the group is involved in trading of cement, manufacturing building materials, and export of machinery and equipment. Has subsidiaries and projects in Qatar, UAE, and Syria.

and conglomerates listed are not only involved in building activities; they also own a range of subsidiary companies that are closely linked to the manufacture and distribution of materials such as cement, steel, aluminium, and other building materials discussed in the preceding section.

A key factor behind the profitability of the firms listed in Table 3.3 is the presence of a low-paid construction sector workforce bereft of political, civil, and social rights. These workers – largely drawn from South Asia – experience very low wages, long hours, and hazardous, substandard conditions of work on construction sites throughout the Gulf. A variety of mechanisms give GCC construction companies considerable power over these workers, including the denial of mobility between jobs, the withholding of workers' passports, and extremely restrictive laws that ban migrant workers in the Gulf from forming unions, going on strike, or engaging in any kind of political protest (see Dito 2014 for detailed discussion of these mechanisms).[17] This is the other side to processes of capitalist class formation in the Gulf, and it carries important implications for how construction firms – and the GCC as a whole – have responded to the recent oil price downturn (see Chapter 7).

Table 3.3 further reveals a clear tendency towards the internationalisation of real estate construction within and beyond the Gulf. The first step in this – evident for virtually all firms examined in Table 3.3 – has been a pan-GCC orientation, most particularly around a Saudi-UAE axis but also increasingly targeting other GCC states. While home markets continue to be their major base, all of these firms have established branches or launched joint ventures in order to better compete in neighbouring GCC states. More notably, particularly in relation to the very largest firms, internationalisation has involved an additional geographical step: expansion to nearby Arab countries such as Egypt, Jordan, Lebanon and Syria and even further afield to South Asia and Turkey. In this sense, the GCC construction sector sharply illustrates Gulf capital's tendency to internationalise across the regional scale.

Developers

The firms listed in Table 3.3 are fully positioned at the core of the real estate boom of recent years, drawing opportunities from the literally

[17] In Bahrain and Kuwait, migrant workers are permitted to join established unions (but not to form their own). In practice, however, there is a great deal of reluctance from these unions to recruit or ally with migrant workers. None of the GCC states (except for Kuwait) has ratified the two key International Labour Organization conventions governing the right to freely form and join worker organisations, organise, and collectively bargain (Convention Nos. 87 and 98).

thousands of contracts available in this sector. But alongside these construction and contracting activities, accumulation in the real estate sector also occurs through another major route: the ownership and development of projects themselves. By launching such projects, developers hope to capture rents that accrue from appreciating land and real estate prices. In the Gulf, a variety of techniques are employed to encourage the continued growth of these prices, including off-plan sales, re-zoning of land, changes to ownership laws that permit ownership by foreign investors (Buckley and Hanieh 2014; Wiedmann 2016), and, perhaps most imaginatively, sea reclamation projects that aim to turn large swathes of Gulf coastline into palatial playgrounds for speculative capital (Shehabi and Suroor 2015).

Unlike construction and contracting, the main developers in the Gulf tend to be state-owned firms that are typically connected to one of the numerous Sovereign Wealth Funds discussed in the previous chapter. Table 3.4 shows the 10 largest developers in the region, their size, ownership structures and regional activities. Similar to the construction firms listed in Table 3.3, these developers also demonstrate a strong tendency towards internationalising their activities. In this regard, two companies stand out for their regional expansion – the UAE's Emaar and Qatar's Qatari Diar. Both rank among the world's largest developers and have been a primary force behind the dramatic transformation of the Middle East's urban space over recent years.

The fact that these developers are in many cases state owned should not be taken to mean that private Gulf capital is excluded from the lucrative opportunities presented by the ownership and development of real estate. Indeed, precisely the opposite trend is true – these state-owned bodies form a critical link between the state's deployment of surplus capital in the built environment and the accumulation possibilities available for the Gulf's capitalist class. This is not only through the contracts that are made available for construction; rather, private Gulf conglomerates are structurally tied to these development firms through joint ventures, share ownership (for those developers that have been listed on regional stock markets), and – in some cases – directorship positions.

The regional giant Emaar provides an archetypal example of these linkages. The company's numerous investments and associated joint ventures across the Gulf provide one mechanism through which the UAE's financial surpluses are joined with private capital (including that of Gulf ruling families). Some of these investments include Dubai Hills Estate (an 11-million-square-metre project jointly undertaken with Merass Holding, a company owned in a private capacity by Dubai's ruler,

Table 3.4 *Leading GCC real estate developers*

Company	Assets (US $bn)	Ownership, corporate activities, and regional expansion
Emaar (UAE)	21.6	The company's major shareholder is the Dubai government, which holds a 29.2% stake in the company via the Investment Corporation of Dubai. The remaining 70% of the company is publicly listed. Emaar is one of the largest developers in the world and controls subsidiaries involved in finance and mortgaging, engineering and consulting, shopping mall management, information technology, management of schools and kindergartens, and provision of utilities such as cooling. The company is a major investor in Dubai Aerospace Industries, which leases and repairs aircraft. In addition to its home market, Emaar has active subsidiaries in Egypt, Morocco, Jordan, Lebanon, Syria, Oman, and Saudi Arabia
Qatari Diar (Qatar)	20	Owned by the Qatar Investment Authority (an SWF), the company has projects and subsidiaries in Egypt, Morocco, Syria, Yemen, the Palestinian Territories, Turkey, and Tunisia.
Jabal Omar Development Company (Saudi Arabia)	12.9	Founding shareholders and board members include the Al-Subeaei family, one of the largest business groups in Saudi Arabia with interests in real estate, banking, petrochemicals, construction equipment, and manufacturing; and the aforementioned Kamel family, which runs the Dallah Al Baraka Group. Another corporate group that owns a significant share (10.3%) of JODC is Makkah Construction and Development, which in turn is controlled by Mohammed Seraifi (18%) and the Saudi Bin Laden Group (11%). Mohammed Seraifi heads the Taiba Group, with interests in real estate, construction, hotel management, agriculture, manufacture, and mining. The Bin Laden group is one of the largest construction companies in the world (see earlier discussion). The General Organization for Social Insurance, a Saudi government organisation, owns 0.3% of JODC. The company is focused on Saudi Arabia.
Aldar Properties (UAE)	9.8	Aldar is 39.38% directly or indirectly owned by the Abu Dhabi government via Mubadala Development Co. (29%), Al-Sariya Commercial (7.6%), and Abu Dhabi Investment Council (2.25%). In addition to real estate, it also operates malls, schools, hotels, and tourist resorts; manages sports facilities; and manufactures building

Table 3.4 (*cont.*)

Company	Assets (US $bn)	Ownership, corporate activities, and regional expansion
		materials such as concrete. Although Aldar is mostly focused on the UAE, it has projects under development in Egypt and Saudi Arabia.
Barwa Real Estate (Qatar)	7.8	Owned by Qatari Diar (45%) alongside other private investors, Barwa is also involved in banking and wealth management, insurance, management of hotels, distribution of fruits and vegetables, and manufacture of building materials, among other activities. Through its various subsidiaries, the company has projects in Egypt, Bahrain, Morocco, Saudi Arabia, and Turkey.
Dar Al Arkan (Saudi Arabia)	6.7	The company was founded by six Saudi business families in 1994 and is now listed on the Saudi stock market. It operates exclusively in Saudi Arabia.
DAMAC Properties (UAE)	6.4	UAE businessman Husain Ali Habib Sajwani holds a 72.22% stake in the company. The company has subsidiaries in Qatar and Saudi Arabia, with projects in Egypt, Jordan, Lebanon, and Iraq.
United Development Company (Qatar)	5.3	The company is listed in Qatar but various state-related funds hold around 34% of the firm. Major Qatari business groups helped establish the company as core investors – including the Al-Mana, Al-Fardan, Abdulghani, and Al-Marri families. In addition to real estate, the company is involved in waste management, infrastructure, utilities, energy, fashion retail, insurance, hotels, and leisure. Its main project is the Pearl-Qatar, an artificial island that spans 4 million square metres and is the first Qatari land in which foreign investors can own freehold property.
Mabanee (Kuwait)	2.0	The company is listed in Kuwait and the largest ownership stake is held by the Al Shaya Group, a major retail group that owns franchises for more than 70 international brands through the Middle East (see later discussion). The company provides contracting services and advertising, manufactures prefab buildings, operates hotels and health clubs, and owns Kuwait's largest shopping mall. It is planning to construct new malls in Saudi Arabia and Bahrain by 2019.

Source: MEED Projects; company financial reports.

Mohammed Bin Rashid Al Maktoum), Emaar Middle East (a joint venture with the Saudi group Al Oula Real Estate Development Holding Company),[18] Emrill Services (a facility management company jointly held with the UAE's Al Futtaim Group; see Table 3.3), Amlak Finance (a financial services firm whose board of directors includes family members from some of the largest business conglomerates in the UAE, such as the Lootah and Arjomand groups), and part-ownership of Galfar Engineering & Contracting Co., Oman's biggest contractor (jointly owned with Omani businessman Salim Saeed Hamad Al Fannah Al Araimi; see Table 3.2). All of these investments leverage Emaar's considerable resources to strengthen privately owned Gulf firms, including those from outside the UAE. They thus provide a further illustration of how state-owned firms help to underwrite the accumulation of private Gulf capital, deepening the latter's ability to expand and extend across the region.

Financial markets represent another means through which Emaar's rents are recirculated to Gulf businesses and other private citizens. Around 70% of Emaar's shares have been publicly held since the company's initial public offering (IPO) in 2000, enabling private capital to draw a share of the developer's activities in the built environment (nearly three-quarters of Emaar's listed shares are held by UAE or other GCC citizens).[19] Importantly in this respect, Emaar has undertaken several IPOs that have involved spinning off profitable parts of the company and listing them as independent entities on regional stock markets. In 2006, for example, Emaar launched an IPO on the Saudi stock market for Emaar the Economic City (EEC), a joint venture between Emaar, the Saudi government, and other private Gulf investors, to develop the King Abdullah Economic City in Saudi Arabia – a mega-project that industry sources have described as the world's largest construction project, worth an astounding US$100 billion (CW Online 2015). In September 2014, Emaar listed its malls division as a separate company on the Dubai Financial Market (DFM) through a sale of 15% of the company. By mid-2016, the resulting company, Emaar Malls, was the third largest on the DFM, with its capitalisation equivalent to more than 10% of the entire market.

Emaar's ownership and management structures reinforce and reflect these tightening connections between the UAE state and private Gulf

[18] Al Oula is controlled by two leading business families in Saudi Arabia, Abdulkadir Al Muhaidib and Sons Group (see Table 3.1) and Abdullatif & Mohammad Al Fozan Company.

[19] Calculated by the author from Dubai Financial Markets data, 28 July 2016.

capital. Prominent Emirati business families have sat on the company's board over the past decade – a member of the Ghurair family (see Tables 3.2 and 3.3), for example, was part of the original board of directors until 2012. Emaar's current chair, Mohammed Al Abbar, is a leading UAE businessperson,[20] and the board also includes a Saudi citizen from one of that country's main business families.[21] For Emaar the Economic City, founding shareholders included a veritable who's who of Saudi Arabia's business elite – including the Bin Laden family, the Dallah Al Baraka Group (controlled by the Kamel family), the Ali Reza family, and, of course, members of the Al-Saud ruling dynasty (Emaar 2006, pp. 19–22). Similar patterns can be found for the other state-owned developers shown in Table 3.4 – Qatari Diar, Aldar Properties, and Barwa Real Estate. In all cases, what we consider as 'state' capital needs to be viewed as highly propitious to the development of Gulf capitalism itself – most particularly in regards to its tendency to internationalise – not an inimical force that undercuts the private sector or is arrayed competitively against it.

Telecommunications

The expansion of the built environment is also closely connected to the growth of new technological industries. Most important in this regard are the large telecommunications companies that provide mobile, Internet, network, and data services across all GCC states. Control of this sector is dominated by a handful of firms. Just nine telecoms operate all mobile and Internet services across the Gulf: Zain (Kuwait), Ooredoo and Vodafone Qatar (Qatar), Etisalat and du (UAE), Saudi Telecom and Mobily (Saudi Arabia), Omatel (Oman), and Batelco (Bahrain).[22] Hundreds of smaller technology companies are linked to these firms as subcontractors, resellers, and service providers. These nine firms play an

[20] Mohamed Alabbar is involved in numerous private companies, including Africa Middle East Resources, which aims to link Africa's extractive industries to Asian export markets; Eagle Hills, an investment and real estate development company; Tradewinds Corporation, a real estate developer in Malaysia and Southeast Asia; and RSH, a pan-Asian fashion retailer. In 2015, Alabbar founded Capital City Partners, which was initially announced as the firm that would lead development of a new capital city in Egypt – this project, however, was later terminated due to contractual disputes.

[21] Ahmed Bin Jamal Bin Hassan Jawa, who also sits on the board of Salam Bank (Bahrain), and runs a private equity firm, Starling Group. He is chair of Disney-Jawa Enterprises, which introduced Disney products to the GCC.

[22] There are three other telecoms in the Gulf that are subsidiaries of the firms listed here: Wataniya Telecom in Kuwait (92% owned by Ooredoo), Ooredoo Oman (55% owned by Ooredoo), and Viva Bahrain (a 100% owned subsidiary of Saudi Telecom).

increasingly pivotal role in the shaping the nature of daily urban life in the GCC. More than simply technological providers, they are driving urban transformation itself, intimately involved in the actual development and design of the core infrastructure for new city spaces.

The critical role of telecommunications firms to the contemporary Gulf is best epitomised in the notion of 'Smart Cities' – an urban development perspective adopted by all GCC states over the last few years. This vision aims at creating urban spaces in which the seamless integration of information and communication technologies penetrates all aspects of daily life. Constant connectivity to home, work, and the shopping mall is said to promise general happiness and better inclusivity for all citizens, while also encouraging an increase in economic activity. This vision is farthest advanced in Dubai, where the emirate's ruler, Sheikh Mohammed Bin Rashid Al Maktoum, announced in early February 2016 that the Smart City concept would make Dubai 'the happiest city on earth'. Appropriately delivered through a three-hour 'Tweetathon', the strategy promised a revolutionary shake-up of government and daily life aimed at promoting 'feelings such as fun, joy, and other hedonistic pleasures' (Smart Dubai 2016). A new ministerial post was announced, a Minister of State for Happiness, who would lead the city's transformation. At a more elemental level, Dubai's Smart City mantra is guided by a totalising vision of urban existence: the city and its residents, forms of play, commerce, and logistical infrastructures are seen as a unified whole – the backbone of which is a network of emerging information and telecommunications technologies.[23]

Dubai's Smart City plan provides a good illustration of the significance that telecommunications firms play in urban transformation. The initial committee established to oversee the project's implementation, the Higher Committee for Smart Cities, brought together the UAE's two telecom providers (Etisalat and du) as private sector representatives, alongside appointees of government ministries (Emirates 24/7 2013). In March 2016, du was appointed as official strategic partner to develop and implement the 'Smart Dubai Platform' – the technological backbone of the project that will link infrastructure and data generated across the

[23] This Smart City concept is not restricted to Dubai. In Saudi Arabia, six new cities are planned that will embody the same concept of technological interconnectivity, in addition to the holy city of Mecca, which is also scheduled for a twenty-first-century upgrade. Five cities across Qatar, Kuwait, and Abu Dhabi are earmarked for a similar transformation, while Bahrain and Oman explore how to follow suit. It remains to be seen where this new orientation of the Gulf's urban development eventually leads, particularly given the fact that it is closely tied to the increased surveillance and securitisation of everyday life.

city within a single integrated system. Likewise, Etisalat has been developing systems that allow Dubai's residents 'to monitor, automate, secure and control their homes remotely from anywhere and at any time' (Etisalat 2015, p. 33).

Although Etisalat and du are considered private companies, the nature of this 'private sector' is more complex than it initially appears. The two firms are publicly listed on the UAE's stock exchanges, but their shareholding continues to be dominated by state institutions or related government funds, with the government owning 60% of each. In the case of Etisalat, the remaining 40% is listed on the Abu Dhabi stock exchange. For du, however, the situation is not as straightforward. While just over 20% of du's stock is publicly listed, a further 20% is owned by Dubai's ruler and the architect of the Smart City Project, Mohammed Bin Rashid Al Maktoum. This ownership, however, is exercised through a network of related companies in a *private* capacity – it is not part of any state holding.[24] Maktoum, moreover, also controls Tecom, the third private firm that sat with Etisalat and du on the Higher Committee for Smart Cities, and whose Dubai Design District is one of the first developments in Dubai being constructed along the 'Smart' lines. These patterns provide further illustration of how state and capital relate in the Gulf: while dominating the state apparatus, Maktoum also forms a core component of the 'private' capitalist class in Dubai. Like the rest of this class, Maktoum's personal accumulation is acutely fused to the patterns and pace of urban development.

In the rest of the GCC, ownership of the major telecommunications companies follows similar arrangements as Etisalat and du: largely state owned, although corporatised[25] and listed on regional stock exchanges. As a consequence, much like their relationship with petrochemical companies and real estate developers, the major Gulf conglomerates are heavily connected to these firms through share ownership, joint ventures, and board directorships. One significant example is the region's third largest telecom by assets, Kuwait's Zain, which is 15% owned by the aforementioned Kharafi group. Mobily, the second largest telecom in Saudi Arabia, has members of the Al Jomaih and Al Saghyir

[24] Maktoum's 19.5% stake in du is held through Emirates International Telecommunications (EITC), which in turn is fully owned by the Dubai Holding Commercial Operations Group. This latter company is 100% owned by Dubai Holding, which is 97% owned by Maktoum. Through EITC, Maktoum also owns (in a private capacity) more than 30% of Tunisie Telecom (see Chapter 5).

[25] This term refers to state-owned firms that are increasingly run in the manner of private companies – embracing 'market-oriented operating principles such as financialized performance indicators, cost-reflective pricing and competitive outsourcing' (McDonald 2014, p. 2).

families sitting on its board. Similar patterns occur across the region, positioning Gulf capital as both a major beneficiary and driver of the new forms of urban development under way in the GCC.

Moreover, echoing once again the trajectories of construction and development firms, there has been considerable international expansion by GCC telecoms in recent years. At the scale of the GCC itself, there has been a high degree of cross-border investment in this sector, expressed through the establishment of subsidiaries or the acquisition of existing players in neighbouring countries. In every Gulf state with the exception of the UAE, firms from a second GCC country operate one of the mobile licences or own a stake in an existing operator. Each Gulf state has either two or three licences in operation, and apart from a Vodafone joint venture in Qatar (actually majority owned by the Qatari government), there are no foreign companies from outside the GCC active in any Gulf state. This has led to a pronounced degree of ownership concentration: the entire GCC market is in effect dominated by just four companies – Saudi Telecom, Qatar's Ooredoo, Kuwait's Zain, and the UAE's Etisalat; these four companies and their subsidiaries operate 11 of the 15 mobile licences in the region.

Expansion to markets outside the GCC has also been highly evident over the last five years. In 2010, international revenue for GCC telecoms stood at around 25% of total revenue. By late 2015, four Gulf operators – Zain, Ooredoo, Batelco (Bahrain), and Etisalat – earned close to 60% of their revenues outside domestic markets, way in excess of the industry standard of 40% (Emirates NBD 2015, p. 4). One of the most active examples of this international cross-border growth has been Etisalat, whose international assets accounted for around two-thirds of their total assets in 2015 (Etisalat 2015, p. 81). Much of this geographical expansion of GCC telecoms has targeted other Arab countries – a dimension I explore in Chapter 5 – but, in addition, Africa and Asia have also been an important focus for internationalisation. Indeed, GCC firms control at least one of the main telecom operators in 18 countries across these two continents: Indonesia, Myanmar, the Maldives, Pakistan, Afghanistan, Sri Lanka, Nigeria, Benin, Burkina Faso, the Central African Republic, Gabon, Mauritania, Ivory Coast, Mali, Sudan, South Sudan, Niger, and Togo. In many of these countries, GCC-owned operators are the market leaders.

Retail and Distribution of Commodities

The 'Smart City' concept – and the role of Gulf telecoms within this – shows that a full understanding of class formation at the urban scale needs to go beyond simple construction and building activities. We must also consider how social existence in Gulf cities is encountered and lived in the everyday, and a further key feature of this is the way in which retail activities are organised. As I outlined in Chapter 2, the GCC has been an important source of global demand for goods produced elsewhere and then exported to the Gulf. Here Gulf conglomerates also play a pivotal role. Given the particular weight of imports in meeting daily needs, Gulf capital acts to mediate the turnover of a commodity circuit deeply enmeshed in global trade – bringing in commodities from outside the GCC, representing foreign brands and goods through a system of agency rights, and distributing these goods to consumers through a dense and highly concentrated network of retail outlets. Control over all these aspects of daily consumption constitutes another route around which the accumulation of Gulf capital takes place.

Many of the large capital groups mentioned in the preceding sections demonstrate these connections to the distribution of consumer commodities and the retail sector (see Table 3.5). Some of these groups originate in the trading activities of early merchants and remain controlled by single families; others are publicly listed on regional stock markets with a wider base of share ownership. All of these conglomerates are highly diversified. In addition to their prominent role as distributors of various consumer commodities such as automobiles, food,[26] and other retail goods, they are also typically involved in activities such as construction and manufacture of building materials, security, logistics, entertainment, tourism, and education. Pointedly, many of these activities are directly reflective of services linked to the actual concrete form that production of the built environment may take – housing, office blocks, malls, hotels, shopping centres, schools, and so forth. The majority of these firms are based in Saudi Arabia, Kuwait, and the UAE, giving a very high proportion of market share to a handful of companies from these countries. Thousands of smaller firms interlock with these firms throughout each individual Gulf country.

Crucial to understanding these retail distribution networks is the GCC's system of agency licences, which give exclusive rights to import and distribute certain commodities. These rights are negotiated with international companies who seek local partners in the GCC, but because they are sanctioned by the state, there is a tight connection between accumulation opportunities in this circuit and proximity to the ruling family. Frequently, these rights pertain only to the domestic market; in other cases they extend across the

[26] Although the Gulf's primary agricultural production is limited, over the past decade it has achieved a growing regional dominance in both food manufacturing and the import and distribution of agricultural products throughout the Middle East. Chapter 4 will explore this sector in more detail.

Table 3.5 *Retail and distribution of consumer commodities*

Main groups	Related companies and investments	Other activities and investments	Regional expansion
Savola (Saudi Arabia)	Afia (100%), edible oils; Herfy (47.6%), fast food; frozen meat and bakery production Al Marai (36.5%), dairy, poultry; United Sugar Company (74%), sugar; El Maleka (100%), pasta; Panda Retail Co. (91%), supermarkets/ hypermarkets	Plastics, real estate, private equity.	Operates and exports across the Middle East. Owns a packaged pasta plant and two sugar refineries in Egypt (responsible for 44% of the company's sugar production). Panda is present in UAE and Egypt.
Kharafi (Kuwait)	Kuwait Food Company, restaurants and agencies for fast-food chains; National Food Company (100%), production of frozen meat and other food products; Gulf Food Industries (100%), production of canned fruits and vegetables, sauces and condiments, edible oil, tuna, and meat; manufacture of packaging products; Gulfa, production of mineral water and manufacture of plastic bottles and caps; Cairo Poultry Company, poultry	Petrochemicals, steel, cement, banking, and real estate	Restaurants and factories located in Saudi Arabia, UAE, Qatar, Bahrain, Oman, Egypt, Jordan, Lebanon, Morocco, Iran, Kazakhstan, and the Kurdistan province of Iraq

Table 3.5 (*cont.*)

Main groups	Related companies and investments	Other activities and investments	Regional expansion
Suleiman Abdulaziz Al Rajhi Group (Saudi Arabia)	Al-Watania Poultry (100%); Al-Watania Agricultural Company (100%), fruit, vegetable, and livestock farms; Saudi Grains & Fodder (100%), import of grains and cereals; Suleiman Abdulaziz Al Rajhi Company for Trade (100%), fast-food restaurants	Real estate; hotels; manufacture of packaged products and building materials; logistics; engineering, procurement, and construction for agricultural projects	Exports grains to Egypt through investments in agricultural land in Ukraine and Poland. Manages land in Egypt.
Kuwait Projects Company (KIPCO) (a vehicle related to Kuwait's ruling family, the Al Sabah family)	Saudia Foodstuffs Company (through KIPCO's subsidiary, the Qurain Petrochemical Industries Company), dairy producer	Banking and financial investments, real estate, industry and manufacturing, petrochemicals, education, and media	Produces, imports, and distributes dairy products across the Middle East. It has 21 depots located in Saudi Arabia, Bahrain, Qatar, Kuwait, and Jordan.
Sultan Center Food Products Company (Kuwait)	Sultan Center Trading & General Contracting (99%), 65 hypermarket and other stores and 8 restaurant chains; Market Vision for Trading (100%), wholesale distribution of foodstuffs and home goods to businesses; Riviera Holding Company (40%), operates hotel in Lebanon; National Real Estate Company	Security and cleaning, logistics, warehousing, maintenance and repair of oil equipment, real estate and facilities management, banking and finance	Stores located in Oman, Jordan, Lebanon, and Bahrain; NREC's developments, including one mall, are located in UAE, Egypt, Lebanon, Libya, Iraq, and Jordan.

Table 3.5 (*cont.*)

Main groups	Related companies and investments	Other activities and investments	Regional expansion
	(30%), malls and other retail development		
Olayan Group (Saudi)	Arabian Food Services (100%), fast-food restaurants; Coca-Cola Bottling Company of Saudi Arabia (40%), production of carbonated soft drinks; Colgate-Palmolive Arabia (49%), importer and distributor of CP products for GCC region; Olayan Kimberly-Clark Arabia (51%), manufacture and distribution of KC products to the GCC; Arabian Paper Products (50%), Middle East's largest supplier of paper cups	Construction and engineering, real estate development, energy and power, banking and finance, oil industry services	Goods produced as agents for Coca-Cola, Kraft, Nestlé, Kimberly-Clark, Colgate-Palmolive, and others are exported through the GCC and elsewhere in the Middle East. Runs franchise for Burger King and other international fast-food chains across Egypt, Jordan, Kuwait, Morocco, Oman, Qatar, UAE, and Lebanon.
Al Ghanim Industries (Kuwait)	Gulf Trading and Refrigeration Company (100%), distribution, warehousing, and transport of food and household goods, including exclusive Kuwaiti distributor for Kraft and Mars; Costa Coffee Kuwait (agents); Wendy's Middle East (agents); Al	Transport, logistics, and warehousing; advertising; engineering and contracting; manufacture of building materials; insurance; banking and finance	In February 2015, acquired exclusive rights to operate Wendy's restaurants across the Middle East. Has 16 restaurants in the UAE and plans to grow to other Middle East and North African countries.

Table 3.5 (*cont.*)

Main groups	Related companies and investments	Other activities and investments	Regional expansion
	Ghanim Automotives (100%), exclusive agency rights in Kuwait for Chevrolet and Cadillac; X-cite (100%), electronics retailer, 17 outlets in Kuwait; Safat Home (100%), home furnishing stores		
Majid Al Futtaim (UAE)	Majid Al Futtaim Properties (100%), 19 shopping malls and 4 hotels; Majid Al Futtaim Retail (100%), Carrefour (agency rights), with 151 supermarkets, hypermarkets, and convenience stores in operation; Majid Al Futtaim Fashion (100%), agency rights for international fashion brands; Majid Al Futtaim Food & Beverages (100%), agency rights for food and beverages; restaurants; Majid Al Futtaim Cinemas (100%), operates 182 cinemas	Finance, healthcare, and facilities and energy management	Exclusive agency rights for Carrefour across the Middle East and North Africa; six malls are located outside the UAE (in Egypt, Lebanon, Bahrain, and Oman); 45 (of 67) of the group's hypermarkets are outside the UAE. A total of 47% of the group's revenue in 2015 was earned outside the UAE.
Fawaz Abdulaziz Alhokair & Co. (Saudi Arabia)	Al Hokair Fashion Retail (100%), largest franchise retailer in Middle East; agencies for	Construction, financial services, health care	Around 30% of the company's retail stores are outside Saudi Arabia; two shopping malls are

Table 3.5 (*cont.*)

Main groups	Related companies and investments	Other activities and investments	Regional expansion
	more than 80 international brands and more than 2,100 stores; Arabian Centres (100%), 22 shopping malls; FAS Hotels (100%), hotels; Food & Entertainment (100%), 23 international and local brands for cafes and restaurants		located in the UAE and Egypt.
Al Shaya (Kuwait)	M. H. Alshaya Company (100%), agency rights for around 70 international brands in clothes, footwear, cosmetics, eyewear, home furniture, cafes, restaurants, and pharmacies; Oriental Hotels Co. (64%), two Sheraton hotels in Kuwait; Kuwait Automotive Imports (50%), exclusive agency rights for Mazda, Peugeot, Michelin tyres, and other automotive brands; Mabanee (34%), mall development company, runs Avenues Mall in Kuwait	Construction, IT, advertising	More than 1,200 stores located across Saudi Arabia, UAE, Lebanon, Oman, Egypt, Jordan, Morocco, Qatar, and Turkey; Mabanee has land in Saudi Arabia and Bahrain on which future malls are planned.

Table 3.5 (*cont.*)

Main groups	Related companies and investments	Other activities and investments	Regional expansion
Al Tayer Group (UAE)	Al Tayer Motors (100%), agency rights for Ford, Lincoln, Ferrari, Maserati, Jaguar, Land Rover, and Ford Trucks; Al Tayer Insignia (100%), franchise rights for 25 luxury fashion, cosmetics, jewellery, and footwear brands; two department stores; restaurants and cafes	Construction, interior design, travel, industrial machinery production, logistics, media	Franchise rights for a number of the group's international brands (Gap, Banana Republic, and others) are GCC-wide; stores operate in all GCC states.
LuLu Group International (UAE)	Al Tayeb Meat Establishment (100%), distribution of fresh meat and poultry; EMKE International (100%), distribution of consumer goods; LuLu Hypermarkets (100%), 127 supermarkets and other stores (32% of UAE retail market); Line Investments & Property (100%), ownership and management of 9 malls; EMKE Commodities, exports agricultural products from Africa to Middle East	Foreign exchange and money transfer, shipping, logistics and warehousing, travel and tourism, IT training	Hypermarkets in all GCC states and four malls in Qatar, Saudi Arabia, Bahrain, and Oman. In 2015, announced opening of a hypermarket in Egypt with plans to construct 10 more by 2018.

Table 3.5 (*cont.*)

Main groups	Related companies and investments	Other activities and investments	Regional expansion
BMMI Group (Bahrain)	Al Osra Supermarkets (100%), 7 supermarkets; BMMI Shops, agents for alcoholic beverages (AB Inbev, Bacardi, Brown-Forman, Diageo, Heineken, and Moët & Chandon); Nader Trading & Refrigerating Company (100%) and Zad Marketing & Distribution (50%), distribution of general food products (20% market share)	Logistics and facilities management (military, government, and corporate clients), hotel management	BMMI distributes food in Qatar and operates a supermarket in Saudi Arabia.
Jawad Business Group (Bahrain)	Jawad International Fashion (70%), clothing and footwear retail stores; agents for international brands; Jawad Service Stations (100%), fuel distribution; food wholesaler and distributor for more than 100 brands; 13 restaurant chains, 600 retail stores, 4 supermarket chains, and 2 malls	Logistics and warehousing, travel, and automobile rentals	Stores in Kuwait, Saudi Arabia, Qatar, and Oman.
WJ Towell (owned by Sultan family, Oman)	Towell Unilever, agents and distributors for Unilever; Enhance	Construction, real estate development, telecommunications, cement, logistics,	Enhance operates in UAE and Kuwait; Gulf

Table 3.5 (*cont.*)

Main groups	Related companies and investments	Other activities and investments	Regional expansion
	(100%), distribution of general food products (largest in Oman); operation of supermarkets; agents for Nestlé in Oman; Gulf Seafoods (100%), seafood processing; Majan Distribution (70%), general food distribution; Towell Auto Centre (100%), agents for Mazda and other international automobile producers	engineering and oil industry services, life insurance	Seafoods in UAE and Saudi Arabia.

Source: Stock exchange data, company websites and news reports.

GCC or the wider Middle East (see, for example, in Table 3.5 the cross-regional franchises operated by Al Ghanim, Kharafi, Olayan, Majd Al Futtaim, and Al Tayer groups). In some instances – such as the Saudi Arabia–based Olayan Group's relationships with Colgate-Palmolive and Unilever – goods carrying international brand names are manufactured under rights in a particular country and then distributed further afield. In all these variations, large Gulf conglomerates lay claim to a certain proportion of commodity value through their strategic alliances with international firms.

The dominance of these groups also extends to the actual point of sale to the consumer, through ownership of retail outlets, supermarkets, and, increasingly, hypermarkets (very large stores that sell a variety of products including food, clothing, and electrical appliances in a single location). These so-called modern retail formats are growing at a very rapid rate and replacing traditional shops – in 2013, modern retail made up more than half of all retail space in the Gulf (Alpen Capital 2015a, p. 10).[27] The large bulk of this type of

[27] According to figures from the government of Dubai, more than half of all food retail sales take place in supermarkets or hypermarkets (Dubai SME n.d., p. 54).

retail is located in the UAE (40% of the GCC's modern retail space) and Saudi Arabia (35.8%), although other Gulf states are increasingly adopting this format. The control of this sector is highly concentrated, with three large Saudi and UAE chains listed in Table 3.5 controlling much of the GCC's modern retail space: Savola's Panda Retail Co., Majid al-Futtaim's Carrefour, and LuLu Hypermarkets. Panda holds the largest share of Saudi Arabia's modern retail area, while Majid al-Futtaim and LuLu command around one-third of the UAE's entire retail market share by value (Alpen Capital 2015a, p. 18). All these chains have expanded outside their domestic market into the wider Middle East.

In addition to such large supermarket/hypermarkets, internationally branded outlets, restaurants, and entertainment venues make up another major sector of retail. These are also organised through the system of agency rights, with a heavy concentration of brands held by a few corporate groups. In Kuwait, for example, the Al Shaya Group – listed in Table 3.5 – owns the agency rights for more than 70 international brands, including Mothercare, H&M, Debenhams, Foot Locker, Harvey Nichols, Starbucks, the Cheesecake Factory, the Body Shop, and Estée Lauder. With more than 2,800 stores retailing these brands, the company operates across all GCC states, as well as Jordan, Iraq, Lebanon, Morocco, Egypt, Turkey, Russia, Poland, and the Czech Republic. Similarly, alongside the Carrefour label, the aforementioned Majd Al-Futtaim controls agency rights for dozens of fashion brands, international hotels, cinemas, and restaurants.

Typically, these international brands are consolidated in malls and shopping centres, further reinforcing the forms of real estate development noted in the preceding section. Following global trends, GCC malls usually contain an 'anchor store' – frequently a hypermarket or large department store – around which the mall owner leases other internationally branded shops. In this manner, the mall developer draws profit from rent, in addition to the sales made in their own franchises. In the case of the Al Shaya Group, for example, which is the largest shareholder in Kuwait's mall developer, Mabanee Development company (see Table 3.4), around one-fifth of its mall stores are tenanted to its own companies (Global Investment House 2016a, p. 2). While ownership of the very largest Gulf malls continues to be dominated by the developers discussed earlier (such as the world's most visited building, Emaar's Dubai Mall), several of the large conglomerates shown in Table 3.5 are heavily involved in the ownership, development, and management of malls. The Majid Al Futtaim, Hokair, LuLu, and Al Shaya groups stand out in this regard, but virtually all the groups noted in Table 3.5 are involved in construction and real estate to some extent. Importantly, as

Chapter 5 will explore further, there is a pronounced expansion of mall development throughout the wider Middle East – it is these same large groups that drive this process of internationalisation.

3.3 Site of Accumulation 3: Banking and Finance

Financial markets and institutions sit at the core of all features of Gulf capitalism discussed earlier. Without the financing provided by these markets, most of the mega-projects that dot the Gulf's landscape would be impossible. For the large conglomerates dominating economic activity in the Gulf, financial markets provide a crucial site through which to shift surpluses across different circuits of capital, and thus fund the expansionary tendencies noted throughout this chapter. For both the retail and real estate sectors, the credit provided by financial institutions (both consumer and corporate) is critical to the continuing circulation of commodities through the urban space. In each of these roles, financial markets intersect with all aspects of daily life in the GCC, and are deeply embedded in the day-to-day reproduction of Gulf capital.

The most important financial markets in the Gulf are stock markets that list both company shares and debt securities. The first of these was formed in Kuwait in 1977, but it took another two decades before all GCC states established their own domestic markets.[28] Today, the largest stock market in the GCC is Saudi Arabia's Tadawul, which represents just over 46% of the Gulf's total market capitalisation (July 2016, US $389 billion out of US$841 billion) (Global Investment House 2016b, p. 1). Qatar and the two UAE markets – the Abu Dhabi Securities Exchange and the Dubai Financial Market – together contribute another 40% of the GCC total. All of these markets grew rapidly from the early 2000s as growing pools of surplus capital found their way to investments in newly listed companies. The pace of growth slowed after double-digit declines in the wake of the 2008–2009 global crisis,[29] but all Gulf markets recovered quickly from that crisis and generally trended upwards until the effects of the oil price downturn set in from 2015 onwards (see Chapter 7).

[28] Kuwait (Kuwait Stock Exchange, 1977), Oman (Muscat Stock Exchange, 1988), Bahrain (Bahrain Stock Exchange, 1988), Saudi Arabia (Tadawul, 1989–2001), Qatar (Doha Securities Market, 1997), and the UAE (Abu Dhabi Securities Market, 2000; Dubai Financial Market, 2000).

[29] One-fifth in the case of Oman; around one-third in Bahrain, Kuwait, and Abu Dhabi; almost one-half in Saudi Arabia; and as much as two-thirds in Dubai (Deutsche Bank 2012).

The increasing weight of financial markets has important implications for the structure of the largest Gulf conglomerates – most markedly in their relationship to the state. I have noted at several points earlier how stock market IPOs have acted to strengthen the linkages between private corporations and the state – allowing Gulf firms (and wealthy individuals) to participate in ownership structures of state-dominated firms after they have been partially listed (e.g. SABIC, Emaar, Barwa Real Estate, and most Gulf telecoms). Likewise, stock markets provide an important route by which the wealth of ruling families is circulated in a *private* form through non-state-owned companies. One extraordinary indication of this can be seen in an analysis of directorship positions for firms on the Qatar Stock Exchange (QSE). Eighty per cent of all firms listed on the QSE have at least one al-Thani family member sitting on their boards (36 of 45 firms) – the vast majority of these individuals occupy their board positions in a private capacity, not as representatives of state institutions.[30] In this manner, investments into firms listed on the QSE help constitute the Al-Thani as a core part of the (private) Qatari capitalist class.

Stock markets also strengthen pan-GCC linkages, with cross-border listings affording one way for companies to expand into neighbouring Gulf countries (Emaar and Etisalat's listings on the Saudi exchange provide two salient examples). Moreover, as I shall explore later in some detail, these markets are essential to understanding the evolving position of GCC capital within the wider Middle East. In recent years, non-GCC Arab firms have increasingly chosen to list on Gulf stock markets, thereby deepening the interlocking of ownership structures across the regional scale. A number of recent agreements between GCC markets and other Arab stock exchanges have formalised these intraregional relationships, thereby constituting GCC financial markets as a critical space around which capitalism in the Middle East as a whole increasingly pivots.

A variety of financial institutions operate within these financial markets, including banks, private equity companies, venture capital, and other asset management firms. These institutions act to pool various sources of surplus capital from wealthy individuals, firms, and governments, which is then redirected to investments in stock markets and private companies or provided as loans for businesses and households. For some institutions, such as many of the region's largest banks, these

[30] Calculated by the author from an analysis of QSE data. Al-Thani members occupy 104 of the total 388 directorship positions across all firms listed on the QSE. It should be noted that Qatar's other large business families also hold a significant portion of board spots – 80 board positions are occupied by individuals drawn from just 10 families (the Al-Kuwari, Al-Mannai, Al-Mana, Al-Marri, Al Kaabi, Al Fardan, Al Mohannadi, Fakhroo, Sulaiti, and Abdulghani).

different types of financial operations are managed through subsidiaries or specialised bank departments. In other instances, financial firms will specialise in particular types of investments, such as the funds run by private equity companies, which target specific industries or geographical regions.

Among these financial institutions, Gulf banks play a leading role. Not only are banks among the largest listed firms on Gulf stock markets – making up more than 55% of the total market capitalisation in Qatar, the UAE, and Kuwait, and just over 75% in Bahrain – they are also instrumental to financial market operations. In addition to lending to corporations and households, banks coordinate IPOs and the issuance of bonds for sale on stock markets, earning fees and commissions that are increasingly central to bank profits (see Chapter 6). Gulf banks are also among the principal buyers of both corporate and government bonds. There is thus a mutually reinforcing relationship between the growing significance of financial markets to capital structures in the Gulf and the power of the largest Gulf banks – a relationship that further strengthens the interdependencies that exist between different fractions of Gulf capital.

The earliest banks in the Gulf were foreign owned and formed under the impetus of British and French colonialism, largely as a means of channelling petrodollar surpluses towards Western markets (Hanieh 2011a, pp. 43–45). Through the 1970s, alongside the establishment of national central banks and the introduction of local currencies, domestic Gulf-owned institutions displaced the dominant position of many of these foreign banks. In some cases, foreign finance capital retained a stake in banks that were taken over by Gulf investors; by and large, however, the biggest and most important Gulf banks were to become domestically owned. Today, this remains the case.

The banking system in the contemporary Gulf is highly concentrated within a few key institutions. Saudi and UAE banks dominate the GCC as a whole – reflecting the geographical arrangement of power in the Gulf itself – with each of these countries holding just under 30% of total Gulf bank assets. They are followed at a much further distance by Qatar (15%) and Kuwait (14%), dwarfing both Bahrain (9%) and Oman (4%). Concentration of bank power is also found at the national scale, with a handful of large banks holding dominance within each country. The proportion of total national banking assets held by the top two banks ranges from around 30% in Saudi Arabia, the UAE, and Bahrain to between 44% and 62% in the case of the three other GCC states (as of the end of 2017). While ownership of banks tends to remain nationally based, there has been a marked tendency for Gulf banks to expand throughout neighbouring GCC states, and in some cases this has led to pan-GCC ownership structures. This is particularly evident in Bahrain's offshore banking sector, where ownership of the top banks is dominated by non-Bahraini Gulf capital, mostly drawn from Saudi Arabia and Kuwait.

Within this clear centralisation and concentration of financial power, Gulf banks constitute a vital element within the wider circuits of capital accumulation. While a high proportion of state ownership marks the banking system as a whole (see Table 3.6), banks tend to be listed on domestic stock exchanges, with large Gulf conglomerates coming to hold direct ownership stakes via this route. In some cases, private Gulf capital groups dominate individual banks – such as the Al Rajhi (Al Rajhi Bank), the Olayan and Muhaidib (Saudi British Bank), Dallah Al Barakah (Al Baraka Banking Group), or Al Ghurair (Mashreq Bank) groups. In other cases, particularly for those banks that are largely state owned, the position of Gulf capital within these institutions is reflected through representation on bank boards. These financial institutions are thus densely interlocked with other parts of the economy, through shared directorships and outright ownership of non-banking subsidiaries. As Table 3.6 demonstrates, many of the major firms and projects encountered throughout this chapter – developers, construction, retail, and telecommunications companies – are directly connected to Gulf banks in this manner.

An excellent illustration of these patterns is shown by the National Bank of Kuwait (NBK), which was established by a group of Kuwaiti businessmen in 1952 as the first locally owned Gulf bank. Today, NBK is the sixth largest bank in the Arab world (by assets) and the largest in Kuwait, controlling more than one-fifth of all banking assets in the country. NBK is listed on Kuwait's stock exchange (indeed, it was the first shareholding company established in the GCC), and is controlled by the most important segments of Kuwaiti capital. Its board of directors, for example, has representatives from the Al Kharafi Group – one of the original founders of the bank – whose construction, food, and retail activities were discussed earlier. Alongside Al Kharafi, other principal owners and directors of NBK include the Al-Bahar, Al-Sager, and Al-Fulaij Groups – each of these conglomerates similarly spans a range of business sectors. NBK is also closely connected to the Kuwaiti state itself – with the government-run Public Institution for Social Security holding a major stake in the company.

Other types of non-bank financial institutions are also gaining prominence in the region. Of particular significance to the themes of this book are private equity (PE) firms, which manage funds for wealthy investors – buying and selling companies and other assets with the aim of eventually

Table 3.6 *Gulf banking systems and interlocking directorships*

Country	Total no. of banks (assets $US bn)	% assets held by top two banks	Top two banks	State ownership	Interlocking directorships
Qatar	17 (329.2)	62.0%	Qatar National Bank	Qatar Investment Authority (51.93%)	Darwish Holding, Buzwair Group, Qatari Diar, Qatar Airways, Ooredoo, Hassad Food Company, Doha Film Institute, Ras Al Khaimah Cement Co., Qatar Shipping Co., Al-Safwa Islamic Financial Services, Qatar Navigation, Qatar Petroleum, Investcorp Bank, Housing Bank for Trade and Finance (Jordan), Doha Bank, Qatar Electricity and Water Co., International Bank of Qatar, Mannai Corporation, Readymix Qatar, Qatari International Real Estate Co.
			Commercial Bank of Qatar	Qatar Holding (16.83%)	Al Fardan Group, National Bank of Oman, United Arab Bank, Qatar Gas Transport, Vista Cargo Services, Abdullah Bin Ali & Partners, Qatar Cinema and Film, United Development Company, Qatar Insurance Company HBH Al Mulla & Sons
Saudi Arabia	20 (624.9)	32.6%	National Commercial Bank	Public Investment Fund (44%), General Organization for Social insurance (GOSI) (10%), Public Pension Agency (10%)	Banque Saudi Fransi, Saudi Telecom, Saudi Arabian Mining Company, Al Mutlaq Group, Al Maimani Group, National Bank of Oman, Saudi

					Investment Bank, Saudi Real Estate Company, ACWA Power, Al Ghandi Group, Al Khaleej Ceramic Company, Dorra Contracting, Al Rajhi Group, DAEM Real Estate Investment, Saudi Arabian Investment Company, Rana Investment Company, National Shipping Company of Saudi Arabia (Bahri), Tabuk Cement Company, National Industrialization Company (Tasnee), Elaf Group, SEDCO Holding Group, Dunia Alaswaf Trading.
			Al Rajhi Banking Corporation	General Organization for Social insurance (GOSI) (10.2%)	Al Rajhi, Al Wataniya Poultry, Yanbu Cement, Gulf Farabi Petrochemical, Tabuk Agricultural Development Company, Raysut Cement, Arabian Cement Company, Bank Audi Syria, Al Baraka Bank Syria, Savola Group, Herfy Food
UAE	40 (608)	36%	National Bank of Abu Dhabi	Abu Dhabi Investment Council (69.2%)	Sabat International Metal, Abu Dhabi Securities Exchange, Abu Dhabi Ports Company, Mubadala Development Company, International Petroleum Investment Corp., Gulf Capital, Al Dhafra Insurance, National Drilling Company, Al Dhaheri Group, Abu Dhabi Commercial Bank, Abu Dhabi National Tanker Co, Abu Dhabi National Hotels, Etisalat, Union National Bank, Aldar Properties, Etihad Airways, ADIA

Table 3.6 (*cont.*)

Country	Total no. of banks (assets $US bn)	% assets held by top two banks	Top two banks	State ownership	Interlocking directorships
			Emirates NBD	Investment Corporation of Dubai (55.6%)	Emirates Airlines, Dubai International Airport, Al Owais Group, Emirates International Bank, Etisalat, Dubai Refreshments, Commercial Bank of Dubai, Al Mulla Group, Al Jazeera Steel Products, Oman Refreshment Company, MH Khoory Group, Dubai Insurance Company, United Foods Company, National Bank of Fujairah, Emirates Islamic Bank, Juma Al Majd Group
Kuwait	38 (303)	43.6%	National Bank of Kuwait	Public Institute for Social Security (5.0%)	Kuwait Cinema Company, Al Argan Real Estate, Mada Telecom, Dubas Electrical Contracting, Al Bahar, SHUAA Capital, National Bank of Ras Al Khaimah, Al Kout Industrial projects, Kuwait Qatar Real Estate Development, Al Saghar, Al Watyah United Real Estate, Kuwait Food Company, Egypt Kuwait Holding Company, Mohammed Al Kharafi & Sons, Al Fulaij
			Kuwait Finance House	Government funds (49%)	Ahli United Bank, Wataniya Telecom, Ahli Bank, Zain Saudi Arabia, Bin Nisf Trading, Kuwait Building Materials Manufacturing, A'Ayan Leasing and Investment, Thunayan Al Ghanim Group.

Bahrain	47 (196.8)	31.6%	Ahli United Bank	Kuwait government (18.1%) Bahrain government (10.1%)	Bahrain Petroleum Company, Bahrain Stock Exchange, Ahli Bank, Tamdeen Real Estate Company, Global Omani Development & Investment Company, United Development Company, Ooredoo, Maraf Al Rayan, Commercial Facilities Group, Kuwait Insurance Company, United Beverage Company, Maersk Kuwait, Al Marzouk Group, Al Ghanim Group of Shipping and Trading, Fluor Kuwait, Kuwait Continental Hotel Company, Lafarg Kuwait, United Aluminium, Kuwait and Energy International Petroleum, Behbehani
			Al Baraka Banking Group	None	Dallah Al Barakah Group, Bank Al Jazira, Saudi Arabia Food Company, ABC Islamic Bank, Jordan Islamic Bank, Najran Cement Company, Al Rajhi, SHUAA Capital, Emirates Islamic Bank, Halwani Brothers, Al Rabiah Trading Company, Banque Saudi Fransi, Ahli Bank
Oman	15 (82.1)	51.1%	Bank Muscat	Omani government funds (38%)	Dubai Group, Dhofar International Development and Investment Company, Dhofar Cattle Feed, Al Salam Bank (Bahrain), Oman Chlorine Company, Falcon Insurance Company, Al Khalij Commercial Bank, Arab Media Group, Gulf Investment Services

Table 3.6 (*cont.*)

Country	Total no. of banks (assets $US bn)	% assets held by top two banks	Top two banks	State ownership	Interlocking directorships
			Bank Dhofar	Omani government funds (27%)	Dhofar International Development & Investment Holding, Omani Packaging company, Hotels Management Company, Housing Bank for Trade and Finance (Jordan), Dhofar Insurance, Port Services, Raysut Cement, LuLu Shopping Centre, Oman Cement, Oman Fisheries Company, Shell Oman Marketing Company, Sohar Poultry Company, Dhofar Cattle Feed

Source: Stock market data and company websites. Interlocking directors indicate when individuals on the bank's board sit on other company boards; these should not be taken as a comprehensive list of all existing interlocks.

exiting the investment and earning above-market returns. In 2015, around US$1 billion was raised by PE funds in the Middle East – the vast majority of which were based in the GCC – and the cumulative funds under management reached $US26.5 billion (MENAPEA 2015, p. 21).[31] PE firms have been very active in the different sectors analysed throughout this chapter. There are, for example, more than 30 real estate–focused PE funds active in the GCC, which together control more than US$3 billion in capital; these funds own residential buildings, urban infrastructure, and land across the GCC – even Abu Dhabi's oldest children's nursery, Humpty Dumpty, is controlled by a PE firm (Al Masah 2015, pp. 47–50).

Gulf PE firms and similar alternative asset management companies are important to later arguments for two key reasons. First, unlike banks, these companies display a very distinct tendency towards pan-GCC ownership structures, with owners and boards of directors drawn from across the Gulf (Hanieh 2011a, pp. 140–145). Through these regional ownership structures, PE firms envelop all major economic sectors as well as state institutions across all GCC states. Second, as we shall see in later discussions, Gulf PE firms have been key players in regional acquisitions outside the GCC. Fund investments in countries such as Egypt, Lebanon, Jordan, and Morocco have been a leading mechanism through which the internationalisation of Gulf capital has unfolded over recent years.

Fully embedded at the core of Gulf capitalism, all of these GCC financial institutions act as critical nodal points for different fractions of Gulf capital and the state, acting to gather and circulate funds through a variety of markets, economic activities, and geographic spaces. This is not meant to imply that finance 'dominates' industry or vice versa; rather, these financial institutions form a pivotal site through which Gulf capital comes to envelop *all* moments of accumulation. Finance is today a fundamental aspect to class formation in the Gulf and the projection of GCC power throughout the Middle East – these themes will form a recurring motif of later chapters.

[31] The PE industry grew very rapidly in the Middle East from its origins in the late 1990s to the boom years of 2006–2007. In 2007 more than $6 billion was raised by PE funds operating in the region, and international PE firms were predicting that the region would become 'the fourth private equity center of the world five to 10 years from now' (Ijtehadi 2007). Following the global crisis, however, Middle East PE experienced a massive crash and fundraising levels shrank by more than 80%, reaching just US$700 million in 2009. Since this collapse there has been a notable recovery of the industry, although levels remain far below those seen in the peak year of 2007 (MENAPEA 2015, p. 5).

3.4 Conclusion

Several key observations emerge from the foregoing discussion. First, across all three sites of accumulation examined, a small number of highly diversified corporate groups are dominant. These groups constitute the primary core of Gulf capital, and their names will reappear frequently in subsequent chapters. Typically, these groups are controlled by prominent business families – such as the Al Kharafi, Olayan, Al Rajhi, Ghurair, Al Futtaim, and Al Shaya – who are active across all moments of the circuit of capital and act through a complex network of subsidiaries and investments. Spatially, there is a hierarchical ordering of these groups within the GCC. The Saudi Arabia–UAE axis is preeminent across most sectors; Kuwait and Qatar form important independent zones of accumulation; while Oman and Bahrain tend to be more subordinated to the accumulation circuits of one or another of their neighbours. Hierarchies are also reproduced through the national scale, with concentration of control and ownership held by a handful of firms that sit atop a base made up of thousands of smaller, local firms. Such differentiation of class power has important implications for understanding how crises have impacted the evolution of capital in the Gulf.

State institutions, sovereign wealth funds, and other government agencies are closely interlaced with all of these conglomerates. This is especially evident for the largest petrochemical firms, real estate developers, telecoms, and banks – among these companies, state-ownership predominates, but private Gulf capital is deeply associated with them through share holdings, joint ventures, and board representation. There is a tight interlocking between 'state' and 'private' capital; privately owned companies often have public officials (including members of the ruling family) on their boards, and, equally, the boards of state-owned companies will include prominent business people. Banks, in particular, play a particularly important role as interlocutors between different fractions of the Gulf capitalist class and the state, drawing together a variety of conglomerates alongside state capital within single-ownership structures. It is thus crucial not to establish an artificial division between the 'state' (or the ruling families) and the capitalist class itself. The ruling families of the Gulf certainly dominate the political apparatus of the state, but they are also intensely involved with the accumulation of private capital. Moreover, movement between the 'public' and 'private' spheres is highly fluid, and individuals from the ruling family will frequently own major private businesses alongside holding positions in the state apparatus (as illustrated by Maktoum's investments in Tecom and du and by the Al-Thani's preponderance on Qatari company boards).

Characterised by these ownership forms, Gulf capital envelops all aspects of social existence in the contemporary Gulf. The urban scale appears as a crucial locus of accumulation, through both the production of the built environment and the circulation of commodities through city spaces. Other scales, however, are no less significant – most of the large conglomerates involved in construction, retail, telecommunications, and banking clearly envision the GCC as a single zone of accumulation (Hanieh 2011a); this pan-GCC orientation is amplified by the densely bundled linkages established through cross-border mergers and acquisitions, direct investments, the spread of agency rights, and – buttressing all of these forms of internationalisation – capital flows into GCC equity and debt markets.

This intrinsic expansionary dynamic is not restricted to the scale of the GCC itself, and here we can return to the theoretical framework with which I opened this book. Cutting across all these moments of accumulation is Gulf capital's propensity to draw the wider Middle East region ever closer. This internationalisation of Gulf capital was fundamentally enabled by the rolling-out of structural adjustment packages in many Arab countries through the 1990s and 2000s, and the subsequent liberalisation and opening up to foreign direct investment flows. Building upon the platforms established through the urban and pan-GCC scales over the past decade, Gulf capital was a principal beneficiary of this neoliberal turn – becoming intimately entwined with the patterns and rhythm of capital accumulation across the region as a whole. Much of this expansion has taken place through the same sectors described in this chapter. In this sense, the dynamics of class formation discussed earlier need to be viewed as constitutive to 'national' accumulation elsewhere in the region – these GCC dynamics exist *internal* to the national scale of other Arab countries, despite the fact they occur in a different geographic location. Simultaneously, the ways in which the Gulf stands in relation to the rest of the Middle East is part of what Gulf capital actually *is*: an integral element of class formation in the GCC itself. It is this internally related production of scale across the Middle East that forms the main object of inquiry for the chapters that follow.

4 From Farm to Shelf

Gulf Agro-Commodity Circuits and the Middle East

This chapter is the first of three that examines a specific sector of GCC capital accumulation and its interconnections with the wider region. I focus here on the agro-commodity circuit, which, as Chapter 3 noted (see Table 3.5), forms an important component of business activities for large Gulf conglomerates such as the Savola, Kharafi, Al Rajhi, and Al Ghurair groups. Understanding who produces food, the routes through which it moves, and how and where it is consumed, can reveal a great deal about broader patterns of power and domination – this is particularly pertinent to the Middle East where the politics of food remains such a prominent theme of social contestation and protest. Utilising the methodological approach outlined in Chapter 1 – i.e. a focus on the mutually constitutive relations that link various scales – I aim to trace the growing weight of Gulf capital in Gulf food systems, the relationship this holds with the internationalisation of Gulf capital throughout global food chains, and the ways in which both these processes are internally related to the development of agro-commodity circuits throughout the wider Middle East.

At a global level, a key element to approaching the question of food is the overarching influence of large agribusiness firms, which now organise the sourcing and marketing of agro-commodities across transnational circuits. The rise of these firms reflects 'increased concentration and centralization in the world food market' – a process that has accelerated through the neoliberal era and that 'has deepened the trend toward monopolistic and oligopolistic control' (Bush and Martiniello 2017, p. 196). The impact of these firms is felt across all moments of the food value chain – from the provision of inputs such as seeds, fertilisers, and pesticides; the ownership of land or contracting-out of food production; the logistics infrastructures that move food across and within borders; through to the supermarkets and retail outlets where food is ultimately marketed to consumers (Friedman and McMichael 1989; McMichael 2009, 2012; Clapp 2014; Bernstein 2016; Chesnais 2016).

In recent years, the power of these agribusiness firms has been greatly extended by the generalisation of neoliberal policies throughout major agricultural producing countries. These measures have led to an increasing concentration of land ownership in the hands of a few producers – concomitant with the erosion of collective or public land rights, the dismantling of guaranteed price supports for key agricultural inputs, the bringing down of trade barriers around the import of food items, and an orientation towards export-oriented agricultural production (McMichael 2012). As a result, farmers in the South have been incorporated into the new global agro-circuits through 'tenuous contract relations, or [by] simply regrouping the dispossessed on agro-industrial estates' (McMichael 2009, p. 154), with ultimate power over food production subordinated to the decisions of vertically integrated agribusiness firms. These types of policies have made it much more difficult for farming communities to reproduce themselves on the land – they have thus been causally linked to migration flows from rural to urban areas and the intensified pressure on farmers to undertake multiple occupational roles (Bush and Martiniello 2017, p. 197).

Export-oriented agriculture and the liberalisation of trade has produced an increasing dependence of many states – including those in the Arab world – on food imports to meet their consumption requirements. The implications of this have been evident over the recent period, most notably during the first decade of the 2000s, as rising prices for grains and other food staples created fears of shortages and put pressure on food import bills. At the peak of this price spike in 2007–2008, a wave of popular protests erupted around the globe – one author documented 25 countries affected by such 'food riots' between September 2007 and April 2008, with dozens killed during government repression of these demonstrations (Schneider 2008, cited in Bush and Martiniello 2017). Such protests not only highlighted the increasing insecurity of millions in the face of rising food prices; they also graphically illustrated the stark reality of a globally integrated food system structured around the profit imperatives of agribusiness and large financial firms.

In the wake of these global protests, many governments and international organisations began to re-emphasise the importance of 'food security' – a concept that first emerged in the 1970s and that sought to ensure that 'all people, at all times, have physical and economic access to sufficient, safe and nutritious food that meets their dietary needs and food preferences for an active and healthy life' (FAO 2006, p. 1). The notion of food security has played an enormously important discursive role in how agricultural production and trade is conceived at a policy level – not least in the Arab world, as I explore in some detail later. At this stage, it suffices to note that the food security paradigm tends to reinforce the separation of food from the systemic realities of capitalism: access to food is viewed through a technical, legal, and market-based lens, and the actual means through which food is produced and made available is thereby abstracted from the relations of power that undergird the food system itself (Windfuhr and Jonsen 2005, p. 15). In this manner, agricultural policies continue to naturalise a 'mainstream development paradigm built on liberalised international agricultural trade, trade-based food security and industrial agriculture and food production by well-resourced producers' (Windfuhr and Jonsen 2005, p. 1). Food security becomes framed around 'the weary policy of comparative advantage', which stresses that 'poor countries should try and generate income that will enable food purchases on global markets rather than focus inward on generating greater autonomy and food sovereignty locally' (Bush and Martiniello 2017, p. 195) – paradoxically, in other words, the policies associated with achieving food security act to deepen the *food insecurity* that arises from the current world order.

The work of scholars in mapping these core characteristics of contemporary food and agriculture – the globally posited nature of food production and circulation, the leading role of transnational agribusiness firms in determining agricultural priorities, the attendant reshaping of social relations on the land, and the discursive shift towards market-based food security – has contributed a great deal to understanding the structure of agro-commodity circuits and their relationship to forms of power within the global economy. Nonetheless, at a theoretical level, much of the literature on these issues has tended to hypostasise conceptual, abstract categories such as the 'global' and 'national' – or, alternatively, 'North' and 'South' – and thereby downplay the multiple, concrete spatialities within which food is produced and circulated. The prominent food scholar Philip McMichael has noted this analytical weakness, implying the need to move beyond a sole focus 'on imperial/national tensions, national/transnational tensions and now transnational/local tensions' towards a reconstruction of the 'historically concrete whole' that does not reify conceptual forms of appearance but takes seriously 'the lens of specific regional processes and articulations' (2016, pp. 661–662).

Heeding this injunction for a more attentive approach to the regional spatiality of food systems, this chapter asks how the dynamics of accumulation through the agro-circuits of Gulf capitalism are internally related to both the global food system and the production and circulation of food across the wider Middle East. I begin by outlining the basic patterns of food production, consumption, and trade in the Gulf, with a particular focus on the two most important countries in this respect: Saudi Arabia and the UAE. I then turn to the embrace of food security policies by all Gulf governments following the 2007–2008 global food price spike. The chapter traces the ways in which these food security policies discursively underpinned a reorganisation of food systems in the Gulf, marked most significantly by the internationalisation of Gulf agribusiness firms into global circuits of agricultural production and circulation. In addition to the purchase of agricultural land across the globe, I show how these internationalisation tendencies need to be viewed across the whole agro-commodity circuit, including the provision of agricultural inputs, storage, processing, trade, and logistics. Taken together, these dynamics have positioned large Gulf agribusiness firms at the core of the entire agricultural value chain in the GCC.

Having established these changes within the Gulf itself, the chapter then moves to examining their ramifications for food systems of other Arab states. I show that the increasing power of vertically integrated Gulf agribusiness firms is acting to more deeply embed other Arab states into the agro-circuits of Gulf capitalism. This can be seen in the changing geographies of Arab agricultural trade, as well as the notable presence of Gulf conglomerates in ownership structures of other Arab agricultural firms (here I focus on the paradigmatic case of Egypt). Taken as a whole, these processes provide an important illustration of how the changing spatiality of accumulation around food in the Gulf is simultaneously reworking food systems across the wider Middle East.

4.1 The Gulf Agro-Commodity Circuit: Food Security and Internationalisation

For many years the biggest agricultural producer and food market in the Gulf has been Saudi Arabia. This agricultural dominance has a long historical pedigree in Saudi attempts to 'master and remake the environment' (Jones 2010, p. 10), as Toby Jones has shown in his superb environmental history of the country. Saudi rulers saw 'authority over the water and the lands that sustained or enabled agriculture' as a key 'means to strengthen and secure their reign' (Jones 2010, p. 24), and thus pursued a range of schemes aimed at building up the country's agricultural sector, particularly domestic wheat production. Although the initiative for such schemes came firmly from within the Saudi ruling family, they also came to rely heavily upon foreign (particularly American) technical expertise.[1] For a time, this orientation meant that the

[1] Jones argues that the centrality of environmental questions to the projection of Saudi power means state–society relations were shaped by much more than just the presence of oil. Instead, Saudi Arabia is 'also a modern technostate, one in which science and expertise, scientific services, and technical capacity came to define the relationship between rulers and ruled' (2010, p. 14).

Kingdom became self-sufficient in wheat and was even exporting surpluses of this key crop[2] – a fact that US officials described as making 'about as much sense as planting bananas under glass in Alaska' (Jones 2010, pp. 231–232). Irrigated crop area rose from 400,000 hectares in 1971 to around 1.6 million hectares by 1992 (Ouda 2014, p. 283).[3] By 2008, however, ecological pressures on the country's scant groundwater reserves led the government to reverse this long-standing policy of supporting irrigated crop production, and wheat farming was scheduled to be completely phased out by 2015. Nonetheless, the country continues to farm other less water-intensive crops such as fruit and vegetables, and food-processing industries have also expanded significantly over the last decade. Today, Saudi Arabia accounts for around 70% of total food production in the GCC and is responsible for just over 60% of Gulf food consumption (Alpen Capital 2015b, p. 16).

Other Gulf states have historically possessed much smaller agricultural sectors, largely due to limited arable land and shrinking renewable water resources. After Saudi Arabia, the UAE is the second largest food producer (15% of the region's total, with most farming land located in the emirate of Abu Dhabi), although the country plays a much more consequential role as the GCC's largest re-exporter of food commodities – indeed, almost half of imported food products are re-exported (Alpen Capital 2015b, p. 11). With its large expatriate population and high levels of tourism, the UAE is also a major food consumer in the Gulf, making up 18.5% of the Gulf's total market (Alpen Capital 2015b, p. 18). After Saudi Arabia and the UAE, Oman ranks third in Gulf agricultural production (around 8% of the GCC total), mostly seafood, vegetables, and fruit, while Qatar, Bahrain, and Kuwait have very small domestic agricultural sectors.

As a consequence of these low levels of agricultural production across the Gulf, close to three-quarters of the region's food consumption is met by imports. Much of these imports consist of basic food commodities such as wheat, sugar, rice, and other grains, for which per capita consumption levels in the Gulf exceed global averages. Importantly, however, as I pointed out in Chapter 3, the dynamics of agro-commodity flows at the pan-GCC scale act to mediate this overall dependency on

[2] For meat, milk, and vegetables, Saudi Arabia was able to meet much of its domestic consumption (60%, 55%, and 73%, respectively).

[3] This policy was closely linked to the emergence of large commercial agricultural capital groups in the Kingdom, supported through state-backed provision of agricultural technology, generous subsidies (including soft and interest-free loans), free land, and government-funded agricultural services. The origin of many of the firms discussed later – such as the Al Rajhi, Savola, and Almarai – date from this period.

food imports. The central characteristic of this is the role of Saudi Arabia and the UAE as principal suppliers of agro-commodities to the other Gulf states. Indeed, for each of the other four GCC states, the combined share of food imports from Saudi and UAE is greater than those from any other state anywhere in the world. In 2015, Saudi Arabia or the UAE ranked as either the first or second food exporter to each of the other GCC states. Remarkably – particularly since these figures include major wheat and meat exporters to the Gulf such as the United States, India, Brazil, and Australia – Saudi Arabia and the UAE were responsible for 53% of the total food export value of the top 10 exporting countries to Oman, 36% for Qatar, 34% for Bahrain, and 24% for Kuwait.[4] These trends not only point to the importance of placing the Saudi-UAE axis at the centre of understanding trends in the wider Gulf, but also have important implications for understanding how the rest of the Arab world interacts with the Gulf as a whole.

With rapidly growing (and increasingly youthful) populations, rising tourist numbers, and the phasing-out of irrigated crop production in Saudi Arabia, the Gulf's dependency on food imports has risen significantly over recent decades – between 2000 and 2007, the region's total food import bill rose from $8 billion to $20 billion (Daniel and Mittal 2009, p. 2); by 2014, cereal imports to the Gulf alone had reached $8.8 billion (AOAD 2015, p. 119). The consequences of this were sharply illustrated through the 2000s, as global food prices began to move upwards from about 2004 and culminated in the sharp price spike of 2007–2008.[5] For the Gulf states, this price spike precipitated a major reorientation of food and agricultural policies. Although at an immediate level the Gulf was relatively insulated from rising prices due to its sizable financial reserves (oil prices were also rapidly increasing over this period), the price spike led at least 25 countries to impose export embargos or restrictions on their food exports, including key agricultural producers such as Russia, Argentina, Thailand, and India (Smaller and Mann 2009, p. 4). Fearing further export restrictions and potential food shortages should prices continue to increase, Gulf policy makers began to

[4] The comparative figures for Saudi Arabia and the UAE vis-à-vis each other are much lower but not insignificant – 5% of the UAE's food imports from its top 10 partners come from Saudi Arabia (which ranks fifth); for Saudi Arabia, 14%, with the UAE ranking third.

[5] Between 2003 and 2008, global food prices for commodities such as dairy, cereals, vegetable oils, and sugar approximately doubled. The reasons for this price rise continue to be debated, but explanations have included financial speculation, drought, the impact of oil prices, growing use of biofuels, and falling food stockpiles.

increasingly highlight the goal of food security – understood as guaranteeing stable, reliable supplies of key food staples – as the principal element of their food strategies (Al-Alami 2012). In the words of Rashid Mohammed bin Fahad, the UAE's Minister of Water and Environment, food security had become 'an immediate priority ... and execution of a core food security strategy is essential to provide a sustainable growth platform' (Malek 2014).

Most accounts of the Gulf's embrace of the food security paradigm have focused on the primary drivers typically articulated in government strategy documents. Paramount in this regard are the ecological challenges noted earlier – specifically, the limited supplies of underground water and arable land (Woertz et al. 2008; Smaller and Mann 2009) – as well as the region's exposure to world price fluctuations given the high dependency on imports. But as the critical food studies literature has emphasised, these food security strategies need to be understood beyond the simple formula of market supply and demand. Most notable for our purposes are the ways in which food security strategies have acted discursively, as a means to justify, explain, and legitimate deep-reaching changes to the Gulf's place in global agro-commodity circuits. In this sense, the food security discourse resembles what Timothy Mitchell has described as a 'logic of distribution' – a way of demarcating and delimiting a particular conceptual field so as to confine thought (and political action) within boundaries that appear as 'common sense' (Mitchell 2011, p. 9).[6] Specifically, the food security discourse – framed around ecological limits and the need to ensure a stable market supply of basic staples – has validated state-led support of the largest capital groups involved in agribusiness activities, helping gird their internationalisation through regional and international agro-circuits, and simultaneously reinforcing their control over domestic agricultural production and distribution.[7] This is not a new feature of GCC

[6] Mitchell discusses this in relation to the making of concepts such as 'democracy' and 'economy' through the mid-twentieth century (see chapter 5 of *Carbon Democracy*).

[7] This should not be taken to imply that ecological and other factors are not pertinent at the level of government policy. It made little rational sense, for example, that Saudi Arabia – one of the most arid countries on Earth – spent decades subsidising the growing of wheat and the maintenance of large livestock and forage farms. But this obviously ecologically disastrous policy becomes perfectly explainable when placed in the context of the development of Saudi capitalism: Saudi agricultural policy was primarily driven by the state's support of Saudi capital – the Al Rajhi, Savola, and other conglomerates that built massive fortunes on state-supported fiscal and ecological subsidies. Indeed, from 1984 to 2000, subsidies for the Saudi wheat program reached $85 billion – equivalent to 18% of its oil revenue over the same period, and thus directly underpinned the rise of Saudi agribusiness (Melly 2013, p. 20).

agricultural policy – Jones notes, for example, in relation to Saudi investment in food production, that 'while rhetorically tied to concerns about national security', government policy has long been about 'lining the pockets of those close to government [and] securing the support of the country's financial elites' (Jones 2010, p. 229) – but what *has* changed is its global dimension. These internationalisation tendencies are evident in the Gulf's acquisition of overseas farmland and primary agricultural resources, alongside the Gulf's growing role in commanding (and constituting) vertically integrated circuits that extend across the production, circulation, and realisation of agro-commodity value. It is to this global expansion that we must now turn.

The Gulf's Global Land Grab?

In the wake of 2007 and 2008, numerous media, non-governmental organisations (NGOs), and academic reports began to speak alarmingly of the Gulf's role in a great global 'land grab' (Daniel and Mittal 2009) – the overseas acquisition of farmland, by which Gulf states aimed to replace domestic production of water-intensive crops with guaranteed supplies of imported food as part of their food security strategies. Although all GCC states embarked on such land purchases, the regional leaders have been Saudi Arabia and the UAE. According to one online database of global land acquisitions, Land Matrix, these two states have concluded deals to buy more than 3.8 million hectares of land since 2000 – an amount that is second only to the United States in transnational land purchases.[8] In comparison to Saudi Arabia and the UAE, the other four GCC states have been much less prominent in overseas land purchases, despite all adopting food security strategies in the wake of 2008. The reasons for this are partly due to their smaller populations and less developed food industries, as well as the distinctive patterns of agro-commodity trade within the GCC noted earlier, in which Saudi Arabia and the UAE act as the key entrepot markets for goods that are then recirculated to the other GCC states. Nonetheless, there have been some land acquisitions by these other Gulf states over recent years, most

[8] These figures must be treated with a great deal of caution. Land Matrix notes that accurate figures are very difficult to obtain as land deals are frequently not transparent, lack established procedures, and negotiations do not take place in the public realm. The organisation relies heavily on unofficial sources and reporting, and the geographic focus is only on deals that target low- and middle-income countries.

notably by Qatar, which in 2008 established a US$1 billion state-owned firm, Hassad Foods, as the primary vehicle for its food security strategy.[9]

A marked feature of these land purchases, particularly for Saudi Arabia and the UAE, is the essential role of state institutions in supporting the international expansion of private companies through subsidies and other forms of financial support. Saudi Arabia, for example, launched the King Abdullah Initiative for Saudi Agricultural Investment Abroad (KAISAIA) in January 2009, which, according to the Saudi Deputy Minister for Agricultural Research and Development Affairs, Abdullah Al-Obaid, sought to encourage 'Saudi Private Investment [to] play in the near future, an active role abroad in enhancing food security for Saudi Arabia' (Obeid 2010, p. 8). As part of this initiative, a US$800 million government firm called the Saudi Agriculture and Livestock Company (SALIC) was established to support firms seeking to invest in overseas lands. In this manner, and further illustrating the nature of class–state relations outlined in Chapter 3, the internationalisation of private capital was earmarked as the primary means of implementing the country's food security strategy, with the Saudi state acting as an essential support for its domestic capitalist class.

The state's role in this process extends beyond simple financial aid for private firms, to encompass a range of diplomatic and political initiatives that sought to encourage target countries to open their land to foreign direct investment from the Gulf. According to the Saudi ministerial committee charged by Royal Decree with implementation of KAISAIA, target countries would be expected to have 'strong political relationships with Saudi Arabia' and be willing to sign investment treaties that protected Saudi investments from any expropriation (Rouli 2010, translation by the author).[10] Changes to local laws were demanded in order to liberalise land ownership laws or make available long-term leases to Saudi investors, provide labour at competitive cost, exempt Saudi firms from custom taxes on agricultural equipment and other inputs, remove income tax on production and processing, and guarantee 'availability of all needed agricultural investment resources including fertile land and abundant water resources that will allow production of large quantities of some of the strategic crops

[9] Qatar's initial response to the global food price rises was focused much more on increasing domestic food production. The Qatar National Food Security Programme (QFNSP) – first announced at the World Summit on Food Security in Rome in 2009 – promised research into the use of new technologies to remove the reliance on underground water aquifers. It was an approach described by two scholars as a 'cornucopian plan to raise self-sufficiency . . . with the help of futuristic farming designs and solar-based desalination' (Keulertz and Woertz 2015, p. 36). Implementation of the QFNSP, however, was marred by technological and environmental barriers, in addition to rivalries between different branches of the ruling family.

[10] Products are focused on staple goods, including wheat, barley, sorghum, corn, and livestock.

such as rice and wheat at sufficient quantity and at low and stable prices' (Wikileaks 2010). Most significantly, target countries were required to grant Saudi investors the right to export no less than half of the product back to Saudi Arabia (Agriculture Development Fund (ADF) n.d., p. 11). In a 2011 newspaper interview with the Arabic-language daily *Al Riyadh*, the Saudi Minister of Agriculture noted that the greatest fear of potential investors was 'change in the investment and financial regimes of the country . . . if the Sudanese government, for example, prevented the repatriation of profits, increased taxes or the currency depreciated . . . these kind of changes are what foreign investors fear the most' (Haidar 2011, translation by the author). Once such fears were assuaged, KASAIA would place the country on a list of approved investment targets and provide funding to the Saudi investor of up to 60% of the value of the project (ADF n.d., p. 4).

Supported in this manner by various state initiatives, Gulf firms initially targeted poorer countries across Asia and Africa for land acquisitions. In these areas, Gulf investments were said to promise a 'win-win' scenario through developing the large tracts of cheap land, plentiful labour, and water resources while guaranteeing the Gulf's food security needs. Hesham Al Shirawi, Chair of the UAE's Economic Zones World, noted that 'Africa has potential for great success in agri-business, which will help supporting food security programmes for many countries that suffer from food shortage production' and called for the establishment of free zones across the continent that 'could be used as storages for all kinds of food products and could also include large livestock farms and factories for packaging and exporting' (Bitar 2013). Likewise, Sultan bin Saeed Al Mansouri, the UAE's Minister of Economy, has marshalled Arab pre-colonial history to make the case for UAE land purchases in Africa: 'We [the Arabs] were at the Cape before the Europeans ... The trade routes were established before the European came. We understand how important Africa is. It is critical for us in terms of food security. We have looked around the world and we feel the solution is in Africa' (Staples 2015).

Initially, the Gulf's first forays into Africa and Asian land acquisitions appeared to meet with some success. Indonesia, for example, agreed to change its investment laws in 2010 – after Saudi investors halted projects in the country – in order to allow up to 49% ownership of staple crops (Mahdi 2010). In the Mindanao region of the Philippines, Saudi investors circumvented local laws intended to prevent the export of staple foods by leasing land through local Filipino subsidiaries, rezoning land as 'unproductive', and producing crops that were similar, but not identical, to those restricted from export (e.g. basmati rice instead of white rice) (Salerno 2011, p. 10). Such practices were facilitated by trade partnerships and agreements between the two countries, as well as new laws established in the Philippines that sought to build up agricultural special economic zones that lay outside the country's domestic legal structure. Similarly, in the UAE, government-backed agencies – most notably the Abu Dhabi Development Fund – extended grants and loans to target countries in Africa and Asia in order to finance the preparation of land for leasing or purchase by private, UAE-based firms. These UAE land deals made headlines post-2008 following a number of high-profile acquisitions, including 800,000 hectares in Pakistan, most of which was bought by the private equity firm Abraaj Capital (see Chapter 6 for discussion of this company), and more than 250,000 hectares in Sudan that were provided to UAE investors for free or at nominal rent (Bundhun 2011).

Nonetheless, despite the global attention garnered by such Saudi and Emirati land purchases across Africa and Asia in the post-2008 period, many of these deals did not materialise or proceeded at a much smaller scale than initially announced. In part, this was due to resistance from local farmers and landowners. In Ethiopia, for example, where the massive Saudi Star conglomerate holds a 60-year lease of 10,000 hectares of land in the Gambella region, armed attacks have occurred on Saudi Star's compound by farmers forcibly displaced from their land.[11] Likewise in Cambodia, the Philippines, and Indonesia, the initial projects announced by Gulf investors have been put on hold or never eventuated due to public protest or a lack of effective guarantee for investments.

The failure of some of the more high-profile land deals has led a number of analysts to question the very notion of a 'global land grab', and the veracity of figures provided by NGOs tracking this phenomenon. However, while it is certainly the case that many of these deals did not move beyond the announcement stage, what appears to have happened over recent years is rather a realignment of target countries, with Gulf investors increasingly seeking land acquisitions in regions deemed more investor friendly. The Middle East has been one important destination of these investments, but in general, instead of poorer countries with weaker investment regimes, Gulf land purchases increasingly turned towards wealthier countries with extensive farming areas and more secure property rights. Saudi companies, for example, now hold nearly 40,000 hectares of arable crops in the Ukraine and Poland (a joint venture between SALIC, the Al Rajhi Group, and the

[11] In protest against their removal from the land, armed protestors attacked the Saudi Star farm in April 2012, killing at least five people. According to Human Rights Watch, the Ethiopian military responded by 'arbitrarily arresting and beating young men and raping female relatives of suspects' (HRW 2012). Saudi Star is owned by the Saudi billionaire Sheikh Mohammed Hussein Al Amoudi, estimated by Forbes to be worth more than $8 billion. Al Amoudi is expected to pay an annual tax of less than $3 per hectare on his land in Ethiopia (Financial Times 2016).

dairy company Almarai); more than 5,500 hectares of land in Arizona and California, dedicated to growing alfalfa as fodder for Almarai's dairy herds (Kim 2016); a 20% stake in one of Brazil's largest cattle farms (Casey 2015); and a majority stake in the former Canadian Wheat Board, which held a seven-decade monopoly on the marketing of wheat in Canada before its privatisation in 2015 (Business Times 2015).[12] By 2013, more than $11 billion of land purchases had been made by Saudi investors in countries such as Argentina, Brazil, Canada, the Ukraine, Egypt, and Sudan (Agrimoney 2013). Likewise, the UAE Ministry of Economy has claimed that Emirati firms had acquired or leased more than 1.5 million hectares of land (Al Makahieh and Sherif 2012), including hundreds of thousands of hectares of farming land across the United States, Spain, Italy, Australia, New Zealand, Brazil, and Serbia.[13]

Perhaps due to this geographical realignment of Gulf investments, popular discussion of Gulf land purchases has received less attention in recent years. There is, however, one significant feature that has been frequently overshadowed in these debates: the wider transformation of the agricultural commodity chain (and associated forms of accumulation) that has accompanied the internationalisation of Gulf agribusiness. A more complete assessment of the Gulf's incorporation into global agro-circuits needs to move beyond a narrow focus on land purchases (or leasing) to examine these other parts of global agro-commodity circuits, including control over agricultural inputs (seeds, fertilisers, farm equipment, and forage), trade, shipping, storage, processing, and distribution. To a large degree, Gulf capital's changing relationship to these sectors carries much more significance than the simple purchase of land, as it presages the interlocking of circuits of both the production *and* circulation of agro-commodities under the control of Gulf capital.

Beyond Land: The Gulf across Global Value Chains

The Gulf's expansion through other parts of the agro-value chain has occurred alongside its acquisition of overseas land, and frequently involves the same major private firms. In this manner, and echoing observations of the critical food studies literature made in other regional contexts, processes of internationalisation underlie a tendency towards

[12] CWB was sold to a consortium of Bunge and SALIC and renamed G3 Global Grain Group.

[13] Similarly, Qatar's Hassad has focused on land purchases in Australia, where the firm owns 14 farms covering an area of 750,000 hectares. In 2015, the company announced that it was also engaged in talks to expand into Brazil (sugar and poultry) and North America (grains).

the vertical integration of a handful of firms within the GCC agro-commodity sector. From farm to shelf, these large firms have come to coordinate each stage of the production and circulation of food, particularly for staple products, with ownership structures that stretch across multiple geographical spaces and sectors. These processes carry important implications for the construction of the wider regional scale (explored in Section 4.3), as they tie together different moments of value realisation, subordinated to the overall tempo of accumulation in the Gulf.

The privately owned UAE firm Al Dahra provides an illustrative example of such forward and backward linkages. The firm has been a leading protagonist in Gulf overseas land acquisitions, and now operates a global land bank of more than 200,000 hectares on which it grows rice, corn, wheat, fruits, and vegetables (mainly potatoes, citrus, dates, and olives), as well as a network of large dairy farms, comprised of more than 1,600 cows. But in addition to this primary agricultural production, Al Dahra's business strategy explicitly points to vertical integration as a core goal, conceived through the firm's involvement 'in the entire agribusiness cycle from farming to marketing and activities in between' through which it hopes to 'Bypass intermediaries ... gain greater control over the supply chain elements ... [and] ensure seamless delivery of products' (Al Dahra n.d.).

This orientation is clearly evident in the range of Al Dahra's business activities. The firm, for example, is heavily involved in the production and marketing of animal feed and forage (alfalfa, grass, and hay), which it supplies to its own farms as well as other livestock producers across the Middle East. Indeed, Al Dahra claims to be 'the largest conglomerate of globally produced, processed and sourced Forage products', and in 2014, close to two-thirds of all the animal feed and forage imported into the UAE was supplied by the company.[14] Reflective of the global nature of Al Dahra's supply networks, the company's animal feed materials are sourced, processed, packaged, and marketed by eight subsidiaries headquartered in the United States, Italy, South Africa, Hong Kong, Egypt, Spain, Saudi Arabia, and the UAE. Quite remarkably, Al Dahra subsidiaries are now the largest forage exporters in the United States, Italy, and Spain.

In addition to animal feed, Al Dahra also operates grain, flour, and rice mills across Europe and South Asia. Once again, these processing facilities are conceived as an integral step within the firm's international trade in agro-commodities: raw grains are sourced from Al Dahra farms and those of other producers, processed into flour and other products, and then marketed to countries across the globe. Within this circuit, the firm places

[14] Calculated by the author from Al Dahra's metric tonnage of fodder imports and UN Comtrade data.

a high priority on being a principal supplier of staples to the Middle East. In 2013, for example, Al Dahra took a 20% stake in Greece's oldest and largest flour producer, Loulis Mills, thereby gaining 'access to a high-level cereals transit hub in Europe [and] enabling it to channel its [Al Dahra's] production from European countries such as Spain, Italy and Serbia into the Middle East'.[15] Likewise, a new rice milling plant in Abu Dhabi that Al Dahra began constructing in July 2015 (the first of its kind in the Gulf) will import rice through a joint venture that Al Dahra holds in India, process this rice in Abu Dhabi, and then export it to other Gulf countries, Africa, and Europe. If these ventures prove successful and Al Dahra establishes itself as a significant global intermediary for grains and other staples, the firm stands to benefit enormously from the Middle East's huge demand for such commodities: 6 of the top 10 wheat importers in the world, for example, are from the Arab world, and Arab countries import 57% of the world's traded barley (Battat et al. 2012, p. xi).

Knitting together these complex circulatory routes is the firm's growing involvement in the logistics sector. In addition to a global network of silos, warehousing facilities, and transport vehicles, the clearest illustration of this logistics turn is Al Dahra's close relationship with Agility, the largest logistics company in the Middle East since 2004 and one of the top 15 global logistics firms (Agility 2014). Al Dahra is the leading shareholder of the Abu Dhabi subsidiary of Agility, and also owns a major stake of Tristar, a UAE affiliate of Agility, which in March 2016 purchased Eships, an important ship owner and operator based in Abu Dhabi.[16] As a result, Al Dahra's operations are increasingly enmeshed with the development of port infrastructures in the UAE; indeed, Al Dahra is now the largest importer at Khalifa Port – one of the biggest ports in the UAE – where the company has established its regional base in order to facilitate 'greater logistical and trading opportunities for [Al Dahra's] business and [to] provide a platform for the expansion and growth', according to the firm's vice-chairman (Khaleej Times 2013).

As with the expansion of Gulf capital into global land ownership, the emergence of Al Dahra – and the consolidation of its control over various moments of the agricultural value chain – has been dependent upon the firm's close connection to the UAE state. Despite its status as a private company, the firm is actually fully owned (in a personal capacity) by Sheikh Hamed bin Zayed Al Nahyan, a member of Abu Dhabi's ruling

[15] Around the same time as its stake in Loulis, Al Dahra announced a $400 million investment in Serbian agriculture.

[16] Eships was purchased by Tristar in March 2016 from the German Oldendorff Group for US$90 million.

family and also head of ADIA (see Chapter 2); in this symbiosis of state power and private capital it thus bears a close structural resemblance to firms such as Tecom and du discussed in Chapter 3. The firm's accumulation has been underpinned through its connection to the state, particularly its access to exclusive contracts for the supply of various agro-commodities to the UAE as part of the country's food security strategy. Al Dahra, for example, along with just two other firms (Agthia and Al Ghurair), controls virtually all the import, storage, and milling of wheat in the UAE. Moreover, since 2007, Al Dahra has held the contract to supply alfalfa and other animal fodder to the Abu Dhabi Food Control Authority (ADFCA), the state body in charge of Abu Dhabi's food security policy; Al Dahra also manages more than 70 forage distribution and warehousing facilities on behalf of ADFCA. As a result of these contractual arrangements, Al Dahra positions itself as 'essentially the official partner of the Abu Dhabi government in achieving the government's long-term food security vision' and to this end 'has created a strategic reserve for emergencies inside the country and at various origins with constant stock rotation' (Al Dahra 2013).

Three other large UAE agribusiness conglomerates – the Al Ghurair Group,[17] Agthia,[18] and the Jenaan Investment Company – display similar patterns of intensifying forward and backward linkages across the supply chain, combined with an orientation towards controlling logistical infrastructures that bind together the internationalisation of productive and commodity circuits. These firms are characterised by varying degrees of state and private ownership, and explicitly view themselves as arms of the UAE's food security strategy. The CEO of Abu Dhabi–based Jenaan Investments Company, for example, has commented: 'The most important thing is to have government support. This enables Jenaan to expand to other countries, such as Sudan or Egypt, and find the best way to invest there. We would not be able to go at this alone or play an important role in the food security plan without the government's support' (TBY 2015). Similarly, the Al Ghurair Group (see Chapter 3) works closely with the UAE government to provide grain supplies across a network of silos and mills located in the UAE, Algeria, Sudan, Lebanon, and Egypt (Beer 2015). As a result of such arrangements, these firms now largely dominate the import, processing,

[17] This Dubai-based group is controlled by the Ghurair family. It owns the largest standalone sugar refinery in the world, Al Khaleej Sugar, and is the UAE's largest importer of raw sugar. Al Ghurair is also a major player in wheat, rice, and food processing (flour, pasta, noodles) and the hospitality industry and manages silos, mills, and refineries across the Middle East and South Asia.

[18] Agthia manufactures, distributes, and markets mineral water, flour, animal feed, juices, dairy products, frozen vegetables, and baked goods.

and distribution (including re-export) of several key staple agro-commodities in the UAE, including wheat (Agthia, Al Ghurair, Al Dahra),[19] rice (Al Ghurair), sugar (Al Ghurair), and animal feed (Jenaan, Al Dahra). Alongside the transnational linkages established by these firms, other large UAE conglomerates continue to play the traditional role outlined in the previous chapter of distribution agents and re-exporters of food and agricultural products sourced from non-UAE producers outside the country.

In Saudi Arabia, patterns of agribusiness development – invariably also framed by notions of food security – likewise illustrate the growing influence of vertically integrated conglomerates over the import and distribution of food staples, concomitant with their tightening linkages to international agro-circuits. All feed barley imported into Saudi Arabia, for example, is controlled by the Al Rajhi Group, which operates tens of thousands of hectares of international farmland across the Ukraine, Poland, Egypt, and Sudan to grow this barley alongside wheat, soya beans, corn, and green fodder. Highly integrated across the value chain, Al Rajhi provides the engineering, procurement, and construction for agricultural projects on these farms; supplies fertilisers, seeds, machinery, and spare parts; owns the trading and logistics networks necessary to export their products to Saudi Arabia and across the Middle East; and runs an extensive bagging and retail distribution network across the Kingdom itself. All of these varied agribusiness activities – a complement to the Group's other extensive financial and industrial interests discussed in Chapter 3 – explicitly tie processes of capital internationalisation to the requirements of Saudi state agro-policy, with the firm noting its objective is to 'globalize Al-Rajhi Group's agricultural business on a long-term sustainable basis while securing specific goals of food security'.[20]

Likewise, Saudi Arabia's Almarai – the world's largest integrated dairy company and seventh largest company on the Saudi stock exchange by market capitalisation – is characterised by patterns of vertical integration extending across domestic and international markets. The firm's major shareholders include the major Saudi conglomerate Savola (36.5%), noted in Chapter 3, as well as a Saudi prince (in a private capacity), Sultan Mohammed Bin Saud Al Kabeer Al Saud (28.7%). Following the Saudi government's decision to shift away from water-intensive farming inside the

[19] There are three main storage and milling sites for the country's grain imports: the Fujairah Strategic Grain Terminal (capacity of 275,000 metric tons), operated by Al Dahra; the Al Wathba Production and Distribution Complex in Abu Dhabi (capacity 50,000 metric tons), operated by Agthia Group; and the Jebel Ali Free Zone (300,000 metric tons), operated by Al Ghurair Group.

[20] www.raii.net/company-overview/.

Kingdom,[21] Almarai pursued an aggressive strategy of overseas expansion, and now owns or operates tens of thousands of hectares of farmland in Argentina, the United States (California and Arizona), Ukraine, Poland, Egypt, and Jordan. Much of this overseas land is devoted to growing feed for its livestock in Saudi Arabia, and as a result, Almarai is now the second largest importer of corn into Saudi Arabia – responsible for around 25% of the Kingdom's entire corn imports in 2014. The firm is also the GCC's leading manufacturer across the dairy, juice, bakery, poultry, and infant formula sectors – holding the highest market share for most of these commodities. As with many of the other firms discussed here, Almarai operates an extensive logistics infrastructure, including thousands of trucks, tankers, and vans, and more than 100 distribution centres spread across the GCC, Jordan, and Egypt – indeed, just under 30% of the company's projected capital investment until 2020 is dedicated to expanding this logistics network, an amount exceeding that earmarked for farming itself (Almarai 2015, p. 3).[22] As in the Al Dahra example discussed earlier, these circulatory routes are increasingly linked to the development of port infrastructures, with Almarai becoming the first tenant of a dedicated processing zone at King Abdullah Port in 2014, from where the firm imports corn, soybeans, and alfalfa for processing and distribution to a variety of domestic and international markets (Beer 2014).

The emergence of such vertically integrated agribusiness firms in Saudi Arabia is closely connected to the country's clear decision to place large agribusiness conglomerates at the centre of its food security strategy. Privatisation across the agro-food sector has been a major contributing element to this, and the likely prospect of this continuing will doubtless accentuate the growing weight of these conglomerates across all moments of the value chain. One recent example is the part-privatisation of Bahri Dry Bulk (BDB), Saudi Arabia's largest grain importing firm, which controls a fleet of massive container vessels that ship food and feed products from around the world. One of Saudi Arabia's major private agribusiness firms, ARASCO,[23] now holds a

[21] In 2015, the Saudi cabinet issued a decision to end green fodder cultivation in the country by the end of 2018.

[22] Almarai has also commissioned the Swiss-based company Swisslog to fully automate its distribution logistics network in Al Kharj, Saudi Arabia.

[23] ARASCO describes itself as a 'feed to food company' and 'a pipeline from plant growers, based elsewhere, to a dairy and meat product supplier of local supermarkets and other retail and food service'. The firm imports around one-half of Saudi Arabia's corn annually, with about 40% for its own use and the remainder retailed to other end users (USGC 2015). Underpinning ARASCO's wide scope of interests across the agro-commodity value chain is the firm's involvement in logistics, including a fleet of 300 trucks, 150 railcars, and a network of warehouses for its own agro-commodities and those of other customers.

40% stake in BDB, and the privatisation is held up by the World Bank as a model for neighbouring Arab countries to emulate (Battat et al. 2012, p. 41). But perhaps the most significant portent of where Saudi agribusiness may be heading is the plan to privatise the Grain Silos Organisation (GSO), a state-owned firm responsible for the storage, milling, and distribution of grain. The privatisation of GSO heralds a seismic change in Saudi grain policy.[24] For the first time in Saudi history, private firms would operate the country's mills and control the distribution of wheat flour; these firms would also be permitted to import their own (non-subsidised) wheat. Beyond the enfeoffment of Saudi food security to private capital, this privatisation of Saudi Arabia's mills could also foreshadow a closer interlocking of Saudi-Emirati agribusiness chains, with two of the large UAE agribusiness firms noted earlier (Agthia and Al Ghurair) emerging as likely candidates to buy these mills. Such linkages have been increasingly evident in recent years, such as the February 2016 announcement that Agthia had entered into a joint venture with the Saudi Olayan Group to distribute Agthia's flour (milled in Abu Dhabi) to the Saudi kingdom (Sahoo 2016).

In summary, over the last decade, the internationalisation of Gulf agribusiness has involved not just the acquisition of overseas land but also the transformation of the wider agro-commodity circuits connecting the global production of food with its consumption in the Gulf. A few key agribusiness conglomerates – centred principally upon Saudi Arabia and the UAE – have emerged as vertically integrated firms involved across all moments of agro-value circulation: primary production, the provision of farming inputs, transport, storage, trade, and the distribution of core food staples through domestic markets. Closely associated with this process is the growing significance of the logistics and infrastructure sectors to GCC agribusiness operations – including road transport, shipping, ports, warehousing, and silo facilities – such that the ownership of agribusiness firms is increasingly bound up with the institutional assemblages of circulation. Internationalisation is thus not something that has occurred 'outside' or external to the national scale; rather, it is intimately connected to a transfiguration of domestic forms of accumulation – marked principally by the increased weight of large capital groups in ensuring the provision of food in the Gulf. These class relations that have emerged around food at the pan-GCC scale thus constitute, in spatial terms, a particular instantiation of global food dynamics.

[24] In Chapter 7 I will situate this proposed privatisation in the context of Vision 2030, a new economic strategy adopted by the Saudi government in 2016.

4.2 Reshaping Middle East Food Systems

These changes to food systems in the Gulf are having a significant effect on agriculture in the wider Middle East. Most fundamentally, the internationalisation of Gulf agribusiness through global agro-commodity circuits – and the associated framing of GCC 'food security' around guaranteed, low-cost supplies of basic food staples – is acting to re-pivot the circulation of food in the Middle East around accumulation patterns in the Gulf. While this process does not fully encompass all Arab countries – notably Morocco and Tunisia, which continue to be more tightly linked to European markets – the realignment of Gulf food systems is shifting regional patterns of agricultural trade, the types of agro-commodities produced, and structures of ownership and control within the sector. This is a food system increasingly articulated at the regional scale – one that revolves around the Gulf as a central attractor, and through which forms of agricultural development in other Arab countries are mediated.

One indication of this reorientation is the changing character of food export markets for major Arab agricultural producers. Over recent years, food exports from non-GCC Arab countries have been topped by Egypt (with $4.66 billion of food exports in 2014) and Morocco ($3.9 billion), followed at a further distance by Jordan ($1.8 billion), Syria ($1.4 billion), Tunisia ($1.3 billion), Sudan ($0.99 billion), Lebanon ($0.82 billion), and Yemen ($0.48 billion) (AOAD 2015).[25] Table 4.1 displays the Gulf's share of total annual food exports (2007–2015) from selected countries in this list (satisfactory longitudinal data are unfortunately not available for all countries). The results are striking. Over the last decade, there has been a pronounced shift in the exports of these producers towards markets in the Gulf – partially reversing historical patterns that saw exports typically go to neighbouring non-GCC Arab states, European markets, or further afield. Between 2007 and 2015, the GCC's share of country exports has more than doubled for Egypt, Jordan, and Yemen. This proportion has also risen in the case of Morocco and Tunisia (doubling in the case of the latter) – albeit from a very small base. Jordan and Yemen now export more than two-thirds of their total food exports to the Gulf, while the levels for Egypt and Lebanon reach around one-third of total exports.

[25] The other non-GCC Arab countries included in the AOAD statistics (with much smaller levels of food exports) are Mauritania, Iraq, Somalia, Djibouti, Palestine, Libya, and Algeria. The main exports from these countries include fruits and vegetables (Morocco, Egypt, Jordan, Syria, and Tunisia), dates (Tunisia), live animals (Jordan and Sudan), dairy products (Egypt and Morocco), fish (Morocco, Yemen, and Tunisia), oils (Tunisia and Egypt), and other processed products.

Table 4.1 *Share of country food exports destined for GCC (%)*

Period	Egypt	Jordan	Yemen	Lebanon	Morocco	Tunisia
2007	12.2	31.1	35.4	37.2	1.6	1.0
2007–2009	19.7	29.8	41.8	37.2	1.4	1.1
2010–2012	24.0	36.4	47.3	36.4	1.1	1.4
2013–2015	26.5	57.4	67.2	35.8	1.3	2.2
2015	31.2	67.5	78.8	37.2 (2014)	1.7	2.3

Source: UN Comtrade database using SITC code 0 (food and animal exports).

Table 4.2 examines Egypt, Jordan, Yemen, and Lebanon in closer detail, illustrating the GCC's market share for the top three agro-commodity exports of each of these four countries. In each case, the commodities listed represent the country's most important agro-exports – ranging from around 43% of all agro-exports in Lebanon to 63%–65% in Egypt, Jordan, and Yemen. In all four countries, there has been an extremely noticeable tilt towards Gulf markets; for the latest year in which data are available, 11 of 12 of the commodities listed in the table saw the GCC holding more than one-third of the total market share. For Jordan and Yemen, the Gulf is approaching 100% of market share for selected commodities. While part of this shift is attributable to the closing-down of markets following the onset of the Syrian crisis in 2011 (particularly for the case of Jordan), the overall volume of production for these agro-commodities has risen very significantly over the same period, indicating that the Gulf is driving greater demand for the core agricultural products of these four countries. In short, in these states, the types and volumes of agro-commodities grown, processed, and exported are increasingly bound up with consumption and demand in the Gulf.

A clear majority of these Arab food exports to the Gulf are destined for either Saudi Arabia (an average share of 54% of total Arab food exports from 2010 to 2014) or the UAE (19%).[26] This trend has held relatively constant over the last decade, despite fluctuation among individual Arab states.[27] The primary position of Saudi Arabia and the UAE as key markets for Arab food exports is not surprising given the large market size

[26] Followed by Kuwait with 12% of exports, Qatar 7%, Oman 5%, and Bahrain 3%. Figures calculated by the author from Comtrade data, average share from 2010 to 2014 (2015 data not used as they are not available for Lebanon).

[27] The only outlier to this is Yemen, which has shifted much more towards exporting to Oman following the onset of the Saudi-led bombing campaign in 2014. In 2015, 36% of Yemeni exports to the GCC went to Oman, reversing historical trends that had seen around 90% of Yemeni exports going to Saudi Arabia and the UAE.

Table 4.2 *GCC market share of top three agro-commodity exports for selected countries (%)*

	Agro-commodity	Share of commodity in total food and beverages exports	GCC share of export market (annual average for period indicated)		GCC share (most recent year)
			2005–2009	**2010–2014**	**2015**
Egypt	Edible vegetables	27.1	19.1	24	35.0
	Edible fruit	26.8	20.8	27.7	36.0
	Dairy products	8.9	33.2	38	43.6
			2006–2010	**2011–2015**	**2015**
Jordan	Edible vegetables	35.9	39.3	59	80.5
	Live animals	13.9	82	96.6	98.4
	Edible fruit	13.3	38.2	48.1	84.9
			2005–2009	**2010–2014**	**2014**
Lebanon	Preparations of vegetables, fruit, and nuts	17.9	26	34.1	36.2
	Beverages, spirits, and vinegar	14.3	19.2	22.2	31.4
	Edible vegetables	11.1	65	70.2	63.4
			2005–2009	**2010–2014**	**2014**
Yemen	Fish and crustaceans	42.7	34.1	50.6	72.9
	Edible fruit	11.9	81.9	90.1	98.9
	Dairy products	10.2	52.9	57.7	64.9

Source: UN Comtrade Database.

of these two countries and the regional dominance of their agribusiness firms; however, it is important to remember that many of the primary food products imported by Saudi Arabia or the UAE may well undergo further processing and then be sold in other Gulf states (or be directly re-exported without value-adding activities). Constituting in this manner an entrepot to the wider GCC, the regional supply chains constructed by UAE and

Saudi firms intercede between the moment of food production in the Arab world and final consumption of food in the Gulf.

I now turn briefly to the other direction of this trade – the food imports of non-GCC Arab countries. These tend to reflect global patterns, particularly for core staples, with a few world producers dominating sales to the region – the United States, Russia, and Ukraine for wheat and cereals; Brazil and Australia for meat; European countries for dairy products. Nonetheless, there has been a significant increase in the proportion of certain food commodities that are either directly imported from the Gulf or are routed to the wider region through GCC re-export zones. According to figures from the UN Comtrade database, more than half of Egypt's imports of vegetable and fruit preparations, for example, were coming from the Gulf in 2015 – a figure that had risen from almost zero in 2000. One-third of Jordan's edible oil imports came from the GCC, an increase from around 2% in 2000. For processed cereal and flour products such as pasta and baked goods, the Gulf is one of the principal suppliers to the region – with a market share of 13% of Egyptian imports (up from 3% in 2000), 18% in Lebanon (up from 2.6% in 2000), 32% in Jordan (up from 14% in 2000), and 53% in Iraq. As a consequence of these trends, the GCC is now a major source of food commodities for several Arab countries. In 2014, for example, the GCC as a whole ranked within the top six exporters of food to Jordan, Iraq, Yemen, and Lebanon; two decades previous, only Yemen was reliant upon imports of food from the Gulf to any significant degree.

These shifting export and import patterns of non-GCC Arab states provide an important indication of how the Gulf's agro-commodity circuits are reorienting food systems in the wider Middle East. Aggregate trends of trade, however, do not capture the full reality of the internationalisation tendencies discussed earlier. They do not reveal, for example, *which* firms are actually producing for Gulf export markets, nor, indeed, how control over the circulation of food commodities within domestic Arab markets is shaped by the growing dominance of Gulf agribusiness firms. Even figures for the import of food staples are to a certain degree misleading, as they ignore the transnational ownership structures noted earlier that may see Gulf firms control the production and distribution of food from third countries – if Al Dahra, for example, directly exported flour to Egypt from its mill in Greece (with wheat sourced from its fields in Serbia), this would not register as a UAE export despite being controlled by a UAE firm. In order to get a fuller picture of these trends, we must turn to a closer examination of how Gulf firms are directly inserting themselves into Arab agro-commodity circuits – whether through purchase or leasing of land, investment flows into other Arab agro-companies, or the cross-border establishment of subsidiaries.

Agribusiness and Gulf Internationalisation: The Egyptian Case

Paralleling all other sectors discussed in this book, the internationalisation of Gulf capital into Arab agricultural and food production has been predicated on the wider neoliberal turn across the region. From the 1980s onwards, agricultural systems in most Middle East states began to undergo a profound transformation, linked closely to the global reorganisation of food production (Bush 2002, 2016; Ayeb 2012; Breisinger et al. 2012; Hanieh 2013). Framed by a range of structural adjustment packages sponsored by international financial institutions, Arab governments began to implement measures such as the privatisation of land and agro-industries and their opening-up to foreign ownership; removal of state control over agricultural prices and the supply of seeds, fertilisers, and other agricultural inputs; and the roll-back of subsidies for basic food items (Hanieh 2013, pp. 78–84). Although the pace of implementation of these policies varied considerably across different Arab countries – and was met with high levels of social unrest – their net result was to increase the polarisation of Arab agricultural systems. Throughout the region, export-oriented agricultural sectors dominated by large corporate firms came to co-exist alongside small-scale subsistence farming and endemic levels of rural poverty (Bush 2016).

As with so much in the Middle East, Egypt was the archetypal example of these changes. The agricultural sector was the initial focal point of Egypt's neoliberal project beginning with Sadat's *infitah* and continuing through the Mubarak era. Both these leaders moved to liberalise agricultural prices by allowing prices for essential inputs to rise to those of international markets, abolishing the state purchase of crop, and permitting private companies to operate in the provision of agricultural services, supplies, and distribution.[28] Mubarak's Law 96 of 1992 revoked Nasser's Agrarian Reform Law and gave landlords the right to evict tenants from the land. As Ray Bush has meticulously documented, these legislative changes precipitated a structural transformation of rural social relations. Liberalisation saw rents increase 300%–400%, and land could be sold

[28] The government eliminated, for example, the compulsory purchase of all crops in 1987 except rice, cotton, and sugar cane. For wheat and corn crops, farmers were offered voluntary purchase at government-set floor prices. Rice marketing was liberalised in 1991 and subsidies for fertilisers were eliminated over 1991–1993. Likewise, other agricultural services such as land preparation and artificial insemination were charged at full cost to farmers. Similar policies were pursued in the rest of North Africa.

without the consultation of tenants (Bush 2004). With more than one-third of Egypt's agricultural area made up of rental lands, more than 1 million people lost their rights to farming – a figure that represented one-third of all Egyptian rural families (USAID 2010, p. 6). Alongside this degradation of rural life, agricultural development strategies emphasised the export of agricultural products.

Such policies were a necessary precondition to the internationalisation of Gulf capital into Egyptian agribusiness; in turn, flows of Gulf capital acted to deepen liberalisation itself, by progressively embedding a market-oriented logic throughout the provisioning of food and strengthening the position of agribusiness interests within decision-making circles of the state. This intertwined process was ultimately bound up with all of the changes to Gulf food systems outlined earlier; Egypt became *the* major platform for Gulf agribusiness firms in the Arab world – with control over the corporate production of food in Egypt oriented both to the provisioning of Gulf supply chains (discursively justified through the 'food security' paradigm) and to providing a lucrative source of capital accumulation through sales in the Egyptian domestic market itself (the largest of all non-GCC Arab countries).

Table 4.3 reveals the extraordinary extent of the Gulf's involvement in the production and circulation of Egyptian agro-commodities. The 27 companies shown in the table hold the dominant market share across all major sectors of corporate-produced food[29] – including dairy and juice, poultry production, edible oils, vegetables and fruit, sugar, grains, and flour. There are a variety of different company and ownership structures evident across the firms listed in the table. In some cases, such as the Egyptian Starch and Glucose Company, GCC-based firms bought into state-owned agricultural companies that had been privatised through stock market IPOs. Food and agriculture-related companies were an early and major focus of such privatisation efforts in Egypt; indeed, between 1994 and 2001, slightly less than 30% of all IPOs of state-owned assets consisted of companies from this sector.[30] By the end of 2016, of the 31 food and agricultural companies listed on the Egyptian Stock Exchange, close to half (14) were either controlled or had

[29] It should be noted that a very considerable proportion of food consumed in Egypt (particularly by the poor) lies outside such corporate food chains (e.g. family-produced poultry, dairy, fruits, and vegetables). Nonetheless, there is an ongoing orientation in Egyptian food policy (both before and after Mubarak) to promote corporate food at the expense of these unregulated sectors. Much of this is tied up with claims around health, cleanliness, and 'modernisation' (see Henderson 2017 for a discussion of these issues).

[30] Calculated by the author using data drawn from Abdel-Shahid (2002, table 5).

Table 4.3 *GCC involvement in Egyptian agribusiness*

Food sector	Company or brand	Ownership
Dairy and juice	Dina Farms (67% of fresh pasteurised milk), largest supplier of raw milk	Owned by Qalaa Holdings (formerly known as Citadel Capital), in which two Gulf groups own major stakes: the Emirates International Investment Company (UAE) and the Olayan Group (Saudi Arabia). A member of the Qatari ruling family has previously served on the board.
	Beyti (20% market share of juices, 19% dairy, and 10% yoghurts)	Almarai (52%)
	Arab Dairy Products Company	Pioneers Holding Company, which in turn is 13% owned by Saudi group Al Muhaidib
	EDAFCO	Kuwaiti-owned Danah Al Safat 100%
	Juhayna (23% of juice market, largest packaged milk producer, 63% market share of plain milk)	Controlled by Pharon Investment Group, in which Saudi businessmen hold a sizable minority share. In March 2017, an investment vehicle controlled by the Saudi Al Rashed Group (see Chapter 3) purchased 6.3% of the company.
Sweets and confectionary	Rashidi El-Mizan (68% of tahini market, 58% of halwa, 15% of jam)	Olayan
Poultry (three companies listed control 50% of commercial poultry market)	Cairo Poultry Company	Americana Group
	Wataniya Poultry	Rajhi
	Misr Arab Poultry	Dallah Al Baraka Group
Cheese	Greenland (24% of cheese market)	Americana Group
	Domty (40% of cheese market)	Largest individual shareholder is member of Saudi Bin Laden family
Starch and glucose	Egyptian Company for Starch and Glucose (25% of starch, 45% of glucose markets)	Americana Group

Table 4.3 (*cont.*)

Food sector	Company or brand	Ownership
Pasta	Al-Malika and Al-Farasha (largest pasta brands with 60% of market share)	Savola Group
Edible oils	Afia International, controls 42% of the market	Savola Group
	Rawabi (largest vegetable ghee product with 25% market share)	Savola Group
	Ajwa for Food Industries (second-largest edible oil producer) also major producer of frozen vegetables	Saudi-owned Jaber Group
Fruits and vegetables	Al Dahra Egypt (major producer of citrus fruits)	Al Dahra
	Farm Frites, largest frozen vegetable producer, holds 90% of the frozen potato market and 22% of the frozen vegetable market; also a major vegetable exporter.	Americana
	Ismailia National Food Industries (fruit and vegetable farms, frozen vegetables)	Largest share ownership held by Saudi-controlled bank
	Egyptian Canning Company (major producer and exporter of top-grade olives)	Americana
Sugar	United Sugar Company and Alexandria Sugar Company (together hold around 50% of all Egyptian beet sugar refining capacity)	Savola
Processed meats	Halwani Brothers (34% of processed meat market in 2015)	Saudi-owned
Grains and flour	Al Dahra Egypt (20,000 hectares of land in Egypt, planning to produce up to 300,000 tons of wheat)	Al Dahra
	Al Rajhi Group (20,000 hectares for wheat and rice)	Al Rajhi Group
	Rakhah for Agricultural Investment and Development (owns 10,000 hectares for grain and fodder production)	Owned by Saudi agribusiness company Jannat Agricultural Investment (linked to Al Rajhi Group)

Table 4.3 (*cont.*)

Food sector	Company or brand	Ownership
	Upper Egypt Flour Mills (largest publicly listed flour mill)	The largest private investor is a Saudi businessman with 15.75% holding; a further 10% is owned by Arab Cotton Ginning, itself controlled by Amwal Al Khaleej (a Saudi private equity firm).

Source: Hanieh (2013, pp. 91–93); Egyptian Stock Exchange; news reports.

significant ownership stakes held by Gulf-based capital groups.[31] In addition to public ownership through the stock market, Table 4.3 also shows the presence of Gulf-related private equity firms in the food sector – of the 16 private equity acquisitions in the Egyptian agrifood sector between 2003 and 2009, 11 involved such PE companies (Dixon 2014, p. 238). Finally, some of the Gulf-based firms listed in Table 4.3 have entered Egypt through establishing subsidiaries or by making direct investments in land, factories, or storage silos.

Unsurprisingly, Saudi capital is predominant throughout the firms shown in the table. Many of these Saudi investors have been encountered earlier; they include, for example, the Savola Group, which dominates the production of sugar in Egypt (50% of all beet sugar refining), pasta (60% market share), and edible oil (42% market share). In 2014, just under a quarter (24.2%) of Savola's total revenue came from sales in the Egyptian market, second only to 35% in Saudi Arabia, as well as one-third of its sale volumes (Savola 2015, pp. 20–21). Indeed, Savola's chief executive noted at the Saudi-Egyptian Business Opportunities Forum in 2016 that Egypt is the 'the very first country Savola Group invests in outside KSA' and that it 'captures the lion's share of Savola's investments' (Amwal Alghad 2016). As noted earlier, Savola is also the largest shareholder of the Saudi dairy company Almarai, whose Egyptian affiliate, Beyti (a joint venture with Pepsi-Cola), holds the number-one position in the branded juice market (Beyti 2014) and 20% of market share across all juices, dairy, and yoghurts (MENAFN 2015). In 2015, Almarai was mooted as a possible buyer of the largest Egyptian confectioner,

[31] Calculated by the author from stock exchange data.

Rashidi El-Mizan, which claims 68% of Egypt's tahini market, 58% of halwa, and 15% of jam; in the end, Rashidi El-Mizan was sold to the Saudi Olayan Group (see Chapter 3) in December of that year. Olayan also owns the Burger King franchise in Egypt. Another major producer of sweets, jams, and meat products is the Saudi-based Halwani Brothers, which holds around one-third of the market for processed meats in Egypt, and earned around 50% of all its total sales from its Egyptian operations in 2015 (Saeed 2016). Saudi investors are also the major shareholders of the largest publicly listed flour mill in Egypt, and Saudi conglomerates such as Al Rajhi and the Kingdom Group own or lease tens of thousands of hectares of Egyptian land for the production of wheat, fruits, and vegetables.[32]

UAE firms have been less active in the direct operation of Egyptian agribusiness firms, but a number of the Emirati conglomerates discussed earlier are major owners of farmland, grain silos, and sugar refineries. Al Dahra, for examples, owns or manages around 8,000 hectares of farms spread over four agricultural projects, which focus on the production of citrus fruits. In addition, Al Dahra holds another 40,000 hectares in Egypt's Toshka project – a controversial land reclamation scheme that was begun under Mubarak and recently revived by General Abdul Fattah Sisi following the military coup in 2013 (see Chapter 8). According to Al Dahra Agriculture's CEO, the company's land bank in Egypt constituted more than 80% of all the land it owned or leased around the world in 2013 (Mahmood 2013, pp. 3–6). Another major Emirati agribusiness conglomerate, the erstwhile Al Ghurair Group, also has significant investments in Egypt, including a network of grain silos (Scott 2015). Reflecting the close relationship between the UAE's food security paradigm and the internationalisation of UAE capital, Ghurair's grain stores are not only marketed within Egypt; an explicit provision of the company's Egyptian investments allows this grain to be drawn upon in the event of shortages in the UAE. Indeed, in 2015, the firm announced it was building an additional silo in Egypt 'as part of the [UAE's] food security strategy . . . the target is to have one and a half year's food supply reserve for the UAE' (Sathish 2015). Al Ghurair also runs a sugar firm, and in 2014, the company won approval from the Egyptian government for the allocation of 60,000 hectares to build a new sugar refinery in the Minya governorate in Upper Egypt; the new refinery will have capacity to

[32] These land sales have been the subject of considerable controversy in the country, with critics accusing the Mubarak regime of selling large tracts of land to Gulf investors at below-market prices.

produce around one-fifth of Egypt's current sugar production and will be aimed at export markets (Stetzel 2015).

Through such internationalisation processes, the accumulation of companies like Savola, Almarai, Al Dahra, and Ghurair have come to depend crucially on the agro-commodity circuits that straddle both the Egyptian and Gulf markets. For this reason, the strikingly high proportion of Egyptian food exports that flow to both Saudi Arabia and the UAE (about 70% of all Egyptian food exports to the Gulf in 2014) is, to a significant degree, actually reflective of value appropriation by firms from these two states that produce in Egypt, and then export their goods to the GCC. The internationalisation of Gulf capital, in other words, complicates any conclusions we may draw from standard trade statistics about the geography of value appropriation – such nationally based statistics give an illusory picture of which firms actually benefit from growing Egyptian exports to the Gulf.

In much the same fashion, Kuwait's considerable levels of food imports from Egypt – constituting, in 2014, nearly half of all the country's food imports from non-GCC Arab states – is partially reflective of profits made by *Kuwaiti* firms through their Egyptian operations. The most important illustration of this is the Kuwaiti conglomerate Americana, which was owned by the Al Kharafi Group for many decades until its sale to a UAE-based private equity firm in 2016.[33] Egypt is a major base for Americana, and the company owns a variety of subsidiaries and affiliates that are market leaders in a wide range of food products. The firm's Cairo Poultry Company (CPC), for example, is a vertically integrated firm that produces animal feed (9%–11% of Egyptian market share), poultry (around 22% of market share, the largest in Egypt), and a distribution network that supplies direct to retailers as well as the restaurant franchises operated by Americana in Egypt. CPC is the largest single user of grain in Egypt (EFG Hermes 2016, p. 10), and contributed more than one-quarter of the value of Americana's global food processing sales in 2014 (Americana 2014, p. 33). In addition to its poultry business, Americana owns the Egyptian Starch and Glucose Company (ESGC), the largest producer of starch, glucose, and corn oil in Egypt, whose products are exported around the Middle East from its factories in Egypt. Americana also controls Egypt's largest frozen vegetable producer (Farm Frites Egypt) and the Egyptian Canning Company (ECC), a major producer and exporter of top-grade olives. Illustrating

[33] Americana was bought by Adeptio, a private equity joint venture set up by a Saudi Arabian sovereign wealth fund, the Public Investment Fund (PIF), and the Dubai businessman Mohamed Alabbar (see Chapter 3). The nature of this joint venture provides further confirmation of the pan-GCC linkages that private equity firms appear to be encouraging in the region (see Chapter 3).

the vertically integrated structure of Americana, the raw produce for Farm Frites and ECC is grown on 2,800 hectares of reclaimed land in Egypt, processed in its Egyptian factories, and then either consumed in the firm's Egyptian restaurant chains or exported across the Middle East. Indeed, in 2012, Americana claimed that its Egyptian-produced frozen potatoes captured 90% of the Egyptian market, 35% in Kuwait and the UAE, 62% in Jordan, 14% of the Saudi market, and more than 40% of the Bahraini and Qatari markets (Americana 2012, p. 42). In this manner, the labour of farmers in Egypt is inextricably tied to the consumption of households across the Middle East; although such spatial linkages may be imperceptible to either side of this relationship, they fully rest upon Americana's deep reach across the regional scale.

Moreover, Americana provides a good illustration of how political relations with Egypt's elite helped consolidate the entry of Gulf capital into the country's agribusiness chains (Roll 2013; Dixon 2014; Henderson 2017). The firm's CEO in Egypt, Moataz Al-Alfi, was considered 'a close associate of the Mubarak family' and a prominent member of the ruling National Democratic Party under Mubarak (Abdelmonem 2011, p. 3). Al-Alfi was also vice president of the Future Generation Foundation (FGF), an organisation established in 1998 by Hosni Mubarak's son, Gamal Mubarak, which aimed at promoting Gamal's image as a leader for the next generation and ran high-profile campaigns making the case for economic reforms in order to bolster the country's 'bold strategy for achieving sustainable economic growth through global competition' (McGann 2008, p. 5).[34] As Egyptian state-owned food companies were privatised through the 2000s, such close linkages to the Mubarak family appeared to pay off for Americana; in the state's divestment of ESCG to Americana in 2004, for instance, the firm reportedly paid only EG£126 million, despite the fact ESCG's assets were valued at more than EG£400 million – a fact revealed only after the ousting of Mubarak in 2011 (Issawi 2011).

Americana's activities within the Egyptian agro-circuit also encompass the sale and retail of food commodities. Much of the food produced by the firm – particularly poultry and vegetables – is consumed by the large network of restaurants and fast-food franchises it operates such as KFC, Pizza Hut, Baskin Robbins, TGI Friday's, Costa Coffee, and Hardees. Indeed, as Christian Henderson (2017) has documented in some detail,

[34] FGF's donors included the Saudi businessman Al Waleed Bin Talal, owner of the Kingdom Group, who donated at least EG£12 million to support its programs. The organisation has been described as a 'lobbying tool of Egyptian businessmen' with a board composed of prominent business people, many of who later held cabinet posts under Mubarak (e.g. Ahmed Ezz, Ahmed El-Maghrabi, and Rashid Mohamed Rashid) (Denis 2012, p. 295).

Gulf-based capital is the dominant force across the modern food retail sector in Egypt, with the majority of the large hypermarket and supermarket chains controlled by the same UAE and Saudi firms discussed in Chapter 3: the Carrefour hypermarket franchise (operated by the UAE's Majd al Futtaim Group), the UAE-owned LuLu Hypermarkets, and Savola's hypermarket chain, Panda, which opened in Egypt in 2015 and has plans to construct 16 more outlets across the country. These stores sell everyday food items as well as other consumer goods, and are particularly significant in that they reflect the intersection between the realisation of value in the agro-commodity circuit and the ownership and operation of real estate.

The examples listed in Table 4.3 should not be taken to imply that other international capital is absent from Egyptian agribusiness. Numerous Western firms – Danone, Kellogg's, Nestlé, Bunge – have significant interests in the sector and, in some cases, have successfully vied with Gulf capital over important acquisitions in the country.[35] Likewise, domestic Egyptian capital itself is also active, particularly in the production of fruits and vegetables and the ownership of private mills. Many of the firms listed in Table 4.3 are joint ventures between Gulf and Egyptian capital, including investment funds controlled by the Egyptian government. Moreover, the important function of the Egyptian military in this sector should also be acknowledged – both as an agro-food producer in its own right and as a joint partner to foreign investments (Marshall and Stacher 2012; Henderson 2017).[36] Industrial action is forbidden across the military's vast business interests, which pay no taxes and benefit from free labour provided by soldiers during their military service (Abul-Magd 2011).

The key point, however, is not to fetishise any competitive antagonisms that may exist between the Gulf and these other capital groups as inherently *national* in character. Competition is always integral to capitalism's functioning, but what is most significant here are the ways in which the internationalisation of Gulf capital expresses a changing spatialisation of accumulation in the sector. The incorporation of Gulf capital into these ownership structures has acted to tie Egyptian capital accumulation in agribusiness more closely to the forms and patterns of accumulation in the Gulf. The internationalisation of Gulf capital is *rescaling* Egyptian agribusiness, more firmly embedding it within the accumulation dynamics of a regional order centred upon the Gulf, and

[35] In 2015, for example, Kellogg's outbid the UAE private equity firm Abraaj to acquire Bisco Misr, one of the leading snack makers in the country. In the same year, Kellogg's also bought Mass Food Group, a leading producer of breakfast cereals in Egypt.

[36] Marshall and Stacher (2012) again use the Kharafi Group as an example of this relationship.

thereby changing the ways agribusiness firms operate (through, for example, encouraging vertical integration and export-oriented production). This reorientation is altering the character of Egyptian capital and its forms of accumulation in this sector, not erasing its presence or subordinating a supposed national bourgeoisie vis-à-vis a foreign one. Gulf firms need to be seen as an integral component *within* – not an opponent *of* – Egyptian class formation.

4.3 Conclusion

While Egypt has been the primary focus of Gulf internationalisation, several other countries in the Arab world have also been drawn more closely into Gulf agribusiness circuits over recent years. In Jordan, for example, the leading companies involved in dairy farming,[37] fruit and vegetable production,[38] processed meat,[39] edible oils,[40] and mineral water[41] are all GCC owned. Similarly, in Lebanon, Gulf-based firms hold controlling or major stakes in the largest dairy producer,[42] one of the top ice cream and juice companies,[43] a grain mill/silo compound with the highest storage capacity of any mill in the country,[44] the biggest nut retailer in the Middle East,[45] soft drink manufacturers,[46] and two of the leading supermarket chains.[47] Food manufacturing in Iraq is also increasingly connected to the Gulf.[48] While the Maghreb countries have been less directly impacted by these internationalisation trends, there are signs that this is changing – with Morocco and Tunisia recently signing deals to

[37] Teeba, a joint venture between Almarai and Pepsi-Cola.

[38] The Rum Agricultural Company owned by the Saudi-based ASTRA group.

[39] Siniora Food Industries, a subsidiary of the Saudi-based Arab Palestinian Investment Company. Siniora claims a 65%–70% market share in Palestine, and 55% in Jordan (Beer 2016).

[40] Jordan Vegetable Oil Company, owned by the Saudi-based ASTRA group, which claims half the vegetable ghee market (Ghawi 2015).

[41] Ghadeer, the largest producer of mineral water, is a joint venture between a Saudi firm and Nestlé.

[42] Taanayel Les Fermes, which is a subsidiary of Kuwaiti-conglomerate Danah Al-Safat, and held around half the licensed dairy market in 2014 (Cochrane 2014).

[43] Bonjus, also owned by Danah Al-Safat.

[44] Al Ghurair's National Flour Mills. Storage capacity data for each of Lebanon's six mills can be found at http://dlca.logcluster.org/display/public/DLCA/LCA+Homepage.

[45] Al Rifai, in which the Qatar First Investment Bank acquired a 35% stake in 2012.

[46] National Beverage Company (manufacturer and distributor of Coca-Cola products in Lebanon), which was bought by the Saudi-based Aujan Coca-Cola Beverages Company in 2014.

[47] Carrefour, a franchise owned by the UAE's Majd Al Futtaim Group, and Spinneys, owned by the UAE's Abraaj Capital.

[48] In June 2014, for example, the Saudi firm Al Safi established a joint venture in Iraq with Danone, which is now one of the country's largest dairy manufacturers.

encourage Gulf firms to enter key agricultural sectors.[49] The implications of these trends are critical to keep in mind given the violent crises currently wracking the region – a point to which I will return in Chapter 8.

These distinctive shifts in the patterning of production and circulation of agro-commodities have ultimately been driven by changes to food systems in the Gulf itself. Most essential to this is the implacable rise of large agribusiness conglomerates, particularly those based in Saudi Arabia and the UAE, to the centre of Gulf food provisioning. These conglomerates typically exist as lucrative arms of wider Gulf capital groups or are closely linked to the private interests of ruling elites. Having emerged during earlier phases of agriculture and food production, they are now pivotal to the ways that food circulates within the Gulf. From overseas farmland, factories, and silos to the growing and processing of food in the GCC itself, the complex agro-commodity circuits constituted and superintended by these conglomerates bind together a variety of spatial scales, subordinating all moments of food circulation to the accumulation imperatives of Gulf capital.

Gulf agribusiness firms, in other words, more and more shape the spatiality of agro-commodity circuits across the Middle East as a whole – articulating different moments of production, circulation, and distribution as they extend across the national, regional, and pan-GCC scales. As such, this chapter has confirmed the complex, mutual co-constitution of spatial scales that have been produced by – and thereby form – the global food system. We need to avoid juxtaposing or reifying any of these scales as bounded 'levels' that operate on one another in a closed and external fashion. Instead, this chapter has stressed the ways in which the class relations that have emerged around the Gulf agro-commodity circuit contain, as an integral part of what they are, particular internal relations with all these other scales.

This shifting spatiality of food in the Middle East has had a critical discursive element, embodied most clearly in the notion of food security. By explicitly tying a stable and guaranteed supply of food to the internationalisation of Gulf capital – including, very significantly, the construction of logistics networks necessary to store and transport food across global supply chains – Gulf food security policies have acted to bolster the position of its own agribusiness firms through international, regional, and domestic markets. The degree to which these conglomerates control

[49] In 2016, for example, Tunisian President Beji Caid Essebsi visited Qatar to sign a deal for a $2 billion fund that would invest in Tunisia's food sector. Strongly echoing the themes of this chapter, a Tunisian delegate noted during the visit that 'Tunisia offers opportunities for Qatar in agriculture, olive oil, dates, sugar, meat, other oils, milk, animal feeds, ... the recent liberalisation in the country has created immense opportunities for investors and businessmen' (Kumar 2016).

the import and circulation of staples within the Gulf means that they have become the primary vehicle for the region's food security strategy, and, in turn, the discursive effect of the 'food security' paradigm has been to strengthen their position within all moments of the agribusiness circuit. In this manner, food security policies form an organic part of the latest phase of Gulf capitalism; the content of these policies – and their effects and implications – is entwined with the wider development of Gulf capital.

For non-GCC Arab states, understanding the nature of the regional food system is crucial to demystifying the technocratic, market-based approaches to food security that continue to dominate policymaking today.[50] The reality is that the Gulf remains by far the most food-secure zone of all Arab countries, and this is due in large part to policies that obfuscate the actual power dynamics surrounding food production and consumption in the wider Middle East.[51] A continued policy trajectory based upon the opening of land and agro-industry assets to private ownership and export-oriented production will only reinforce the place of Gulf agribusiness within regional food systems. Given the already highly polarised distribution of food (and hunger) in the Middle East, such an eventuality does not bode well for the future.

[50] See, for example, the 2011 *Arab World Initiative for Financing Food Security Project*, supported by the World Bank, in which it was claimed that 'an export-oriented agricultural development strategy centered on high value crop production is generally the most effective way to valorizing scarce arable land and water resources and ensuring food security' (World Bank 2011).

[51] Indeed, by 2016, the GCC states took all top six places in the FAO's ranking of regional food security, while other Arab states fell far behind. Of course, there are other highly significant reasons for such disparities; frequently, however, these too are also hidden by the obfuscation of the food security discourse. Perhaps most striking in this regard is the case of Yemen, the most food-insecure country in the region, which continues to reel from a devastating two-year bombing campaign led by neighbours championing the need to ensure food security for all Arab states. The Yemeni case is a salient reminder that narratives of food security narrowly couched in terms of market supply and demand serve to mask the often all-too-violent real-world causes of hunger (see Chapter 8).

5 The Arab Built Environment, Accumulation, and the Gulf

Over the last three decades, the Middle East has followed much of the rest of the world in moving towards market-based models of urban planning in which the interests of private-sector developers take priority (World Bank 2005; Daher 2011). A neoliberal (re)imagining of the urban has seized the visions of city planners and national governments, centred upon the private provisioning of housing, land, and infrastructure and the construction of spectacular mixed-use 'mega-projects' targeting wealthy residents and foreign tourists (Barthel and Vignal 2014). The resulting proliferation of heavily guarded gated communities, high-end malls, and new tower blocks has come to mark city landscapes in North Africa and the Levant – an urban form often compared to that found in Dubai and other Gulf cities (Hvidt 2009; Barthel 2010; Sims 2010; Parker and Debruyne 2011; Vignal 2014). Such regional emulation of the Gulf also extends to architectural and artistic styles – a pastiche of Islamic and modern, designed to repackage the 'traditional' as aesthetic prop for a newly envisioned corporate-led urban future.

Nonetheless, alongside these changes, huge zones of informal housing and marginalised neighbourhoods not only persist but continue to grow (Daher 2007; Elsheshtawy 2008b; Bayat and Biekart 2009). Poorer urban areas have also been deeply impacted by neoliberal intervention, with 'slum upgrading' projects seeking to marketise informal dwellings in peri-urban settings, thereby facilitating their eventual transfer to private developers (El-Batran and Arandel 1998; Sabry 2010; Sims 2010; Bogaert 2011). The resulting spatial inequalities of everyday urban life – 'cities of extremes', in the words of Bayat and Biekart (2009) – have seen significant social protest emerge around policies such as slum evictions and land rezoning, changes to rent-control laws, and the sale of land to foreign investors at below-market prices. At the same time, authoritarian governments have attempted to instrumentalise communities of the urban poor, 'turn[ing] segments of subaltern migrant populations into buffers for the regime' (Ismail 2013, p. 891). With an estimated 56% of the population in the Arab world living in cities and an expected doubling of urban residents by 2050 (IOM 2015, p. 3), all of these themes illustrate just how central the quotidian experience of the urban is to contemporary political and social life in the Arab world.

In this chapter, I explore how these transformations of the non-GCC Arab urban scale intersect with shifting patterns of capital accumulation across the regional scale. As Brenner and Schmid have recently noted, one of the problems with much of the urban studies literature is a tendency 'to equate the urban with [a] singular, bounded spatial unit ... coherently delineated relative to some postulated non-urban "outside"' (Brenner and Schmid 2015, p. 166). Instead, they argue, we need to pay much more attention to 'the multiple sociospatial configurations in which [urban] agglomerations are crystallizing under contemporary capitalism, as well as to the transnational, inter-scalar and often extra-territorial webs through which their developmental pathways are mediated' (p. 162). I hope to contribute such an analysis here, through exploring how forms of capitalism in the Gulf are internally related to the nature of urban spaces across the broader Middle East.

Drawing upon the analysis of Gulf capital and the built environment outlined in Chapter 3, I argue that the trajectories, tempo, and forms of development at the Arab urban scale are more and more interlaced with the dynamics of accumulation emanating from the GCC – or, put differently, the logics of the GCC scale are increasingly interiorised within the urban scale of the wider region. This entanglement is closely connected to the internationalisation of the Gulf's surplus capital into the built environment of other Arab states – a process of 'capital-switching', to borrow David Harvey's useful term, in which a solution to the obstacle of overaccumulation in one area is sought through geographical and sectoral diversification in another. In this manner, Arab urban change can be viewed as much more than just a contingent imitation of a Gulf 'model' or a hypermodern vision advanced by city planners; rather, it expresses a deeper shift in both the forms and spatiality of capital accumulation across the entire region. By bringing in the regional scale and positing patterns of Arab urban development as a 'form of appearance' of these regional alignments, we can thus avoid a kind of 'methodological cityism' that privileges the city as the sole scale of urban research (Brenner and Schmid 2015, p. 162).

In making this argument, I seek to deepen two key theoretical points made throughout this book. First, the process of pan-regional capital-switching through the Arab urban scale both requires – and simultaneously acts to drive – regulatory change aimed at loosening any barriers to investment in the built environment. The recent rolling-out of neoliberal urban policies across most of the Arab world is thus intimately wrapped up in – as both a magnet *for* and effect *of* – the internationalisation of Gulf capital. This is true for all the sectors analysed in this book, but it is *particularly* significant for the urban scale due to the inherent spatial fixity of the built environment. Second, echoing the observations of the previous chapter, I will show that these cross-scalar capital flows are altering the nature of class structures in the Arab world – more deeply interlacing Gulf capital with the accumulation of other Arab capitalist classes. There are a variety of mechanisms through which this occurs, but precisely because of the centrality of the built environment to capital accumulation, the urban scale emerges as a key spatial site for the intertwining of class structures across the region.

Empirically, this chapter largely focuses on Egypt, Jordan, Lebanon, Morocco, Tunisia, and Palestine, where urban development has taken centre-stage within wider processes of economic reform. Following a brief discussion of neoliberal urban policy across these countries, I begin by tracing the regional evolution of *large housing and commercial real estate projects* – clearly a major element in the production of urban space. The incorporation of GCC-based capital into this sector is examined in three respects. The first of these is the extent to which Gulf capital is an owner, developer, or major contractor in these projects. In all these roles, Gulf firms lay principal claim to rents involved in the production of the built environment. The second is the Gulf's incorporation into local ownership structures of major Arab real estate companies through, for example, minority investment stakes. These companies can be figured as core components of domestic 'national bourgeoisies' – but through these cross-border ownership ties they become just as much intercalated with the accumulation of Gulf-based capital. Finally, this section examines the interesting case of diaspora capital in the Arab world – displaced populations that have historically developed their base of accumulation outside their home country, and increasingly within the Gulf, while retaining historic ties to their national homelands. For this diaspora capital, the straddling of accumulation across the regional scale often takes place through activity in the built environment. Taken together, these three geographically varied forms of production of the built environment convey a strong sense of how the Gulf is implicated in the transformation of the Arab urban scale.

The second half of this chapter moves beyond the simple physical construction of buildings and real estate. In this respect, I turn to the *production of major infrastructural work*, specifically power, water, and transport utilities (PWT) and telecommunications networks. These elements of the built environment are no less essential to capital accumulation than housing and commercial real estate, even though they have received much less scholarly attention (outside the Gulf). Although PWT has generally not been subject to privatisation to the same degree as other parts of the built environment, it has become a major focus of intervention for international financial institutions over the last few years. Gulf capital plays an increasingly important role in driving this trend towards the private provisioning of essential urban infrastructure. For Arab telecommunications, GCC-based firms – the same ones mapped in Chapter 3 – are absolutely dominant in the ownership of major telecoms and mobile networks. These infrastructural questions lie at the frontier of how urban spaces may be changing in the wake of regional crises, mass displacement, and the reassertion of neoliberal development models post-2011. The analysis in this chapter thus forms an important precursor to discussions of potential future trajectories of the Middle East in Chapters 7 and 8.

5.1 Producing the Built Environment: Real Estate Development and the GCC

At a global level, it is widely acknowledged that the urban scale constitutes a critical node to the elaboration, experimentation, and contestation of neoliberal policymaking (Brenner and Theodore 2002; Peck et al. 2010, 2013; Aalbers 2013). With the generalised shift towards market-led development models through the 1990s and 2000s, private firms have been placed at the centre of how cities are built and the kinds of urban planning that governments prioritise. Urban governance policies aim principally at widening private sector involvement in the built environment, through measures such as the privatisation of land and public housing, the lifting of rent caps, the deepening of mortgage markets, private provision of infrastructure services, and the incorporation of private real estate developers and financial institutions into city and municipal decision making (Lizarralde 2014). It is at the urban level where the social effects of neoliberal policies are often most acutely felt – through, for example, the displacement of municipal services, housing provision, and public administration to market-based actors; rising land and rent prices; and the resultant exclusion and marginalisation of large swaths of the urban population. All of these trends mean that cities now comprise 'strategic targets and proving grounds for an increasingly broad range of neoliberal policy experiments, institutional innovations, and political projects ... incubators for, and generative nodes within, the reproduction of neoliberalism as a living institutional regime' (Theodore et al. 2011, p. 25).

Within this 'urbanization of neoliberalism' (Theodore et al. 2011, p. 24) global investment flows remain central to how city-level processes develop. Much of the needed capital investment in the built environment is of a very great magnitude and has a lengthy turnover time that can run into decades (particularly for large infrastructure projects) – costs that often lie beyond the ability of local governments and domestic investors. And unlike other movable commodities, buildings and infrastructure 'have to be built or assembled *in situ* on the land' (Harvey 1999, p. 233) – this spatial fixity means that urban development depends critically upon attracting perpetual inflows of international investment, with cycles of urban growth resembling 'speculative carousels [that] are sustained as long as the promises for securing future value entitlements are maintained' (Swyngedow 2010, p. 315). Given the persistent reality of overaccumulation and the presence of growing pools of surplus capital seeking above-average rates of return, international investors can switch into the built environment as a 'fix' for sluggish profit rates in other sectors (Harvey 1999).[1] A range of constantly shifting performative strategies seeks to encourage such flows, articulating and modelling cities as spaces of entrepreneurialism, networks, creativity, and innovation – with cities ranked and refashioned as 'sites of up-scale living, consumption, and hyper-competitiveness' (Anderson 2014, p. 13). The laying-down of new infrastructure and transport routes and the development of tourist 'spectacles', help to underpin such discursive projections, promising locational advantages and the hope of ever-increasing returns on investment. Moreover, precisely because these dynamics are international, the logic of spatial competitiveness innervates urban planning processes across all geographical spaces (Oosterlynck and González 2013).

In sum, the built environment cannot be exported; capital must come to it – in amounts of increasing size, enmeshed in cross-border flows, and mediated through neoliberal regulatory change. The Middle East has not been immune from such global trends. Through the 1990s and 2000s, a range of transformations in major cities across the region saw housing and land markets progressively liberalised and municipal planning authorities increasingly oriented towards private sector firms – both domestic and international – as the principal levers of urban growth. In earlier phases of

[1] Such switching processes, however, are always temporary, unstable, and cyclical. As real estate prices inflate and subsequently collapse, capital withdraws and new geographical areas are sought for investment – the switching process begins anew in continuing cycles of uneven development. While the precise dynamics of capital switching remains a point of contention in the literature, the global phenomenon of real estate bubbles over the past two decades confirms the fact that the massive amounts of capital have indeed sought profit-making opportunities in the built environment.

development, construction of housing and land ownership had been dominated by powerful state-owned agencies. The neoliberal turn deemed these organisations as inefficient and a drain on government expenditure, and thus sought to restructure them as policymaking bodies rather than direct providers of housing or land. In this manner, the functions of these housing agencies could be 're-aligned with the countries' objectives of promoting public-private partnership' as the World Bank was to put it, with the 'auctioning of public land and privatisation of housing production companies [as] high priorities' (World Bank 2005, p. viii). The pace of change varied considerably between countries, but all governments moved perceptibly towards embracing the commodification of land, housing, and urban infrastructure.

In Jordan, for example, a 2002 World Bank loan transitioned the country's public-sector housing agency, the Housing and Urban Development Corporation (HUDC), from a 'direct land and housing provider to a policy-making and development-facilitating body' (World Bank 2002, p. 2). The proportion of urban dwellings in Jordan owned, managed, or controlled by public authorities fell from around 12% in 1993 to almost zero a decade later (World Bank 2005, p. 61). In Tunisia, following a structural adjustment program that began in 1986, a housing policy strategy saw the private sector put forward as a core provider of housing. In 1989, the government owned National Housing and Savings Fund (*Caisse Nationale d'Epargne Logement* (CNEL)) was transformed into an autonomous corporation (the Housing Bank), which was eventually part-privatised (UN-HABITAT 2011, p. 13). Similar restructuring of state housing and land agencies took place in Morocco, Egypt, and the Palestinian Authority. By 2005, a comparative study of land ownership across seven Arab countries found that around 95% of housing construction was carried out by the private sector in Tunisia, Jordan, and Lebanon, and levels of public ownership of housing stock in Egypt and Morocco were less than those found across European states (World Bank 2005, p. 15). In Egypt, private financing of land development grew dramatically from US $2.6 million in 2005 to $526 million by 2009 (UN-Habitat 2010, p. 77).

Linked to this shift towards private provision of housing, Arab governments also moved to dismantle restrictive rental control laws that had been inherited from Ottoman times or instituted in earlier periods by Arab nationalist governments. These laws gave tenants considerable rights over occupancy, including fixed rent prices, and made it extremely difficult for property owners to pursue eviction procedures. The full commodification of property in city centres required the roll-back of these laws – without the ability to increase rents and evict tenants, property could not be easily sold on the market. In Lebanon, for example, a 2012 law reversed an earlier set of laws (Rent Acts nos. 159 and 160 of 1992) that had protected a significant number of Beirut residents from rent inflation and eviction. The new law would liberalise rents over a period of six years, and led one scholar to note the possibility of 'massive evictions towards the periphery ... [and] the rise of social and territorial inequality between gentrified central urban areas and peripheries coping with a substantial influx of pauperised families' (Marot 2012). Similarly in Jordan, a series of laws enacted from the 1980s onwards progressively undermined the rights of tenants by expanding the ability of landlords to evict them in the name of redevelopment, as well as raise rents – such measures drew explicitly on World Bank recommendations and led to 'a dramatic reorganization of property rights, especially in older neighborhoods' (Hourani 2014, p. 642). Reforms such as these have had a significant impact on historic centres of Arab capital cities – particularly Cairo, Amman, and Beirut – and have been met with considerable social protest.

These moves towards market-driven housing and real estate policy have shaped the dominant form of urban real estate development in the region: large-scale mega-projects, high-end residential and commercial tower blocks, gated communities, and massive shopping complexes, aimed at the wealthiest layers of society (and, relatedly, a skewing of infrastructural priorities towards these projects) (Barthel and Planel 2010). According to one Arab analyst, this new form of urban development led to 'urban geographies of inequality and exclusion and spatial and social displacement of second-class citizens ... in favour of first-class tourism developments and real-estate ventures' (Daher 2007, p. 275). Numerous such examples can be seen across the Arab world: the Abdali and Marsa Zayed Projects in Jordan, Solidere in Lebanon, Rawabi City in Palestine, Tunis Financial Harbor in Tunisia, Dream Farms, and the gated communities of Uptown Cairo, Marassi, Mivida, and Al-Burouj in Egypt (Makdisi 1997; Parker 2009; Debruyne 2013; Mango 2014). All of these and similar projects are characterised by a combination of private ownership (sometimes through public-private partnerships), an orientation towards upper- and middle-class consumption, and the central role of state authorities in establishing an enabling regulatory environment and providing subsidies for land and capital – including, in some cases, expropriating the property of small landowners for the benefit of large private developers (Mango 2014, p. 16). At the same time, this reorganisation of city space was guided by 'authoritarian vision[s] of urban renovation', which – as Konrad Bogaert has meticulously documented in the case of Casablanca – involved both an 'attempt to remodel [the] city centre according to global market requirements' while simultaneously turning 'the urban territory into a more calculable and governable space ... to improve control over urban residents and their movement ... increas[ing] the velocity of urban life ... and [reducing] people's capacity to stand still, wonder, think and – if necessary – mobilize' (Bogaert 2011, p. 718).

Significantly, however, this shift in the character of urban development emerged alongside the amassing of large levels of surplus capital in the states of the GCC. As I discussed in Chapter 3, construction and real estate development constitute a major source of accumulation for the dominant capitalist groups in the Gulf. Virtually all of the large Gulf conglomerates are involved in these activities to some degree, whether at the level of construction and contracting or through investment in project development. Concomitant with the liberalisation of land and housing markets in the rest of the Middle East, these firms have expanded their activities beyond local Gulf markets – seeking opportunities to invest in high-end real estate projects within neighbouring Arab countries. In this manner, patterns of urban development in the Middle East have come to reflect the global trends outlined earlier – as the urban scale emerged as a major locus of neoliberal restructuring across the region, the internationalisation of Gulf capital acted to propel and deepen these restructuring processes, internalising itself within the forms of urban development extant across the wider Middle East.

The extent to which Gulf capital has driven the transformation of Arab urban spaces is powerfully confirmed in Table 5.1, which presents data on 119 major real estate projects (housing, office blocks, and mixed-use

Table 5.1 *Large-scale real estate projects in selected countries, 2008–2017*

	No. of projects	Government-owned projects	GCC-related projects	Value of projects ($US mill)	Value of GCC-related projects (US mill)	GCC-related projects as % of total value
Algeria	4	3	1	8,377	5,900	70.1
Egypt	61	7	19	93,776	41,526	44.3
Jordan	14	4	10	16,645	15,008	90.1
Lebanon	29	0	9	12,428	6,608	53.2
Morocco	10	2	4	3,483.8	2,315.2	66.6
Tunisia	1	0	1	3,000	3,000	100
Total	119	16	44	137,709	74,357	54

Source: Calculated from Zawya Projects Database; projects from January 2008 to March 2017 valued at over US$100 million.

developments) across six non-GCC Arab countries. The figures in the table are drawn from a regional construction and projects database, and include those projects worth more than US$100 million that were either completed or ongoing between January 2008 and March 2017. The data reveal some very clear characteristics of the regional project market. First, Egypt and Lebanon are the principal leaders in large real estate construction outside the Gulf, with 90 of 119 projects located in one of these two countries – although Morocco and Jordan also rank highly. Second, the impact of neoliberal change on the built environment is evident – only 13.4% of contracts across these six countries (16 of 119) were for government-owned projects. The development of large-scale Arab urban real estate is, in other words, almost completely driven by the private sector.

Beyond these general characteristics, Table 5.1 also lists those projects in which a GCC-based firm is the owner, developer, or main contractor (denoted as GCC-related projects), i.e. a form of internationalisation whereby GCC-based conglomerates directly expand into the real estate sector of other Arab countries. The data show the remarkable impact of the Gulf on the Arab built environment – nearly 40% (46 of 199) of all large-scale real estate across the six countries is owned, developed, or built by a GCC-based company, and these projects represent more than half of the total value of the project market. Indeed, even in the case of the 16 government-owned projects, 5 were public-private partnerships between Arab governments and Gulf investors (both projects in Morocco, and 3 out of the 4 in Jordan).[2] The Gulf-related projects recorded in Table 5.1 include billion-dollar gated communities in Egypt, Jordan, Morocco, and Lebanon; shopping malls and hotels; and massive office towers across the region. Many of the same Gulf conglomerates encountered in Chapter 3 are involved in these projects, including Emaar, Qatari Diar, DAMAC Properties, Majd Al Futtaim, Fawaz Hokair, Olayan Group, Al Kharafi, and Arabtec. For all of these firms, the wider Middle East provides an important and profitable source of income beyond their domestic markets in the GCC.[3]

[2] In Morocco, these public-private partnerships (PPPs) involve the Saudi conglomerate Kingdom Group (owned by Waleed bin Talal) and Wessal Capital (a joint venture of Saudi, UAE, Qatari, and Kuwaiti capital along with the Moroccan government). In Jordan, the three PPPs noted involve Saraya Aqaba, a subsidiary of the UAE-based Saraya Holdings.

[3] The annual financial statements of these firms typically do not present an exact breakdown of income or profits from individual markets. Their financial reporting, however, does indicate a significant increase in general cross-border expansion, within which non-GCC Arab countries figure prominently. Emaar, for example, held 42.5% of its assets outside its home market in 2016, up from 26% in 2009. More than 6% of

A whole range of regulatory changes underpinned and encouraged this internationalisation of Gulf capital. Alongside the measures noted earlier, chief among these was the privatisation of state-owned land, which enabled the sale or leasing of large tracts to Gulf investors, frequently at very low prices that did not reflect market value.[4] Beyond the sale of land, Gulf residents have also been a major source of market demand for buildings, apartments, and villas in completed real estate projects. A striking example of this is the $136 million Green Valley Project in Morocco, which was announced in March 2016 by the UAE-based firm Green Valley Group Real Estate. Green Valley will contain 350 villas (each measuring between 231 and 297 square metres) as well as pools, health facilities, a sports complex, gardens, shopping centres, and restaurants. According to the company's chairperson, projects such as this are explicitly geared at 'satisfying the needs of UAE and GCC nationals in the Emirates and beyond' (Capital Business (CB) n.d.) and are part of the firm's 'strategy to offer GCC nationals the opportunity to invest in properties outside the Gulf region' (Arabian Business 2016) – to this end, Green Valley operates dozens of companies involved in contracting, construction, and real estate brokerage across the UAE, Qatar, Lebanon, Egypt, Morocco, Turkey, and Syria (CB n.d.). Indeed, visitors to Dubai in early 2017 could see large billboards lining the city's

DAMAC's revenue came from outside the UAE in 2016, compared with only 1% in 2014. The one firm for which more fine-grained figures are available is the Majd Al Futtaim Group – a UAE company noted in Chapter 3 as a leading retailer, mall operator, and agent for the Carrefour franchise. In 2016, more than 16% of Majd Al Futtaim's total revenue came from its operations in Egypt, Jordan, Lebanon, and Iraq, and in 2015, the Group held 12.5% of its total assets in non-GCC Arab countries – a figure that had risen from only 3.8% in 2011.

[4] In some cases, such land sales provided lucrative opportunities for corrupt state officials to make money as brokers of these deals – a fact that has come to light in court cases against Gulf firms in Egypt following the overthrow of Mubarak in 2011. In 2011, for example, Egyptian courts annulled a 2006 deal between DAMAC and the Egyptian government for the sale of 30 million square metres of land on which a resort complex was planned. It was alleged that the tourism minister at the time, Zuheir Garranah, had sold the land at very low prices without any process of public bidding. DAMAC was fined and ordered to return the land, and an Interpol arrest warrant was requested against the firm's chairman Hussain Al-Sajwani. In response, DAMAC took the Egyptian government to the International Centre for Settlement of Investment Disputes, arguing that the post-Mubarak government was conducting 'a political vendetta against investors who entered into land sale agreements with the State under the former government' and that the firm could not be held responsible for the actions of corrupt Mubarak-era ministers (Issac 2011). In 2013 the dispute was settled, with DAMAC agreeing to pay the price difference between the purchase price and its estimated value. Similar cases have been raised and settled against the Al Futtaim Group and a range of other Gulf investors (see Chapter 8). Such cases confirm the ways in which the expansion of Gulf capital across the regional scale has been intimately linked to the authoritarian character and corrupt practices of Arab leaders.

main highway advertising Green Valley villas for sale in Morocco.[5] Similarly, a Lebanese real estate agent interviewed for this book stated that the vast majority of demand in Beirut for new apartments – as well as the tourist footfall driving shopping mall expansion – came from the GCC, particularly the UAE and Saudi Arabia.[6]

The Built Environment and Arab Capital

The 'GCC-related' data shown in Table 5.1 only cover those firms fully controlled by Gulf investors that are operating in the countries listed. In addition to these companies, however, a more indirect route of internationalisation can be found: the holding of minority stakes by Gulf capital in what are typically thought of as non-GCC, Arab construction and real estate firms. This form of internationalisation is typically not considered in the literature but is essential to fully mapping and understanding the different actors involved in accumulation within the built environment. Most specifically, it illustrates the ways in which Gulf capital has become deeply incorporated within the class structures of other Arab countries through the route of construction and real estate activities.

f we take Egypt, for example, two of the largest real estate companies in the country – the Talaat Moustafa Group (TMG) and the Sixth of October Development and Investment Company (SODIC) – are well-known 'Egyptian' companies listed on the Egyptian stock market. By the end of the Mubarak era, these two firms were the largest private landholders in Cairo, and had benefitted enormously from the sell-off of state land, often at below-value prices (Deutsche Bank 2010, p. 17). In both cases, however, it was the incorporation of Gulf capital into the companies' ownership structures that marked the expansion of their real estate activities (Hanieh 2013, p. 142). Today, the largest shareholding in TMG is held through a joint venture ultimately controlled by the Egyptian Talaat Moustafa family and the Bin Laden family in Saudi Arabia (Blom 2013, p. 11). In the case of SODIC, the two largest shareholders (with more than 25% of the company's stock between them) are also from Saudi Arabia (the Olayan conglomerate and Suleiman Bin Abdullah Abanumay). In addition to TMG and SODIC, two other prominent Egyptian real estate firms are closely linked to Gulf-based capital: the Rooya Group (majority-owned by Pioneers Holding Company for Financial Investments, in which the Saudi Muadib family

[5] Author's observation, February 2017.
[6] Interview with sales agent at a Lebanese real estate firm, March 2016, Beirut.

holds the second largest share ownership) and the Golden Pyramids Plaza Company, which is 20% owned by the Saudi investor Abdulrahman Sharbatly. If these four companies – TMG, SODIC, Rooya, and Golden Pyramids – were to be included in the GCC-related category shown in Table 5.1, the proportion of Gulf-related projects in Egypt would rise to a staggering 70%.

These types of minority investments by Gulf capital in national real estate firms are a common feature encountered across other Arab states. Table 5.2 displays the number of real estate firms listed on the stock markets of Egypt, Jordan, Morocco, Palestine, and Tunisia and, for each of these markets, the number of these firms that have at least 20% of their shares held by GCC-based investors or at least two board members who are from the GCC. The table also shows the proportion of total market capitalisation in the real estate sector held by these GCC-linked firms. In this manner, the table reflects the degree to which GCC capital has become 'indirectly' enmeshed with accumulation in the built environment across these four Arab countries. We have here a different mode of internationalisation in the real estate sector: the interiorisation of Gulf capital within other Arab class structures.

The results are particularly evident in Egypt and Jordan, where more than one-fifth of all listed real estate firms are linked to the GCC, and which constitute 60% and 39%, respectively, of all market capitalisation in the sector (pointing again to the fact that it is the largest firms that are related in this manner to the GCC). In both these countries, four out of the largest seven listed real estate companies are closely associated to Gulf capital. These patterns are highly pertinent in that they disrupt the way that a 'national bourgeoisie' (*ra'as al mal al watani*) is usually thought of in the region. For the real estate sector – which, we must remember, has been a

Table 5.2 *Listed real estate firms*

	No. of listed real estate firms	No. connected to GCC capital	Proportion of firms connected to GCC (%)	Proportion of market capital held by GCC-linked firms (%)
Egypt	35	8	22.9	59.5
Jordan	40	8	20	39.40
Morocco	6	1	16.7	15.80
Palestine	10	0	0	0
Tunisia	4	1	25	27.80

Source: Country stock exchanges.

central moment of accumulation for all Arab capitalist classes – many of the most important firms that we are accustomed to viewing as Egyptian, Jordanian, and so forth actually need to be conceived of through a multi-scalar lens. While they may certainly constitute some of the most significant firms in their respective countries, their patterns of accumulation and ownership are deeply tied to accumulation in the GCC.

The Role of Diaspora Capital

The outlier in Table 5.2 is evidently Palestine, but here we see a third route through which the production of the regional built environment is linked to the GCC: the centrality of the Gulf as a space of accumulation for non-GCC Arab diaspora capital, which then takes on real estate and other activities in their home countries (or the wider region). Both Palestine and Lebanon exemplify this trend, two countries where – due to war, conflict, and occupation – 'national' bourgeoisies have tended to emerge in the diaspora and then later returned to their home countries. In both instances, the Gulf remains a critical zone of accumulation for these capitalist classes – indeed, in some prominent examples, Lebanese and Palestinian capitalists have been granted citizenship of Gulf states.

I begin with the case of Palestine. There are three main Palestinian real estate developers – the Palestine Real Estate and Investment Company (PRICO), Massar International, and Amar Real Estate – which, between them, fully drive the planning, development, and management of new residential and commercial neighbourhoods. In this context, the Palestinian Authority has conceived its role as facilitating the accumulation of these companies – providing 'external infrastructure', 'attracting Arab and regional investments' (SOP 2014, pp. 52–53), and – perhaps most significantly – laying the institutional groundwork for the development of a mortgage market through the Palestine Mortgage and Housing Corporation (see Chapter 6). The ownership structures of PRICO, Massar, and Amar reflect the profound influence of a Palestinian capitalist class closely connected to the Gulf. PRICO is a subsidiary of the Palestine Development and Investment Corporation (PADICO), a large holding company controlled by three individuals from the Masri family – Sabih, Munib, and Bashar Al Masri.[7] Sabih Al Masri is a Saudi citizen, whose major business is the Arab Supply and Trading Corporation (ASTRA) that was founded in Saudi Arabia in 1967 and is now one of the largest privately owned

[7] PADICO controls a very significant proportion of the Palestinian economy, including the Palestine Stock Exchange and the main Palestinian telecommunications company (see later discussion).

conglomerates in the Kingdom with important agricultural interests in the wider region (see notes 38 and 40, p.143).[8] Sabih's cousin Munib is frequently described as the 'world's richest Palestinian' – he is also deeply involved in economic activities in the GCC, through his engineering and oil services company, EDGO.[9] Bashar al-Masri is the nephew of Munib, and in addition to his joint control of PADICO/PRICO, owns Massar International. Massar's flagship project is Rawabi City, a $1 billion real estate development that is the largest private sector project in Palestine and is jointly owned with the firm Qatari Diar, noted in Chapter 3.

After PRICO and Massar, the third major Palestinian real estate developer is Amar. Amar is a fully owned subsidiary of the Palestine Investment Fund (PIF), another large holding company that was established in 2003 with the aim of consolidating Palestine Liberation Organization (PLO) investments within the Palestinian territories. PIF is closely linked to the Palestinian Authority (the organisation's highest supervisory body, the General Assembly, is appointed by the Palestinian president), and is often referred to as Palestine's sovereign wealth fund. Nonetheless, despite this relationship to nascent Palestinian state structures, PIF is also tightly bound to the Gulf – indeed, to a significant degree, the organisation can be seen as forming an institutional bridge between the internationalisation of Gulf-based capital and state formation in Palestine (Hanieh 2011b).[10] PIF's head, Mohammed Mustafa, served as economic adviser to the Kuwaiti Government for economic reform and privatisation, and also as an adviser to the Public Investment Fund for Saudi Arabia (APIC 2014, pp. 25–26). Another board member, Tarek Aggad, is a Saudi-based Palestinian businessman closely involved in a range of firms throughout Palestine – as with Sabih Masri, Tarek Aggad holds Saudi citizenship.[11] The founder and CEO of a UAE-based

[8] ASTRA initially supplied Saudi Arabia's military with food and other provisions, expanding over the following decade into construction work as well as the distribution and manufacture of fertilisers, pesticides, and seeds throughout the Middle East and North Africa. Much of Sabih Masri's fortune – and ASTRA's growth – was due to his close linkages with the Saudi state; during the 1990–1991 Gulf War, for example, he was contracted by the Saudi government to provision US and Coalition troops.

[9] Although EDGO is based in Jordan, the principle source of its profits derived from contracts with foreign companies to provide equipment, maintenance, drilling, and engineering support in the Gulf's oil and gas industry.

[10] In an interview in Ramallah in 2014, I was told by a member of PIF's General Assembly that a principal goal of the organisation is catalysing FDI flows from the Gulf to Palestine, with a particular focus on real estate, finance, and telecom projects. Interview with member of PIF General Assembly, January 2014, Ramallah.

[11] The Aggad Group is one of the largest companies in the Gulf. It was founded by a Palestinian from Yaffa, Omar Aggad, who after exile from Palestine went to Saudi Arabia where he eventually gained Saudi citizenship. Today, the group holds the sole

private equity firm, Genero Capital, also sits on PIF's board. Other large Palestinian conglomerates whose owners are tied to accumulation in the Gulf – including the Masri-controlled PADICO – are likewise represented on the board.[12] These patterns demonstrate how – regardless of initial appearances – accumulation in the Palestinian real estate sector is interlocked with the Gulf through the mediation of Palestinian diaspora capital.

A similar role for Gulf-based diaspora capital can be seen in the case of Lebanon, most specifically in the large proportion of real estate activities that involve firms connected to the family of former Lebanese Prime Minister Rafic Hariri. Hariri has been described as 'businessman-representative of the Saudi Royal Family' (Hourani 2010, p. 298), a role in which he developed his Saudi-based real estate firm, Saudi Oger, into one of the region's largest developers (Baumann 2017).[13] In Lebanon, the Solidere redevelopment of Beirut is almost exclusively controlled by the Hariri family, as is the building of Amman's new downtown centre, the Abdali Project (in partnership with Kuwaiti firms). Similar to the Masri and Aggad examples just noted for Palestine, the Hariri family holds both Saudi and Lebanese citizenship and, with the core of its business empire located in Saudi Arabia, remains just as much a part of the Gulf capitalist class as Lebanese. Moreover, the particular spatialisation of accumulation embodied by diaspora capital groups such as the Hariri and Masri is also an important feature of how the Gulf penetrates regional political structures – an issue that I will return to in Chapter 8.

In these cases, we see the centrality of the Gulf itself as a space for accumulation for other Arab capitalists, thereby facilitating the incorporation of these capitalists into Gulf class structures while further tying real

distribution rights for Chrysler and Dodge throughout Saudi Arabia. In telecommunications, it has the exclusive distributor rights for Motorola and Siemens. It is involved in the manufacture and distribution of pharmaceuticals, software and IT, elevators, and aluminium. The chairman of Aggad, Omar Aggad, was a founding board member of the Saudi British Bank where he served for 23 years. He is also a board member of the Bahraini-based Investcorp Bank.

[12] Another example is Samer Khoury, whose family controls the Consolidated Contractors Company (CCC). CCC's initial capital accumulation occurred through its close partnership with the largest engineering company in the United States, Bechtel. For much of its history, CCC has been headquartered in Athens, but its major revenue and largest projects are based in the Gulf region. Indeed, at the beginning of 2013, more than half of all of CCC's 63 largest ongoing projects in the world were located in the GCC. These included work on one of the largest airport projects in the world (Midfield Terminal of the Abu Dhabi International Airport, awarded in 2012), construction of the world's largest gas-to-liquid project in Qatar, and work on the Dubai Mall, the largest shopping mall in the world.

[13] In mid-2017, Saudi Oger collapsed following a pull-back in Saudi construction spending. I will return to the firm and its demise more fully in Chapter 7.

estate development in the wider region to the GCC. There are indications, moreover, that this process is broadening beyond displaced diasporas. If we consider, for example, contracts awarded to the two largest construction companies in Egypt, the Arab Contractors (AC) and Orascom Construction (OC), the value of their projects located in the GCC exceeds by many billions those won in their home country over the last two decades.[14] Reflective of this, OC announced in early 2015 that it would move its primary share listing to Dubai, and keep only a secondary listing in Cairo – a move that raises the future possibility of changes in the firm's ownership structures. These and other examples – including a November 2014 agreement between Cairo and Dubai to formerly link their capital markets – point to the ways in which Gulf markets increasingly shape patterns of class and accumulation within the wider Arab built environment.

5.2 Power, Water, Transport, and Telecommunications

Alongside the construction of real estate and the types of mega-project developments discussed in the preceding section, a critical element to understanding the Arab urban space is the role and place of infrastructure. Infrastructure encompasses both physical things – e.g. railways, buses, roads, and ports – and those 'elements of urban form that mediate the physical and spatial with the social and economic' (Tonkiss 2014, p. 2) – i.e. the political, legal, and institutional apparatuses and modes of organisation that enable these things to circulate and function. Precisely because infrastructure plays this bridging role between the physical and the social, its impact is felt across all aspects of urban life – functioning as signifier of 'modernity', a site of capital accumulation, a constitutive element to social relations of inequality, and a focus of struggle (McFarlane and Rutherford 2008, p. 363). In the Gulf, all these diverse aspects to infrastructures' configuration of the urban scale can be found – including, most notably, its role in demarcating and symbolising political power, as the work of Stephan Ramos on Jebel Ali Port in Dubai has shown (Ramos 2010, pp. 107–137).[15] The development of Gulf infrastructure, moreover, was a key site that enabled the penetration of capitalist social relations, norms, and practices throughout the Arabian Peninsula in the mid-twentieth

[14] From 2003 to December 2015, AC won $25.5 billion worth of contracts in the GCC and $15.2 billion in Egypt; for OC, US$68 billion in the GCC compared with US$52 billion in Egypt. Calculated by the author from the MEED Projects database.

[15] Ramos shows how the construction of Jebel Ali (and an associated industrial zone) was utilised by Dubai's ruler Sheikh Rashid as a means of territorial demarcation – and thereby symbolic power – from the neighbouring emirate of Abu Dhabi.

century (Khalili 2017);[16] in this sense, a study of infrastructure is essential to understanding how economic, political, and social practices actually come into being – not least at the urban scale.

Given this significance, what role does Gulf capital itself play in the ownership and control of infrastructure across the wider Arab region? In addressing this question, I will focus on two sectors: (1) urban utilities, specifically power, water, and transport (PWT), and (2) telecommunications networks. Both these types of infrastructure are essential to day-to-day social life in urban areas, and, as Chapter 3 discussed, they have formed an important aspect to the accumulation of Gulf capital within the GCC itself. Outside the GCC, these infrastructure sectors represent a rapidly growing and lucrative source of profits; in North Africa and the Levant, for example, the total value of all PWT projects launched from 1991 to 2015 reached US$642.2 million, exceeding the value of real estate construction contracts issued over the same period (US$628.1 million).[17]

For the PWT sector, there were over 650 projects carried out across seven Arab countries between 1998 and 2015 (see Table 5.3). The large majority of these (60%) have been contracted since 2010, indicating that despite the global downturn of 2008–2009 and the eruption of the Arab uprisings in 2011, there has not been a significant decline in project numbers. Egypt is the regional leader, with the majority of its projects related to the power sector. Algeria, Jordan, and Morocco have also launched a large number of projects – although these are skewed more towards transport and water. Lebanon, Tunisia, Libya, and Syria have tendered significantly fewer contracts in PWT, with the combined value of their projects making up only 6.2% of the total value of projects launched across the seven countries.

The vast majority of PWT projects in North Africa and the Levant are owned by state or government entities. Indeed, of the 659 projects carried out in the PWT sectors from 1998 to 2015 (the same ones examined in Table 5.3), only 58 (8.8%) of them were privately owned (either fully or partially). The majority of these privately owned projects (around 60%) were located in either Egypt or Jordan, with Morocco and Lebanon making up the bulk of the remainder. Algeria, Syria, Libya, and Tunisia have relatively few privately owned PWT projects to date.

[16] In this respect, Laleh Khalili argues that US military institutions took a particularly prominent position in wielding their 'infrastructural power' as a means to deepen 'racialised regimes of labour, capitalist modalities of property ownership, [and] an assemblage of laws, regulations, engineering standards, contracts and practices'. This process was instrumental to integrating the Gulf into the global economy through the twentieth century (Khalili 2017, pp. 17–18).

[17] Calculated by the author from the MEED Projects database.

Table 5.3 *Country breakdown of power, water, and transport projects*

	No. of projects	Sector breakdown (no. of projects)			Total value of projects ($m)	Average project value ($m)
		P	W	T		
Egypt	199	101	35	63	116,060	583.20
Algeria	158	58	30	70	182,684	1,156.00
Jordan	111	42	41	28	17,401	156.80
Morocco	86	32	8	46	45,762	532.12
Lebanon	40	2	17	21	3,547	88.68
Tunisia	28	7	5	16	7,490	267.5
Libya	25	14	9	2	8,986	359.44
Syria	12	6	0	6	4,039	336.58

Source: MEED Projects Database; data from 1998 to 2015.

This lack of private ownership in PWT points to the fact that although privatisation has been a major element of neoliberal reform in the Arab world since the 1990s, divestment of state assets has tended to focus on industry, real estate, and finance, rather than urban utilities infrastructure (Hanieh 2013). Nonetheless, this feature of the urban scale appears to be changing. Over the last five years, international financial institutions have been placing considerable pressure on Arab governments to adopt new regulations regarding public-private partnerships (PPPs), a form of privatisation through which governments offer long-term (often multidecade) contracts for private firms to operate public services. There are a variety of different kinds of PPPs that differ on what the private firm is expected to provide, payment structures, and how the ownership of the underlying asset is distributed between the government and private sector; but, at a global level, PPPs have grown considerably over the last decade, encouraged by the large pools of surplus capital seeking new investment outlets and state-guaranteed returns (Bayliss and Van Waeyenberge 2017).

The growth of PPPs in the Arab world is a relatively new phenomenon but one that is extremely important in relation to the arguments of this book. As I will show in Chapter 8, much of the impetus for PPP legislation has come in the period following the aftermath of the 2011 Arab uprisings, as international financial institutions returned to the region with loan packages that insisted on infrastructure privatisation as part of their conditionalities. Particularly noteworthy in this regard is the entry of the European Bank for Reconstruction and Development (EBRD) to the Middle East, which began operating in the region for the first time in its history following the 2011 revolts. The EBRD was founded in Europe in the wake of the collapse of the Soviet Union; one of its major aims is the encouragement of infrastructure PPPs, a goal that it has heavily emphasised in its activities throughout the Middle East post-2011.

As a consequence, several Arab states have moved to adopt new PPP laws, the passage of which has been accompanied by explicit calls to widen privatisation efforts to specifically target urban infrastructure. Not surprisingly, Egypt has been the regional leader in this regard, with a PPP law (Law no. 67 of 2010) drawn up under Hosni Mubarak and awarded the world's best PPP law by the World Bank in the same year (MEED 2015). Immediately after the 2011 uprising, the government's PPP unit collapsed, but it has since regained prominence following a 2013 military coup and has broadened its scope to encompass a wider array of urban services. The head of the Egyptian PPP unit recently announced that the Nile River bus fleet in Cairo will be tendered for private sale, as well as 1,000 public schools and other services such as healthcare, sanitation, social housing, and transport. Similarly, in Morocco, a PPP law enacted on 24 December 2014 heralded a diversification of privatisation efforts towards private-sector contracting in urban areas; electricity, infrastructure, urban transport, water, waste management, public lighting, hospitals, justice, police stations, universities, and schools have been highlighted by government spokespeople (Linklaters 2015, p. 2). Both Jordan and Tunisia have also recently passed PPP laws (in 2014 and 2015, respectively).

These efforts appear to be having a marked impact on the trajectory of direct private ownership in the PWT sectors. Strikingly, of the 58 private-sector PWT projects launched in the region between 1998 and 2015, 48 were announced since the 2011 Arab uprisings. As we shall see in Chapters 7 and 8, this development mirrors a similar trend in the GCC, and Gulf-based companies have been major beneficiaries of the privatisation of PWT projects in the rest of the Arab world. Indeed, GCC firms are the owners, operators, or developers of more than half of the 58 private-sector PWT projects across the eight countries listed in Table 5.3, a level of involvement that far exceeds that of US, European, or other international capital.[18] In the case of Jordan, for example, one-third of electricity distribution, two-thirds of all wind and solar projects, and the country's major airport are fully or partially owned by firms connected to the GCC. GCC

[18] This should not be taken to mean that Western firms do not benefit significantly from such projects. As was noted in Chapter 2, European and US firms play a major role as consultants for activities such as high-end engineering, design, and architectural or legal functions. EU firms have won more than one-third of all consultancy contracts for PWT in the region since 1998, and close to 80% of all contracts won by non-Arab foreign firms.

capital also dominates private-sector involvement in logistics (particularly seaports) and energy production in Lebanon and Egypt.

Much like the example of agribusiness discussed in the previous chapter, Gulf-based state institutions have heavily supported the expansion of GCC capital into urban infrastructure across the region. This has largely occurred through the provision of Gulf bilateral development aid for water, power, and other infrastructure with contracts that are frequently won by Gulf firms. Significant in this regard is the development aid provided by institutions such as the Saudi Fund for Development (SFD), the Abu Dhabi Fund for Development (ADFD), the Kuwait Fund for Arab Economic Development (KFAED), and the (Saudi-based) Islamic Development Bank.[19] This mutually reinforcing relationship between aid and the internationalisation of Gulf capital into PWT infrastructure is critically important to keep in mind given the predicted scale of reconstruction that will likely follow the current conflicts across the region – a point that I shall return to in Chapter 8.

Telecommunications

Ownership of telecommunications infrastructure – a pivotal and fast-changing element of the twenty-first-century city – has undergone significant transformation across the Arab world in recent decades. For most of the twentieth century, the telecommunications sector was dominated by state-owned companies that regulated, owned, and operated fixed-line telephony and data services. Beginning in the late 1990s, however, Arab governments began a process of liberalisation that aimed at separating the regulatory and operator functions of these state firms while awarding licences to private companies for mobile and Internet. By 2015, Algeria, Tunisia, Egypt, Morocco, Iraq, Syria, Palestine, and Jordan had privatised many of the services previously run by state-owned operators. This process was strongly encouraged by the World Bank and other international institutions, which argued that telecom liberalisation and deregulation were necessary precursors to wider productivity reforms and efficiencies, most particularly in transport, finance, and trade (Rossotto et al. 2005).

The results of this liberalisation are shown in Table 5.4, which lists ownership structures and market share for all the fixed-line and mobile

[19] In 2015, for example, ADFD sent the largest proportion of its aid to Jordan (around 25% of total ADFD aid) – most of this went to transport and logistics projects for which UAE-based firm were major beneficiaries (UAE Ministry of Foreign Affairs and International Cooperation 2016, p. 143). Two such projects are the Amman Development Corridor (a major highway project around Jordan's capital city) and a new port terminal for liquefied gas in Aqaba – both of these projects were built by UAE companies.

Table 5.4 *Telecom operators in selected Arab countries, 2017*

Country	Fixed-line operator	Mobile licence operators (market share)	Ultimate ownership of mobile operators
Algeria	Algerie Telecom (state owned)	Djezzy (14.74%)	Algerian government and Orascom Egypt
		Mobilis (44.85%)	Algerian government
		Ooredoo (40.41%)	Ooredoo (Qatar)
Egypt	Telecom Egypt (state owned)	Mobinil (35.1%)	Orange (France)
		Vodafone (41.6%)	Vodafone (UK)
		Etisalat Misr (23.3%)	Etisalat (UAE)
Iraq	Iraqi Telecommunication and Post Company (state owned)	Zain (29%)	Zain (Kuwait)
		Korek (24%)	Agility (Kuwait) 24%
		Asiacell (37%)	Ooredoo (Qatar) 64%
Jordan	Jordan Telecom (Orange and minority share held by Jordanian government)	Zain (35%)	Zain (Kuwait)
		Umniah (32%)	Batelco (Bahrain)
		Orange (33%)	Orange (France)
Lebanon	Ogero Telecom (state owned)	Touch (53%)	Zain (Kuwait)*
		Alfa (47%)	Orascom Telecom* (Egypt)
Morocco	Maroc Telecom (Etisalat UAE)	Maroc Telecom (47%)	Etisalat (UAE)
		Orange Morocco (33%)	Orange (France)
		Inwi (20%)	Government 69%, Zain 31%
Libya	Hatif Libya (government)	Libyana (n.a.)	Libyan government
		Madar Al Jadeed (n.a.)	Libyan government
Palestine	Paltel (PADICO, a holding company controlled by Al Masri family, see pp. 158–159).	Jawwal (72%)	PADICO (Palestine)

Table 5.4 (*cont.*)

Country	Fixed-line operator	Mobile licence operators (market share)	Ultimate ownership of mobile operators
		Wataniya (28%)	Ooredoo (Qatar)
Syria	Syrian Telecommunications Establishment (government)	MTN (n.a.)	South Africa
		Syriatel (n.a.)	Majority Syrian-owned with minor shares held by Saudi and UAE investors who are also represented on the board
Tunisia	Tunisie Telecom	Tunisie Telecom (34.5%)	Tunisian government 65%, Mohammed Bin Rashid Al Maktoum (Dubai ruler) in private capacity, 35%
		Orange (21.3%)	Orange (France)
		Ooredoo Tunisie (44.2%)	Ooredoo (Qatar)

* Firms are owned by Lebanese government but managed by Zain and Orascom.

telecom operators across 10 Arab countries. There are several striking features of this data. First, for fixed-line telephony, the incumbent state-owned telecoms have been fully or partially privatised in Morocco, Jordan, Tunisia, and Palestine, but remain under state control in the other six states. Gulf-based capital groups have been the major beneficiaries of this privatisation in Morocco – after the UAE's Etisalat took control of Maroc Telecom in 2014[20] – and Tunisia, where around one-third of Tunisie Telecom is privately owned by Dubai's ruler, Mohammed Bin Rashed al Maktoum (through Dubai Holding). For Jordan, the state-owned incumbent was bought by the French company Orange, following its sale in 1999. In the case of Palestine, PADICO, a holding

[20] Maroc Telecom was initially sold to the France's Vivendi following privatisation in 2001, but then bought by Etisalat in 2014.

group associated with the erstwhile Masri family (see earlier discussion) operates all fixed-line services.

Table 5.4 also shows licences awarded for mobile services – an extremely important sector not only for direct communication, but because access to the Internet across all these countries overwhelmingly takes place through mobile devices rather than fixed-line connections.[21] The data confirm the tremendous expansion of Gulf capital into mobile services over the past decade. Of the 26 mobile licences present across the non-GCC Arab world, 14 are either fully or partially owned by GCC groups, and for Iraq, Jordan, Morocco, and Tunisia, GCC-owned telecoms control the largest share of the entire mobile market. Gulf telecoms own at least one of the mobile licences in each of the eight Arab countries where these services are not state owned. State ownership persists in Libya – where no licences have been awarded to private firms – and Lebanon, where foreign companies operate the country's two mobile licences through management contracts with the government-owned telecom (including one held by Kuwait's Zain).[22]

This expansion of Gulf capital into the wider Arab telecommunications market has largely occurred through the acquisition of subsidiary or associate companies by the same Gulf telecoms discussed in Chapter 3. Most notable in this respect are Qatar's Ooredoo, the UAE's Etisalat, and Kuwait's Zain, which between them operate more than one-third of all licences in the countries shown in Table 5.4 (10 of 26). As a result of this expansion, each of these Gulf telecoms now draws a considerable share of its revenue from across the Arab region. In 2015, for example, Ooredoo reported that 27% of its customers and 35% of its revenue came from its operations in Iraq, Tunisia, Palestine, and Algeria (Ooredoo Annual Report 2015). For Zain, 41% of the group's customers were located in Iraq, Jordan, and Lebanon in 2016, while Iraq and Jordan earned 43% of the company's revenue – indeed, revenue from Iraq alone exceeded that in the company's home market of Kuwait (Zain 2016a, p. 20). Similarly, for Etisalat, around one-quarter of the firm's revenue came from its operations in Morocco and Egypt in 2015 (Etisalat 2015, p. 79). Pointedly, however, this regional expansion has not necessarily reduced barriers to access for much of the Arab world's population – in Tunisia, for example, the World Bank has recently

[21] According to the ITU, the number of mobile broadband subscriptions in each of the countries listed in Table 5.4 ranges between two and eight times those with fixed broadband subscriptions (www.itu.int/).

[22] The Lebanese government has been reluctant to pursue full privatisation due to the fact that telecommunications makes up the state's third largest source of income, after customs and VAT.

estimated that a household in the bottom 40% income bracket would need to spend around 44% of its disposable income to afford mobile services (World Bank 2015a, p. 90).

These ownership structures are quite opaque, and have often involved an apparent attempt to localise the firm's 'national' identity and downplay the dominant role of Gulf telecoms. In the case of Morocco and Tunisia, for example, the names of the market leaders (Maroc Telecom and Tunisie Telecom) bear no sign of Gulf capital's involvement. Remarkably, however, the undersea cables that actually connect these two North African countries to the Internet backbone lie largely under the control of Gulf firms – a fact that is little recognised or commented upon.[23] Likewise, in Palestine, the mobile licence operated by Ooredoo is marketed under the name 'Wataniya' (National); somewhat ironically, this seemingly Palestinian brand is a subsidiary of a UAE firm, which in turn is a subsidiary of a Kuwaiti firm, which is ultimately owned by Qatar's Ooredoo. In Iraq, Ooredoo's subsidiary Asiacell – which holds the largest market share in the country – brought the famous Iraqi singer Kathem Al Saher onto its board as its 'brand ambassador' in 2015.

Such opacity is extremely important to unpack, however, because of the role these telecoms play in articulating the relationship between the Gulf and the wider region. Beyond the question of revenue, there are two important sides to this articulation. First, non-GCC Arab telecom markets are beginning to form a strategic platform for further expansion of Gulf capital into other neighbouring regions outside the Middle East, particularly Central and West Africa. An excellent example of this is shown by Maroc Telecom, Etisalat's subsidiary, which holds nearly half of the mobile market share in Morocco and is the largest listed company on Morocco's stock market. Utilising Maroc Telecom as its acquisition vehicle, Eitsalat has established subsidiaries and associates in Benin, Gabon, Burkina Faso, Ivory Coast, Mali, Togo, Mauritania, Niger, and the Central African Republic. Indeed, in the last quarter of 2015, more than 40% of Maroc Telecom's revenue came from these nine countries (Etisalat 2015, p. 24). This regional expansion is partly a result of geographical proximity and shared francophone heritage, but it is also acting to respatialise the infrastructure assemblages of Central and West Africa – with Maroc Telecom's African subsidiaries directly integrated into the Moroccan firm's fibre-optic networks, submarine cables, and money transfer systems (Etisalat 2015, p. 40). In this manner, Morocco's

[23] In Morocco, the country's sole connection to the Internet is controlled by Maroc Telecom. For Tunisia, there are four undersea cables: three are controlled by Tunisie Telecom and one is jointly run by Ooredoo and Orange.

tightening incorporation into Gulf capitalism appears to be reshaping telecommunications across the wider African continent, pivoting the patterning of infrastructure and accumulation around a subregional scale that – while ostensibly centred upon Morocco – is ultimately controlled by UAE capital.[24]

Second, the regional influence of Gulf-based telecoms holds significant implications for patterns of everyday urban life in Arab cities. As I have discussed in Chapter 3, these networks increasingly drive contemporary visions of urban planning, in which all aspects of social life are envisioned through a ubiquitous and pervasive technological connectivity. Although such Smart City concepts are not as advanced in other Arab countries as they are in the GCC, the Gulf's dominant role in mobile communications and Internet connectivity means that Gulf firms will likely shape the character of these types of urban development strategies in years to come. This is made all the more probable given the weight of Gulf firms across other parts of the built environment – indeed, many of the GCC-built urban mega-projects mentioned in this chapter – including Abdali, Rawabi, Al Burouj, and Mivida, are billed as 'smart'. Over recent years, a number of Gulf telecoms have made significant investments in Smart City–related firms, clearly linking these purchases to their regional expansion.[25]

Future industry projections will likely only accentuate this deep insertion of Gulf telecoms into everyday urban life. One critical example of this is the so-called Internet of Things (IoT), which – in line with global trends – now forms a core element of strategic planning for most Gulf telecoms. IoT is closely related to the concept of Smart Cities, and envisions a world in which decision making is automated through software applications that aggregate and process a continual stream of data across a wide range of different economic sectors and activities (indeed, the Softbank Vision Fund story that opened Chapter 1 is primarily aimed

[24] The US government also heralds Tunisia as a 'strong potential regional IT hub' for Africa due to its excellent connectivity to the Internet backbone (www.export.gov/article?id=Tunisia-Telecommunications-Equipment-Services). In this context, the role of Gulf firms in the ownership of the country's undersea cables that I noted earlier – as well as the market dominance of firms such as Ooredoo in mobile services – may mean a similar positioning of the country as a subregional platform for the expansion of Gulf capital through the wider continent.

[25] One example of this convergence between urban development, telecommunications, and regional expansion was a February 2016 announcement by Zain that it had made a strategic investment into neXgen, a leading Smart City advisory firm based in the UAE. According to the Kuwaiti telecom, the partnership aimed at 'delivering smart city services to governments and mega real estate developers facilitating the deployment of smart city solutions and managed services across Zain's regional footprint' (Zain 2016b).

at the purchase of such technology). Ooredoo, Zain, and Etisalat have all identified the IoT as a main focus of their regional expansion over the next few years, and to that end have launched partnerships with international firms to develop the necessary technical infrastructure and software platforms (Ooredoo 2016; Zain 2016b; Etisalat n.d.). In a recent white paper prepared by Etisalat, the firm highlighted 14 sectors – described as 'verticals' – that would form the basis of its IoT strategy; these include smart cities, surveillance, manufacturing, extractive industries, agriculture, retail, finance, utilities, logistics, and transportation (Etisalat n.d., p. 9). Etisalat envisions a future in which it supplies the technological infrastructure to enable and coordinate the data processing and automation of tasks across all of these sectors; 'IoT is in our DNA', according to the firm's Chief Technical Officer, Hatem Bamatraf, and the firm views this area as one of the three main pillars of its strategic growth through 2020 (Etisalat n.d., p. 5). Although the IoT vision may appear as a utopic (or dystopian?) technological dream, most important for our purposes is how such a strategy promises to reinforce the power of Gulf capital at the regional scale. As I have shown throughout this book, *all* the key economic activities prioritised by Etisalat are dominated by Gulf capital; coupled with the wider trends towards privatisation of PWT infrastructure, the convergence and automation of these sectors through Gulf-controlled telecommunications networks will only bolster such dominance.[26]

5.3 Conclusion

The analysis of these various components of the built environment – the production of housing and commercial real estate, PWT infrastructure, and telecommunications – demonstrates that the pace and character of urban change in the Arab region is powerfully shaped by the accumulation of GCC capital. This reveals something very significant about how we should understand neoliberalism in the Arab world. The market-first urban policies that unfolded throughout the region through the 2000s were presupposed by the internationalisation of Gulf capital; it was this cross-scalar act of capital switching that both enabled and reinforced the

[26] We must also remember that alongside the increasing insertion of technology into our daily lives, there has been a parallel increase in attempts to control and monitor communications. Given the widespread attempts by Arab governments to restrict popular access to websites, social media, and communication applications, Gulf-based firms may become increasingly complicit in such repressive measures (indicated, for example, by Etisalat Misr's shutting down of Internet access in Egypt in late January 2011, reportedly at the behest of the Mubarak government).

commodification of the Arab built environment, endeavouring to overcome the inherent spatial fixity of this sector. The regional embrace of neoliberal urbanism is thus much more than simply a set of policies that accentuated the vastly exclusionary character of the Arab city; it is a process that has more closely fastened the rhythm of all Arab urban development to the tempo of Gulf capitalism. The nature of neoliberal policymaking has been shaped by these internal relations of space and scale across the entire region.

Similarly, we need to view processes of 'national' class formation around the elements of the built environment as fundamentally pan-regional in content. Numerous examples from the foregoing analysis confirms this point: the enmeshing of prominent Arab construction and real estate firms and Gulf capital, the straddling of accumulation by diaspora capital groups across the GCC and their home markets, and the dominance of GCC capital in construction, infrastructure, and telecommunications networks. In all of these examples, we see the ways in which the social relations underpinning (national) class formations are increasingly articulated at a pan-regional level. The built environment emerges as a prime site for this enmeshing of the regional and urban scales precisely *because* it is such a central moment for 'national' capital accumulation; simultaneously, due to its intrinsic spatial fixity, it remains an intensely significant locus for internationalisation.

In this context, future trends remain unpredictable and highly contingent on the region's overall economic path. The apparent renewal of global economic worries and the decline in oil prices that began in 2014 have raised questions about the sustainability of the types of urban development models discussed earlier. Nonetheless, we should not read this as necessarily implying any fundamental reversal of the trends analysed in this chapter. Urban development is always subject to the inherent instability of the 'speculative carousels' (Swyngedouw 2010, p. 315) that follow the perpetual search for profit in this sector. Moments of crisis, therefore, may precipitate waves of devaluation of fixed capital in the urban sphere, but the consequences of this cannot be predetermined – they depend heavily on levels of social struggle and the relative balance of political forces. David Harvey has spoken of 'switching crises' that emerge at such moments, with capital attempting to displace these devaluations onto other sectors and geographies. In the Arab region, such a resolution portends a rise in social conflict at the urban scale – with processes of uneven urban development intensifying as capital seeks to displace the impact of crisis onto the poorest city dwellers. Most importantly, as I will discuss in Chapter 8, the massive destruction and human displacement caused by conflicts in countries that have not featured prominently in the preceding narrative – e.g. Syria, Libya, Yemen, and Iraq – constitutes another, much more violent form of capital devaluation throughout the built environment. The trajectories of regional reconstruction in the wake of these wars will be acutely shaped by the patterns traced throughout this chapter.

A critical issue that emerges from this conclusion is the way in which collective struggles around the profoundly uneven Arab urban landscape are inseparable from the hierarchies of the regional scale. Gulf-based capital may have emerged as the dominant fraction of a regionally articulated capitalism, but the exclusionary and marginalising effects of this dominance are telescoped throughout all scales. When residents of Beirut challenge the dramatic reversal of long-standing rent control laws, or poor Egyptians protest their eviction from informal housing communities in Cairo, they challenge not only aspects of national urban policy, but also the ways in which the priorities of urban development have become increasingly subordinated to the dynamics of regional accumulation. These regional dynamics stand behind the making of the urban space – not necessarily in an explicit or overtly causal sense, but in a way that nonetheless holds potent political meaning for future urban struggles. Any effective concept of the 'right to the city' in the Arab context thus needs to be framed as much more than a concern with localism or the specificities of a particular urban place, but one that is necessarily bound up with challenging wider structures of regional power.

6 Spaces of Financialisation in the Middle East*

A common thread to the preceding chapters has been the critical role of finance and financial markets to the forms of capital accumulation within the Gulf. We have seen how equity and debt markets act to circulate capital through different sites of accumulation, bridging a range of activities, economic actors, and geographic scales. These financial markets have facilitated the channelling of petrodollar revenue from the state to the capitalist class, permitting the largest Gulf conglomerates to tap into wider pools of surplus capital and thereby fund further expansion at both the domestic and international levels. Alongside this expansion, financial markets have profoundly shaped processes of class formation in the Gulf, with ownership structures across all the key sectors analysed earlier – industry, real estate, retail, agribusiness, and so forth – interlocked through the boards of banks and other financial institutions.

In this chapter, I expand the discussion of Gulf finance to explore its growing influence on the rest of the Middle East. I approach this analysis through the concept of *financialisation* – a term employed by scholars to describe the ever-growing weight and significance of financial motives, markets, actors, and institutions within contemporary capitalism (Epstein 2005, p. 3; Marois 2012). In recent years there has been a rich academic debate around this concept, focused on understanding the implications of financial markets for the operation of capitalist firms (both financial and non-financial), households, and individuals (Boyer 2000; McNally 2009; Bellamy-Foster 2010; Fine 2010; Lapavitsas 2013). Building upon these debates, I ask here to what degree the changes typically associated with financialisation are found across the wider Middle East, and how these changes may be connected to financial markets in the Gulf.

In this regard, there are three key claims of the general literature on financialisation that need emphasis. The first of these is that financialisation

* This chapter expands upon an earlier version first published as 'Absent regions: spaces of financialisation in the Arab world', *Antipode*, **48**(5), 1228–1248 (Hanieh 2016).

is a process that brings fundamental changes to how accumulation takes place across *all* firms – not only the financial sector (Krippner 2005, p. 182). On the one hand, this *financialisation of the non-financial* signifies a change in how profits are generated – with business calculus shifting towards the maximisation of stock price and 'shareholder value', rather than simply the sale of commodities (Crotty 2005, p. 88; also see Froud et al. 2000). With non-financial firms connected more tightly to financial markets, financial assets become much more central to balance sheets and income generation. It also means a change in the way that non-financial firms typically fund themselves – coming to rely more on the issuance of equity and debt securities or through their own profits, rather than traditional bank borrowing (Lapavitsas 2013, pp. 219–222). All of these dynamics impact internal firm organisation and management goals, as well as the wider tendency to crisis in capitalist economies.

A second important feature of financialisation is the transformation in how individuals and households reproduce themselves on both a day-to-day and long-term basis (Albo et al. 2010; Fine 2010; Lapavitsas 2013). Closely associated with the erosion of social provisioning of housing, education, health care, and aged care under neoliberalism, households have become increasingly dependent upon financial markets to ensure basic needs. This is reflected in the substantial growth of mortgage and housing finance, the increasingly direct linkage of pensions to the fortunes of capital markets, and the rise of various forms of market-based insurance as a means of managing risk. Lapavitsas notes that this process constitutes a 'financialization of personal revenue ... through which the financial sector [mediates] the private provision of goods and services to households' (Lapavitsas 2013, p. 240). Another indicator, therefore, of the degree of financialisation within any economy is the growth in lending for mortgages and personal consumption purposes (and their relative weight in overall loan volumes).

Connected to these changes in both non-financial firm and household behaviour is a third major characteristic of financialisation – a transformation in the operations of banks. Here, commercial banks have tended to move away from a focus on corporate lending towards a direct role in mediating financial markets. They have become the nexus between financial markets and other capitalist firms, assisting the latter through the issuing of bonds, equities, and derivatives. Dos Santos has shown empirically that that this transformation is reflected in the rising importance of 'non-interest income' to bank profits (Dos Santos 2009). Through their mediating role with financial markets, banks make money through fees, commissions, and their own proprietary fund management rather than lending directly to corporations. At the same time, as individuals have been pushed onto a dependence on the market, banks play another mediating role around 'access to housing, durable consumer-goods, education, and increasingly health-care, through insurance-, mortgage- and other individual loans' (Dos Santos 2009, p. 182). Revenue from the lending to individuals and households thus becomes increasingly central to bank profitability.

The political economy literature exploring these claims has largely focused on examining the characteristics of financial markets within single national economies. In this respect, a number of contributions to the financialisation debates by geographers have questioned the spatial boundedness of these studies. Echoing the core theme of this book, one of the key critiques made by the geography literature is the relative neglect of the spatial/scalar dimensions of financialisation – there is a need to 'financialise space and space financialisation', as French et al. have noted, and address the 'glaring lacuna at the heart of the financialisation project; that is, its relatively uncritical approach to the role of space and place within monetary and financial processes' (2011, p. 805). As such, we should be wary of 'geographically anaemic' approaches to financialisation (Christophers 2013, p. 192), which treat national economies as spatially bounded and methodologically divorced from international flows of capital. Instead, an understanding of financialisation needs to move beyond the notion that 'explanations of "national" economic outcomes' can be found 'exclusively in "national" economic dynamics' (Christophers 2013, p. 243), and embrace 'a more geographically sensitive reading of the myriad of processes associated with financialization … and the new financial spaces and practices to which it is giving rise' (Hall and Leyshon 2013, p. 832).

In a related sense, a further critique of the general financialisation literature has been its relatively limited set of case studies, which typically focus on the core capitalist countries – particularly the United States, United Kingdom, and Japan (and to a lesser degree, France and Germany). As is widely acknowledged within the literature itself, there has been little written on what financialisation looks like outside the advanced core. The work that has been done in this regard has been restricted to a handful of countries, notably, Brazil, South Korea, and Turkey – and has largely focused on how these countries are inserted into global financial flows, rather than mapping the specificities of their own domestic financial markets (Bonizzi 2014).[1] Arab countries have been almost completely absent from the debates on financialisation – 'falling

[1] See Bonizzi (2014) for a useful literature review.

off the map' as Bassens et al. have similarly noted in regard to world systems theory and Islamic financial services (2010, p. 37).

Taking on board these two critiques of the financialisation literature – its methodological nationalism and geographical lacunae – this chapter aims to contribute to the wider debates on finance through the lens of the Middle East. The chapter is organised in two main parts. In the following section, I assess the degree to which financialisation can be said to exist in the region, and its impact on key sectors and institutions. Drawing in part upon an original study of the balance sheets, annual reports, and shareholder information of around 300 banks and non-financial firms (using both Arabic and English sources), I develop a range of indicators that demonstrate these trends – including the relative growth in financial assets, the changing behaviour of non-financial firms, and the composition of bank lending and bank income. The second section extends this analysis beyond the frame of the national scale, demonstrating the weight of Gulf capital in these processes and arguing that financialisation must be understood alongside the rescaling of accumulation and a shifting balance of class power across the region. Much as I have shown in the previous two chapters, this has important implications for how we approach the concept of financialisation in general, and its relationship to processes of class formation.

6.1 Assessing Financialisation in the Arab World

From the 1950s to the 1980s, banking and the financial markets of most non-GCC Arab countries were dominated by the state – capital markets were anaemic or non-existent, interest rate levels and the supply of credit generally government controlled, and foreign financial institutions largely excluded from Arab markets. Egypt, for example, nationalised its 27 banks following the 1952 revolution – merging these into four state-owned banks that would direct credit to targeted sectors such as industry, agriculture, and housing. In Morocco, Jordan, Tunisia, and Algeria, interest rate ceilings were set by the state, and banks were compelled to lend to state institutions. The only exception to this generalised condition of 'financial repression' – as the International Monetary Fund repeatedly described the region's financial system through the 1990s – was Lebanon, where the banking system remained largely market based. Here, on the back of wealth from ruling families in the Gulf, the Palestinian diaspora, and business elites fleeing 'Arab socialism' in neighbouring countries, Lebanese banks acted as a conduit for investments in Western markets – constituting 'a central node linking

European powers and the increasingly dependent economies of the Arab states' (Hourani 2010, p. 296).[2]

Through the 1990s and 2000s, however, this picture was to change appreciably. Due to its linkages with all economic activities, the financial sector formed a strategic lever for wider neoliberal reform and thus a principal element of structural adjustment packages. As these measures were rolled out across the region, financial markets were progressively liberalised, with privately owned banks (both foreign and domestic) increasing their influence in most Arab countries. By early 2015, the average market share of state-owned banks in non-GCC Arab countries sat at 38% of total banking assets, down from 56% in 2001.[3] As I have illustrated at numerous points in earlier chapters, burgeoning stock markets also emerged across the region, in which foreign investors were active, and became closely linked to deepening privatisation trends as the sell-off of state-owned assets occurred through stock market IPOs. Moreover, a number of mutual funds, insurance companies, and other non-banking financial intermediaries were launched in several Arab states. At the level of monetary policy, government ceilings on interest rates were lifted and market-based provision of credit expanded considerably (see Canakci 1995). Again, these aggregate trends hide significant variation, most notably in Algeria, Syria, and Libya where financial systems remained largely under state control through the early 2000s – but even in these three countries, the effects of 'financial deepening' were felt.

Given these trends, what do the standard measures of financialisation indicate for the region? Table 6.1 shows five typical indicators used to measure the magnitude, growth, and relative importance of the financial sector: (1) financial system deposits (a measure of the size of deposits held in banks and other financial institutions), (2) deposit money banking sector assets (a measure of bank claims, i.e. loans to non-financial public institutions, the private sector, and governments), (3) domestic credit provided by financial sector (the proportion of domestic credit that comes from the financial sector), (4) the share of financial firms in total stock market capitalisation, and (5) stock market profits.

The first indicator in Table 6.1 shows financial system deposits as a proportion of GDP, which measures the size of all checking, savings, and time deposits held in banks and other financial institutions as a ratio of a country's total economic activity. It is considered an important measure of financialisation as it reflects the level of resources available to the financial

[2] This situation continued until the 1975 Civil War and the rise of Bahrain as an alternative offshore banking centre.

[3] Calculations for 2015 using Bankscope Database; 2001 figure from Farazi et al. (2011).

Table 6.1 *Selected indicators of financialisation*

	Financial system deposits (% of GDP) (average for selected periods)			Deposit money bank assets (% of GDP) (average for selected periods)				Domestic credit provided by financial sector (% of GDP) (average for selected periods)		Share of financial companies in total market capitalisation (total profits)
Country	1997–2001	2002–2007	2008–2013	1995–1999	2000–2004	2005–2009	2010–2014	2007–2008	2014–2015	2015
GCC Countries										
Saudi Arabia	16	18	24	40	44	47	46	6	11	36% (40%)
Bahrain	51	31	70	53	51	59	86	53	83	76% (73%)
Kuwait	77	58	63	94	78	63	66	68	74	67% (61%)
UAE	n.a.	n.a.	75	60	42	67	84	67	91	58% (72%)
Oman	n.a.	28	33	38	43	36	48	31	53	43% (51%)
Qatar	n.a.	43	50	n.a.	55	50	78	51	102	59% (60%)
Non-GCC Countries										
Egypt	63	77	64	71	80	73	65	81	92	38% (69%)
Jordan	81	100	94	80	88	102	105	113	106	53.5% (74%)
Lebanon	n.a.	n.a.	223	115	161	151	157	180	201	–
Morocco	53	65	83	51	62	73	88	90	110	40% (48%)
Tunisia	44	46	53	52	64	59	73	65	88	51% (75%)
Algeria	26	47	51	35	39	33	37	–8	29	n.a.
Libya	n.a.	23	49	n.a.	31	10	n.a.	–55	n.a.	n.a.
Syria	32	54	n.a.	36	35	34	n.a.	18	n.a.	n.a.

Source: Financial deposits and bank assets data from World Bank Global Financial Development database; domestic credit data from World Bank World Development Indicators (for this item, claims on the central government are a net item, which is why the figures for Libya and Algeria are negative in the 2007–2008 period); stock market data calculated from country stock exchanges (September 2015). Lebanon has not been included in stock market data as its exchange is very small and all companies are related to the finance or real estate sector.

sector for lending. This ratio has increased very significantly across all listed countries, with the exception of Kuwait and Syria. The growth in this ratio has been particularly marked for non-GCC Arab countries – through the most recent period shown in the table, Egypt, Jordan, Lebanon, and Morocco have recorded deposits-to-GDP ratios higher than most GCC states.

Similarly, all Arab countries with the exceptions of Kuwait and Egypt have seen a sharp increase in banking sector assets over the last two decades, indicating a growth in the amount of credit provided by banks to both governments and the private sector. Through 2010 to 2014, four Arab countries had banking sector assets exceeding 85% of GDP (compared with only two countries in the 1995–1999 period). Once again, this increase has been particularly notable in the non-GCC states, where four countries – Jordan, Lebanon, Morocco, and Tunisia – experienced a rise greater than 20 percentage points in this ratio, compared with only Bahrain that had a similar level of increase among the GCC countries. The third indicator shown in Table 6.1, the level of domestic credit provided by the financial sector, also confirms the emerging financial depth of Arab countries. A higher domestic credit level as a proportion of GDP is used as a measure of bank growth, because it reflects the extent to which savings have become financialised (i.e. mobilised as credit to other economic sectors through the mediation of the financial system) (World Bank 2003, p. 277). This ratio has grown very considerably across all countries for which data are available (except for Jordan, where it nevertheless remains very high at over 100%).

Table 6.1 also points to the relative weight of financial companies on Arab stock markets. The proportion of market capitalisation represented by the finance sector ranges from just over 35% in Saudi Arabia, where (as discussed in Chapter 3) oil-related companies predominate, to 75.7% in Bahrain. In 6 of 10 countries, more than half of all stock market capitalisation is constituted by these companies. Even more strikingly, 7 of 10 countries have more than 60% of total stock market profits earned by financial companies. For Bahrain, Jordan, the UAE, and Tunisia, close to three-quarters of all profits in listed companies are connected to finance. In some countries this ratio has increased extremely rapidly – in Egypt, for example, finance-related profits constituted 11.2% of profits in 2005, 27.9% of profits in 2009, and reached 69.4% of total listed profits in 2015. For Jordan, the financial sector's share of total market profits jumped by nearly 25 percentage points between 2009 and 2015.[4] Moreover, for non-GCC states it is noticeable that the share of

[4] Calculated from stock exchange data.

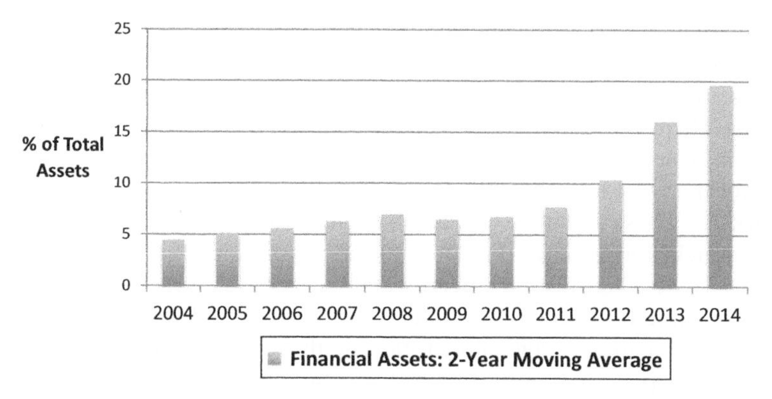

Figure 6.1 Financial assets as percentage of total assets for 22 non-financial companies.
Source: Calculated from consolidated banking sheets (2003–2014) of Saudi Telecommunications, Savola, SABIC, Almarai, Saudi Electricity, Zain, Du, Agility, DP World, Qatar Electricity, Bahri, Nakalat, Air Arabia, Batelco, Tasnee, Omantel, Gulf Cement, SAFCO, Dana Gas, Arab Potash, Telecom Egypt, and Industries Qatar.

bank profits significantly exceeds the share of bank capitalisation – banks, in other words, are much more profitable relative to the size of their capital base than non-financial firms.

Accordingly, it appears from these standard indicators that there has been a definite growth in the magnitude and weight of the financial sector across the Arab world. As noted earlier, however, an important feature of financialisation – perhaps more significant than simply the relative size of the financial sector – is the way in which it changes accumulation patterns for *all* firms, including the non-financial sector. What happens when we turn to examining this 'financialisation of the non-financial'? Unfortunately, the kinds of data that researchers have used to measure this trend in other contexts are not directly available in any consistent or longitudinally satisfactory manner for the Arab world. I have thus developed an alternative indicator (Figure 6.1) that attempts to capture the degree to which 'non-financial' firms are enmeshed with financial markets. These data draw upon the publicly available consolidated balance sheets for 22 of the largest non-financial companies across the GCC, Egypt, and Jordan (three key financial markets in the region). Taken together, these companies make up around one-half of both the total market capitalisation, and total assets, for the top 100 non-financial companies across these countries. These firms have been selected not only because of their size and influence, but also because all of them have been encountered at various points in earlier chapters – they include the largest Arab firms operating in the chemical and minerals, food, telecommunications, utilities, ports, logistics, aircraft, and cement sectors. Using their audited annual balance sheets from 2003 to 2014 (in Arabic, where English is unavailable) I have determined the proportion of company assets that are dependent upon or linked to financial markets. These include: equities available for sale, short-term investments held for trading, derivatives, and investments in associate companies. These figures have been weighted according to the company's market capitalisation (in US dollars) for the specified year, and then the two-year moving average of the total calculated. The aim of this exercise is to develop a proxy indicator for non-financial companies' income – and thus accumulation – that depends upon financial markets/instruments rather than simply revenue arising from the production and sale of commodities.

Figure 6.1 strongly suggests the growing centrality of financial markets to Arab non-financial companies. The proportion of financial assets to total assets grew from around 4.5% in 2003/2004 to 19.5% in 2013/2014 – a remarkable and very sharp jump for just 10 years. The Kuwaiti logistics firm Agility (noted in Chapter 5 as a major shareholder of the Iraqi telecommunications firm Korek Telecom, and in Chapter 4 for its relationship to Al Dahra in agribusiness trade) provides a good illustration of these general trends. The firm reported in 2003 that its financial assets represented around 1.8% of its total assets; by 2014, this had risen to 13.4%. Similarly, the Jordan-based Arab Potash Company attributed around 10% of its assets to various investments in 2014 (including securities and investments in associate companies) – up from around 5% in 2010.[5] It should be emphasised that these companies are market leaders in their respective sectors, and a study of smaller or medium-sized companies may not show identical trends; but the figures appear to confirm that financial markets play a much more important role in the business strategies of the region's most significant non-financial firms. This shift has been particularly notable over the latest five-year period shown earlier, but interestingly there was surprisingly little decrease in this ratio during the financial crisis of 2008–2009 – despite the fact that all Arab markets experienced double-digit declines at this time. This resilience to crisis is perhaps an indication that financialisation represents more than simply an efflorescent market phenomenon, but actually marks a permanent shift in how accumulation takes place in the region.

[5] Arab Potash Company, Consolidated Financial Statements 2010 and 2014.

Changing Role of Banks?

The final set of indicators for financialisation concerns the transformation in the operation of financial institutions – particularly banks – over the last quarter of a century. As noted earlier, one important measure of this is the proportion of non-interest income to total income for commercial banks, which reflects the changing position of banks as mediating links to financial markets (Dos Santos 2009). For banks in the Arab world, this ratio has fluctuated much more sharply than the other data discussed earlier: moving rapidly upwards from 1998 to 2007 and then dropping again in the period following the 2008–2009 global economic crisis and the recent Arab uprisings. Nonetheless, despite these fluctuations, the overall proportion has generally trended upwards, with non-interest income reaching close to 35% of banking income across Arab countries during the 2010–2013 period, up from just over 27% in 1998–2001 (Hanieh 2016). Only Egyptian banks witnessed a significant decline between these two periods.[6] In this sense, a greater proportion of non-interest income – achieved through fees, commissions, and bank's own trading of financial instruments – is an expected corollary to the financialised turn of Arab capital in general.

At the same time, household borrowing has become much more central to the loan profiles of banks. In Egypt, for example, the ratio of bank loans to households versus those made to private businesses stood at around 41% in 2016; in 2010, it was only 28% (CBE 2017b). Likewise, the Central Bank of Jordan has noted in its 2015 Financial Stability Report that 'there is a tendency in the banking sector to increase lending to households at the expense of corporate sector' (CBJ 2015, p. 25), with the proportion of bank loans going to corporations dropping from 51% to 38% between 2010 and 2015. Over the same period, bank lending to households has increased from 18% to 23% (CBJ 2015, p. 25). In Tunisia, bank loans to households made up over 30% of total bank lending in 2016, a figure that has increased from around 20% in 2006.[7] Personal consumption loans also constitute a significant proportion of bank assets in Qatar (29%), the UAE (32%), Saudi Arabia (26%), and Jordan (26%).

An extremely significant factor behind this growth in bank lending to households is the expansion of mortgage markets – a trend that is closely connected to the changes in the built environment that were analysed in

[6] In Egypt, the proportion of non-interest income fell by around 20 percentage points in both 2008–2009 and 2010–2011.

[7] IMF, Financial Access Survey, http://data.imf.org/.

the preceding chapter. For the non-GCC Arab states, numerous policies have sought to increase the volume of mortgages provided to households by commercial banks. A key example of such strategic interventions is the creation of secondary mortgage facilities aimed at providing financial institutions with access to greater liquidity for longer-term lending.[8] This was first trialled in Jordan in 1996, with the establishment of the Jordanian Mortgage Refinance Company (JMRC) supported by a World Bank loan and USAID. The company was established with majority ownership by 12 private banks alongside a minority stake held by the Jordanian government. JMRC has two main functions: first, to provide refinancing for mortgage loans originated by major banks and financial institutions in Jordan at a level equivalent to up to 85% of the loan value, and second, to offer long-term bonds for sale to investors as a means of supplying capital for JMRC's refinancing operations. The second of these activities was explicitly aimed at directing the considerable amount of capital held by pension, retirement, and insurance funds into the built environment. Following its establishment, the number of active mortgage lenders increased from one to eight (Hassler 2011, p. 25), and in 2011 JMRC was listed on the Amman Stock Exchange. Secondary mortgage facilities have also been established in Palestine in 1997 (the Palestine Mortgage & Housing Corporation (PMHC))[9] and Egypt in 2006 (the Egyptian Mortgage Refinance Company). Following the 2011 uprisings, the World Bank and Arab Monetary Fund, as part of the MENA Transition Fund, have launched projects in Tunisia and Morocco to support the establishment of similar refinancing companies (World Bank 2013).

Although uneven, these efforts have appreciably deepened the provision of mortgages and real estate–linked borrowing over the last decade. In Jordan, mortgage loans as a proportion of (current) GDP reached 18.1% in 2015, up from around 16% in 2010. This latter ratio – a standard measure of the penetration of housing finance – has increased even more sharply in Lebanon (11.8%–19%), Morocco (10.7%–16%), and Tunisia (13.3%–18%). Although perhaps exaggeratedly, it has been claimed that in Tunisia 'an astounding 40 per cent of the income of the active

[8] Strongly backed by international financial institutions, relevant policies have included the liberalisation of credit markets, setting up an institutional framework enabling commercial banks to lend for real estate activities, the full privatisation of housing banks (Jordan), the partial opening up of these banks to private ownership (Lebanon, Tunisia, and Morocco), the ending of any privileged access to credit for state-owned lenders (Algeria, Lebanon, Morocco, and Egypt), the removal of interest rate ceilings, and the entry of new banks and financial institutions (including international lenders) into mortgage provision.

[9] PMHC is controlled by firms linked to the Masri and Khoury families (see Chapter 5). Bashar al Masri is chair of the board.

population' goes towards paying mortgage debt (UN-Habitat 2011, p. 63); one regional expert has spoken of the country's 'almost total reliance on mortgage-based financing' where '93 per cent of housing unit acquisition ... is financed through the country's banking system' (UN-Habitat 2011, pp. 62–63). While Egypt has been slower in this regard (partially related to extremely high levels of poverty and the widespread levels of informal housing estimated at 37% of all urban areas (Ahram Online 2015)), the volume of mortgage loans increased 16-fold between 2006 and 2013, growing from a meagre EG£300 million (US$42.6 million) to EG£5 billion (US$710 million) (World Bank 2015b, p. 15). The number of mortgage providers had also increased from 2 to 12 by 2011 (Oxford Business Group 2014, p. 223). Moreover, in February 2014, the Egyptian government announced a major stimulus package worth EG£20 billion, aimed at encouraging banks to massively expand the amount of mortgage lending (World Bank 2015b, p. 18). Taken alongside the general expansion in commercial real estate development, this deepening of mortgage markets provides major financial institutions with significant profit-making opportunities. This 'real estate–finance nexus' (Buckley and Hanieh 2014) is an essential component to the other trends discussed in Chapter 5, not least in the role played by GCC banks in intermediating mortgage payments throughout the Arab world (see later discussion).

6.2 Rescaling Financialisation

The data analysed earlier must be treated with some caution – statistics for the region frequently lack depth and there are significant gaps in coverage. Cross-country comparisons are not always possible due to different underlying variables. It is also important not to overstate these trends. For many of the standard indicators typically used to measure 'financial deepening' by international financial institutions – the penetration of non-bank financial institutions (pension and mutual funds, insurance companies, and so forth), the depth of corporate debt markets, and the ability to trade futures and derivatives[10] – the Arab world lags behind other regions. Nonetheless, we should not think of financialisation as a closed process with a definitive endpoint, but rather as an ongoing feature of contemporary capitalism. In this respect the conclusions are clear: the principal characteristics of the Arab financial system – from the magnitude of the financial sector to the

[10] Aside from Kuwait, future and options trading have not been possible in Arab stock markets. The NASDAQ Dubai exchange launched a derivatives market in 2008, but as a result of the global crisis it did not succeed and the last contract was traded there in 2011.

behaviour of non-financial firms and the changing role of banks and bank lending – all confirm that the trends of financialisation noted in the general literature are applicable to the region itself.

But given these trends, what can we learn about financial transformations in the Middle East if we unsettle the methodological nationalism implicit in many of the indicators examined earlier, and consider financialisation through the lens of other scales? The overall context for addressing this question is framed by the patterns of class formation traced in Chapter 3 – namely the dominant position of large Gulf business conglomerates, for which the financial circuit has played such a critical role in buttressing accumulation, and also in conjoining different fractions of capital, the state, and a range of economic activities. Similar to the other sectors mapped in Chapters 4 and 5, Gulf finance has also internationalised over the past decade – becoming increasingly entangled with, and acting to shape, financial circuits throughout the wider regional scale. From this perspective, financialisation is as much a reflection of scalar processes linked to the internationalisation of capital, as it is simply a quantitative growth or change in the ways that financial markets intermediate the behaviour of firms and individuals at the national scale.

Table 6.2 illustrates this process through examining merger and acquisitions (M&A) data for banks, insurance, and financial services in nine Arab countries outside the GCC. The data capture the relative weight of GCC, European, and North American capital flows[11] into the Arab financial sector from 2006 to 2015 (first quarter). The results confirm both the dramatic internationalisation of Gulf finance capital over the last decade and the Gulf's weight in the regional finance circuit. In all countries, with the exception of Morocco, the overwhelming proportion of capital flows into the finance sector has come from the Gulf. Taken in total across the nine countries, 65% of the 14.3 billion euros of foreign investment in the financial sector over this period originated from the Gulf, with most of the remainder (31%) coming from EU-28 countries. North American investment has been negligible.[12] If Morocco is excluded from these figures, the Gulf's proportion reaches a staggering 72.7% of total investment originating from the three zones. The opening-up of Arab financial markets, in other words, has been primarily and overwhelmingly characterised by the internationalisation of Gulf finance capital.

Table 6.3 provides further corroboration of this process and its implications for banking at the national scale. The data are drawn from an

[11] Virtually all FDI flows into the region originate from one of these three blocs.

[12] In this respect, the figures in Table 6.3 may be slightly misleading as they do not differentiate investment that is made via EU headquarters of US firms.

Table 6.2 *M&A investments by origin in selected country financial sectors, 2006–2015*

Country	Total M&A investment from GCC, EU (28), and North America (millions of euros)	GCC share (%)	EU (28) share (%)	North America share (%)
Algeria	716.8	82	16.7	1.3
Egypt	6,363.4	62	31.7	6.4
Jordan	1,644.4	95.2	0.94	3.8
Iraq	655.3	95.7	4.3	0
Tunisia	787.4	79.4	20.6	0
Libya	718.5	76.6	23.4	0
Morocco	3,407.8	41	59	0
Syria	89.4	97.6	2.44	0
Yemen	1.8	100	0	0

Source: Zephyr M&A Database; figures for financial sector only.

Table 6.3 *GCC-related banks in Arab banking systems*

Country	Total no. of banks	No. of non-government-owned banks	No. of GCC-related banks	Share of total country bank assets held by state-owned banks (%)	Share of total country bank assets held by GCC-related banks (%)	Share of total non-government bank assets held by GCC-related banks (%)
Jordan	18	18	12	0	86	86
Syria	15	13	10	70	24	81
Palestine	6	6	2	0	63	63
Egypt	37	28	17	50	30	59
Lebanon	35	35	26	0	51	51
Yemen	11	8	3	37	29	45
Algeria	19	13	7	88	5	45
Tunisia	36	33	11	30	18	25
Iraq	31	29	6	61	8	19
Libya	16	10	4	72	7	26
Morocco	26	22	0	16	0	0

Source: Calculated from Bankscope database, bank annual reports, and websites. Figures for Palestine do not include Jordanian banks (all of these are GCC-related and are highly influential in the Palestinian market).

examination of shareholder structures and boards of directors for 250 banks across the 11 listed countries. It shows the degree to which these banks are 'GCC related' – defined as a bank that fulfils one or more of the following characteristics: (1) GCC shareholders control 20% or more of the bank's shares, (2) a minimum of two GCC investors sit on the board of directors, and (3) the bank is a subsidiary of another GCC financial institution. In this sense, the data reflect the degree of cross-border, intraregional enmeshing of class relations within banking. The results reveal that banks closely connected to GCC capital completely dominate the non-state-owned banking systems in Jordan, Syria, Palestine, Egypt, and Lebanon. In each of these states, GCC-related banks hold more than 50% of all non-state-owned bank assets – reaching a remarkable 86% in the case of Jordan. In Yemen, Algeria, Tunisia, Iraq, and Libya, GCC-related banks also hold a significant share of non-state banking assets – ranging from 19.3% to 45%. In four of these latter countries (Yemen, Tunisia, Iraq, and Libya), GCC investors hold more of the banking sector than any other foreign country (for Algeria, French-related banks hold 52% of non-state banking assets). Morocco is the only outlier in the data shown, but there are indications that this may be changing with the introduction of new regulations permitting Islamic financial institutions to operate within the country (see later discussion). Moreover, Table 6.3 shows that in those countries where high levels of state-ownership persist (Algeria, Libya, Iraq, and Syria), the GCC's proportion of overall bank assets is considerably less than that within the non-state banking sector alone. In those states where the private ownership of banks is most advanced – such as Jordan and Lebanon – GCC-related banks have overwhelming predominance. Bank privatisation, in other words, is intertwined with, and reinforced by, the internationalisation of GCC finance capital.

The GCC-related banks analysed in Table 6.3 are often the largest and most important financial institutions in their respective countries – a fact confirmed by their weight in regional stock markets. Of all the banks listed on stock markets across Lebanon, Jordan, Egypt, Tunisia, Palestine, Syria, and Iraq, six of the largest seven (by market capitalisation) are GCC related.[13] Strikingly, GCC-related banks constitute 57% of the entire market capitalisation of all banks listed on these seven markets. The 10 largest GCC-related banks alone control just under 40% of all listed banking assets in these seven countries. Moreover, the weight of GCC finance capital in Arab markets appears to be deepening

[13] Calculated from stock market data.

despite the regional crises of recent years – in Egypt, for example, three large banks listed on the stock market have been taken over by GCC banks since 2013.[14]

The internationalisation processes captured in Table 6.3 take place in two main ways. First, mirroring the patterns of other sectors, GCC banks have established direct subsidiaries in neighbouring Arab markets, sometimes through listing on the stock market of the target country. Numerous Gulf banks now operate across the region in this manner, including the largest bank in Qatar (Qatar National Bank, operating in Lebanon, Egypt, Syria, Iraq, and Tunisia), the UAE (Emirates-NBD, operating in Egypt), Saudi Arabia (National Commercial Bank, operating in Lebanon), Kuwait (the National Bank of Kuwait, operating in Egypt, Iraq, and Lebanon), and Bahrain (Al Baraka Bank, operating in Lebanon, Egypt, Tunisia, Jordan, Algeria, and Syria).[15] Of the 10 largest GCC-related banks listed on the stock markets of the countries in Table 6.3, five are direct subsidiaries of GCC banks. While all these Gulf banks remain principally focused on their domestic and other GCC markets, the revenues drawn from other Arab markets can be significant – the National Bank of Kuwait, for example, reported that around 19% of its net operating income in 2016 came from its Middle East operations outside Kuwait (NBK 2016, p. 28).

More common than the establishment of cross-border bank subsidiaries, however, are Gulf investments – by either bank or non-bank capital – into already existing Arab banks. Much like the real estate and agribusiness examples examined in Chapters 4 and 5, this second form of internationalisation may lead to majority control or involve a minority interest; in all cases, it represents an important means through which Gulf capital interlocks with other Arab business groups. An illustrative example of this is the case of Bank Audi, Lebanon's largest bank (by assets) and an extremely influential financial institution across the Arab world.[16] The bank was founded in 1962 (in its present form) by the

[14] These banks were BNP-Paribas (Egypt) (bought by UAE-based Emirates-NBD), National Societe General Bank (bought by Qatar National Bank), and Piraeus Bank (bought by Kuwait's Al Ahli Bank).

[15] Other Gulf banks with subsidiaries in Arab markets are the Abu Dhabi Islamic Bank (Iraq, Egypt), Al Rajhi Bank (Jordan), Bank of Sharjah (Lebanon), Burgan Bank (Tunisia and Algeria), and the Ahli United Bank (Egypt, Iraq, Libya).

[16] Bank Audi has expanded aggressively through other Arab countries in recent years, with operations in Egypt, Jordan, Iraq, and Syria as well as the Gulf and Turkey. According to its 2015 Annual Report, nearly 40% of Bank Audi's assets were located in Middle East countries outside Lebanon in 2015 (including Turkey) (Bank Audi Annual Report 2015, p. 102). Strikingly, 14% of its loans and 17% of its net profits were due to Egypt alone in 2015 (Bank Audi 2015, p. 43).

Lebanese-based Audi family and some Kuwaiti investors. In 2004, it merged with a bank controlled by another prominent Lebanese business family, the Saradar Group, in what was then the largest banking merger in Lebanese history. In 2014, however, the Saradar Group sold its stake in the bank. Today, four Gulf investors hold around 30% of the bank's shares: the Kuwaiti Al Sabbah and Al Homaizi families,[17] a member of the Abu Dhabi ruling family, and the Al Hobayeb family from Saudi Arabia. All of these investors share control of the bank with the Audi and other influential business families (including the Palestinian Khoury family; see note 12, p.60).[18]

Another major shareholder in Bank Audi is FRH Investment Holding, an investment vehicle owned by Fahd Hariri, the youngest son of former Lebanese prime minister Rafic Hariri and brother of the current prime minister, Sa'ad Hariri. The Hariri involvement in the Lebanese banking sector provides further confirmation of the influence of Gulf-based diaspora business groups in shaping Arab capitalism. Alongside its stake in Bank Audi, the Hariris – who, as noted in the previous chapter, hold both Saudi and Lebanese citizenship – also control Bankmed, Lebanon's sixth largest bank by assets, as well as two other smaller banks (the Saudi Lebanese Bank and Medinvestment Bank). Moreover, for a decade, the Hariri family was the leading shareholder in the Arab Bank, the largest bank in Jordan and one of the most important financial institutions in the Middle East. In December 2016, however, the family sold its 20% stake in the Arab Bank to a consortium led by another example of Gulf-based diaspora capital, Palestinian businessman Sabih Al Masri, part of the Masri family who were mentioned in Chapter 5 as the principal investors in PADICO, the holding company that controls the leading real estate firm PRICO and the main Palestinian telecommunications company, PALTEL, among other assets.[19] Masri's newly acquired dominance in the Arab Bank – alongside the Hariri involvement in Bank Audi and BankMed – points once again to how such diaspora business groups act to bridge accumulation in the Gulf and regional capital structures.

[17] The Al Sabbah are the ruling family of Kuwait. Suad Al Homaizi, one of the directors and major shareholders of Bank Audi, was married to a member of the Al Sabbah family.

[18] www.bankaudigroup.com/group/shareholders-related1.

[19] Alongside the Masri stake, investors from Saudi Arabia, Kuwait, Qatar, and Bahrain also hold significant proportions of the Arab Bank's shares. Sabih al Masri also stands out for his dominant position in the fifth largest bank in Jordan, the Cairo Amman Bank (CAB). He owns around 5% of CAB directly, but through Al Masira Investments (wholly owned by the Al Masri family) and other investment vehicles his total holdings reach around 34%.

Whether through the establishment of subsidiaries or direct investment, the internationalisation of Gulf capital into the financial sector has become a critical enabler to the Gulf's growing insertion into wider state and class structures in the Arab world. Banks are frequently the most highly interlocked of all firms in the economy (Krippner 2005), and through their ownership (full or partial) of Arab banks, Gulf capital groups can extend their influence through a range of non-bank sectors. Typically, this initially involves activities that are closely related to finance – such as insurance and real estate development – conducted through subsidiaries established by banks for these purposes. Indeed, almost all of the Gulf-related banks analysed in Table 6.3 own such subsidiaries, many of which are dominant in their respective sectors. In some cases, however, banks may also control an array of other industrial and service sector companies that are far removed from traditional banking – in this manner, Gulf capital's control over the banking sector serves as a conduit for its penetration of the wider economy. A particularly suggestive example of this is the Jordan Islamic Bank (JIB), which is the third largest Jordanian bank (by assets) and operates more than a dozen non-financial companies involved in private universities, pharmaceuticals, the manufacture of steel pipes, real estate, technology, insurance, and chemicals. JIB is a subsidiary of the Al Baraka Banking group, a financial company based in Bahrain that is controlled by the erstwhile Saudi businessman Saleh Kamel and whose interests extend across real estate, media, logistics, and trade (see Chapter 3).[20] Many of the non-financial firms controlled by JIB are market leaders; indeed, five of these rank within the Forbes top 50 Jordanian firms (Forbes 2013). In this manner, Kamel's control over JIB represents a powerful – although largely hidden – mechanism for his deep involvement in all parts of the Jordanian economy.

Banks also form a principal institutional linkage between private capital and state elites. Bank boards frequently contain politicians (both current and former), as well as representatives of state-owned companies, pension, or investment funds. The Lebanese academic Jad Chaaban has exhaustively analysed this phenomenon in the case of Lebanon, showing that 18 of the 20 Lebanese banks he examined have major shareholders linked to political elites; these elites, moreover, exert substantial influence over the banks' board of directors – according to Chaaban, 15 of 20 banks have a chair of the board linked to politicians (Chaaban 2015, p. 11). Bank Audi once again provides a good illustration of these characteristics of state/capital relations. In

[20] The Al Rajhi Group also owns a 7% share of Al Baraka.

addition to the Hariri connection noted earlier, the bank's current chair (and one of its founders), Raymond Audi, was appointed Minister of the Displaced in the Lebanese government following Israel's attack on Lebanon in 2006.[21] Another board member, Marwan Ghandour, was vice-governor of the Central Bank of Lebanon between January 1990 and August 1993. The internationalisation of Gulf capital into Lebanese banks acts to bring the Gulf even closer to political elites such as these. In this manner, Lebanese banks not only reinforce elite cohesion within a highly fractious polity – a function of the banking system that scholars of post–Civil War Lebanon have long noted (Moore 1987) – they also serve as a key site for Gulf capital's incorporation into a state–capital relation centred upon the banking system.

This connection with the state is further reinforced through the financing of public debt. In line with the trends noted earlier, most Arab countries now issue domestically traded debt on their financial markets and have come to depend heavily on these markets for state financing (as opposed to external borrowing) (Garcia-Kilroy and Silva 2011, p. 9). One of the consequences of this is that interest repayments on public debt have become a major drain on government spending. Egypt stands out in this regard, with interest repayments on domestic debt as a proportion of government expenditure reaching 27% in 2015 – more than total government spending on housing, education, and health combined – and up from 21% in 2011 (IMF 2016a). Most of Egypt's spending on interest payments (97%) flows to banks, financial institutions, and other investors operating in domestic markets (Egypt MoF 2017), and such high levels of domestic debt servicing can also be found for other countries.[22] *In the context of the trends analysed earlier, the Arab state thus increasingly mediates the transfer of national wealth to large Gulf-related banks through the servicing of domestic debt.* This is confirmed through an analysis of bank balance sheets. In 2015, for example, Jordan's Housing Bank for Trade and Finance – Jordan's second largest bank, majority owned by the Qatar National Bank (QNB) (34.5%) and a Kuwaiti real estate firm (18.6%) – reported that 35% of its gross income in 2015 came from its Jordanian treasury holdings (HBTF 2015, p. 97). QNB's Egyptian subsidiary, QNB-AlAhli, reported that 23% of its financial assets were composed of Egyptian treasury bills in 2015, and that 52% of its interest income came from these instruments (QNB 2015,

[21] Audi served during 2008 and 2009.

[22] Interest payments as a proportion of government expenditure reached the following for the years indicated: Jordan 11.8% (2015), Tunisia 6% (2012), Morocco 10.9% (2015), and Lebanon 31% (2014).

pp. 49, 59). For Bank Audi, 37% of its financial assets (measured at fair value) in 2015 were made up of treasuries or Lebanese sovereign Eurobonds (Bank Audi 2015, p. 112). In addition, Bank Audi holds a significant number of government bonds from other Arab states, particularly Egypt.

These patterns indicate how Gulf banks' centrality to Arab financialisation signifies a regional entwinement of class and state structures, such that the Gulf is increasingly interiorised within these structures at the national scale. This should not be viewed simply as a predatory, hostile takeover of other Arab capitalist classes. Gulf capital groups certainly benefit from this – as numerous examples from this chapter indicate – but considerable advantages often extend to non-GCC Arab capitalists. Gulf capital's involvement in many of the banks analysed in Table 6.3, for example, has enabled leading Egyptian, Jordanian, and other Arab business groups to embark on their own processes of expansion and internationalisation.[23] Reflecting trends analysed for other sectors, the future trajectories of these non-GCC Arab capitalists are increasingly predicated on their ties to the Gulf region. In short, GCC financial circuits are not external to the national scale of other Arab countries but, rather, should be seen as internally related to processes of class and state formation across the entire region.

Other Forms of Gulf Finance

Beyond conventional banking, it is necessary to mention two other forms of Gulf finance capital that hold important implications for processes of financialisation and internationalisation at the regional scale. The first of these are private equity (PE) and other types of asset management firms, which – as I noted in Chapter 3 – act to pool and mobilise the savings of high-net-worth individuals and large firms. The GCC is the center of the Middle East's PE industry, and, in comparison to the banking system, this form of Gulf finance demonstrates a much greater degree of pan-GCC ownership ties. PE firms play a growing role in the financialisation of Gulf economies, and, as with Gulf banks more generally, their influence is felt across both financial and non-financial sectors.

[23] One example is the Bank of Palestine, founded in 1960 by the Gaza-based Al Shawa family. In 2008, the Kuwaiti conglomerate MA Kharafi & Sons became the Bank of Palestine's largest shareholder, taking 9% of the bank's capital, with the Al Shawa family retaining a significant holding. Following this investment, the Bank of Palestine significantly expanded, increasing its number of branches by more than 50% in five years, and becoming the leading Palestinian bank in the West Bank and Gaza Strip.

The most significant of these PE firms is the UAE-based company Abraaj Capital, which is worth an estimated $9 billion and is reportedly the largest global investor in emerging markets outside Brazil, Russia, India, and China (McBride 2015). Like all PE firms, Abraaj works through attracting money into its funds, which it then uses to target other companies for purchase, while making aggressive use of the relevant tax laws to maximise profits. In many cases Abraaj will take a controlling stake in these firms – the company notes that it holds a majority share of nearly half of its portfolio companies (McBride 2015) – restructure them, and then sell them off either in full or in part at some point in the future. Abraaj's investments are spread widely across globe, including the Middle East, and have targeted sectors such as logistics, health, education, agribusiness, retail, energy, and infrastructure. In some of these cases, Abraaj's investments have led to a consolidation of ownership within the same sector – such as its entry into the private hospital sector in Egypt, in which four large private hospitals were brought under a single Abraaj-owned umbrella. In other cases – such as Spinneys, the Egyptian supermarket chain noted in Chapter 4 – Abraaj's strategy has been to encourage the regional expansion of firms that it has purchased.

Most of these investments lie outside the financial sector. But PE firms such as Abraaj nonetheless play a significant role both in deepening the financialisation tendencies discussed earlier and in strengthening the position of Gulf business conglomerates within regional ownership structures. This is most clearly seen in what typically happens to firms following their purchase. In many cases – following a period of downsizing and rationalisation – PE firms seek to take their acquisitions public through listing them on regional stock markets. In doing so, they encourage the financialisation of non-financial firms – share prices become the core metric of a company's valuation, and newly listed firms increasingly depend upon the issuance of equity and, especially, debt securities for their day-to-day operations. In some instances – such as Abraaj's IPO of the Jordanian logistics firm Aramex – stock market listing will take place in the Gulf rather the company's country of origin; the company's previous owners, moreover, may be absorbed into the management structures of the PE firm.[24] In this manner, PE not only forms an important vehicle for extending the influence of Gulf capital throughout

[24] Aramex was acquired by Abraaj in 2002 for US$65 million. In June 2005, following three years of restructuring, it was listed on the Dubai Financial Market, raising US$270 million through the IPO. Today, Aramex is one of the largest logistics firms in the Middle East, and the company's founder, the Jordanian Fadi Ghandour, is a board member of Abraaj.

many of the sectors mapped earlier; it also reinforces the important role of Gulf financial markets in binding different fractions of Arab capital across the regional scale.

The second important form of Gulf finance beyond conventional banking is Islamic finance (IF). Islamic banks market *sharia*-compliant products that do not involve earning interest or any investments that are said to violate Islamic principles. At first glance this interdiction on interest-bearing products may appear to contradict the notion of financialisation described earlier, but in practice, IF instruments closely resemble their non-Islamic counterparts. In the case of Islamic mortgages, for example, the bank buys the property on behalf of the individual client. The client then buys it back by paying higher instalments (*murabahah*) or through monthly payments that involve a repayment of the purchase price and a 'rent' until the property is fully owned (*ijara*). For Islamic bonds (*sukuk*), the bond-holder technically does not lend money; rather, they own a share of whatever their money was used to purchase, and earn income from profits generated by that asset or rental payments made by the *sukuk* 's issuer. At the end of the term, the issuer buys back the share of the asset owned by the lender (equivalent to paying the principal). Even forms of forward contracts exist within Islamic finance (*salam* and *istisna'*), despite the Islamic principle that commodities should not be exchanged prior to their coming into existence. In all these cases, as with any standard circulation of money capital and the accrual of interest, the original money advanced sees an increase over time.

According to the Islamic Financial Services Board, an international standard-setting body for IF based in Malaysia, only four Arab countries have 'systematically important' IF sectors (where Islamic assets constitute more than 15% of total banking assets): Saudi Arabia (51.3%), Kuwait (38%), Qatar (25.1%), and the UAE (17.4%) (IFSB 2015, p. 9). There are no non-GCC Arab countries that fall into this category. Nonetheless, IF holds great significance for the internationalisation trends discussed earlier. The GCC is seen as a global centre of IF – alongside Malaysia – and IF appears to be emerging as a possible route through which GCC capital will more fully enter those countries in which GCC-related banks have historically been less prominent. One example of this is the case of Morocco, where Islamic banks have traditionally been banned due to the monarchy's fear of Islamist movements. In January 2015, however, the country enacted legislation permitting IF institutions to operate. This move was explicitly conceived as a means to 'attract Gulf money' (Golcer 2014, p. 4), and the Qatar International Islamic Bank (QIIB) – Qatar's third-largest Islamic bank – was the first to announce a joint venture with a large Moroccan bank, CIH Bank, for an

Islamic bank in which QIIB would hold 40% of assets. Similarly, in Tunisia and Jordan, all of the Islamic banks currently in operation are Gulf owned or controlled. How this regional expansion of IF develops in the future remains an open question – partially related to trends I will discuss in Chapters 7 and 8 – but IF is certainly viewed by many traditional proponents of 'financial deepening' (including the World Bank)[25] as a means to widen the penetration of finance across the region; in this context, any regional growth of IF would undoubtedly be steered by GCC-based banks and further entrench these banks in Arab financial markets.

6.3 Conclusion

Taken together, these resolutely spatial dimensions of financialisation in the Arab world indicate both the consolidation of the power of GCC capital at the level of the regional scale and, simultaneously, the interiorisation of this class within other Arab states. Viewed from the perspective of the regional scale, the key features of financialisation outlined earlier – the growing size and weight of financial assets and financial profits, the increasing importance of financial income for non-financial firms, the changing nature of bank lending, and so forth – can all be understood as reflecting, enabling, and girding this projection of regional power by Gulf-based capital. Financialisation in the Arab world thus signifies not only the assertion of financial markets within individual states, but a rescaling of accumulation itself, the imbrication of *all* scales within regionally articulated circuits dominated by the Gulf.

The processes have strengthened the weight of GCC banks and other institutions vis-à-vis their Arab counterparts, a trend indicated in the divergent regional distribution of financial wealth and power. In 2000, for example, banks located in the GCC held 62% of all banking assets in the Arab world.[26] By 2014, this figure had reached 71.7%. The pre-tax profits of GCC banks constituted 70% of all Arab bank profits in 2012–2014, up from an average of 57% in 2007–2008. Even those characteristics of bank income directly associated with financialisation indicate this polarisation – in 2014, more than 70% of all non-interest income earned across the entire Arab banking system flowed to GCC-based

[25] In 2015, for example, the Arab Monetary Fund and the World Bank launched a project aimed, in part, at promoting Islamic finance in the region.

[26] Calculated from Bankscope database. Countries included are Algeria, Bahrain, Egypt, Iraq, Jordan, Kuwait, Lebanon, Morocco, Oman, Palestinian Territory, Qatar, Saudi Arabia, Syrian Arab Republic, Tunisia, United Arab Emirates, and Yemen.

banks. Most pointedly, these 'national' figures do not take into account the ways in which GCC-based capital has expanded through the forms of internationalisation indicated in Tables 6.2 and 6.3 – at a purely quantitative level, they thus considerably understate the actual position of the GCC within Arab financial markets.

This dominant position of Gulf banks looks set to strengthen given a recent spate of cross-border bank mergers and acquisitions within the GCC itself. In July 2016, for example, Abu Dhabi's two largest banks, the National Bank of Abu Dhabi and First Gulf Bank, approved a merger that saw the creation of First Abu Dhabi Bank, one of the biggest financial institutions in the Middle East. Following these successful negotiations, it was widely reported that two other mergers were under consideration: the Abu Dhabi Commercial Bank with Union National Bank, and the Abu Dhabi Islamic Bank with Al-Hilal Bank. In December 2016, three important Qatari banks – Masraf Al Rayan, Barwa Bank, and the International Bank of Qatar (IBQ) – launched negotiations for a merger that will create Qatar's second largest bank after Qatar National Bank. This merger will create yet another large IF institution headquartered in Qatar, and thus potentially presages Qatar's growing influence in this field at a regional scale.[27] Two substantial Omani banks –Bank Dhofar and Bank Sohar – also pursued merger talks through 2016, which, however, were unsuccessful. These trends have continued through the early part of 2017, with the Bahraini-based Gulf Finance House confirming in March that it hoped to create a financial group worth $2.5 billion following a merger with the UAE-based firm, SHUAA Capital.

This unprecedented wave of banking mergers will consolidate control over the Gulf's banking sector in fewer but more powerful hands, increasing the size, weight, and influence of Gulf banks both domestically and across the wider Middle East. This has important implications for understanding the pan-regional linkages explored earlier. All major economic sectors and activities – construction and real estate, infrastructure, agribusiness, telecommunications, manufacturing, and so forth – depend heavily upon financial institutions to mediate investment flows, issue equity and debt instruments, and oversee M&A activities. The centrality of Gulf capital to Arab financial institutions thus places it at the nexus of the wider economy, reinforcing the general patterns discussed for other sectors.

[27] Both Masraf Al Rayan and Barwa Bank are Islamic institutions, but IBQ currently follows conventional banking principles. Qatari regulations do not allow a lender to operate both standards, so IBQ would have to convert its business to being *sharia*-compliant for the deal to go ahead.

More generally, approaching financialisation from the perspective of the regional scale reveals why analyses of financial processes need to move beyond a view of the national scale as a self-enclosed and 'natural' spatial container of social relations. When we measure, for example, the rapid growth in consumer and real estate lending in Jordan, we are also seeing the manner in which GCC finance capital increasingly intermediates Jordanian social relations.[28] When we observe the growing proportion of financial profits on the Egyptian stock market, we are simultaneously mapping how Egyptian capitalism has become closely enmeshed with circuits of accumulation in the GCC. Financialisation, to employ one of Marx's favourite concepts, constitutes a 'form of appearance' of this shifting spatialisation of accumulation, a renascent reworking of space and scale, such that the dynamics of accumulation and class formation emerge anew. Beyond the direct implications for scholars concerned with the political economy of the Middle East, these examples hold potentially useful insights for other geographical locations. Their specificities will clearly differ from place to place, but the Arab world provides a compelling argument for more careful attention to these emerging spaces of financialisation.

[28] Once again, this is closely connected to the changes in the built environment discussed in Chapter 5. For example, the largest mortgage provider in Jordan is the Housing Bank for Trade and Finance (HBTF), which was established by the government in 1973 to provide housing finance, but was converted into a fully commercial bank in 1997. As noted earlier, HBTF is controlled by Qatar National Bank (35%) and a Kuwaiti firm (18%) – the expansion of mortgage provision in Jordan is thus fully connected to Gulf-based finance. Likewise, in Lebanon, the main mortgage provider is Credit Libanais, whose largest shareholder is a Bahraini firm (35%). For Palestine, the biggest lender (and the second largest private-sector employer) is the Bank of Palestine – in which a Kuwait investor is the largest shareholder. All of these examples reveal how the real estate–finance nexus is a major moment of accumulation for GCC-based capital groups at the Arab urban scale; Gulf capital thus emerges as a principal beneficiary of both the *production* of the built environment and its *financialisation*.

7 Visions of Capital

The GCC and the 'New Normal'

Much of the narrative of this book has unfolded against the backdrop of a lengthy period of rising global oil prices, stretching from the beginning of the 2000s up until mid-2014.[1] By 2016, this more than decade-long trajectory of high oil prices appeared to have definitively ended. After peaking at around $110 per barrel in June 2014, oil crashed to an average of just over $40 per barrel through 2016 – its lowest level since 2003. The plunge has been attributed to a variety of causes – including increased supply of non-conventional oil sources and slowing global demand[2] – but regardless of why it occurred, the impact on oil producers has been severe. Despite attempts by the Organization of Petroleum Exporting Countries (OPEC) and non-OPEC countries to raise prices through coordinated cuts in oil output, there has been little sign of the market returning to earlier highs, with oil struggling to move over $52 per barrel during the first half of 2017. Market analysts now predict that oil traders

[1] Aside from short-term fluctuations, the only exception to this generally rising trend was a six-month decline in the midst of the 2008 global economic crisis.

[2] Perhaps the most important of these changes is the growing significance of 'non-conventional' oil supplies – those that are harder and more expensive to extract than the conventional fossil fuels. Of particular relevance here is US shale oil, crude oil that is held in shale or sandstone of low permeability and is typically extracted through fracturing the rock by pressurized liquid (hence the term 'fracking'). Between 2009 and 2014, the production of US shale oil tripled, propelling the United States into the top rank of oil producers globally. At the same time as these new oil sources came on line, there has been slowing growth in world demand for energy in general, and oil in particular. This is most notable in China, which as Chapter 2 discussed, constituted the most significant source in energy demand growth globally throughout the preceding period. From 2010 to 2014, the growth in Chinese total primary energy consumption averaged around 6.4% annually, a figure that dropped to 3.4% in the 2014–2016 period. This moderation of Chinese energy consumption growth was, in turn, reflective of a wider downturn in global economic conditions – most notably a slowing (and in some cases, recessionary turn) in emerging markets, which had been the primary engine of the sputtering economic growth since the Great Recession of 2008–2009. Other important factors connected to the oil price decline include the move towards renewable energy sources, the phasing out of some hydrocarbon-intensive technologies, and the persistently high levels of oil inventories.

and producers face an extended period of low prices and slowing demand, a prognosis commonly described as the 'new normal'.[3]

This slump poses major economic challenges for the GCC. In June 2017, the World Bank estimated aggregate GCC growth for 2017 would reach only 1.3% – the lowest since the global crisis of 2009 and comparable to levels of around 8% just five years earlier (World Bank 2017a, p. 6). Plummeting growth has coincided with emerging current account deficits from 2015 onwards. For the GCC as a whole, the IMF reported that the current account balance fell to a deficit of 2.0% in 2016, compared with an average surplus of 17.3% between 2000 and 2013 (International Monetary Fund (IMF) 2017a, p. 17). With declining oil prices, government revenue has also dived, falling in 2016 to around half the levels of 2013 in Kuwait, Oman, Saudi Arabia, and Qatar.[4] In October 2016, the IMF anticipated that Gulf governments would need to find around $475 billion in order to fund their expected cumulative fiscal deficit between 2016 and 2021, a daunting prospect that implied significant budget restructuring (IMF 2016b, p. 8).

My goals in this chapter are to analyse how Gulf governments have responded to this new economic environment and to ask what this response may mean for the future development of Gulf capitalism. Much of the discussion will focus on a series of economic 'visions' put forward by Gulf governments in the wake of the oil price decline. Drafted with a view to diversification away from oil and heralding significant cuts to government spending, these visions have been supplemented since 2015 by numerous strategic and sectoral blueprints aimed at making such goals a reality. Although these plans are still in early stages of implementation, many of the proposed changes touch upon elements of the Gulf's social model that have previously been considered out of bounds by ruling families and policymakers. In part, they have also altered how the leading Gulf conglomerates relate to the state (particularly in Saudi Arabia). This is a potentially historic shift – not only promising major transformations to social and economic structures in the Gulf, but also holding profound

[3] The IMF has predicted an average of only $53 in 2017 and $56 in 2018. The 2017 forecast is up 24% from the oil price in 2016, but successive predictions by the IMF were revised down through the first half of 2017. Part of the difficulty in assessing short- to mid-term oil prices is the uncertainty related to instability among major producers, such as Venezuela, Iraq, Libya, and Nigeria, which may cause disruptions in global supply.

[4] IMF WEO 2017 Database, government revenue in national currency, estimated levels for 2016 compared with 2013. The decline in general government revenue as a proportion of GDP has been slower but still pronounced (more than one-third for most GCC countries).

implications for the GCC's place in the regional economy and the dynamics mapped throughout earlier chapters.

In the context of this highly significant moment – riven by contradictions, contingency, and instability – I will investigate these new economic strategies through the lens of class–state relations and forms of capital accumulation in the Gulf. Specifically, I will argue that while these plans may ostensibly appear as a managed and 'technocratic' response to an economic downturn caused by low oil prices, they are better viewed as a state-led attempt to utilise this conjunctural crisis as a means to transform and deepen the general conditions of capital accumulation. In this sense, my argument closely follows a range of Marxist accounts that point to how crises are often seized as moments of opportunity by capitalist states – a chance to restructure and push forward change in ways that were previously foreclosed (Cypher 1989; Huws 2012; Oguz 2013) and significantly extend the reach of the market in a range of economic sectors that have hitherto been largely state dominated. At the same time, such policies carry with them an implicit threat of further marginalisation for poorer citizens and migrant worker populations in the Gulf. For the latter, in particular, the downturn has meant a sharp deterioration in both already limited rights and living conditions.

In making this argument, my vantage point in this chapter moves away from the regional focus that dominated Chapters 4 to 6. But as I have repeatedly emphasised, we need to understand what happens within the GCC as a principal driver of developments through the wider Middle East. If my core thesis proves to be correct – i.e. that the policy response to the economic downturn will strengthen the weight of the large GCC conglomerates within their national and pan-GCC contexts – then the dynamics of accumulation analysed earlier will be greatly magnified. In this sense, although my focus here is largely restricted to the GCC itself, the argument can be seen as a prefigurement of future developments at the regional scale. This is all the more important to keep in mind given the multiple crises currently unfolding throughout the rest of the Middle East, a question that I will return to in Chapter 8.

This chapter is divided into three main sections. The first examines the broad strategic orientation towards private-sector growth enunciated by all Gulf states since the beginning of the economic downturn. In this respect I pay particular attention to Saudi Arabia – the focal point of the economic changes in the Gulf – where I trace the substantial expansion in plans for privatisation and public private partnerships (PPPs), and look at the relationship this holds to the emergence of new political actors and a changing articulation of state power. I then compare these trends in Saudi Arabia with other countries in the GCC, illustrating that across the region such measures are aimed at widening the sectoral reach of private capital into emerging frontiers of accumulation – including, most notably, education, health, and renewable energy.

The second section turns to the other critical side of these economic strategies, a realignment of government budgets and fiscal policy. Here, we can see a shift in both sources of government revenue and modalities of state financing, as well as a series of austerity measures that are unparalleled for the Gulf. Following a discussion of bond and *sukuk* issuance in the Gulf, my analysis highlights three key elements to this fiscal reorientation: cuts to project spending, reduced public sector employment costs, and the introduction of new taxes and tariffs. In looking at these policies, I pay specific attention to what they mean for both citizen and migrant worker populations in the Gulf. Moreover, alongside the significant social implications of these policies, I demonstrate that they must also be understood beyond the simple goal of reducing government spending; they are integral to the actual 'making' of markets – a necessary precursor to the opening-up of new spheres of capital accumulation throughout the region.

The final section of this chapter looks more closely at what these changes have meant for Gulf capital itself. Despite the economic downturn, an examination of both firm profits and the evolution of private wealth levels in the region strongly suggests that the Gulf's capitalist class has fared remarkably well over the recent period. There are, however, important shifts taking place. What we appear to be seeing is an increasing differentiation within the capitalist class – a growing dominance of the Gulf's largest conglomerates and a simultaneous weakening of smaller capitals. In this sense, the Gulf's response to the economic downturn provides a potent indication of the class interests that continue to underline policymaking in the GCC.

7.1 Putting Capital First: Privatisation, PPPs, and the Gulf's New Vision

In early July 2015, the new terminal of Madinah International airport[5] opened as gateway to the Muslim world's second holy city. Inaugurated in a visit by the Saudi leader, King Salman bin Abdulaziz Al Saud, the opening was significant in many respects. Following a fierce bidding war in 2011, a consortium of the Turkish firm TAV and domestic

[5] Also known as Prince Mohammed bin Abdulaziz International Airport. Mohammed bin Abdulaziz was one of the sons of the founder of the Saudi kingdom, Ibn Saud, and died in 1988. Outside the Kingdom, he was perhaps best known for ordering the public execution of his 19-year-old granddaughter in 1977 for alleged adultery.

groups Saudi Oger and the Al-Rajhi Group had won the 25-year contract, financing the deal through $1.2 billion in Islamic loans. This was Saudi Arabia's first fully fledged PPP, and Madinah would be the first airport in the country to be built and operated by a private company – it was also the first PPP in history to be entirely financed through Islamic lending instruments. Beyond these milestones, however, perhaps the most striking feature of the airport launch was its coverage in the Saudi press. Championed by a new king only six months into the job, the Madinah Airport PPP received wall-to-wall media attention, an opening salvo of a plan that not only aimed at privatising all 27 Saudi airports, but that also foreshadowed an imminent change in Saudi Arabia's economic direction.

Less than one year after the opening of Madinah Airport, King Salman's newly appointed Deputy Crown Prince, Mohammed bin Salman, unveiled an 84-page strategic document known as Vision 2030. Mohammed's meteoric rise to power had come courtesy of his father, King Salman, who had taken over the reins of the Saudi state following the death of his predecessor, King Abdullah, in January 2015. Popularly known by his initials, MBS, Mohammed had held no significant ministerial positions until Salman took the throne. With his father now heading the country, MBS was made deputy crown prince – behind his half-brother, Crown Prince Mohammed bin Nayef – as well as minister of defense and secretary general of the Royal Court. His position as second in line to the throne, however, was to last barely two years. In April 2017, a surprise decision by Salman saw MBS elevated to crown prince ahead of his brother – a change in succession that led observers of Saudi royal intrigue to quickly dub the young king-in-waiting as 'the world's most powerful millennial'.

As part of his rapid ascent up the Saudi hierarchy, MBS also became chair of the newly established Council for Economic and Development Affairs (CEDA), a powerful government body charged with drawing up Vision 2030. Launched on 25 April 2016, Vision 2030 projected a future Saudi Arabia that is 'the heart of the Arab and Islamic Worlds, the investment powerhouse, and the hub connecting three continents' (Kingdom of Saudi Arabia (KSA) 2016a, p. 9). In introducing the document, MBS pledged to break the 'country's addiction to oil' and dramatically increase private sector activity from 40% of GDP in 2015 to 65% by 2030. This would be achieved through privatisation of government services, the embrace of world markets, and increased global competitiveness. As one of Saudi Arabia's leading banks noted in a May 2016 report, Vision 2030 promised that 'the next chapter of [Saudi Arabia's] growth will be spearheaded by the private sector' and that a comprehensive privatisation programme would 'jumpstart the process of offloading state companies … streamline government processes and policies, and create a strong business environment wherein the private sector could thrive' (Saudi British Bank (SABB) 2016, p. 2).

Vision 2030 was followed in June 2016 by the National Transformation Program 2020 (NTP), a more detailed blueprint of the precise reforms that the country would adopt through 2020. Described in the *Financial Times* as akin to 'Saudi Thatcherism' (Kerr 2016), this $72 billion plan outlined 178 strategic objectives across 24 Saudi ministries and government institutions (KSA 2016b, p. 15). Underlining all of these objectives was the goal of placing private capital at the centre of the Saudi economy. By 2020, the NTP pledged that the private sector would control 100% of power-plant electricity generation (up from 27% in 2015), 70% of ports (up from 30%), 52% of desalinated water provision (up from 16%), 50% of railways (up from 5%), 35% of health spending (up from 25%, with a 1200% increase in health sector revenue from private firms), 15% of education (up from 6%), and 10% of the country's judicial facilities (from zero) (figures drawn from KSA 2016b).

Such an expansion of the private sector's reach would be achieved through two main mechanisms. First, the Saudi government announced plans to roll out PPPs for many key government services. By April 2017, PPP contracts had been signed for four more airports in addition to Madinah (Yanbu, Taif, Hail, and Al-Qassim), while the Saudi government declared that all the country's airports would be privatised by 2020. PPPs were likewise identified for all unfinished rail projects in the country – including the Saudi Landbridge,[6] the Mecca Metro, and urban rail projects in Jeddah, Medina, and Dammam – and in mid-2017 it was announced that a long-awaited 75-kilometre rail and road causeway with Bahrain would also be built through a PPP. In addition to such transport infrastructure, Saudi PPP plans encompassed a range of new sectors that

[6] This 1,600-kilometre cross-country railway aims to link the port cities of Jeddah (on the Red Sea) and Dammam (on the Arabian Gulf), passing through the Saudi capital Riyadh. The project provides a powerful confirmation of many of the features of the regional scale examined throughout this book, most notably the ways in which the Gulf's central position in global supply chains is connected to domestic infrastructural change. Linking cities, ports, and industrial zones, the railway seeks to both reinforce Saudi Arabia's position as a key node in global trade and to speed up the turnover time of global commodities through the country. The CEO of Saudi Railway, the firm in charge of the project, notes: 'The goal is to transport goods arriving from Europe, meaning that they can then be shipped to the East and vice versa. Currently, for goods coming from China, for example, instead of going around the peninsula, then through the Suez Canal, they can use this line. This saves a huge amount of time and, of course, time is money' (Business Year (TBY) 2014).

had previously been dominated by state-ownership, including education (with 300 schools expected to be offered as PPPs through 2018), health care (PPPs planned for the building of up to 3,000 medical facilities), and social housing (the first-ever PPP was launched by the Ministry of Housing in June 2016).

The other means of encouraging such private sector growth was an ambitious plan to sell off state firms. More than 140 major state-owned firms would be identified for IPOs by the Saudi government, including the Saudi Electricity Company, the Saline Water Conversion Corporation (the largest producer of desalinated water in the world, with bids for privatisation advisers under way as of mid-2017), the Saudi Postal Authority, and the Saudi Grains Organization (SGO). Each of these firms dominates its respective sector (as Chapter 5 noted in relation to SGO), and any steps towards privatisation – even if only partial – will appreciably extend the influence of private capital and therefore the logic of market profitability within these critical areas. Even the Saudi Stock Exchange, the largest in the Middle East, was earmarked for sale. Beyond these large firms, the Saudi government would also announce plans to sell smaller, individual government assets. All meteorological centres, public hospitals, and pharmacies are being studied for privatisation. Saudi Arabia's top dozen football clubs will also be sold off – with plans for their sale approved by the Council of Ministers in November 2016.

The most shocking privatisation news, however, came with the announcement that up to 5% of Saudi Aramco would be sold through the Saudi Stock Exchange and a second international market (yet to be identified). The drive to sell Aramco is largely driven by MBS and it has shaken financial markets globally; analysts have valued the company at $2 trillion, making the sale worth an estimated $100 billion – the largest stock market listing anywhere in history and far surpassing the $25 billion IPO for the Chinese company Alibaba in 2014 (Farrell and Parasie 2016). If the expected valuation of Saudi Aramco proves correct, the company would be the largest and most valuable in the world with a market capitalisation greater than Exxon, Apple, Berkshire Hathaway, and Google combined (Ambrose 2016). Frequently described as Saudi Arabia's 'crown jewels', the proposed IPO has generated considerable debate in the usually docile Saudi press and on social media – with the hashtag 'Mohammed has sold the chicken' trending on Saudi Twitter accounts through early 2017 (in response, MBS described those opposed to the sell-off as engaging in 'communist thinking'). Given this opposition and the climate of low oil prices, some market watchers have been sceptical that the proposed listing will actually happen. Nonetheless, the Saudi government is moving determinedly ahead with the IPO, appointing advisers and beginning the process of selecting a secondary international market (with London, New York, or an Asian market as front-runners).

But perhaps even more significant than the sums involved in the Aramco IPO is what will happen to the company post-privatisation. All proceeds from the IPO are earmarked for the Public Investment Fund (PIF), which will then be converted into a sovereign wealth fund also holding the government's remaining portion of Aramco shares. This will make PIF the largest SWF in the world by a very large margin. In the process, PIF will become a major element of Vision 2030's goal of 'encourag[ing] [Saudi Arabia's] major corporations to expand across borders and take their rightful place in global markets' and 'unlock[ing] strategic sectors requiring intensive capital inputs' (KSA 2016a, pp. 7, 42). In this sense, the planned IPO provides a powerful expression of the fundamental trends mapped in earlier chapters: Aramco would no longer simply be the world's biggest oil firm; it is now envisaged as the primary revenue source for a newly repurposed SWF, unambiguously linked to the internationalisation and expansion of the very largest domestic Saudi conglomerates.

Reconfiguring the State: Foreign Consultants and Centralisation of Power

Throughout this book I have consistently emphasised the close alignment between Gulf economic policymaking and the accumulation of the Gulf's capitalist classes. The foregoing discussion of Vision 2030 and the NTP confirms that such an orientation will continue. Nonetheless, the push towards diversification and private-sector growth has been accompanied by significant changes to *how* decisions are made within the Saudi state, and the ways in which lines of authority and power are constructed. As part of this, new political actors and state institutions have emerged alongside the development of Vision 2030 and the NTP – such a reinstitutionalisation of state power aims at promoting the speedy implementation of these plans, while simultaneously embedding market-driven logic more solidly within the state apparatus. At the same time, this process has involved a disruption to the preexisting balance of forces within the Saudi ruling family – and the relations between important sectors of Saudi capital and the state.

An oft-noted and very important feature of this is the growing weight of international management consulting firms in inspiring the direction of Saudi economic planning. Indeed, Vision 2030 'seems to have come courtesy of the "Ministry of McKinsey"', according to Saudi bureaucrats who point to the influence of one of the world's leading consulting companies, McKinsey & Co., on the principles underlying the new strategy (Saif 2016). This is not a new relationship (or one confined to Saudi Arabia), but McKinsey and other international consultants are located at the centre of economic change in the country. Indeed, a market research firm that tracks the consultancy industry claims that the growth in Saudi Arabia's consultant commissions is the fastest in the world – and, following Vision 2030, 'the focus is on Saudi like never before ... Consultants are working to transform an entire country' (Bloomberg 2016).[7]

In other cases, international firms are directly managing core components of Vision 2030 and the NTP. Perhaps the starkest example of this is the February 2017 contract awarded to the massive US engineering firm Bechtel, tasked with establishing and running a cross-government oversight office called the National Project Management Organization (NPMO) (*Mashroat*). NPMO's role is to manage the capital expenditure of projects proposed in the NTP and to push forward the privatisation process (Fahy 2017) – 'reducing inefficiencies and trimming costs', according to media coverage of Bechtel's successful bid (Reuters 2017).[8] As an institution that spans different state bodies and thus displaces power upwards from individual ministries, the establishment of the NPMO aims at imposing a universal logic of cost cutting (to be achieved primarily through privatisation and PPPs) across the entire government. Bechtel's leading position within this process reflects the firm's long and intimate relationship with the Saudi ruling family and other Middle East elites (Vitalis 2007, pp. 74–76) – this connection, however, is now one formally institutionalised within the Saudi state.

Such consulting contracts are extremely pertinent to understanding how policies are formulated in Saudi Arabia (and the rest of the Gulf). The heavy involvement of foreign consultants helps to explain why these strategies carry such a marked discursive resemblance to market-oriented economic planning found in other parts of the world, and further buttresses earlier arguments regarding the recirculation of the Gulf's financial surpluses to Western companies. But such contracts should not be

[7] Alongside McKinsey – which has grabbed the largest share of Saudi consultancy contracts, according to news reports – other major international players include the Boston Consulting Group (BCG) (working on developing Saudi Arabia's secondary mortgage markets), Oliver Wyman & Co, Deloitte, and PricewaterhouseCoopers LLP.

[8] The NPMO was formed by the Ministry of Economy and Planning (MEP) in 2015, as part of the latter's mission to assist different ministries achieve the targets of Vision 2030. The first strategic objective of the MEP (as outlined in the NTP) is the privatisation of government services and assets (KSA 2016b, p. 26).

taken to mean that international firms are simply *imposing* economic strategies on Saudi Arabia. There exists a very real domestic social base for such policies, constituted primarily by the political and economic elites traced in preceding chapters. In an interview conducted for this book, a consultant employed by a leading firm active in the Gulf describes the close alignment between such elites and global consultancy firms:

> The goals of improving efficiency, increasing productivity, and trimming redundant positions within the public sector are all key elements to our work in the Gulf. But should we describe consultancies as 'the evangelist' that drives these changes? I don't think so. The state officials that employ us have very often circulated through positions in multinational companies, or have MBAs from Western business schools. They share the same world-view as us. There is also the constant push from the World Bank and IMF. If we take health care in Saudi Arabia, for example, the World Bank produced a report in which they presented themselves as experts, then McKinsey came out with a report also taking about health care, then MBS includes the corporatisation of health care in Vision 2030. They are all on the same train, and then you see the entry of health insurance providers in the Saudi market, in the UAE market, and so forth. It's all part of the same kind of self-reinforcing rhetoric. MBS is cut from the same cloth as McKinsey. He's a Harvard guy, our team has met him multiple times, he is really with it, he's not just some bureaucrat, we speak about him in the same language as we would a CEO. So I'm not surprised at what he's doing – obviously there is a political element to it as well – but he's doing what every CEO does when they come into their position. But while we've always worked for governments and done these things, we've never done it at the speed and the number of projects as we've seen under MBS. He has been a windfall for consultancy firms.[9]

A key element to this restructuring process involves bringing practices and benchmarks of corporatisation found elsewhere in the world to the Gulf. But rather than a simple one-to-one transposition of models from Western states, this process involves a more nuanced global comparison that takes into account local conditions:

> Everyone is asking for the best practice, it's an aspirational game. Everyone wants to know what's the newest thing that's going on. But it's not a colonial thing of wanting to be like the colonial masters. Rather it's about what can we learn from where capital flows most freely and most quickly, and how we can make the most money out of it. To do this – Gulf governments need to compare themselves to countries that are different enough that there is a change that they can aspire to, but, at the same time, similar enough so that they can copy. So very often, we're

[9] Interview with UAE-based consultant, October 2017, London.

talking about places like Malaysia and Turkey – 'muslimish' countries but further along the path of liberalisation.[10]

Drawing upon Ong's notion of 'flexible citizenship', Ahmad Kanna has insightfully described the professionals that populate many of Dubai's leading firms (both state owned and private) as 'ideal cadres of the city-corporation' (Kanna 2009, p. 213), who construct place-specific neoliberal norms of governance as 'processes of working through local structures of meanings rather than of Western or foreign influences imposed from above or outside by states' (Kanna 2009, p. 213). In much the same way, consultants in the Gulf play a key role in articulating a vision of development that fully internalises neoliberal perspectives in a manner that appears simultaneously as 'local'. According to my informant:

This is why so many consultants on the ground are Western-educated Arabs. You want to be white enough, but also Arab enough. Those of us who possess this kind of insider/outsider position thrive in the consultancy world. I can pretend to know about what's happening in Japan because I'm kind of Western, but at the same time I'm Arab. It's this constant process of translation. It's internationalized practices with an Arab face.

However, the ideological alignment of Gulf state elites with such a corporate-centred worldview should not be taken to mean that there is no resistance within the state apparatus to liberalisation. Very often, mid-level managers are highly reluctant to see standardised rankings for employment remuneration, cutbacks to departmental budgets, or clear identification of public sector roles – the imposition of such 'New Public Management' metrics threatens to undermine the power of state managers whose social influence partially derives from their ability to provide employment and offer bonuses to employees that often earn many multiples of a base salary.[11] For this reason – concurrent with the growing influence of international consultancy firms on the modalities of

[10] Interview with UAE-based consultant, October 2017, London. Interestingly, these patterns are also cascading throughout the wider region as a result of the internationalisation processes traced in this book. My informant noted, for example, that several large companies in the UAE require their executives to relocate to other Arab countries in order to generalise corporate change across their entire regional network. Such intraregional experience is now a prerequisite for career progression into the so-called C-suite (e.g. chief executive officer (CEO), chief operations officer (COO), and chief financial officer (CFO)).

[11] Interview with UAE-based consultant, October 2017, London. In this interview, my informant noted one case in the UAE, where a mid-level manager refused to define the roles of up to 2,000 employees of a particular department, for fear this might mean potential redundancies. He noted that in the Gulf it is common for bonuses and other allowances to make up around 70% of a government salary, with the base salary making up only 30%.

economic planning – the recent policy shifts in the Gulf have involved a centralisation of decision making within dominant institutions of the state. Simultaneously, state structures have been reorganised to minimise overlapping centres of influence or potential sites of resistance, thereby better facilitating the drive to liberalisation.

Emblematic of this reorganisation is the rapid rise of now–Crown Prince Mohammed Bin Salman and the power he has amassed as head of CEDA. In previous years, discussion of economic matters had been dispersed across a dozen different Supreme Councils, which encompassed various strategic sectors. These were dissolved by royal decree following King Salman's ascension and replaced by CEDA, thereby focusing economic strategy in a single powerful institution chaired by MBS. Twenty-two key ministers sit as members of CEDA, many of whom were explicitly appointed because of their private-sector experience; indeed, a study by one Arabic-language financial website found that up to 40 board members of prominent Saudi firms resigned from their corporate posts at the time King Salman came to power in order to take up positions in government ministries (Argaam 2015). New ministers with extensive corporate backgrounds included Almarai's (see Chapter 4) former CEO, who became Minister of Agriculture, as well as the ministers for education, labour, social affairs, housing, and health.

While CEDA sets the broad vision and strategy for privatisation, it also oversees the work of other new committees charged with drawing up concrete blueprints for the sale of state assets. Most important in this respect is the National Centre for Privatisation and Public Private Partnership (NCP), established in April 2017, and which reports directly to CEDA. NCP is frequently described as Saudi Arabia's 'PPP unit', and along with eight Supervisory Committees established in the key sectors identified for privatisation, it holds the responsibility for the practical execution of privatisation over the next decade – including the development of legal, financial, and marketing regulations for those entities identified for sale. With the power to push privatisation residing at a supraministerial level within the state apparatus, structures such as this aim to reduce the ability of any existing sectoral interests to slow down the pace of sell-offs.

Alongside the formation of CEDA as the 'supercommittee' overseeing economic change, a very important shift took place in the composition of government ministries themselves. The sectors deemed as highest priority for privatisation were amalgamated within single, larger ministries, controlled by powerful ministers fully committed to the new economic direction. This sectoral consolidation would enable the privatisation and reform programme to be driven more directly through a handful of strategic individuals, who were now wholly responsible for these different areas, in contrast to the previous, more disparate structure that had seen competing and contradictory interests operating across various ministries.

The most significant example of this ministerial restructuring is the creation of the Ministry of Energy, Industry and Mineral Resources (MEIMR), which now supervises oil, gas, petrochemicals, electricity, and industry. In the past, responsibility for electricity had been held by the Ministry of Electricity and Water – now abolished by Salman's royal decrees – while industry had been located under Ministry of Commerce and Investment. By bringing electricity and industry together under the newly formed MEIMR, many of the crucial sectors targeted for price liberalisation and privatisation – electricity, industry, renewable energy, oil, gas, and petrochemicals – would be housed under a single roof.

The new minister placed in charge of MEIMR, Khalid bin Abdulaziz Al-Falih, clearly illustrates the increasing power of carefully selected actors within the Saudi state apparatus. Al Falih has extremely close links to major international firms – serving, until 2015, as the only person from the Arab world on JPMorgan Chase's International Council, alongside two dozen other international political and business figures including Tony Blair, Henry Kissinger, and Condoleezza Rice.[12] Much like MBS, Al Falih wields influence across a range of highly strategic positions within the Saudi state. In addition to his role as head of MEIMR, Al Falih was appointed chair of Saudi Aramco in April 2015, replacing the octogenarian incumbent, Ali Al Naimi, who had led the organisation for more than two decades. As head of Aramco, Al Falih is steering the part-privatisation of the most important company in the country – simultaneously, as the Minister of Energy, Industry and Mineral Resources, he is driving the changes to utility pricing (see later discussion), the privatisation of the Saudi Electricity Company and other industrial firms, and the push towards a private-sector-based renewable energy market in the Kingdom. Significantly, Al-Falih also chairs the Saudi Industrial Development Fund (SIDF), an important government entity that provides soft loans to the private sector for expansion and upgrading of assets, as well as the Saudi Industrial Property Authority (MODON), which has responsibility for the oversight and development of industrial cities and technology zones. By controlling these multibillion-dollar institutions, Al-Falih plays a major role in channelling wealth to the large Saudi business groups, and, in this sense, he directly mediates the relationship

[12] It should also be noted that in mid-2017 JPMorgan Chase was appointed as one of the three international financial advisers for the Aramco IPO (along with Morgan Stanley and HSBC).

between state and private capital in the Kingdom. This role, moreover, is set to take on a qualitatively new level given the aforementioned objectives behind the part-privatisation of Saudi Aramco (chaired by Al Falih), and its absorption into the Public Investment Fund (on whose board Al Falih sits). Indeed, according to one Gulf-based banker: 'While MBS may be the power behind the throne, Khalid is the major actor behind economic restructuring. He has a vision and his influence is felt everywhere – Aramco, the Ministry, and PIF. There are no longer a thousand cooks.'[13]

Emerging Frontiers of Accumulation

Pointing to previous strategic proclamations that have failed to take root or achieve their stated objectives, some sceptics have expressed doubt about the privatisation targets of the NTP and the ability of the Saudi government to implement such a far-reaching transformation in a few short years. Such criticisms, however, can miss the essential point: regardless of the actual numerical targets met through these plans, what matters is what they tell us about the trajectory of economic strategy and the primary concerns of the Saudi state. They should be taken to 'indicate a direction of travel rather than a forecast' (Kinnimont 2017, p. 11), and, in this respect, the line of march is clear: the ultimate priority remains the growth and expansion of the Saudi private sector, enabled through a streamlined and newly repurposed state.

Although dwarfed by the scale of privatisation proposed by Saudi planners, other GCC states have also put forward similar strategic 'visions' over the last few years, strongly emphasising the need for economic diversification and the prioritisation of private-sector growth.[14] Numerous partnerships with the private sector have been tendered or are in the pipeline across these GCC countries (see Table 7.1). As with Saudi Aramco, major state-owned companies have been identified for IPOs – this is particularly notable in Kuwait, where several of the key subsidiaries of the national oil company are earmarked for privatisation. Oman is also planning IPOs for its oil firms, state-owned postal company, national airline, and electricity distribution, and has passed laws mandating all insurance companies to be publicly listed.[15] Likewise, in

[13] Interview with UAE-based investment banker, February 2017, Dubai.

[14] These are National Vision 2020 (Qatar), Vision 2020 (Oman), and Vision 2030 (Bahrain, Kuwait, and the UAE).

[15] Moreover, Omani law now requires all PPPs in the power and water sector to list part of their shares on the Muscat Stock Exchange.

Table 7.1 *PPPs and privatisation planned or under way (as of August 2017)*

Qatar	The Qatar National Development Strategy for 2011–2016 (published in March 2011) explicitly highlighted PPPs as an important part of investment strategy, particularly noting projects associated with the 2022 FIFA World Cup. Following the publication of this strategy, a PPP Ministerial Working Group was established to identify possible PPP projects. A PPP law is under consideration and expected to be finalised during 2018. One World Cup stadium, Ras Abu Abood, is reportedly being considered for PPP. In the water and power sector, four projects are currently being developed or planned as PPPs, with the first contract signed in 2015 (Ras Laffan). In October 2016, the Ministry of Economy and Commerce and Ministry of Education and Higher Education jointly sought private-sector interest for the construction and operation of 10–12 public schools on a PPP basis. Hospitality, logistics, real estate, and medical facilities are also being considered for PPPs.
Bahrain	Although Bahrain does not have specific PPP legislation, it was the first country in the GCC to undertake a PPP for social housing in two projects worth $1.5 billion signed with private developers in 2012 and 2015. The country has also announced that it will develop a liquefied natural gas terminal as a PPP (the first such PPP in the Middle East), and also has a waste-to-energy PPP project under tender. In addition, the privatisation of the country's telecom network infrastructure was announced in 2017. Bahrain's health strategy (2015–2018) is largely framed around the use of PPPs for health infrastructure development.
UAE	Due to the more decentralised nature of the UAE, each emirate operates differently with regard to PPPs. In 2015, Dubai introduced its inaugural PPP law, and in 2016 agreed on its first PPP project, a deal to build the world's largest automated carpark. Two further PPPs are currently under development in Dubai: a 15,000-square-metre mixed-use real estate project connected to one of the Emirate's busiest metro stations, and a $3.4 billion deep tunnel sewerage scheme. Dubai is also planning a significant expansion in PPPs for hospitals and other medical facilities. Beyond Dubai, PPPs have been undertaken for airport expansions (Sharjah, Abu Dhabi), a desalination plant (Fujairah), the world's largest concentrated solar project (Abu Dhabi), medical facilities and schools (Abu Dhabi), and an energy and waste management plant (Sharjah). In 2017, the federal UAE Cabinet issued a resolution outlining procedures for partnership between federal entities and the private sector, as well as a manual to assist federal entities in developing PPPs. The fuel distribution unit of Abu Dhabi's oil company, ADNOC, was listed in an IPO in 2017, and plans are under way to also sell the state-owned aluminium producer Emirates Global Aluminium.
Kuwait	Kuwait adopted a new PPP law in 2015 and as of August 2017 had a pipeline of 28 PPP projects in place. The first PPP was awarded in 2013 (Az Zour Electricity and Water Plant); five others in water, waste, and energy are under tender (August 2017). Bids are under evaluation for the Kuwait Schools Project, which will see nine schools operated by private companies through a PPP. PPPs have been awarded for hospitals, and discussions are occurring around delivering a national railway and a metro system for Kuwait City as PPPs. In addition, four major subsidiaries of Kuwait Petroleum Corporation are under consideration for 20%–30% sale (Kuwait Petroleum International, Kuwait Foreign Petroleum Exploration Company, Kuwait Oil Tanker Company, and the Petrochemical Industries Company).

Table 7.1 (*cont.*)

Oman	The Sultanate's ninth five-year plan (2016–2020) highlights the importance of PPPs in acquiring, financing, and developing projects. As of 2017, there were eight PPPs in water and desalination in development or under tender. The country has also successfully agreed an equity investor for Sultan Qaboos Medical City, a health care–focused city complex that will include three PPP hospitals, specialist clinics, hotels, retail outlets, and residential areas for patients and staff. PPPs have also been announced in logistics, infrastructure, and services at the newly developed Khazaen Logistics Hub and Port of Duqm. The redevelopment of the Port Sultan Qaboos Waterfront (announced in 2016) is also planned as a PPP. In 2017, Oman announced that it would launch IPOs for the Salalah Methanol Company (a subsidiary of the Oman Oil Company), Muscat Electricity Distribution Company, Oman Post, Oman Air, and non-core subsidiaries of Petroleum Development Oman.

Source: GCC vision documents and news reports.

late 2017, the Abu Dhabi government listed the fuel distribution unit of its state-owned oil firm, ADNOC, in what was the largest IPO seen on the Abu Dhabi stock exchange in more than a decade; the UAE has also confirmed an IPO for state-owned Emirates Global Aluminium, one of the biggest aluminium producers in the world (see Chapter 3). This unprecedented wave of public listings is intended to deepen stock market capitalisation and will likely strengthen the trends discussed in Chapter 6 – most notably, the financialisation of non-financial firms and the ongoing centrality of share ownership as a route for domestic capital accumulation.

In all cases, wide-ranging regulatory changes around foreign ownership and PPPs are central to enabling these processes. Both Kuwait and Dubai, for example, introduced new PPP laws in 2015, while in Qatar and Oman, government spokespeople say that PPP legislation is in advanced stages of preparation.[16] In other areas of the Gulf, governments have chosen to facilitate PPPs through more general investment legislation. The regulatory frameworks for these laws are being directly imported from abroad, most notably from British firms that are the dominant players in drafting legal codes for privatisation in the Gulf. This illustrates yet another avenue of foreign involvement in the Gulf's economic reform and further confirms the significance of the Gulf's

[16] In the case of Dubai, this was the first law specifically dealing with PPPs, and since that time several projects have been tendered; Kuwait, on the other hand, has revised an earlier law from 2008, the main effect of which was to extend the rights of foreign ownership.

commercial services market to global firms (see Chapter 2). It may, however, pose potential obstacles down the road; one lawyer interviewed for this book described the Gulf PPP legislation as a 'dog's breakfast' – a mismatch of British privatisation law and Gulf legal codes that could create significant problems if any of these projects are challenged in court.[17]

A striking feature of the PPPs listed in Table 7.1 – echoing the similar trends for Saudi Arabia mentioned earlier – is the emergence of new investment frontiers for private capital across the Gulf. During the pre-2015 period, the limited number of PPPs in the Gulf had largely focused on water and power generation – so-called independent water and power projects, which saw private firms take contracts to build and operate electricity- and water-generation plants. This sector continues to be important, but the new phase of PPP expansion in the Gulf is characterised by a marked shift in the types of activities for which governments envisage private-sector participation. Three new emerging sectors particularly stand out in this regard: education, health, and renewable energy.

In education, the market for privately run institutions in the GCC is said to be the fastest growing in the world, worth around US$15 billion in 2014 (Lione 2014). Private schools now make up more than one-fifth of all school enrolments in the Gulf, and grew at around three times the rate of public school enrolments between 2009 and 2014 (Alpen Capital 2016a, p. 13). Industry analysts see education as 'a huge opportunity for the private players' due to the region's rapidly growing young population and high income levels (Alpen Capital 2016a, p. 8). I noted earlier Saudi Arabia's plans to significantly increase private-sector participation in the education sector, and the Saudi Education Minister has stated unequivocally that

> the ministry views the private sector as the driving force for the development of education in the Kingdom … We will broaden the range of privatization by not only opening investment opportunities for schools but also for small and medium educational establishments and school management offices and services. We will also open the door for non-educational investments such as food companies to operate school cafeterias. Saudi Gazette (2016)

Similarly, both Kuwait and Qatar have recently tendered large PPP projects for schools (Table 7.1); the UAE has a long-standing reliance on such partnerships in schooling, including PPPs for more than 170 Abu Dhabi schools (Abu Dhabi Digital Government Gateway (ADDGG) 2017).

[17] Interview with lawyer working for an Arab construction firm active in the GCC, June 2017, London.

Many of these private schools are owned by foreign firms, including from countries such as the United States and United Kingdom – in 2015, the UAE hosted the highest number of foreign schools in the world (511 schools), while Saudi Arabia and Qatar came in globally at fifth and fourteenth, respectively (Alpen Capital 2016a, p. 9). But domestic Gulf conglomerates have also been prime beneficiaries of the opening-up of this sector, and now operate throughout the private education market regardless of what their traditional core activities may be. Following a range of M&As since 2014, we can find several of the large firms mentioned throughout this book that manage or are invested in schools; these include the Al Rajhi Group, Al Habtoor Group, Boubyan Petrochemicals, the Kuwait Finance House, the National Commercial Bank, Al Khabeer Capital, the Kingdom Group, and Gulf Finance House (GFH 2016).

The health sector is similarly seen as holding substantial opportunities for private capital – with market value estimated to grow from US$40.3 billion in 2015 to US$71.3 billion by 2020 (Alpen Capital 2016b, p. 8). Part of the reason for this is the Gulf's staggering rate of metabolic disease, including cancer, obesity, and diabetes – indeed, excluding small island states, GCC countries filled the top five spots for diabetes prevalence in the world in 2015 (20–79 years, age adjusted) (World Bank data). In this context, the growth of private health care – including through the use of PPPs – is seen as a highly lucrative market for both Gulf and international firms. Saudi Arabia, the UAE, Kuwait, and Oman have all launched PPPs for hospitals and other medical facilities since 2015, while Qatar and Bahrain have identified the health sector as a major target for future private-sector growth. Moreover, GCC countries are also looking to develop themselves as hubs for medical tourism – illustrated by the development of Dubai Healthcare City and Oman's Sultan Qaboos Medical City.

The renewable energy market is a third key sector identified in all GCC vision documents. A major focus of Saudi Arabia's Ministry of Energy, Industry and Mineral Resources, for example, is the expansion of renewable energy, and to this end, the King Salman Energy Initiative was launched at the same time as Vision 2030. Khalid Al Falih is the animating force behind this initiative (although he also remains a strong proponent of fossil fuels). According to one executive of a leading energy consulting firm, Al Falih's position at the centre of oil, electricity, and industry signifies that 'the paralysis brought about by a multitude of competing entities is to be replaced by a central, top-down governance structure', and these changes potentially mean a 'game changer for the prospects of renewable energy in Saudi Arabia' (Borgmann 2016). Indeed, at a speech at a renewable energy forum in Saudi Arabia in April 2017, Al Falih noted that the Saudi government planned to launch 60 renewable energy projects by 2023, which will meet 10% of the country's electricity supply by that time (Business Year (TBY) 2017).[18]

The UAE has been the other leading force in the expansion of renewable energy markets. Abu Dhabi targets 7% of its electricity supply to be met by renewables by 2020, while Dubai is planning for 'clean energy' to supply 25% of the market by 2030 and 75% by 2050.[19] Dubai's Clean Energy Strategy was launched in November 2015 and allocated $163 billion in investments for the sector, including more than $27 billion of cheap loans for private investors. In bids received for solar PPPs since 2015, the UAE has broken the world record three times in terms of the low cost of power offered by competing consortia. The UAE has also become the headquarters of the International Renewable Energy Agency (IRENA), the first time that an international intergovernmental organisation has been located in the Middle East (and a move with significant ramifications for regional politics, as I will discuss in Chapter 8).

There are other emerging sectors of privatisation also prominent across the Gulf – such as water desalination, transport, and logistics – and taken alongside education, health, and renewable energy, these new frontiers promise a major expansion in the opportunities for private capital. As these plans move forward, they will certainly benefit international firms – particularly in the kinds of consultancy and high-end engineering activities delineated in Chapters 2 and 5. But if the patterns of PPP and privatisation deals to date are any indication, domestic Gulf conglomerates look set to profit significantly from state divestment. Since 2015, virtually all successful privatisation deals have been won by Gulf conglomerates either alone or as part of consortia; indeed, according to some market players this is no accident – many of the sales seem to be reserved for well-connected firms that hold privileged access to the state and ruling families.[20] In this manner, the immanent alignment of state and private capital remains an enduring element of the current economic environment. Moreover, as I will discuss in some detail in Chapter 8, this

[18] Saudi Arabia also plans to expand its nuclear energy capabilities through the launch of at least two nuclear reactors.

[19] This includes what Dubai describes as 'clean fossil fuels', nuclear, and gas. According to the country's strategy, renewable fuels will make up 44% of the total clean energy supply by 2050.

[20] One employee of a firm that has successfully bid on PPPs in the Gulf told me in an interview for this book: 'We would be negotiating over the terms of the bid and then someone would come and tell us "so-and-so has met with someone from the royal family, and it's been decided". All of these deals happen behind closed doors – it's about who you know not what you can do.' Interview with lawyer working for an Arab construction firm active in the GCC, June 2017, London.

process is synergic with the opening-up of these same new sectors of accumulation across the wider Middle East. As has so often been the case over recent decades, the consolidation of Gulf capital in its national locale is inseparable from its expansion through the regional scale.

7.2 Fiscal Policy, Austerity, and the Making of Markets

Closely related to these private sector–oriented visions are major changes to budget policies, including both sources of funding and patterns of government spending. In the immediate wake of the oil price decline through 2015, GCC states initially sought to cover government expenditure through drawing upon some of the considerable financial assets built up over the past 15 years, including government deposits in commercial banks. These asset sales met an estimated 80% of financing needs through 2015. In 2016, however, this was to change. Seeking to preserve their global asset base and fearing that withdrawal of government deposits might place liquidity pressures on local financial markets, Gulf governments switched away from asset drawdowns towards the issuance of government debt. In 2016, more than $102.4 billion in new bonds (including *sukuk*) were issued in the GCC, up from $65.1 billion in 2015 and far in excess of the average $36.8 billion offered annually between 2006 and 2014 (Markaz 2017, p. 4).[21] These bonds include both corporate and sovereign (government) debt, as well as domestic and international issuances.

At the international level, Gulf governments offered more than US$38 billion worth of international securities for sale in 2016, a level of sovereign bond issuance that is unprecedented for the GCC (World Bank 2017a, p. 17). These bonds have met with strong international demand given a global environment of overaccumulation and the search for higher returns, making the Gulf a central player in emerging market debt – in 2016, around 14% of total emerging market debt issued internationally came from the Gulf (Grifferty 2017). At a global level, the GCC has offered 5 of the 10 largest emerging market bonds since 1995; 4 of these have been issued post-2015 including the world's largest ever emerging market bond by Saudi Arabia in October 2016 (worth US $17.5 billion) (World Bank 2017a, p. 15).[22] Such sales have important

[21] These figures include corporate issuance. In 2016, GCC government (sovereign) bonds made up around two-thirds of total bonds and *sukuk* issued. For 2016, around 90% of GCC sovereign debt was issued on international markets (by value).

[22] In March 2017, Oman issued a Eurobond that met more than 70% of its 2017 fiscal requirements, while Kuwait borrowed US$8 billion in its first international bond placement.

ramifications for the financial patterns outlined previously. For one, the issuance of sovereign debt more closely links the Gulf to international financial markets, and – because sovereign bonds can help investors better price 'risk' in the region – it is seen by private firms as a necessary step in the expansion of corporate debt.[23] In 2016, Gulf corporate entities issued just over $36 billion in bonds and *sukuk*, an increase of more than one-third on 2015 (Markaz 2017, p. 5). Many of the large firms mentioned in earlier chapters have been involved in such issuance, including the Saudi Bin Laden Group (a $266 million *sukuk*), Almarai ($426 million *sukuk*), Majid Al Futtaim ($500 million *sukuk*), Ooredoo ($500 million bond), Kuwait Projects Holding Company ($500 million bond), DAMAC Real Estate ($100 million *sukuk*), and Etisalat ($400 million bond). If such trends continue, we will likely witness a further reinforcement of the financialisation processes noted in Chapter 6, with non-financial firms increasingly looking to financial markets for funding.

Moreover, growing reliance on bond issuance could potentially increase the Gulf's weight in global and regional Islamic financial markets. Although conventional debt continues to make up the largest proportion of total debt issuance in the GCC (particularly for international bonds), Islamic bonds have also seen considerable growth since the oil price decline. In April 2017, the Saudi government offered a US$9 billion *sukuk* on international markets – the largest dollar-denominated international *sukuk* ever sold at a global level.[24] Following a new Saudi government plan announced in mid-2017, this was followed by issuance of Islamic bonds on the domestic market in late July 2017 (worth $4.5 billion). GCC-based Islamic banks, in particular, will disproportionally benefit from such domestic offerings because, compared with conventional banks, they tend to hold a higher proportion of low-yield cash on their balance sheets due to a lack of *sharia*-compliant investment options (Moody's Investors Service 2017, p. 2).[25] With such higher-yield Islamic bonds now being made available, Islamic debt issuance will likely act to strengthen Islamic banks, while also consolidating the role of public debt as a mechanism through

[23] Financial analysts understand this through the development of domestic 'yield curves' for debt, which would allow companies to develop benchmarks for their own issuances.

[24] These levels will likely grow as investment firms increasingly include GCC Islamic bonds within global bond indexes. JPMorgan, for example, announced in August 2016 that it would include some *sharia*-compliant bonds from the GCC in its emerging market bond index for the first time from October 2016, a move that will likely boost international appetite for these securities.

[25] Moody's notes, 'As of March 2017, Saudi Islamic banks' holdings of cash and placements with SAMA and banks equalled 20% of their total assets, versus 16% for conventional Saudi banks, while their investment portfolios accounted for only 8% of their asset base, versus 20% for conventional Saudi banks' (2017, p. 2).

which the state increasingly underpins the accumulation of domestic financial institutions more generally (see Chapter 6).

At the same time as these bond and *sukuk* issuances, GCC governments also vowed to cut government expenditure through a range of different areas. The scale of fiscal austerity initially discussed was very large: for the GCC as a whole, the IMF calculated that an average 25% reduction in spending would be needed to balance budgets in 2016 – individual figures for Bahrain, Saudi Arabia, and Oman all reached over 30% (based on a price of oil of $50 per barrel) (IMF 2016c, p. 18). Although actual levels fell short of this, all GCC governments introduced policies aimed at reducing government spending and finding new sources of revenue. There are three instructive examples in this respect: cuts to project spending, reduced public sector employment costs, and the introduction of new taxes and tariffs. Each holds significant implications for GCC residents – both citizens and migrants – and also provides a highly revealing clue to the trajectories (and intent) of the new vision strategies.

Cuts to Project Spending

A major initial focus of cutting government expenditure in the Gulf was the reduction of public spending on construction and infrastructure projects, a trend that began in 2015 and further accelerated through 2016. According to industry trackers, 2016 was the first time in more than a decade that the GCC projects market registered negative growth – measured by the net gain of new contract awards ($105 billion) versus the value of project completions ($166 billion) (Foreman and Rademeyer 2017, p. 76). The drop was particularly severe because of an unprecedented simultaneous decline in all the Gulf's major markets – Saudi Arabia, the UAE, and Qatar – with cuts mostly targeting construction and transport projects. These cuts created major problems for some large construction firms, including regional leaders such as Saudi Bin Laden and Saudi Oger, who were faced with a sudden halt in government construction jobs and significant delays in receiving payments for work already under way.

There are two key aspects to these cuts to project spending that are often overlooked in analyses that focus simply on their implications for government budgets. First, they have played an important discursive role to the simultaneous rolling-out of PPPs, with privatisation often justified as a means to achieve the reductions in project spending outlined in the various strategic documents. This is one reason why the language of 'project management' – and its emphasis on cost cutting through privatisation and outsourcing – has been such a prominent feature of government restructuring since 2015 (perhaps best exemplified by Bechtel's NPMO contract in Saudi Arabia). In turn, many construction firms have sought to deal with the slowdown in government spending by diversifying into the PPP market, bidding on contracts for the long-term management of infrastructure and services rather than simply short-term building projects. As the president of one of the leading construction firms in the Gulf puts it, 'the lack of government funds' means 'no option but to move into privatisations [sic] as a means of securing sizeable construction jobs at reasonable prices' (Foreman 2017, p. 18).

Second, project spending cuts have had critical implications for migrant working classes in the Gulf, as construction firms responded to shrinking government expenditure by shutting down projects or placing them on hold and, in the process, firing hundreds of thousands of workers. Government-backed campaigns to deport migrants began at the same time, most evidently in the Gulf's largest labour market, Saudi Arabia, where millions of workers have been expelled since the economic downturn began. The Saudi government describes these workers as 'violators' (*mukhalif*) – they include tens of thousands laid off without pay following cuts to construction spending, and others who did not have the proper work permits or who had fled their official sponsors due to abuse. Between November 2014 and March 2015, the government reported that workers were being sent home at the astonishing rate of 2,000 people per day (HRW 2015); by the end of 2015, the Interior Ministry claimed that more than 1.2 million workers had been removed from the country since the beginning of 2014 (Akhbar24 2015). Many of these workers – typically from South Asia, Yemen, Ethiopia, and Somalia – were beaten and abused while in detention and awaiting deportation (HRW 2015).[26] A further deportation campaign, dubbed 'A Nation without Violators', was announced on 19 March 2017, which sought to secure the removal of an additional 1 million migrant workers from Saudi Arabia (of a total migrant population of 9–12 million, this figure represents around 10% of the official non-citizen workforce). By end July 2017, more than 600,000 workers had left the country as part of this new campaign, according to media reports (Anderson 2017). With the Gulf's lowest paid workers reeling from such measures, the Saudi government simultaneously stepped in to pick up the costs of higher-paid

[26] Human Rights Watch reported that many 'returned to their home countries destitute and with no means to buy food or pay for transportation to their home areas' and that they had faced 'arbitrary confiscation of their personal property, which authorities refused to allow them to take' (HRW 2015).

(mostly Western) construction managers and engineers left stranded by the halt to project spending.

One result of such redundancies and deportation campaigns has been a startling drop in remittance flows from the Gulf between 2015 and 2017. In the case of Saudi Arabia, for example, remittance levels fell in absolute terms by more than 13% during the first quarter of 2017 compared with the same period in 2015.[27] Moreover, the pace of this decline appears to be accelerating. Saudi news reports noted that June 2017 had seen a plunge of 34.5% in remittance outflows compared with a year earlier, the highest fall witnessed throughout the preceding 11 months (Mohammed 2017). Saudi Arabia is the world's second largest source of remittances (after the United States), and any prolonged slowdown in its employment of migrants could have a potentially severe impact on labour-sending countries.[28]

These patterns illustrate a key feature of the Gulf's class structure: the particular nature of labour in the Gulf – specifically the reliance on a large body of non-citizens drawn from surrounding countries – enables the GCC to effectively displace a large part of the impact of economic downturn onto their migrant labour force through forced redundancies and deportations (Hanieh 2011a). Unlike most other countries, the GCC does not face the prospect of major social unrest from workers as a result of mass layoffs in construction or a halt to government spending on new building projects. By extension, this means that the effects of the crisis are heavily felt in the regions from which these workers come. This

[27] Calculated by author from SAMA Monthly Bulletin, June 2017, table 17, p. 152. There was a 6.5% decline between Q1 2017 and Q1 2016.

[28] Data from countries in Asia confirm the likelihood of such a scenario. India, the world's largest remittance recipient and with more than half its overseas workforce located in the GCC, saw money remitted globally by migrant workers drop by around 9% in 2016 compared with 2015 (World Bank, Bilateral Remittance Matrix 2015, www.knomad.org/data/remittances). Similarly, Bangladesh saw an 11.1% annual decline in remittances in 2016 (reaching the lowest levels since 2011), while Nepal registered a 6.7% drop (World Bank 2017b, p. 26). The State Bank of Pakistan's monthly data on remittances from June 2017 showed a 24.7% drop in remittances from Saudi Arabia compared with one year earlier; remittance levels had also fallen by 4.6% from the UAE over the same period. For Bangladesh, the levels of remittances received from Saudi Arabia plunged by 22% in the first half of 2017 compared with the same period in 2016; there was an even higher drop in remittances received from the UAE (23.5%) (Bangladesh Bureau of Manpower, Employment and Training, Remittance Inflow Tables 2016 and 2017, www.bmet.gov.bd). The number of Sri Lankan workers departing for the Gulf fell by 13.3% from 2014 to 2015 – a dangerous trend for a country in which nearly 90% of all migrant departures are to the Gulf (Sri Lankan Bureau of Foreign Employment 2015, p. 17). And in the Philippines, media and government agencies have estimated that up to 1.7 million overseas workers were threatened with displacement due to slowing economic growth in the Middle East (TESDA 2017).

spatial displacement of crisis has been a critical element to how Gulf states (and Gulf capital) has attempted to deal with the oil price decline; it thus needs to be viewed as functional to the actual implementation of the vision documents themselves.

Reducing Public Sector Employment Costs

Together with a reduction in project spending, a second major element to Gulf vision documents has been the goal of reducing the size and cost of public sector workforces. Similar to the patterns just discussed in the construction sector, migrant workers bore the initial brunt of such changes, suffering heavy job losses across state and para-statal firms.[29] But moving forward, the paring back of public sector work could significantly impact Gulf citizens, who have traditionally found employment in better-paid public-sector jobs rather than in the private sector. Indeed, one of the performance indicators outlined in Saudi Arabia's NTP pledges an extraordinary 20% reduction in the proportion of workers in the public sector by 2020 (KSA 2016b, p. 42), with a concomitant increase in citizen employment in the private sector. Other ways of trimming public-sector employment costs have also been explored. In 2016, for example, Saudi Arabia cancelled allowances and bonuses for state employees – a move that caused significant consternation among the citizen population (leading King Salman to reverse the decision in March 2017).[30] Similarly, Oman has implemented a hiring freeze in the public sector, and Kuwait has announced targets to reduce public sector wage growth and the layoff of thousands of workers in government ministries.[31]

As with the cuts to construction spending and the associated shift to PPPs, the goals behind these labour market transformations are closely linked to the process of privatisation. In order to keep costs down for private sector employers, the expectations citizens hold around the types of work they undertake as well as wages and benefits must be significantly curtailed – and this implies substantial erosion in public-sector job

[29] GCC media through 2016 and 2017 reported large-scale job losses across firms such as Qatar Rail, the Abu Dhabi National Energy Co. (around a third of oil and gas jobs, and more than half of staff at its headquarters), Etihad Rail (30% of jobs), Qatar Petroleum (3,000 jobs), Abu Dhabi's National Oil Co. (nearly 10% of staff), and the National Bank of Ras Al-Khaimah (250 jobs) In all of these cases, Gulf governments have explicitly announced that only migrant workers would lose their jobs.

[30] In June 2017, a further announcement was made that all benefits and allowances would be back-paid.

[31] In December 2017, local Kuwaiti newspapers reported that just under 2,400 employees at the Ministry of Awqaf and Islamic Affairs would face redundancy.

opportunities and conditions, and a convergence of the employment cost of citizens with that of the cheaper, non-citizen labour force currently preferred for private-sector work. Once again this is an explicit target of Saudi Arabia's NTP, which pledges a sharp reduction in the differential cost of employment between citizens and non-citizens from 400% to 280% by just 2020 (KSA 2016b, p. 56). Such a shift will be a politically difficult measure for Saudi Arabia to implement; it is, however, widely understood as a critical element to moving the privatisation process forward.

This goal of increasing levels of citizen private-sector employment intersects closely with the removal of migrant workers from the Gulf. To this end, governments have enacted a range of new restrictions on employment of non-citizens in an attempt to push citizens into the private sector. In Saudi Arabia, these laws include reducing the employment of non-Saudis in retail outlets – such as mobile phone shops, car rental agencies, groceries, and malls – and it is now not unusual to see Saudi citizens working in areas that were previously the domain of migrant workers (e.g. driving taxis).[32] Nonetheless, the rate of growth of citizen employment in the private sector still remains well below targets set by the Saudi government, and citizen unemployment levels have risen. In the first quarter of 2017, unemployment rates for Saudi citizens reached 12.7%, the highest level in well over a decade (Saudi General Authority for Statistics, www.stats.gov.sa/en/814). Hardest hit have been Saudi women – over one-third of the female population is now unemployed, a figure that has doubled since the beginning of the 2000s. Unemployment rates in Oman also reached 12% in 2017, up from only 5% in 2013. In 2011, young Omanis engaged in major protests and clashes with police due to the lack of jobs; a possible repeat of such disturbances continues to animate debates in the Omani press and political circles (Valeri 2015).

Moreover, as with much of the rest of the Middle East, the prospect of rising citizen unemployment is particularly serious given the so-called youth bulge evident across the Gulf. The proportion of the population under 25 ranges from a low of 25% in Qatar to a high of 50% in Oman. In the Gulf's largest and most important labour market, Saudi Arabia, 46% of the population was under 25 in early 2017, according to figures

[32] One of the consequences of this policy is the shutting-down of smaller retailers who cannot afford the (still) relatively higher pay expected by citizens – further encouraging the concentration of market power in the hands of larger capital (indeed, a 2017 law explicitly restricted the issuance of retail licences to larger firms) (http://gulfbusiness.com/saudi-ban-foreign-workers-grocery-shop-jobs/).

from the country's Statistics Unit.[33] Youth unemployment rates also stand at levels considerably higher than overall unemployment – again, this is particularly evident in Oman and Saudi Arabia, where 50.8% and 30.1% of youth were out of work respectively in 2016 (according to International Labour Organization estimates).[34] These demographic trends mean that a growing number of jobs need to be created moving forward – for Saudi Arabia, it is estimated that by 2030 the number of new Saudis expected to enter the labour market stands at nearly twice the total number of Saudi citizens in work as of 2017 (Kinnimont 2017, p. 9).

The potential repercussions of such labour market transformations are huge, and citizen youth could now face a generational decline in public-sector job opportunities and thus a very different future from their that of parents. For ruling elites, navigating the tight line between cutting public-sector employment and other forms of government provision, while attempting to maintain a social base of citizen support, is a complex and difficult task. Such tensions promise increased cleavages and differentiation within the citizen population, which, moreover, must be overlaid on existing social tensions – such as youth alienation (Oman and Saudi Arabia), sectarian patterns of rule (Bahrain), elite contestation in the political sphere (Kuwait), internal ruling family rivalries (Saudi Arabia and Qatar), and geographic inequalities within individual Gulf countries (Saudi Arabia and the UAE). As a result, we should not be surprised by reversals and hesitancy in implementing such labour market transformations moving forward (such as the turnaround on the Saudi decision to cancel bonuses for state employees) – but neither should we rule out the possibility of citizen protest against such measures.

New Taxes and Tariffs

A final prominent feature of the Gulf's new fiscal policies has been a sharp increase in tariffs for key consumer commodities such as petrol, electricity, and water, and the introduction of new fees for a wide array of services. Although many of these measures only target non-citizens (see Table 7.2), they also hold significant implications for the citizen

[33] In the UAE it stands at 34%, while it is 35% in Bahrain and 40% in Kuwait.

[34] These figures record the percentage of the labour force aged 15–24 out of work but actively seeking a job. It should be noted that these rates include the entire labour force (including non-citizens) and thus cannot be directly compared with the earlier cited figures for citizen unemployment. Figures from World Development Indicators Database (databank.worldbank.org).

Table 7.2 *New fiscal measures in the GCC*

	Taxes and fees	Fuel, electricity, and water tariffs
Saudi Arabia	Increased fees for passports, driving licences, and resident permit renewals for domestic workers New fees (US$2133) for multiple entry visas New fees that will rise to US$100 per month by 2020 for non-citizens to bring in dependents (per dependent)	Increase in prices (ranging from 10% to 134%) across fuel, electricity, and water to businesses and households
UAE	Abu Dhabi introduced new 3% fee on housing rental contracts for foreigners	Floated petrol prices in line with oil price Increased water and electricity tariffs by 170% and 40%, respectively (Abu Dhabi)
Kuwait	New fees for issuance and renewal of foreign worker permits A 160% increase in health insurance fees for foreign workers	Increase in petrol prices from 41% to 83% depending on fuel grade New tariffs on water and electricity
Oman	Increased income tax; greater visa fees and new airport departure taxes	23%–33% increase in petrol prices depending on fuel grade Water tariffs increased for government, commercial, and industrial users
Bahrain	Increased visa fees Increase in alcohol and tobacco taxes	Up to 60% increase in petrol prices Electricity and water tariffs adjusted for non-domestic users
Qatar	Increased alcohol licence fee for foreigners	30% percent increase in petrol prices Water and electricity prices raised and tiered according to consumption

Source: Adapted from Arab Gulf State Institute in Washington (AGSIW) 2017; International Monetary Fund (IMF) 2016b, p. 13; news reports.

population – particularly in the area of fuel and energy costs, which have traditionally been heavily subsidized across the Gulf. Since 2015, all GCC states have moved rapidly to liberalise the prices of these utilities; in some cases, tariffs have increased by up to 170%. Plans to introduce a GCC-wide value-added tax – the first time in history for such a tax in the Gulf – will also impact citizens and non-citizens alike.

A point that is often overlooked in discussion of these new policies is the fact that they are not only a means to reduce government spending or increase revenue – they are essential to the actual *making* of new markets in the Gulf. A key example of this is the question of increased tariffs for electricity, water, and petrol; beyond budgetary savings, such increases are a necessary step in any move towards utility privatisation. Without bringing consumer prices up to a level that can make utility ownership profitable, it is difficult to convince private capital to invest in these sectors. This goal is explicitly recognised by industry analysts[35] and goes a long way towards explaining why the question of subsidy reform has received such emphasis in the new economic strategies and in the advice provided by international financial institutions. Moreover, liberalisation of energy prices is seen as a necessary move towards the development of private sector involvement in the renewable markets – a fact acknowledged in Saudi Arabia's Vision 2030 (Kingdom of Saudi Arabia (KSA) 2016a, p. 49). As a leading renewable energy consultant has noted in relation to Saudi Arabia: 'If fuel and electricity subsidies continue to be reduced, there will be a strong case for distributed solar energy ... The first step in this direction has already been taken with the steep increase in electricity tariffs at the beginning of 2016' (Borgmann 2016).

This 'market creating' effect of fiscal policy is clearly evident in other sectors, which, moreover, also demonstrate the differential impact of these policies on non-citizens. In Kuwait, for example, a new law saw the introduction of large health insurance fees for foreign workers (increasing by 160%) and the announcement that non-citizens would be banned from accessing the country's public hospitals. One of the leading voices pushing for these measures is Safa al-Hashim, a Kuwaiti businesswoman and the country's sole woman parliamentarian, who in comments reported in the local press sought to cast the segregation of health facilities as part of 'achieving social justice for citizens' (Al-Alas 2017).[36] In practice, however, the main effect of these measures is to forcibly induce demand for private medical and insurance services from foreign residents (particularly significant in a country where 70% of the population are non-citizens). It is noteworthy that as these legal changes were enacted, the government was simultaneously moving to privatise its medical services, exemplified by a PPP initially valued at around $1 billion – the largest in the history of Kuwait – that saw the creation of

[35] One such analyst has noted, 'A key part of facilitating a broader role for private players in the region's power and water markets will be the reduction of subsidies to ensure the price consumers pay for utilities is reflective of what is used and the cost to produce it' (Roscoe 2016).

[36] Numerous Kuwaiti doctors opposed the measure as discriminatory and racist, and amidst the debate one of these perceptively noted that Hashem was acting as if 'pressure on the human rights of foreigners' was the 'solution to the economic crisis' (Al-Alas 2017).

the Kuwait Health Assurance Company (KHAC) (Kuwait Life Sciences (KLSC) 2015, p. 11). The PPP contract was eventually won by the local Arabi Group following a bidding war between major private conglomerates in Kuwait,[37] and a deal to build the first of three private hospitals to be run by KHAC was signed in August 2017.

Likewise, the introduction of laws across the GCC that make health insurance mandatory for foreigners and their dependents is seen by industry analysts as extremely positive for the growth of private health sector. Between 2013 and 2016, such laws were phased in for Saudi Arabia, Abu Dhabi, and Dubai, while Kuwait and Oman are in the final stages of developing similar regulations. At the same time, new laws – such as one passed in Saudi Arabia in December 2014 – allow non-medical firms to own and operate health facilities for the first time. A founder of one private hospital in Oman has commented: 'Once medical insurance becomes more widely available and mandatory, it will drive significant growth to this sector. In addition, governments in the GCC are encouraging the privatization of medical care and services. Both these factors when coupled together create an environment of significant growth and innovation' (Alpen Capital 2016b, p. 7).

Like the other fiscal policies discussed earlier, the introduction of such measures illustrates the ways in which forms of government expenditure and income are inextricably linked to the goal of encouraging private sector growth. These policies are not only about dealing with the 'new normal' of lower oil revenue and attempting to balance budgets; they are also an essential part of the strategic orientation towards private capital that underpins all Gulf vision documents. The impact of these policies may be differentially felt across citizen and non-citizen populations, but – taken as a whole – they embody a radical reworking of Gulf capitalism that aims ultimately at expanding the sphere of private sector activity.

7.3 Gulf Capital and the Downturn

In 2017, the Gulf's economic downturn claimed its most high-profile corporate casualty with the collapse of the Saudi construction giant Saudi Oger. The firm has been noted numerous times as a key illustration of the links that exist between accumulation in the Gulf and Arab diaspora capital. Owned by the family of assassinated Lebanese Prime Minister Rafic Hariri, Saudi Oger's extremely close relationship to individuals within the Saudi

[37] Groups involved in the bid included two Kuwaiti firms frequently noted throughout this book, Agility and KIPCO. The PPP also saw a 50% share of KHAC offered through the Kuwaiti stock market, further illustrating the tendencies discussed in Chapter 6.

ruling family is renowned among the country's business circles. Despite these linkages, the firm was hit hard by the slump in construction contracts and delayed government payments that followed the economic downturn. By late July 2017 the company was unable to meet at least $3.5 billion in debt obligations, and was forced to shutter amidst acrimonious accusations of mismanagement and corruption. More than 30,000 Saudi Oger employees were left stranded without pay, many of whom were subsequently swept up in the Saudi government's migrant deportation campaigns.

In the wake of the collapse, commentators described the fall of Saudi Oger in portentous terms, symbolic of the 'dramatic reordering of the business climate under Crown Prince Mohammed bin Salman' and 'a demonstration of what the current environment requires' (Nereim et al. 2017). Yet while such descriptions may capture the market-shaking significance of this incident, it is important not to conflate the end of one firm with the general trajectory of the GCC's capitalist class. Saudi Oger may no longer exist, but the geographically and sectorally diversified nature of conglomerate ownership mapped in earlier chapters means that the Hariri family's multi-billion-dollar wealth has been largely ring-fenced from these particular difficulties.[38] Moreover, Saudi Oger's misfortunes may have had as much to do with its particular allies within the Saudi ruling family than any market downturn. Traditionally, the firm's main link to the Al-Saud has been through Prince Abdul Aziz bin Fahd, who has been pushed to the side following the coming to power of King Salman.[39]

Indeed, the apparent marginalisation of the Hariri family by the new king and his crown prince, Mohammed Bin Salman, points to a reconfiguration of the long-standing relationships between certain parts of the Saudi capitalist class and the Saudi ruling family. Striking confirmation of this occurred in November 2017, with the shock move by MBS to detain more than 200 leading business people and members of the ruling family under the slogan of fighting corruption. The latter included prominent Saudi capitalists, including Al Waleed Bin Talal, Bakr Bin Laden, and Saleh Kamel. Those arrested were not taken to prison but held in the five-star Ritz Carlton Hotel in downtown Riyadh – where a storm of social media rumours alleged torture and mistreatment of those detained. Somewhat ironically given the Hariri family's apparent marginalisation by MBS, the palatial detention facility had actually been built by Saudi Oger some years previously.

[38] This observation was pointed out to me by a lawyer who has worked closely with the firm on bids in the Gulf.

[39] Some commentators have also pointed to Saudi displeasure with Sa'ad Hariri's ability to uphold their interests in Lebanon – a premise that appeared to receive some confirmation following the surprise resignation (later put on hold) of Hariri from the position of Lebanese prime minister in Saudi Arabia in November 2017 (see Chapter 8).

At this stage, it appears that the motivations for these detentions have much to do with the reinstitutionalisation of state power described earlier in this chapter – most particularly the centralisation of state power in the hands of MBS and his closest allies, and an attempt to weaken rival branches of the ruling family. It is notable that the business leaders arrested are closely associated with wings of the Saudi ruling family outside the Sudairi lineage. In addition, MBS appears to be attempting to displace criticism of his economic reforms and the ongoing war in Yemen (see Chapter 8) by playing to popular resentment against Saudi Arabia's richest businesspeople. Given the political conditions in the country, it is difficult to measure such popular sentiments with any certainty, but if Saudi-based Twitter and social media accounts are any indication, then the move appears to have been met with a measurable level of support by Saudi citizenry. Finally, an important factor within this has been an attempt to raise funds from the Saudi capitalist classes – those detained have been offered their freedom in return for billion-dollar payments (Kerr 2017). In this sense, the detentions can be seen as akin to 'forcible taxation' in a country where corporate taxes are non-existent.

These shifting alliances within and between the Saudi state and capitalist class need to be situated in the increasingly differentiated impact of the economic downturn on capital accumulation in the Gulf. Despite the slowing growth and cuts to project spending, the largest Gulf firms have weathered the economic storm with resilience, faring much better than smaller capitals and the average Gulf citizen (or migrant worker). One indication of this can be seen in the trajectory of profits for firms listed on Gulf stock exchanges. Table 7.3 shows the change in total reported profits for all listed companies across the Gulf from 2015 through to the first quarter of 2017. It illustrates that the aggregate profits of firms listed on the five largest Gulf stock exchanges (Saudi Arabia, Dubai, Abu Dhabi, Kuwait, and Qatar) registered significant declines in 2016 in comparison with 2015 – ranging from a 2.7% drop in Kuwait to 12.2% in Qatar. Only in the much smaller markets of Bahrain and Oman did the balance sheets of firms remain relatively healthy. However, if we disaggregate these firms according to market capitalisation, a striking pattern emerges: the economic downturn has had remarkably different effects on firms depending upon their size. The most powerful firms – those within the top 10% of firms ranked by stock market capitalisation – were relatively unaffected by the downturn through 2016. In Dubai and Kuwait, these large firms actually managed to register a considerable growth in profits in 2016 compared with the previous year, while profits earned by smaller companies showed double-digit declines. In Saudi Arabia, Abu Dhabi, and Qatar, aggregate profits of the largest companies

Table 7.3 *Change in reported profits of listed firms (%)*

	2015–2016 (%)			Q1 2017 compared with Q1 2016			Proportion of total market capitalisation held by top 10% of firms	
	All firms	Top 10% of firms	Bottom 90% of firms	All firms	Top 10% of firms	Bottom 90% of firms	31 Dec 2016	31 Dec 2013
Saudi Arabia	−6.2%	−2.0%	−18.9%	42.1%	55.1%	1.2%	70%	66%
Dubai	−6.4%	7.3%	−33.8%	−10.5%	5.6%	−37.7%	62%	62%
Abu Dhabi	−8.7%	−2.3%	−43.9%	8.3%	13.1%	−13.1%	77%	68%
Kuwait	−2.7%	6.2%	−29.4%	3.0%	4.0%	1.0%	71%	72%
Qatar	−12.2%	−0.7%	−22.0%	−0.8%	12.7%	−13.2%	56%	56%
Bahrain	28.2%	34.2%	18.1%	14.5%	16.7%	10.7%	59%	55%
Oman	13.4%	14.3%	11.5%	−34.0%	−8.8%	−75.6%	60%	61%

Source: Calculated from GCC stock exchange data and company reports; top 10% of firms ranked by market capitalisation (2016).

fell only slightly, while the rest of the market was very badly hit. Indeed, in Saudi Arabia, Abu Dhabi, Dubai, and Kuwait, none of the firms within the top decile registered a loss in 2016, while more than 15% of smaller firms fell into the red for that year.[40] In Bahrain and Oman where markets performed well, profits of the largest firms grew at a much more rapid pace than the bottom 90% of firms.

Table 7.3 also compares the net profits reported by companies in the first quarter of 2017 with those made in the same period a year earlier. Here, there has been a marked improvement in most markets across the Gulf. This recovery, however, has been largely limited to the biggest firms; these market leaders have generally recorded significant increases in their profits through 2017 (with the exception of firms in Oman). In contrast, smaller firms have struggled considerably – barely making a net profit in Saudi Arabia and Kuwait, and seeing double-digit declines in all other markets (with the exception of Bahrain, where a $10 billion fund established by other GCC states in the wake of the country's 2011 revolt has continued to prop up project spending).[41]

The final column in Table 7.3 shows that alongside this very uneven impact of the downturn on different firms there has also been a shift in the concentration of capital held by the largest companies. For the important markets of Saudi Arabia and Abu Dhabi, the proportion of total market capital held by the top 10% of firms has increased significantly since the year prior to the oil price decline (2013). Although it is too early to predict how such market concentration might evolve over coming years, it is clear (at least in some markets) that the slowdown has had the effect of increasing the relative weight of a handful of very large firms. Taken as a whole, the figures in Table 7.3 illustrate that the Gulf's largest firms have performed relatively well throughout the downturn, while their smaller peers have struggled to maintain profitability in the new economic conditions.

These trends are highly revealing and help in more fully interpreting the impact of the oil price decline on corporate power structures in the GCC. The top decile of firms illustrated in Table 7.3 encompasses many of the conglomerates discussed in this book, including the major banks, telecoms, real estate developers, and agro-industrial companies. Of course, profit rates for individual companies fluctuate year by year and some large companies have indeed suffered declines, but the general trajectory is clear: regardless of the considerable retrenchment in public

[40] Calculated from stock exchange data.

[41] The fact this fund has continued to operate, despite the more general cuts to public spending across the Gulf, provides strong evidence of the political fears that the popular uprising in Bahrain provoked among neighbouring GCC states.

spending and the related plunge in construction activity described earlier, the core of Gulf capital has continued to grow throughout the slowdown. As with economic downturn more generally, crisis has acted to increase competitive tendencies in the Gulf, consolidating market power in the hands of the largest firms at the expense of weaker capitals.

The figures shown in Table 7.3 are limited to firms that are publicly listed and thus do not include all of the large privately held Gulf conglomerates (such as Saudi Oger). There is suggestive evidence, however, that notwithstanding the declining oil price, owners of such conglomerates have also prospered. According to data on the fortunes of the billionaire and ultra-high-net-worth class in the Gulf, overall private wealth has increased significantly since 2014. Indeed, the most recent study of the Wealth-X database, a renowned tracker of the world's billionaires, shows that despite a global fall in both the absolute number and collective wealth of billionaires across the world in 2016 – the first annual decline since the 2008 financial crisis – wealth levels in the Gulf have actually increased. Aside from North America, the Middle East was the only region in the world that registered a growth in the number and total wealth of billionaires during 2016, with the vast majority of the Middle East's billionaires located in the GCC (Wealth-X 2017).[42] Saudi Arabia and the UAE ranked number 9 and 10 in the world, respectively, for the absolute number of billionaires, each holding more billionaires than countries such as France, Italy, Spain, or Australia. The collective wealth of these 109 Saudi and Emirati billionaires reached $332 billion. Remarkably, the Saudi-UAE axis now holds the fourth largest number of billionaires in the world (behind the United States, China, and Germany) and – excluding the wealth held by US billionaires – makes up just under 7% of the total wealth held by billionaires across the world.

Such figures support the argument that there has been little dent in the fortunes of the Gulf's wealthiest individuals in the wake of the oil price decline. Beyond the billionaire class, data for the private wealth held by ultra-high-net-worth individuals (those with net disposable private wealth of more than $100 million) provide further evidence for how elites in the Gulf have fared during the economic downturn. According to the 2017 annual report of the Boston Consulting Group, an advisory company that tracks

[42] The Wealth-X report divides the world into seven regions: North America, Europe, Latin America and the Caribbean, Africa, the Middle East, Asia, and the Pacific. This figure for increasing wealth in the Gulf actually refers to billionaires across the entire Middle East, but the vast majority of total Middle East billionaires are located in Saudi Arabia, the UAE, Israel, and Turkey (161 of 169). Israel and Turkey experienced significant declines in the number and wealth of their billionaires during 2016, so it can be assumed that the overall increase in Middle East billionaires came from the GCC.

private wealth globally, GCC ultra-high-net-worth individuals experienced a very sharp rise in their wealth through 2016. Growth rates in ultra-high-net-worth individuals' private wealth averaged just under 12% across the six Gulf states, ranging from a 6.7% rise in Saudi Arabia to a lucrative 23% growth in Qatar (Boston Consulting Group (BCG) 2017).[43] At the same time, the absolute number of millionaire households also increased across all Gulf states, most notably in the UAE and Oman, where levels grew by nearly 6%. It should be noted that other studies have found a simultaneous drop in per capita citizen wealth across the Gulf between 2015 and 2016 (Credit Suisse 2016, pp. 91–98); placed alongside the prodigious growth in the wealth of high net worth individuals, this demonstrates once again the differential impact of the downturn on citizens in the region.

This growing prosperity of the Gulf's ultra-rich affirms the patterns of capital accumulation I have mapped previously – as the Boston Consulting Group noted in their 2017 Annual Report, Middle East billionaires are particularly distinguished by 'the international diversification of their investment and business holdings', tending to hold a much higher proportion of their wealth in offshore financial centres or other overseas investment. In 2017, nearly one-quarter of the Middle East's private wealth was held offshore – a figure that was the second highest of any region in the world (just behind Latin America) and that constituted 18% of the world's total offshore private wealth (BCG 2017, p. 14). Of course, all the provisos about such data discussed in Chapter 2 must be kept in mind, but the evidence strongly suggests that the internationalisation of Gulf capital – coupled with the particular policy orientation of Gulf states since the downturn began – has enabled the wealthiest layers of Gulf society to endure the downturn with little negative impact on their bottom line.

7.4 Conclusion

Given the ongoing nature of the economic downturn, all of the policies and trends discussed here remain in flux. Whether the various targets and goals are ultimately met remains an open question, dependent upon factors such as the future price of oil, political developments in the GCC, and the overall direction of the global economy. Nonetheless, as MBS's November 2017 detention of Saudi princes and corporate leaders indicates, this is indisputably a moment of change, one that heralds a significant reinvention of state–class relations in the Gulf and associated

[43] Ultra-high-net-worth individuals are defined as those with more than US$100 million. Figures for the other GCC states are Bahrain (7.6%), UAE (8.8%), Oman (14.6%), and Kuwait (9.6%).

patterns of capital accumulation. At the same time, in both word and deed, the ultimate priority of Gulf policymaking remains one of supporting the growth and expansion of private markets, with crises – both real and manufactured – wielded to restructure economic activities in ways that appeared previously off limits. In this respect, however labile and destabilising they may be, the strategic transformations currently under way in the GCC are best seen as 'visions of capital': the new normal marks an intensification of potentialities latent in the old – a moment in which the paths examined throughout earlier chapters will be further extended.

Those who stand to lose within this framework are poorer citizens and, of course, the Gulf's large migrant workforce. The former are threatened with an undermining of the type of state–citizen compact that has characterised the Gulf for many decades, in which citizens are overwhelmingly employed in public-sector jobs with much better pay and conditions than most private-sector workers. Coupled with the cuts to social spending and the introduction of new taxes, the erosion of benefits traditionally associated with citizenship will have volatile and serious ramifications. This is particularly true for Saudi Arabia and Oman, where large and youthful citizen populations face the prospect of a significant decline in living standards and a potentially historic change in their relationship to the state.

For migrant workers, the situation is even more precarious. The drop in migrant remittance flows and the associated policies that are causally linked to it – deportations, mass redundancies, wage cuts, and deepening attacks on migrant rights – are essential to interpreting both the effects of the current economic downturn and the Gulf's particular response to it. As with other moments of crisis historically – notably the 2008–2009 global economic crash – what we appear to be witnessing from the vantage point of 2017 is the partial displacement of crisis to neighbouring zones through the channel of migrant labour (Hanieh 2011a, pp. 177–180). If this continues for any sustained period of time, it could have critical implications for labour-sending countries. Across South Asia, for example, remittance inflows are greater than 5% of GDP in Pakistan, Bangladesh, Sri Lanka, and Nepal (based upon 2016 figures), and the vast majority of overseas workers from these countries – approaching 90% in some cases – are located in the Gulf.[44]

[44] Moreover, these aggregate figures need to be differentiated on a subnational basis – certain geographical areas within countries tend to be much more tightly linked to Gulf labour markets than others. Remittances to India, for example, constitute a relatively low level of the country's overall GDP. But for the Indian state of Kerala, a major source of migrant workers to the GCC, remittances are estimated to make up more than 36% of the net state domestic product and are a vital component of household consumption (World Bank 2017b, p. 27).

In this sense, any analysis of the Gulf's response to the economic downturn cannot be confined within the borders of the national scale.

These trends illustrate the close linkages between crisis, economic downturn, and the delineation of class power in the Gulf. While the oil price decline has had – and will likely continue to have –a serious impact on the GCC's aggregate economic health, the full implications of this must be viewed through the specificities of class formation in the Gulf. The kinds of transformations under way in the GCC – ostensibly propelled and legitimated by the economic downturn – are principally aimed at augmenting, extending, and deepening the boundaries of capitalist markets. Significantly, however, all of these intense changes to the Gulf's economic and social structures are occurring at a time in which the wider Middle East region is reeling from multiple, severe shocks – from the devastating wars in Syria, Yemen, and Libya to the reassertion of authoritarian rule and the return of old elites in countries such as Egypt and Tunisia. Closely linked to these explosive conditions is the reappearance of schisms within the GCC itself; most notably demonstrated in the 'cold war' that emerged between Qatar and the Saudi-UAE axis during the first half of 2017. The Gulf's fortunes, both literally and figuratively, are increasingly bound up with these political flashpoints and the trajectories of the wider regional scale. It is to these questions that the final chapter turns.

8 Future Paths and Political Ends

The stream of inquiries began in mid-2017. It had been three years since the two brothers' agro-industry factory in Lebanon's Beqaa Valley ground to a halt due to the war in neighbouring Syria. But around June, they began to receive requests from visitors interested in purchasing the factory. Most of these visitors came from intermediaries representing Saudi agribusiness firms and other investors, including the massive Al Marai. At least ten such offers were made through June and July 2017. Other neighbouring businesses were also being approached – farms, as well as factories for agricultural produce and food-related industries involved in bottling, plastics, and packaging. It wasn't simply Saudi firms – Kuwaiti, Emirati and Qatari investors were fanning out across this rich agricultural area in search of business opportunities, offering rock-bottom prices for assets abandoned because of the war. A constant refrain heard from these eager investors was the chance promised by reconstruction in Syria – they saw this as an opportune moment to place themselves at the centre of the Beqaa's agro-industries – a key link to rebuilding agricultural chains in a post-conflict Syria.

This story, recounted to me through an intermediary in Lebanon in mid-2017, illustrates an incongruous feature of the violent crises currently wracking the Arab world: alongside mass displacement and widespread destruction, new business openings are being sought out and fought over, and private investors are beginning to look to the prodigious material prizes promised in the phase of reconstruction with keen interest. The experience spoken of is but a small microcosm of the investment opportunities that are expected to materialise in the coming period. Very conservative estimates from 2016 put the cost of rebuilding infrastructure alone at $300 billion to $400 billion for just Syria, Yemen, and Libya.[1] Abdullah Dardari, appointed as Senior Advisor on Reconstruction to the World Bank in February 2017, claims that the business

[1] The cost of rebuilding Syria's infrastructure have been estimated by the IMF at between $100 billion and $200 billion (Gobat and Kostial 2016); that of Libya at $200 billion (World Bank 2016) and Yemen at $15 billion (AlAraby 2016).

opportunities arising from this expenditure will position the Middle East as the only 'centre of growth in the world economy in the next ten years' (Saoud 2016, p. 19). While undoubtedly an exaggeration, such an assessment is nonetheless highly revealing – illustrating the huge value of reconstruction costs, as well as their potential effects on the region's economies over the coming period. Coupled with the spending in those countries less directly affected by conflict, the projected economic boom is unprecedented in both scope and scale.

These forecasts are a direct corollary of a wave of social destruction unique in modern Middle East history. Central to this crisis are the many millions of people pushed across borders or displaced within their own countries, which today make the Middle East the site of the largest forced displacement since the Second World War. Remarkably, Iraq, Yemen, and Syria together accounted for more than half of all internally displaced persons (IDPs) worldwide in 2015 (World Bank 2017c, p. 26). The epicentre of this displacement is Syria, where more than 11.5 million people – half the country's pre-conflict population – have been pushed from their homes (World Bank 2017c, p. 18). More than one-third of this number have been driven outside the country's borders, while Syria now ranks second in the world for the number of IDPs (after Colombia). In addition to this devastating mass displacement, around half a million people have been killed and more than a million injured; indeed, the proportion of the Syrian population killed in the war has reached the same level as the 1980–1988 war between Iraq and Iran – a protracted, bloody conflict that ranks as the longest conventional war of the twentieth century, and whose physical and psychological effects continue to haunt subsequent generations. If the war in Syria had not taken place, the country's population should have reached close to 26 million people by 2015; its actual level today stands at almost 28% less than this number (World Bank 2017c, p. 18).[2]

[2] The scale of such casualties and displacement has torn apart the livelihoods of millions of Syrians. The UN Economic and Social Commission for West Asia estimates that the unemployment rate reached more than two-thirds of the Syrian population in 2015, while the number of people living below the poverty line now encompasses more than 85% of the population (World Bank 2017c, p. 18). More than one-third of the population have only limited access to basic food. Around half of Syrian children are not in school, according to UNICEF, and the rate of child marriages has increased dramatically among refugees (UN Women 2013). The bombing of hospitals and medical facilities, lack of pharmaceuticals, and shortage of medical personnel has meant the reappearance of diseases that had previously been eradicated; vaccination levels have dropped to less than 70%, and in some areas are non-existent (World Bank 2017c, p. 20). All of these horrific figures represent aggregate numbers and thus considerably understate the actual predicament facing many Syrians – across the most affected areas and population groups (particularly those who are displaced), the actual situation is much, much worse.

Of course, Syria is not the only country in the Middle East wracked by such destruction. Yemen is experiencing what UN officials describe as the 'world's largest humanitarian crisis' following a Saudi-led (and US/British-backed) bombing campaign that began in 2015 (UNICEF 2017). This is an 'entirely man-made catastrophe', according to a report issued by the UN Human Rights Council in early September 2017, which has killed more than 10,000 civilians and seen more than 3 million of the country's 28-million-strong population displaced in just over two years of fighting (UN OHCHR 2017). Such high levels of displacement put considerable pressure on both those who have fled and their host communities – in some areas of the country, the number of IDPs and other refugees makes up around 20% of the entire population (OCHA 2016, p. 14). These figures need to be overlaid on an already chronic humanitarian crisis that existed prior to the bombing campaign. More than half the Yemeni population lacks reliable access to sufficient quantities of food, drinking water, sanitation, and basic healthcare – in 2016, the absolute number of food-insecure people in Yemen was the second highest in the world (after north Nigeria), with levels increasing by one-third since 2014 (Food Security Information Network (FSIN) 2017, pp. 21, 114). Up to 7 million people were at the risk of famine in March 2017, and – coupled with the destruction of medical facilities and hospitals – easily treatable diseases such as cholera are spreading rapidly, particularly among vulnerable populations such as IDPs and children (Office for the Coordination of Humanitarian Affairs (OCHA) 2016, p. 30).[3]

Likewise, violence continues to cascade throughout Iraq and Libya where the numbers of displaced make up approximately 10% of the population, and people in need of protection and humanitarian assistance exceed 30% (WHO 2016; OCHA 2017). The territory of both these countries has been fractured into divided enclaves, with their shattered social structures ruled over by different centres of power and armed groups – an outcome of war that foreshadows the possible futures of Syria and Yemen. Moreover, the effects of such conflicts are not confined to those countries directly suffering internal violence; the resulting displacement has also deeply shaken Lebanon, Jordan, Tunisia, and Egypt, countries already host to significant refugee communities before the onset of the current wars. Never before has the Middle East faced such simultaneity of conflict – affecting millions of people across all countries in the region.

[3] Indeed, the number of people who had contracted cholera in Yemen reached the 1 million mark by the end of 2017, the largest figure for any country since records began – and one even greater than the 2011 outbreak in Haiti (Guardian 2017).

In this concluding chapter, I seek to place these conflicts and the dynamics of the current political moment in the context of the Gulf and the patterns of regional accumulation traced throughout this book. I have argued that forms of capitalism in the Gulf – always co-constituted within the making of global capitalism and the particular position of the United States within this – are acutely bound up with the changing character of the regional scale. The Middle East has become increasingly affixed to the ebbs and flows of accumulation in the Gulf, tying the nature of Arab class and state formation to the exigencies of the largest Gulf conglomerates and the machinations of the Gulf's political power. The multiple crises seen across the Middle East directly reflect how this structure evolved since the region-wide revolts that began in 2010 and 2011 – a wave of popular uprisings that has set in train a scramble to both reassemble the hierarchies of the regional system and to shape its future paths. Echoing arguments made in previous chapters, this is another illustration of 'crisis as opportunity', an attempt by various powers – prominent among them the Gulf states – to remake the Middle East in a manner that simultaneously preserves and extends what went before. Yet precisely because this is a moment of such extreme flux and uncertainty, all the contradictions of the regional scale are profoundly accentuated, with deepening tensions emerging both within the GCC itself and between the Gulf and other regional and international powers vying for influence.

Beginning with the context of the Arab uprisings, the first part of this chapter outlines the constantly shifting political alignments of the Gulf over recent years, focusing in particular on the Saudi-UAE conflicts with both Iran and Qatar, as well as the increasingly open alliance between Saudi Arabia, the UAE, and Israel. Each of these relationships is mediated through an array of political forces within different Arab states, and must always be situated in the ever-important position of the region to global capitalism and the forms of US power. The second part of the chapter turns to the political economy dynamics underlying how the Gulf and other actors are engaging with the current moment – a factor that is typically ignored or downplayed in relation to interstate rivalries. Here, building upon the analysis of previous chapters, I look at the renewed penetration of the region by international financial institutions (IFIs), as well as the question of humanitarian support and reconstruction aid. I argue that the manner in which the political transitions and crises are being addressed – shaped by the modalities of loans and aid flows coming from both within and outside the region – is acting to intensify the neoliberal trajectories of past years. Within this response to crisis, the Gulf's role remains paramount.

8.1 Remaking the Middle East?

I have foregrounded this chapter with the violence in Syria, Yemen, and elsewhere not only to convey the scale of social destruction unfolding in the region, but also because these conflicts tell us how far things have moved from the hope initially embodied in the popular uprisings that began in 2010. Throughout their first phase – which saw the immediate overthrow of Ben Ali in Tunisia and Mubarak in Egypt, and the rapid spread of mass protests across all Arab states – these uprisings sought an end to authoritarian rule and expressed widely felt aspirations for a new political order (Bogaert 2013; Hanieh 2013; Beinin 2015; Achcar 2016). Although the demands of participants were varied and cut across different social groups, the remarkable manner in which these protests leapt across borders and touched every area of the Arab world – from Morocco to the Gulf – demonstrates the commonalities of lived experience throughout the region. This was the single most powerful expression of popular anger against the established political class since the post-war Arab nationalist struggles; in this sense, the mass protests forcefully destabilised – whether consciously or not – a regional system that had been nearly four decades in the making.

Precisely because of their regional orientation, the Arab uprisings appeared as a particularly serious challenge to US imperial strategy – and that of other Western states – in the Middle East. Through the late twentieth century, this strategy had come to rely upon three main pillars of regional support – Israel, the GCC, and a range of Arab client regimes – each with their own distinctive relationships to the core powers of the global economy (Hanieh 2013, ch. 2). For the Arab client states in particular, the West's economic, political, and military support would help underpin authoritarian governments that had little interest in upsetting the regional order – epitomised most visibly in the decades-long rule of individuals such as Mubarak and Ben Ali. The GCC came to play a critical role within this regional arrangement of power, in terms of both its unique multidecade strategic connection to the United States and its own significant interests across other Arab states.

The stability of these political arrangements, however, was thrown sharply into question following the popular uprisings that unfolded across the region through 2011 and onwards. The profound destabilisation caused by the uprisings was not only seen across North Africa and the Levant but also felt overtly in the Gulf – with protests in Bahrain, Oman, and other Gulf states directly expressing social and economic grievances and confronting the entrenched position of ruling families. In the Gulf these protests were largely quashed, most notably through the

2011 Saudi-led intervention in support of Bahrain's monarchy – but across the wider Middle East, the uprisings threatened to overturn the particular regional hierarchies superintended by the Gulf. Arab authoritarian rulers were a functional element to maintaining this hierarchical structure; it was no accident that as the power of these rulers and their coterie of business allies appeared to stumble through 2011 and 2012, many were to seek refuge in the GCC.[4]

In this context, the second phase of the uprisings saw a determined effort by Arab political and economic elites, Western countries, and other powers vying for regional influence to remake the Middle East in a way amenable to their continued interests. The crises that have emerged since that time are a direct consequence of this effort, which can be summed up in two interconnected objectives: (1) an attempt to crush the popular aspirations of the uprisings and protect (and extend) the socioeconomic structures that preceded the uprisings, and (2) the connected bid by major international and regional powers – including, but not limited to, the United States, EU, Russia, the GCC, Iran, and Turkey – to project their own influence over this newly fashioned regional order. A multiplicity of political, economic, and military efforts has underpinned these two goals, including direct intervention in the wars under way across the region, as well as the support and funding of governments and political movements deemed to best represent the rival interests of contesting powers. As has been seen so often throughout the preceding chapters, moments of crisis are also moments of change and fluidity. The leading forces within the region have sought to embrace this malleability – not only to preserve the fundamental features of the regional political economy, but to also mould a future advantageous to their own perceived interests.

The GCC has emerged as a key protagonist within these dual processes. From the wars in Syria and Libya – where different Gulf states have supported a range of varying factions – to the catastrophic bombing of Yemen, the Gulf has been the main Arab political force involved in these conflicts. The GCC did not directly initiate these wars – each has its own roots in the political struggles that emerged in the wake of the uprisings – but it has powerfully shaped their subsequent trajectories. Intervening through both direct and indirect means, the various Gulf

[4] Tunisian President Ben Ali fled to Saudi Arabia; his wife, Leila Trabelsi, left for Dubai (although not before removing more than a ton and a half of Tunisia's gold from the central bank); while Ben Ali's daughter and son-in-law, businessman Mohamed Sakher El Materi, fled to Qatar. Yemeni president Ali Abdullah Saleh sought refuge in Saudi Arabia. News reports also noted that a large number of Egyptian businessmen flew to Dubai during the course of the revolution in 2011.

states have attempted to project themselves as the dominant regional powers in the Middle East. In doing so, a whole series of sharp regional ruptures and new political alignments have been generated.

One of the most significant of these emergent tensions is the escalating conflict between Saudi Arabia and the UAE, on one side, and Iran, on the other. In popular accounts, this conflict is often explained through a sectarian lens – pitting the Gulf's Sunni leaders against Iran's Shi'a faith. But while there has been significant repression directed against Shi'a communities in the GCC states – notably in Bahrain – the antagonism with Iran cannot be reduced to a simple religious schism. The explosive growth in sectarianism over recent years has much more profane political roots stretching back to the 1979 Iranian revolution and the 1980s Iraq–Iran War, through which Iran emerged as the principal rival of Saudi hegemony in the Gulf (indeed, one of the main justifications for the initial formation of the GCC in 1981 was precisely this rivalry). Since this time, both Iran and the Gulf states have consistently wielded Islam for very political reasons – as a means to promote their regional influence and isolate political opponents. For Saudi Arabia, this took place through the building of a global network of mosques and religious schools inspired by a Wahhabi version of Islam, and the sponsoring of various Islamist political movements. In the case of Iran, it has been the long-standing alliance with Shi'a movements in Lebanon through the years of the Lebanese Civil War, which led to the founding of Hezbollah in 1985, and, later, Iranian support to the Assad government in Syria, and Shi'a movements and religious scholars in Iraq. Such instrumentalisation of Islam is not confined to Saudi Arabia or Iran – it can be found throughout the Middle East (and beyond). It is deeply connected to the weakening of Arab leftist and secular nationalist forces since the 1980s (Achcar 2002) and – a fact that is often not well understood – the emergence of new fractions of capital that have used religious discourse as a means of building cross-class hegemonic projects (Amel 1986; Balkan et al. 2015).

In the post-2011 struggle to redraw the Middle East map, both the GCC and Iran have intensified this pattern of deliberately fostering sectarian conflict for political ends. This became particularly evident following the ascendance of King Salman to the Saudi throne, and his appointment of Mohammed Bin Salman as defence minister and crown prince. Both father and son have consciously heightened the Gulf's conflict with Iran, and have found a reliable and enthusiastic ally in the crown prince of Abu Dhabi, Mohammed bin Zayed bin Sultan Al-Nahyan. Acting through this united front, Saudi Arabia and the UAE have sought to use the rivalry with Iran as a means to step up their own direct intervention in the region, thereby implanting themselves at the centre of any eventual political transitions or settlements. The ramifications of this interregional conflict are expressed across all countries in the Middle East, but they are most intensely felt in Yemen, Syria, Iraq, and Lebanon – four countries that, to varying degrees, remain outside the Gulf's full orbit of control.

One example of this is the 2015 Saudi war against Yemen, which was orchestrated and led by MBS in his position as defence minister. This conflict is a palpable demonstration of the extreme inequalities that today characterise the regional scale, with the border between the two countries marking the division between the poorest and richest zones in the Middle East. The bombing campaign aimed to restore to power the Saudi-backed Yemeni president, Abd Rabbuh Mansour Hadi, who became the country's leader in 2012. Hadi had been ousted in March 2015 by a Yemeni political movement located in the north of the country, the Houthis, who were acting in partnership with the country's previous ruler and former Saudi ally, Ali Abdullah Saleh (infamous for describing his more than three-decade rule over Yemen as akin to 'dancing on the heads of snakes'). After he was forced from power, Hadi fled to Riyadh, and the subsequent Saudi bombing campaign has used the claim of Iranian influence over the Houthis as its key justification (Al Jubeir 2016). This allegation plays largely a mobilising and ideological role – in reality, the Houthis embrace a radically different brand of Shiism than Iran, and have long-standing grievances against the Yemeni state that both predate the current conflict and have little to do with Iran.[5] Nonetheless, the ways in which the conflict has been framed by Saudi media as well as the country's political leaders demonstrate the pernicious functionality of anti-Iranian sectarianism – and its utility in deepening Saudi influence over Yemeni politics.[6]

Likewise, in the case of Syria, the Gulf states' support of various opposition forces and armed groups has primarily aimed at placing themselves upfront as the key interlocutors in the political future of the country, rather than showing any genuine concern with the Syrian uprising. This uprising was an integral part of the revolutionary wave that cascaded across the

[5] The Houthis – known officially as Ansar Allah [Partisans of Allah] – follow the Zaidi branch of Shi'ism, while Iran represents the Twelver branch (recognising twelve legitimate successors to the Prophet Mohammed). The Houthis have fought for greater political and economic rights in Yemen for several decades, with war first breaking out with the central government (then headed by Ali Abdullah Saleh) in 2004.

[6] The Saudi bombing campaign has been strongly supported – both materially and logistically – by the United States, first under Obama and now to an even greater degree by the Trump administration. The United Kingdom has also provided support for the attack.

region in 2011; protestors confronted the extreme authoritarianism of the Assad family, who had ruled the country for four decades and had used this position to plunder billions of dollars' worth of state assets for themselves and close allies (particularly following a liberalisation process that begun to take root through the 1980s and 1990s). The Gulf came late to the Syrian conflict, with Saudi Arabia, the UAE, and Qatar all initially condemning the protest movements and expressing fulsome support for Bashar Al-Assad's continued rule (Phillips 2016, p. 65). But as the violence intensified through 2012 and 2013, the Gulf states began to seek out various elements of the opposition in order to counter the Iranian (and Russian) support that was the mainstay of survival for the Assad regime. Coupled with the deliberate sectarian turn of this regime and its bloody repression against the Syrian population –made possible only through Russian and Iranian backing – the GCC involvement in Syria worked to undermine the popular, democratic character of the Syrian uprising.[7] Moreover, all of these factors helped create a fertile ground for the rise of various Islamic fundamentalist groups, such as ISIS.[8]

Up until this moment, the tensions between Saudi Arabia and Iran have largely been expressed through these other conflicts in the region. But the antagonisms grew considerably through the latter part of 2017, most notably after the shock resignation of Sa'ad Hariri as Lebanese prime minister on 4 November. The resignation was 'put on hold' a few days later, but the fact that it was announced in Riyadh provided a stunning confirmation of the close relationship between Saudi power and Lebanese politics noted frequently throughout this book.[9] In a thinly veiled reference to Iran's support for Hezbollah in Lebanon, Hariri warned: 'Wherever Iran settles, it sows discord, devastation and destruction, proven by

[7] The popular character of the uprising is perhaps best illustrated by the *tansiqiyyat* (coordinating groups) found across the country in the early years of the revolution, which sought to organise the uprising and defend communities from regime attacks. They were heavily repressed through targeted killings and forced disappearances by the Syrian military and intelligence forces.

[8] The ideological and organisational roots of such groups predate the conflict in Syria and are particularly connected to the successive US-led wars and occupation of neighbouring Iraq in the 1990s and 2000s – but their recent growth has found nurture in a country where all foreign actors (including the Gulf and Iran) have elaborated their intervention through sectarian means.

[9] The particular ways in which the Hariri family's accumulation stretches across multiple spaces while remaining firmly dependent upon Gulf capitalism is essential to understanding this political relationship. As a confidential memo from the US Embassy in Beirut was to note in 2006, because 'a major part of the Hariri fortune remains based in Saudi Arabia', Saudi Arabia held 'considerable financial leverage over Saad'. Indeed, the US Embassy went on to give credence to a widespread rumour that the Saudi government was deliberately paying Saad Hariri's firms at a slow pace in order to keep him 'a bit financially squeezed and thus susceptible to Saudi influence'.

its interference in the internal affairs of Arab countries . . . the hands that you have wickedly extended into [the region] will be cut off' (Barnard 2017). Concurrent with Hariri's resignation, Yemeni Houthi rebels fired a missile at Riyadh's airport; the missile was successfully intercepted, but a statement by the Saudi-led Arab military alliance fighting in Yemen described the attack as 'a blatant and direct military aggression by the Iranian regime' (Al Arabiya 2017). Where these increasingly bellicose accusations may lead remains an open question, but the possibility of a direct conflagration between two of the most well-armed militaries in the region – one that would undoubtedly draw in other states such as Israel, the United States, Egypt, and Russia – would have catastrophic consequences for the entire region.

Conflicts in the GCC

Closely connected to this dangerous brinkmanship, numerous schisms have also emerged within the GCC project itself. The most serious recent example of such internal GCC tensions came with the announcement, made on 5 June 2017, that Saudi Arabia, the UAE, Bahrain, and Egypt were suspending diplomatic ties with Qatar. The decision to shut down much of Qatar's maritime and land trade and halt flights by major Gulf air carriers – including Emirates, Gulf Air, FlyDubai, and Etihad Airways – reverberated across the Middle East. Qatari citizens living in Saudi Arabia and the other participating Gulf states were given two weeks to return home. The UAE outlawed any expression of sympathy for Qatar – including through Twitter – and offenders were threatened with jail terms of up to 15 years. Other governments closely linked to Saudi Arabia and the UAE quickly expressed support for the blockade, including the Tobruk-based House of Representatives in Libya (one of the country's warring governmental factions), the Saudi-backed Abd Rabbuh Mansour Hadi government in Yemen, and the Comoros, Mauritania, and the Maldives.[10]

[10] Not all GCC states or other regional actors supported the blockade. At the time of writing, Oman has allowed Qatar-bound ships to use its ports in place of Saudi Arabia and the UAE – while Kuwait has been engaged in frantic diplomatic efforts to diffuse the tensions. Only Bahrain has stood fully behind Saudi Arabia and the UAE, and this is largely due to the long-standing dependence of the ruling Al Khalifa monarchy on Saudi Arabia. Turkey has offered support to the embattled state including a promise to send troops to a Turkish military base located in Qatar, and Iran has pledged to send food and water, an attempt to overcome the closure of Qatar's sole land border with Saudi Arabia. Despite attempts by Saudi Arabia to bring on board other countries with large Muslim populations – such as Senegal, Niger, Djibouti, and Indonesia – these have largely been rebuffed. Arab countries such as Morocco, Algeria, and Tunisia have also rejected support for the blockade.

These moves followed months of hostile articles in US and Gulf media, and a range of aggressive statements by US, Saudi, and UAE officials alleging Qatari financing of Islamist groups and growing ties with Iran. One of the major protagonists in this campaign was the UAE ambassador to the United States, Yusef Otaiba, frequently described as 'Washington's most powerful ambassador' (Ahmed 2017). Since the beginning of the Arab uprisings, Otaibi had worked the corridors of power in Washington, warning about the threat that the popular revolts posed to the established order in the region, and claiming that Qatar was supporting movements and individuals hostile to Saudi Arabia and the UAE. This anti-Qatar campaign was taken up by former US government officials and think tanks, notably the neoconservative Foundation for the Defense of Democracies (FDD) – a prominent supporter of the 2003 invasion of Iraq – which convened a high-profile seminar on 23 May 2017 to discuss Qatar's relationship with the Muslim Brotherhood and the Trump administration's policy options. At this gathering, former US Secretary of Defense, Robert Gates, called on the US government to consider relocating its large and strategically significant Al-Udeid airbase from Qatar if the country did not cut its ties with groups such as the Muslim Brotherhood and Hamas. According to hacked emails released shortly after the FDD meeting, Gates's comments were supposedly encouraged and reviewed by Otaiba – indeed, one of the putative triggers for the Saudi-UAE blockade was this email leak, which revealed Otaiba's cosy relationship with Gates, FDD, and other Washington figures close to the Trump administration. Gulf media outlets accused Qatar of being behind the leak, an allegation that was denied by the Gulf state.

Together with support of the Muslim Brotherhood, both the UAE and Saudi Arabia claimed that Qatar had increasingly sought to strengthen ties to Iran over the early months of 2017. One piece of evidence offered for this rapprochement was the claim that Qatar recently paid $700 million to Iran in order to secure the release of 26 Qatari royals who had been kidnapped in Iraq in 2015 and had been held in Iran for a year and a half (Solomon 2017). This story – which also allegedly involved a separate payment of up to $300 million to Al Qaeda–aligned groups in Syria – was denied by Iraqi prime minister, Haider al-Abadi, who stated on 11 June that no money had been disbursed and Qatari funds remained in the Iraqi central bank. For its part, Saudi Arabia also pointed to a 23 May statement published on the state-owned Qatari News Agency containing comments from Qatar's leader, Tamim bin Hamad Al-Thani, who, during a graduation speech for National Guard officers at the Al Udeid military base, allegedly praised Iran and criticised other Gulf states who were seeking to brand the Muslim Brotherhood as a terrorist organisation. In response, Qatar claimed that the website carrying these comments had been hacked and that no such statements had ever been made – an assertion later supported by the FBI (Wintour 2017).

As part of its attempt to pressure Qatar, Saudi Arabia has sought to utilise the large and divided nature of the country's Al-Thani dynasty to cultivate a base of opposition from within the ruling family and among other Qatari tribes. A number of Qatari exiles with strong business and personal ties to Saudi Arabia have subsequently come out against Tamim Bin Hamad Al-Thani, most of whom are supporters of Qatar's former ruler, Sheikh Khalifah bin Hamad Al-Thani, who was deposed by Tamim's father in 1995.[11] Other dissidents whose Qatari citizenship had been revoked following a failed coup attempt in 1996 have also expressed opposition to the current emir.[12] Nonetheless, notwithstanding the fact that these opposition figures have received considerable attention in Saudi-owned media outlets – and were reported in early October 2017 to be planning a government-in-exile – they appear to have gained little support or traction within Qatar.

These moves highlight the main political fissures of the GCC project noted in preceding chapters. Despite the shared interests of different Gulf states, the GCC integration project did not extinguish their competitive rivalries; instead, a sharp hierarchy of political and economic power has marked the GCC since its inception, with the main pivot revolving around a Saudi-UAE axis. As I have discussed in some detail, these two countries have formed the core zones of capital accumulation in the Gulf and are the main mediating link between other Gulf states and the wider world market. Dominated by this Saudi-UAE axis, the other smaller Gulf states have felt themselves partly marginalised within the GCC's wider political and economic structures, muscled out by their two larger neighbours.[13] Qatar, in particular, with its tiny citizen population (only 313,000 citizens in a total population of 2.6 million) and its enormous wealth arising from its role as the world's largest exporter of liquefied natural gas, has particularly chafed at this hierarchical structure.

[11] Two examples are Sultan bin Suhaim Al-Thani, who is the nephew of Khalifah bin Hamad Al-Thani, and Abdullah bin Ali Al-Thani, a descendent of Qatar's founding ruler.

[12] These include up to 6,000 members of the Al Ghafran clan of the Al Murrah tribe, who had their citizenship revoked in 2005 as a result of their role in the 1996 attempted coup. They currently live in Saudi Arabia.

[13] The exception to this is Bahrain, which has been closely integrated into the Saudi-UAE axis. The ruling Al Khalifa monarchy depends ultimately upon Saudi financial, political, and military support (as shown by the Saudi-led intervention in Bahrain during the uprisings of 2011).

The tremendous uncertainty of the post-2011 regional environment has heightened these tensions within the GCC project. One consequence of this has been Qatar's attempt to carve out an autonomous regional policy for itself, and achieve a relative independence from Saudi Arabia and the UAE. Doha's attempted projection of power has occurred through financial and political support for different movements and governments across the region, and also its hosting of a variety of exiled individuals and political parties – these include the Muslim Brotherhood, Hamas, and the Taliban; the popular Egyptian cleric Sheikh Yusuf al-Qaradawi, who hosts regular and widely watched TV shows on Qatari channels; and individuals such as the Palestinian intellectual Azmi Bishara (now a Qatari citizen). In addition to such support, Qatar utilises an extensive media network to promote its regional interests (notably Al Jazeera and its affiliates, and, more recently, the daily newspaper and TV channel Al Araby Al Jadid, launched in early 2015).

As so often has been the case, as shown throughout this book, the archetypal example of how these tensions play out at the regional scale can be seen in Egypt, where through 2012 and the first half of 2013, Qatar acted as the primary backer of the Muslim Brotherhood. The Muslim Brotherhood was the most organised and deeply rooted political force in Egypt, and was viewed by much of the population as largely untainted by the Mubarak regime. In 2012, it won power in the country's first post-Mubarak elections, and the party's candidate, Mohammed Morsi, became the country's president. Qatar's capacious support of the Muslim Brotherhood was an attempt to bolster the Gulf's state own influence in Egypt; on the ground, however, it meant little deviation from the economic and social policies of the Mubarak period. In the context of massive popular discontent with the Muslim Brotherhood through 2013, the Egyptian military and the old elites associated with the Mubarak regime reversed this political arrangement, launching a bloody coup against Morsi and his supporters. Once again, the Gulf was the leading force behind the coup government, this time expressed through Saudi, UAE, and Kuwaiti support to the new president, General Abdel Fattah el-Sisi. An estimated total of US$12 billion was initially pledged by these three states in the wake of Morsi's ouster, and Gulf backing of Sisi has continued since that time in a variety of forms, including subsidised supplies of oil, loans, promises of massive investments, and the deposit of Gulf financial reserves in the Egyptian Central Bank (see later discussion).

Similarly, in the case of Tunisia, the GCC rift has been an important factor in the political transition that followed the departure of Ben Ali. Qatari overtures began after the victory of a coalition headed by the Islamist party Ennahda in the October 2011 elections. Ennahda is widely viewed as close to Qatar (and Turkey), and through 2012, Qatar provided Tunisia with large amounts of funding, including a $1 billion loan, half of which would go to strengthening the Tunisian Central Bank asset position (Bouazza 2012). The loan was equivalent to around 20% of Tunisia's external financing needs for that year, and came on the back of a visit to the GCC by then-Tunisian president Moncef Marzouki, where he urged the Gulf to invest in Tunisia and offered visa-free access for Gulf citizens travelling to the country. In addition to this loan, Qatar agreed to 10 other major investments worth billions in total – including funding for a $2 billion oil refinery that could potentially expand Tunisia's refining capacity fourfold (Al Masdar 2012). Part of the reason for such investments was Qatar's interest in making use of Tunisia as a potential gateway to Libya (where Qatar and Saudi/UAE have again taken up different sides) (Ulrichsen 2014, pp. 14–15). Further sign of the warming ties between Qatar and Tunisia was shown in the Gulf country's decision to expel Ben Ali's son-in-law, businessman Mohamed Sakher El Materi, who had sought refuge in Doha after the 2010 revolution – Qatar did not send him back for trial in Tunisia, however, but, rather, allowed him to travel to the Seychelles where he was granted residency.

Qatar's influence in Tunisia was cast into question following the 2014 parliamentary and presidential elections, which saw the defeat of Ennahda and the emergence of the Nidaa Tounes party as the leading political force. The victory of Nidaa Tounes represented a partial return of the old elites, and was accompanied by a reorientation of the country's relationship to the GCC. Although the polarisation of political alliances has not been as sharply manifest in Tunisia as it is has been in Egypt – partly related to Nidaa Tounes's more pragmatic foreign policy, as well as its decision to include Ennahdha in a ruling parliamentary coalition – there has nonetheless been a perceptible tilt towards Saudi Arabia and (to a lesser extent) the UAE. This has included a bilateral military cooperation agreement signed with Saudi Arabia in December 2015, followed by Tunisian participation in a Saudi-led joint military exercise held in the northeast of Saudi Arabia in February 2016. Large-scale Saudi investments have also been pledged, including Tunisia Economic City, a $50 billion project that is planned to stretch over 90 square kilometres and contain 15 smaller cities focused on sectors such as media, logistics, health care, and sports. The Tunisian government's sensitivity towards its ties with Saudi Arabia was indicated in November 2016, when the Tunisian Minister for Religious Affairs, Salem Abd El Jalil, was sacked for criticising Saudi Arabia's Wahhabi doctrine; a terse statement from the prime minister's office noted that El Jalil's dismissal came because he had shown 'lack of respect for government work ... and touched principles of Tunisian diplomacy' (Reuters 2016). Tunisia, however, has not aligned with Saudi Arabia and the UAE in their dispute with Qatar – pushing for reconciliation and calling on 'the brothers in the Gulf to find a solution that can satisfy all sides' (Jahanawi 2017).

These internecine rivalries are nothing new to the Gulf's fractious ruling families, but the Saudi/UAE decision to isolate Qatar has certainly marked a significant ratcheting-up of tensions within the Gulf. Nonetheless, these divisions cannot be understood separate from the fundamental dynamics of the GCC project; as I have repeatedly emphasised throughout this book, this is a bloc of states that is deeply integrated into a US-aligned power structure, has been a major beneficiary of neoliberal change in the Arab world, and has become more and more intertwined within the region's political dynamics in the post-2011 context. These commonalities of the GCC continue to sharply demarcate the bloc *as a whole* from the rest of the Arab world, despite the deep fissures between Saudi Arabia/UAE and Qatar.[14] The divergent strategies of GCC member states towards specific political forces in the Middle East is about calculated expediency and a pragmatic assessment of how best to further their individual regional influence, always within the framework of reordering the region in a way amenable to their collective dominance. Both tendencies need to be kept in mind when assessing the current conjuncture: a strong unanimity of interests that underpin the Gulf states' position atop the regional order (fully supported by – and in support of – Western powers) and, simultaneously, the very real presence of rivalries and competition between these states, ultimately reflected in different visions of how to redraw the map of the Middle East.

. . . and Israel

A further conspicuous feature of this post-2011 redrawing of the Middle East map is the move to normalise political and economic relations between Israel and the Saudi-UAE axis. Reflecting the three pillars of Western power

[14] The lukewarm reaction of the United States and other Western powers to the Saudi/UAE blockade is one illustration of this. Trump expressed implicit support of the blockade, claiming that the actions were a result of his meetings in Riyadh on 20 May 2017, but this is by no means the universal view in Washington, with other US officials – notably US Secretary of Defense Rex Tillerson – calling for an easing of the blockade and a peaceful solution as it was hindering US military efforts in the region. Indeed, in early November 2017, the US government approved a $1.1 billion military deal with Qatar, noting that the deal supported 'the foreign policy and national security objectives of the United States. Qatar is an important force for political stability and economic progress in the Persian Gulf region. Our mutual defense interests anchor our relationship' (Defense Security Cooperation Agency (DSCA) 2017).

described earlier, this move towards normalisation has been a long-standing objective of US and European policy in the region – particularly evident through the 1990s and the Oslo negotiations between Israel and the Palestine Liberation Organization (Hanieh 2013). The Saudi/UAE conflict with Iran and the still-unfolding outcomes of the Arab uprisings, however, have pushed this rapprochement forward in ways that appeared unimaginable a decade ago. One illustration of this was US president Donald Trump's first international trip in May 2017, which saw him visit first Saudi Arabia and then Israel (flying directly between the two), a travel itinerary that perfectly encapsulated the key US strategic priorities in the Middle East. Despite a muted response at the official level, several prominent Israeli leaders openly endorsed the Saudi-UAE actions against Qatar – echoing Israel's growing convergence with the two Gulf countries on many of the key political questions in the region (most significantly, that of Iran). Numerous direct ties involving political, commercial, and military activities have become openly apparent in recent times.

In late March 2017, Israeli newspapers reported that Israeli and UAE pilots flew alongside one another during the Iniochos exercise, a joint military training session held in Greece between 27 March and 6 April. Iniochos also saw the participation of US, Greek, and Italian air forces, and according to a US Air Force press release, the exercise sought to strengthen 'relationships, maintain joint readiness and interoperability, and reassure our regional Allies and partners' (Ahronheim 2017). This was not the first time such joint exercises took place. In August 2016, Israel and the UAE also met at the US Air Force's Red Flag aerial combat exercise in Nevada, along with Pakistan, Spain, and Jordan. The public nature of these exercises points to the increasingly brazen openness of military coordination between Israel and the UAE – something that would have not been possible a few short years ago.

Another indication of warming relations came with the November 2015 announcement that Israel would open a diplomatic mission in the UAE capital, Abu Dhabi. This mission was formally assigned not to the UAE but to the International Renewable Energy Agency (IRENA), an organisation noted in Chapter 7 as an important symbol of the UAE's turn to renewable energy markets. As the first Israeli diplomatic presence in the Gulf state, the mission's establishment has been described by Israeli officials as a 'diplomatic breakthrough', the ground for which was prepared in 2009 by Israel's vote for Abu Dhabi as the site for IRENA's headquarters (against the other contender, Germany) (Times of Israel (TOI) 2016). An explicit condition of this vote was that Israel would be permitted to establish a publicly acknowledged presence in the UAE – the office is also widely understood to act as an embassy for Israel's expanding ties in the Gulf.

Ties between Israel and Saudi Arabia are also increasingly public. Israeli media reported in mid-2015 that the two countries had held five clandestine meetings since early 2014 (TOI 2015). In June 2015, the then–director general of the Israeli ministry of foreign affairs, Dore Gold, spoke together with retired Saudi general Anwar Eshki in a public event at the US-based Council on Foreign Relations. In 2016, Eshki, who has also served in the Saudi foreign ministry, led a delegation of Saudi academics and businesspeople to Israel where they met with leading Israeli politicians and military figures. Similarly, in May 2016, former Israeli national security adviser Yaakov Amidror held a public discussion with the former Saudi intelligence chief Prince Turki al-Faisal at the Washington Institute for Near East Policy (Abdelaziz 2016). Such public appearances could not have happened without the approval of the Saudi ruling family.

Moreover, regional negotiations between Israel and Saudi Arabia almost certainly took place as part of a 2017 decision by Egypt to transfer two islands in the Red Sea to Saudi control.[15] The proximity of these islands to Israel, and the fact that they could affect Israel's shipping routes, means that the agreement represents – at least at a de facto level – Saudi consent to the 1979 Peace Agreement between Egypt and Israel, which guaranteed Israel full maritime rights in the Red Sea. Indeed, a white paper from the Israel-based Begin-Sadat Center for Strategic Studies noted that 'the very fact that Saudi Arabia now undertakes to uphold in practice the obligations assumed by Egypt under the peace treaty means that Israel's place in the region is no longer perceived by Arab leader Saudi Arabia as an anomaly to be corrected' (Lerman and Teitelbaum 2016).

Such diplomatic relations between Israel, Saudi Arabia, and the UAE are further reinforced by commercial and economic ties – most evident in the security, surveillance, and high-tech sectors. A significant example of this is Israeli participation in Abu Dhabi's mass-surveillance system, Falcon Eye, which was installed throughout the emirate in 2016. Billed as a key element of the 'Smart City' strategy discussed in Chapter 3, Falcon Eye consists of thousands of linked security cameras and other surveillance devices, and was reportedly sold to Abu Dhabi in 2011 by Swiss-based firm Asia Global Technology (AGT). AGT is owned by Israeli-American businessman Mati Kochavi, and the system itself was developed by AGT's Israel-based subsidiary Logic Industries (Ferziger and Waldman 2017). A spokesperson for Logic told the Israeli newspaper *Haaretz* in 2008 that all the firm's

[15] This highly controversial move was approved by the Egyptian parliament in mid-2017 despite an earlier court decision that ruled the transfer illegal. It provides a very clear illustration of Egypt's increasing integration into Saudi Arabia's political and economic orbit.

activities 'are carried out in coordination with and under the guidance of the [Israeli] Defense Ministry and all its divisions' (Melman 2008). According to news reports, Kochavi has sold more than $6 billion worth of security infrastructure to the UAE (Ferziger and Waldman 2017).

Likewise, Israeli firms involved in surveillance and security are also marketing their services to Saudi Arabia. Israel's largest private military company, Elbit Systems, is reported to have sold missile defence systems to Saudi Arabia through its US-based subsidiary Kollsman Inc., a fact that came to light in early 2015 following the mysterious death of a Kollsman employee while troubleshooting one such system in the Saudi town of Tabuk (Globes 2015). Saudi Aramco has also purportedly contracted Israeli firms for cybersecurity, and according to Shmuel Bar, the founder and CEO of the Israeli-owned company Intuview, the Saudi royal family has even used his company for public opinion research.[16] Israeli media have also stated that the country has offered Saudi Arabia its Iron Dome military technology to defend against rocket attacks from Yemen (Ferziger and Waldman 2017).

These trends are not isolated to Saudi Arabia and the UAE. The Bahraini king issued a declaration in September 2017 that denounced the Arab boycott of Israel and announced the country's intention to allow Israeli citizens to visit the country – such a public announcement would not have happened without Saudi consent. The post-2011 context has also seen further rapprochement between Israel and key Arab states such as Egypt, Jordan, and Morocco. As Israeli prime minister Benyamin Netanyahu observed in early September 2017, the 'things that are happening today between Israel and the Arab world are unprecedented. Cooperation on a wide range of issues are [*sic*] occurring behind the scenes, more than at any time in Israel's history' (Jerusalem Post 2017).

Nonetheless, a precondition for the drawing-together of these historic pillars of Western power in the region is some form of Palestinian acquiescence – a 'green light' for the normalisation of relations between Israel and the Saudi-UAE axis. For this reason, the imbrication discussed throughout this book of Palestinian capital accumulation with the GCC carries important political implications, not least of which is a tendency for Palestinian decision making – largely driven by the same elite interests connected to the Gulf – to become subordinated to this realignment of regional power. The single major obstacle to this process remains the aspirations of the wider Palestinian population – including the millions of Palestinian refugees scattered across the Middle East – who are increasingly alienated from a

[16] Bar is a former intelligence officer in the Israeli Army and has worked in the Israeli office of the prime minister.

political course directed by Ramallah, Riyadh, and Abu Dhabi. The regional question, in other words, looms ever large over the political trajectories of the national scale.

8.2 Neoliberal Redux?

Taken together, all these developments point to how the Gulf's increasingly predominant weight in the Arab world is linked to a broader reshaping of the regional political system, one that sees a growing convergence of interests between the historic bases of Western power in the region. Yet much analysis of these ever-shifting political rivalries and alliances tends to downplay a concurrent element to contemporary regional politics: an attempt to refashion the Middle East's economic structures such that the general direction of economic liberalisation established through earlier decades not only remains unchallenged, but is further intensified. I have stressed in earlier chapters the interlacing of the political and economic spheres, and this relationship remains paramount to understanding all of the interstate rivalries discussed earlier. It can be seen in the evolving orientation towards post-conflict reconstruction in countries such as Syria, Yemen, Libya, and Iraq – which I shall return to shortly – as well as in the economic policies pursued by states that have not faced such high levels of internal violence. Long-established IFIs, such as the World Bank and IMF, are leading the push for these economic objectives, while working alongside institutions new to the region. Crucially, the GCC states have been the most important regional actors supporting these IFI efforts – their role in this regard needs to be seen as an inseparable part of their political machinations across the region. *Indeed, it is precisely through these economic relations that the Gulf's political influence is largely articulated.* Moreover, in line with the core arguments of this book, the Gulf is also emerging as one of the principal beneficiaries of these new economic arrangements.

These trends were evident from the very first months of the uprisings, and are perhaps most clearly encapsulated by the IFI-led Deauville Partnership, an initiative launched at the May 2011 G8 summit in France that promised up to US$40 billion in loans and other assistance towards Arab countries 'in transition'. The core premise of the Partnership was a redoubled effort towards market opening in five target countries – Egypt, Tunisia, Jordan, Morocco, and Libya – with goals such as 'remov[ing] existing structural impediments', encouraging a 'vigorous private sector' as 'the main engine for job creation', and pursuing 'regional and global economic integration [as the] key to economic development' (European Bank for Reconstruction and Development (EBRD) 2012). Strikingly reminiscent of how the political and economic crises of the 1970s and 1980s had opened the path to structural adjustment in the region, the post-2011 crises were viewed as an opportunity to extend the policy trajectories of past regimes. As the European Investment Bank noted not long after the overthrow of Ben Ali and Mubarak, 'moments of political change can also represent an opportunity to reinforce or improve already existing institutional frameworks' (European Investment Bank (EIB) 2011, p. 12).

Backed by initiatives such as the Deauville Partnership, IFIs moved to expand their position in the region with the offer of new loan agreements and other forms of assistance that were in essential continuity with past programmes. Table 8.1 shows such lending programmes for four key IFIs operating in Egypt, Jordan, Morocco, and Tunisia between 2012 and 2017. There are several salient features of these programmes worth emphasising. First, as is typical in such approaches, there is a clearly coordinated and mutually reinforcing effort shown in the policy priorities across each of the IFIs shown in the table. The IMF has played a chief role in delineating the general direction of macroeconomic and fiscal policy; this has involved an emphasis on fiscal austerity (particularly subsidy and pension reform), the liberalisation of financial and labour markets, changes to taxation systems, and the introduction of legislation to better facilitate PPPs (Hanieh 2015b). Precisely because of their association with past regimes, these new structural adjustment packages were initially met with considerable resistance by popular movements (particularly in Egypt and Tunisia), but between 2013 and 2017 a range of new agreements were inked with governments across the region.

The other IFIs listed in Table 8.1 have reinforced the IMF's general strategic orientation through supporting a larger number of smaller-sized projects within specific sectors. Many of these projects have aimed at providing technical assistance for new regulations around governance and subsidy reform, as well as expanding private-sector involvement in areas such as transport, energy, and water. In this respect, it is striking how the kinds of sectors prioritised for private-sector expansion coincide precisely with those emphasised in the GCC vision strategies discussed in Chapter 7. Once again, we can observe how shifting forms of accumulation in the Gulf are closely intertwined with broader regional patterns.

Within this, the activities of the European Bank for Reconstruction and Development (EBRD) are particularly noteworthy. This bank was established in 1991 alongside the collapse of the Soviet Union with a core mandate of encouraging privatisation and the deepening of private markets in Eastern Europe. Up until 2011 the EBRD had never been active outside Europe, but following the overthrow of Ben Ali and

Table 8.1 *IFI engagement with selected Arab countries (2012–2017), loan values, and policy targets*

	International Monetary Fund (US$ billion)	World Bank (US$ billion)	European Bank for Reconstruction and Development (billion euro)	European Investment Bank (billion euro)
Egypt	2012–2014: 0.0 2015–2017: 4.1 Currency devaluation and adoption of a flexible exchange rate system; raise in fuel and electricity prices; new VAT; encouragement of PPPs in energy sector; new civil service law aimed at reducing wage bill and reducing hires; one-stop shop for business licensing; launch of 5-year IPO programme targeted at banking and financial services, oil and gas, petrochemicals, building materials, and real estate development; abolishment of industrial licensing except for industries related to 'vital public interests'	2012–2014: 1.7 2015–2017: 3.0 Energy subsidy reform, housing finance, fiscal consolidation, power, rural sanitation, microfinance, urban transport infrastructure	2012–2014: 0.8 2015–2017: 1.5 Power and energy (including renewable), credit lines for local bank lending, vertical integration of agribusiness	2012–2014: 0.8 2015–2017: 1.9 Transport, energy, credit lines for local bank lending
Jordan	2012–2014: 1.3 2015–2017:0 8 Greater reliance on PPPs, freeze in government hiring (outside education and health), reduction of threshold for personal income tax, increase in	2012–2014: 0.9 2015–2017: 0.9 Energy and water; labour market reform; judicial reform; refugee displacement; micro, small, and medium enterprise development	2012–2014: 0.3 2015–2017: 0.6 Power and energy (including renewable), waste and wastewater, real estate and tourism, credit lines for local bank lending	2012–2014: 0.1 2015–2017: 0.1 Water, renewable energy, private equity

Table 8.1 (*cont.*)

	International Monetary Fund (US$ billion)	World Bank (US$ billion)	European Bank for Reconstruction and Development (billion euro)	European Investment Bank (billion euro)
	electricity and water prices, easing of rules around foreign property ownership, special economic zones (including for refugees), vocational training			
Morocco	2012–2014: 0.0 2015–2017: 0.0 Morocco currently lacks IMF loans, although it negotiated a two-year precautionary and liquidity line arrangement worth $3.42 billion in July 2016. As of August 2017, this has not been accessed.	2012–2014: 2.7 2015–2017: 2.1 Solar power, waste, transport, capital market development, renewable energy, education reform	2012–2014: 0.4 2015–2017: 0.6 Port upgrades, power and energy, natural resources, credit lines for local bank lending	2012–2014: 1.7 2015–2017: 0.4 Water, waste, agribusiness
Tunisia	2012–2014: 1.1 2015–2017: 1.0 Reduction in budget deficit, cut of government wage bill, cut of subsidies, increase in prices for electricity and gas, pension reform, reduction in size of civil service, new PPP and investment laws	2012–2014: 1.1 2015–2017: 1.4 Governance, entrepreneurship, transport, export development	2012–2014: 0.2 2015–2017: 0.1 Credit lines for local bank lending, agribusiness	2012–2014: 0.8 2015–2017: 0.6 Transport, water, credit lines for local bank lending, telecommunications

Sources: Data from IFI annual reports and project databases; IMF figures are for total funds dispersed over period shown; World Bank figures show principal value of loans or grants. Figures cover up to August 2017.

Mubarak, the bank announced that it would begin operations in Egypt, Jordan, Tunisia, Morocco, Lebanon, and Libya. Its primary objective remained unchanged: to utilise the moment of 'transition' as a means to inspissate private-sector growth, particularly through the use of PPPs in sectors such as infrastructure, energy, and water. As the EBRD's president Thomas Mirow put it in the lead-up to the bank's discussions on opening headquarters in Egypt, 'The EBRD was created in 1991 to promote democracy and market economy, and the historic developments in Egypt strike a deep chord at this bank' (Reuters 2011). Since that time, the Middle East has become a prominent focus of the bank's operations. In 2016, EBRD lending to Egypt, Jordan, Morocco, and Tunisia made up 14.5% of the Bank's total investments across a total of 35 recipient countries; Egypt ranked third among all the Bank's recipients, just behind Turkey and Kazakhstan (EBRD 2017, p. 2).

The EBRD's financial support has been notably propitious for GCC companies operating across the countries listed in Table 8.1. More than one-third of all private sector projects funded by the EBRD in the Middle East since 2011 have involved GCC companies – a proportion far in excess of firms from any other country or region.[17] We can also observe a widening of Gulf accumulation through new sectors that parallel those discussed in preceding chapters; of the 27 EBRD-funded private power and energy projects in Jordan, Egypt, Morocco, and Tunisia, 13 are linked to Gulf-based firms, most of which are also market leaders in the Gulf itself. Indeed, according to a PPP specialist interviewed for this book, Gulf energy firms view the support of institutions such as the EBRD to their Middle East expansion as closely related to their consolidation within the GCC itself. The contracts won in countries such as Egypt, Morocco, Tunisia, and Egypt not only provide profitable opportunities in these individual countries, but also help bid up company valuation more generally; this is particularly important for future IPOs in the Gulf, and acts to better position these firms for the opportunities expected in the wake of the GCC reform plans.[18]

At a broader level, a critical part of the renewed push towards economic liberalisation has been the financial support extended by the GCC to neighbouring Arab countries. The value of such GCC support runs into the many tens of billions of dollars, and has occurred through a variety of interconnected routes, including direct budgetary assistance, the placement of GCC financial assets in other Arab central banks, the provision of subsidised oil and gas, and investment funding for particular

[17] Calculated by author from the EBRD Project database, figures as of August 2017.
[18] Interview with PPP legal expert, February 2017, Dubai.

projects. All of these types of support need to be differentiated along the lines of inter-GCC rivalry noted earlier, but, taken as a whole, they have been predicated on Arab governments undertaking deep-seated changes to their economies in the manner envisioned by the IFI strategies. In this sense, the loans and grants from the GCC need to be seen as working in a mutually reinforcing fashion with the efforts of various IFIs – without the GCC, international financial institutions would not have been able to enter the region in such a decisive manner post-2011.

These aspects of the GCC role can be observed very clearly in the case of Egypt. In 2014, the IMF estimated that Saudi Arabia had provided US $7.8 billion to Egypt in the immediate wake of the 2013 military coup that brought Sisi to power; this included an interest-free deposit of $2 billion in the Central Bank of Egypt, oil and gas subsidies worth another $3.8 billion, and a cash donation of $2 billion (IMF 2014, p. 51; figures for 2013/2014). In addition, the UAE and Kuwait had given $10.6 billion in total – mostly in the form of Central Bank of Egypt deposits and energy products (IMF 2014, p. 51). A year later, this was followed by Saudi pledges of a further $4 billion at the Egyptian Economic Development Conference (EEDC) held in Sharm El-Sheikh during March 2015. This large-scale investor conference had been proposed by late King Abdullah bin Abdulaziz al-Saud during a congratulatory visit to Sisi in Cairo in June 2014. At the Development Conference, Kuwait and the UAE each promised an additional $4 billion on top of their initial support to Sisi, while Oman offered $0.5 billion – Qatar was conspicuously absent from the gathering due to its backing of the ousted Morsi government (Thompson 2015). Although numerous projects proposed at the Development Conference are unlikely to move forward at the scale initially announced, there has nonetheless been a considerable increase in the levels of both private and state-backed Gulf investment in Egypt; for the fiscal year 2015/2016, GCC FDI inflows to Egypt reached $2.15 billion – a figure double that recorded in 2009/2010, just prior to the overthrow of Mubarak.[19]

One of the most revealing components of these financial flows is the deposit of GCC funds in the Central Bank of Egypt. According to the Bank's figures, GCC deposits held in Egypt increased from $7 billion in 2014 to $13 billion in 2015. By 2016, the value of deposits had reached $16.8 billion (Central Bank of Egypt (CBE) 2017a, p. 44).[20] These deposits are transforming the nature of Egypt's external debt relations – remarkably, by 2016, Egypt owed Saudi Arabia, the UAE, and Kuwait more than the total it owed to all IFIs, or any other country or region in the

[19] Figures from the Central Bank of Egypt, Monthly Statistical Bulletins (various years).
[20] These are deposits from Saudi Arabia, the UAE, and Kuwait.

world (CBE 2017a, p. 31).[21] Mirroring the historical role of international debt in institutionalising the power of creditors over poorer nations, such financial obligations have substantially increased the GCC's influence on the Egyptian state. Despite the fact these deposits are provided at relatively low (and sometimes zero) interest rates, Gulf deposits make up a very large proportion of Egypt's foreign reserves, and are thus critical to the country's ability to import goods, manage exchange rates, boost liquidity in case of crisis, and allow Egypt to borrow money on international markets at reasonable rates. Precisely because of these essential functions of a country's reserve position, GCC creditors wield tremendous sway over Egyptian politics and economic policy – if any displeasure with the direction of such policies is felt, the threat to withdraw deposits could generate a severe crisis in Egypt's financial markets.[22]

In this context, GCC deposits (and other forms of financial flows) have undoubtedly been a major factor influencing the trajectory of Egyptian economic policy under Sisi. In the three years following the coup, the Egyptian government devalued its currency by around one-half and implemented a floating exchange rate – a key demand of large business groups and international institutions. Likewise, electricity tariffs and retail prices for gasoline were both significantly increased (by 40% and 35%, respectively), a move explicitly aimed at 'help[ing] the power sector attract private investors' (much like the GCC subsidy reform discussed in Chapter 7) (Crisp 2015, p. 14). The Sisi government also adopted a new civil service law designed to reduce wage costs and the size of the public sector, and agreed to privatise key state-owned companies in banking and financial services, oil and gas, petrochemicals, construction, and real estate. These (and other) measures were all preconditions for a $12 billion IMF loan; once implemented, the loan agreement was signed in November 2016.[23]

[21] In 2013, by far the largest proportion of Egypt's medium- and long-term public debt had been made up of bilateral loans from Paris Club countries (31% of total medium- and long-term debt) and IFIs (28%). By 2016, this pattern had radically shifted. Egypt's debt to Saudi Arabia, the UAE, and Kuwait – and this includes only debt resulting from deposits in the Central Egyptian Bank – had come to constitute 32% of the country's total debt. Paris Club debt had fallen to 20% and IFI debt stood at 30%.

[22] These deposits are not bonds and are generally provided for a limited period of time (e.g. three to five years). In November 2014, for example, Egypt was forced to return a $2.5 billion deposit to Qatar following the latter's displeasure with the ouster of Morsi.

[23] Importantly, another precondition for the IMF loan was the demand that Egypt first find an additional $6 billion in loans from other bilateral sources, most of which came in the form of further GCC deposits. The introduction of new PPP arrangements, efforts to increase the penetration of mortgage financing for low-income housing, and the establishment of special economic zones are further examples of economic policy changes made in the lead-up to the IMF agreement.

Closely connected to these economic shifts – indeed, a necessary corollary of them – has been the sharpening authoritarianism of the Egyptian state itself. At its most obvious, this has included escalating levels of violence and internal repression that far exceed that of the previous Mubarak regime – more than 2,000 people were killed during the 2013 coup and its immediate aftermath; tens of thousands have been imprisoned for political reasons; media and public criticism have been highly restricted; and a new law passed in February 2015 defines anyone who acts to 'disturb public order' or 'harm national unity' as terrorist – a definition that would presumably include the millions who took to the streets in 2011 (Fahmy 2015). In addition to such overt forms of repression, Egyptian lawmakers have introduced regulations that directly counter the democratic aspirations of the 2011 uprising, particularly in the area of public oversight over foreign investment. New laws now prohibit citizens or any third party from legally challenging contracts signed between investors and the state (Butter 2015), nullify earlier court rulings that sought compensation for property sold off by the Mubarak regime at below-market prices (Charbel 2015), and outlaw any future nationalisation of foreign investment (EY Global 2017). Business analysts and Egyptian political activists alike widely agree that these changes were specifically designed with Gulf investors in mind; indeed, the vast majority of the Mubarak-era deals challenged after 2011 have involved GCC companies – by 2017, virtually all of these had been resolved in favour of their Gulf owners.

Although Egypt remains the single most important exemplar of these processes, it is by no means unique among Arab governments. The precise institutional arrangements differ from place to place, but economic liberalisation in the other countries listed in Table 8.1 has also been largely steered through a partnership between IFIs and the GCC. This includes hefty flows of Gulf investment – similarly predicated on privatisation and the opening-up of new sectors – as well as several billion dollars' worth of budgetary support and central bank deposits (in the cases of Jordan and Tunisia).[24] And as with the Egyptian case, IFI-led structural adjustment has been closely entwined with hardening authoritarianism and repression of social protest through the years that followed 2011. The economic packages listed

[24] In Jordan, for example, the GCC extended just under $4 billion in budget grants over 2013 and 2014 (this includes Saudi and Kuwaiti grants for budget support, as well as capital grants to the Ministry of Finance and Central Bank of Jordan). Although this level has dropped since the oil price decline, GCC grants are still expected to make up just under half of the total external grants received by Jordan between 2016 and 2018. These Gulf grants are critical to Jordan meeting its budgetary expenditure – from 2016 to 2018, they are projected to make up more than one-fifth of all external budget financing, a category that includes loans from the World Bank, EU, and other international organisations (IMF 2017b, p. 53). In the case of Tunisia, it is Qatar that placed deposits in the Tunisian Central Bank.

in Table 8.1 mark a fundamental rejection of the popular aspirations for 'bread, freedom and social justice' that brought millions out on the streets in 2011. State-backed violence, stifling of dissent, and GCC support to those in power have all been instrumental factors in this reversal.

Humanitarian Crises and Reconstruction

This determined effort to reassert and expand neoliberal development trajectories provides a revealing clue to where the Middle East may be heading in the wake of the current violence. Returning to the juxtaposition that began this chapter – the intersection of crises and the opening up of new spaces of accumulation – it is clear that major international donors and IFIs are seeking to leverage the destruction and displacement wrought since 2011 as a means to recuperate and deepen the spread of market relations. Crises, as noted in the previous chapter, are also moments of opportunity – and the ways in which these opportunities are seized will substantially shape the political map of the Middle East over coming decades.

This dialectic is well illustrated in how international actors have dealt with one of the most severe humanitarian challenges facing the region – the displacement of millions of Syrian refugees across countries such as Lebanon, Jordan, and Turkey.[25] This displacement has placed enormous pressures on both refugees themselves and their host communities. In the case of Lebanon, for example, it is estimated that the population has increased by a staggering 25% since the onset of the war in Syria; Jordan has also seen a very large increase in numbers of Syrian refugees, now estimated at more than 650,000. These two countries now host the highest proportion of refugees of any place in the world (World Bank 2017c, p. 26). Support to this refugee population – both directly and in dealing with its broader impact on the host country – has come in the form of billions of dollars' worth of international aid and the influx of a large number of humanitarian organisations into the region.

One of the little-noted consequences to this massive expansion of humanitarian activity is the way in which it is reinforcing the weight of the GCC within the wider circulatory and logistics routes of the Middle East. As Rafeef Ziadah has shown, the GCC states have positioned themselves as the single most important hub for humanitarian aid flows throughout the region (Ziadah 2017). Dubai, in particular, has marketed

[25] I use the term 'refugees' here, although it is important to note that not all those displaced are officially categorised as such. In Lebanon, for example, laws passed in 2015 and 2016 have made it very difficult for Syrians to register as refugees or obtain official residency documents.

the use of its established logistics capabilities to attract major international humanitarian organisations. Indeed, virtually all the humanitarian assistance to the key conflict zones in the Middle East is now coordinated through Dubai's International Humanitarian City (IHC) – a free zone situated within a wider logistics corridor that includes Al Maktoum International Airport and Jebel Ali Port. IHC acts as the central base for nine UN organisations, including the World Food Programme, United Nations High Commissioner for Refugees (UNHCR), Office for the Coordination of Humanitarian Affairs (OCHA), UNICEF, and the United Nations Development Programme (UNDP), as well as more than 40 other international NGOs – it is now the 'world's largest humanitarian logistics hub' and has seen its area triple in size since 2011 (National 2017). Pairing with Gulf-based logistics firms – notably the erstwhile Agility (see Chapter 4) – international humanitarian organisations use IHC as the core for the warehousing, dispersal, and management of humanitarian aid throughout the Middle East (and further afield). The UNHCR, for example, holds its largest global stockpile of relief items such as blankets, tents, and mosquito nets at IHC, through which it can serve 350,000 people (Sahoo 2014). Given the massive volume of goods that move through IHC – a direct consequence of the Middle East's numerous humanitarian crises – the free zone acts to position private Gulf-based firms at the centre of humanitarian provision (through subcontracting for the transport and management of these relief shipments), while also further consolidating Dubai's logistics and transport facilities as the backbone of regional commodity flows.[26]

At a more general level, flows of humanitarian assistance in the Middle East are also increasingly tied to – and used to legitimate – development strategies that emphasise further economic liberalisation. Perhaps the clearest example of this was shown at the 'Supporting Syria and the Region' conference, a meeting held in London in early February 2016 that brought together all of the major international donors to pledge support for Syrian refugees. Pointedly, the conference explicitly identified its primary objective

[26] Interestingly, Saudi Arabia is also attempting to vie with the UAE for this aid 'business' – an indication that competitive rivalries between the two states continue to exist despite their strong political alliance. Moreover, the Gulf has emerged as a major humanitarian donor in its own right – with much of this aid directed at Egypt, Jordan, and Yemen. In Jordan, the UAE actually operates its own camp for Syrian refugees (Mrajeeb Al Fhood), while the other GCC states both fund and directly provide health care, food, and shelter. The case of Yemen is particularly contentious given the Saudi-led bombing campaign under way since 2015. Despite being leading protagonists in the conflict, Saudi Arabia and the UAE are the largest providers of humanitarian assistance to Yemen – supplying around 43% of all global humanitarian aid to the country from 2015 to mid-2017 (UN Financial Tracking Service, https://fts.unocha.org/countries/248/donors/2015).

as 'turning the Syrian refugee crisis into a development opportunity' (OECD 2016), through financial aid for programmes that 'expand investment, promote exports and public-private partnerships' (Jordan Times 2017). Although the conference was billed as a humanitarian event in support of refugees and host countries – indeed, according to then-UK prime minister David Cameron, it raised the most amount of humanitarian funds ever in a one-day appeal – the vast majority of pledges came in the form of non-concessionary loans by international financial institutions, chiefly the World Bank, European Investment Bank, the EBRD, and the Saudi-based Islamic Development Bank. The total amount of such loans promised at the conference reached US$41 billion (of which only $1.7 billion were earmarked as concessionary), compared with US$11.4 billion in bilateral humanitarian support.[27] In this manner, the promotion of IFI structural adjustment (and the inevitable ties of debt associated with this) was actually recast as a form of humanitarian assistance.

Jordan, as one of the principal host countries of Syrian refugees, has experienced this twinning of humanitarianism and neoliberal reform most directly. Speaking at the 2016 EBRD Annual Meeting and Business Forum, a Jordanian government representative noted that the Supporting Syria conference committed Jordan to improving its 'business and investment environment' and to 'taking forward a detailed plan on measures and structural reforms needed in this regard ... [including] incentives that can be offered to domestic and international investors' (EBRD 2016, p. 3). In this context, the language of humanitarianism has been a major discursive factor behind privatisation in Jordan, including recent PPPs in energy, wastewater, and education (typically justified on the basis of satisfying the needs of Syrian refugees),[28] as well as plans to establish special economic zones targeting refugee camps, thereby making Syrian labour available for local and international investors. Perhaps in recognition of the Jordanian government's enthusiastic pairing of humanitarian crisis and economic liberalisation, the country will also be the venue for the 2018 annual meeting of the EBRD's Board of Governors, the first country in the Middle East to ever host such an event.

An analogous discursive mobilization of the Syrian refugee crisis can be seen in other parts of the Middle East. Mouayed Makhlouf, the Middle East and North Africa head of the International Finance Corporation (the private sector arm of the World Bank), has linked his institution's

[27] www.supportingsyria2016.com/news/co-hosts-statemtent-annex-fundraising.

[28] See, for example, the Wadi Arab Water System II, the Hashemite Kingdom of Jordan Ministry of Water and Irrigation Water Authority of Jordan, Environmental and Social Impact Assessment Study, November 2015.

'championing of PPPs for the past seven or eight years' directly to the influx of Syrian refugees, arguing, 'If you look at places like Jordan, Lebanon, and to a certain extent Iraq, in some places populations have increased by 30 percent or more, so demand on public services has increased manifold ... The need is greater than ever for the private sector to step up to fill the gaps the public sector has not been able to fill' (Anders 2016). Similarly, in the field of education, the schooling crisis facing Syrian refugee children has been utilised as a means to promote PPPs in schools across Lebanon, Jordan, and Turkey. Framed once again in the language of humanitarian support, private educational firms have sought to provide 1 million school places across these three countries in the form of PPPs (Novelli 2016, p. 16).

Such trends confirm that humanitarian support, as numerous scholars have argued, is never neutral – it is closely bound up with both the phase of direct intervention in conflict as well as the ability to influence the patterns of reconstruction that follow (Bello 2006; Fassin 2007; Duffield 2014). Both the language and practice of humanitarianism is setting up a post-conflict scenario in which market logics have already become firmly entrenched in the course of managing the effects of the conflict itself. Conflict, in other words, can act as a driver of liberalisation and the creation of markets, a chance to push forward new policies that reshape expectations, change social norms, and shift patterns of accumulation in ways that were previously blocked (Cramer 2006). In this sense, violent conflict 'should be regarded as the emergence of alternative systems of profit and power, rather than simply the breakdown of a system' (Turner 2017).

There is every sign that this same capital-centred approach will continue to drive the next phase of reconstruction in Syria, Yemen, Libya, and Iraq. Indeed, the World Bank puts this perspective bluntly and forcefully, arguing:

> A particular way for the reconstruction program to be people-led is to crowd in the private sector. A post-conflict government will have neither the resources nor capacity to rebuild the economy. But the private sector can – and will – be the engine of growth in the aftermath of the war. The government should promote a dynamic business environment and institutional reforms, based on a consensus emerging from an inclusive dialogue on reconstruction, so that the power of the private sector can be unleashed. Privileging the private sector will also be important in facilitating the return of refugees, many of whom abandoned their businesses during the war. Finally, a dynamic private sector is the strongest antidote to a resumption of conflict. World Bank (2017c, p. 44)

Once again, we encounter the trope of private sector 'dynamism' acting as synecdoche for the universal good – the key to ensuring citizen participation, the rights of those displaced, and even promising the end of conflict. As I have frequently pointed out, such a perspective obfuscates more than it clarifies. By projecting the neutrality of capital investment and property ownership – absenting actual relations of power both within and across borders – such a vision promises a future shaped by and for the interests of those who already hold market dominance. If this trajectory is overlaid with the regional political dynamics described earlier, a post-conflict scenario emerges that amplifies all of the principal trends mapped throughout this book – as major poles of accumulation and political power in the Middle East, the Gulf and its capitalist classes are particularly well positioned to benefit from this fecund moment.

There are several indications of such an eventuality. As the vignette that began this chapter illustrates, Gulf capital is attempting to situate itself as a chief player within post-conflict markets. Building upon their established dominance in areas such as finance, agribusiness, construction, and retail, Gulf conglomerates are well placed to further consolidate their position across the regional scale. In newly emerging sectors of private capital involvement that are most significant for reconstruction – notably, power, water, energy, and logistics – these same Gulf conglomerates are ascendant. The massive infrastructure needs of devastated zones across Syria, Iraq, Yemen, and Libya look set to strengthen these patterns – especially if such reconstruction is based upon an invocation of 'private-sector dynamism'. The example of Yemen – where the UN has recently decried Saudi Arabia's 'willful destruction' of $19 billion worth of infrastructure – is instructive here. If the rest of the region is any guide to the direction that reconstruction will take in a post-conflict Yemen, Gulf-based firms stand poised to reap massive riches from this deliberate damage to the country's infrastructure, estimated to be worth around half of the country's 2013 GDP (OCHA 2016, p. 8).

These potentials will almost certainly be reinforced by the extension of Gulf financial support to countries undergoing reconstruction. As has been seen in the case of Egypt, this support can come in a multiplicity of forms, including bilateral investment flows, central bank deposits (indeed, Saudi Arabia has already placed $1 billion in the Yemeni Central Bank), subsidised oil and gas, and development aid. Large GCC-based institutions such as the Saudi Fund for Development, the Abu Dhabi Fund for Development, the Kuwait Fund for Arab Economic Development, and the Islamic Development Bank are already active across the region and will certainly play a major role in determining where post-conflict funding goes and on what it is spent. As I have noted in earlier chapters, funding from these institutions typically focuses on large infrastructure projects, agribusiness, and financial reform – any further support to these sectors as part of reconstruction efforts will undoubtedly continue to bolster the expansion of large Gulf conglomerates throughout the Middle East (alongside the more generalised goals of promoting economic liberalisation and regional integration).

Of course, there is no foregone conclusion as to how successful the Gulf's ambitions may be in moving forward. The concrete form of reconstruction (and its beneficiaries) will be shaped by the competitive struggles between the different Gulf states and the particular configuration of political power that marks the end of these wars.[29] International firms – and states – will play a prominent part within the new markets that emerge, likely through the types of consultancy and engineering activities highlighted in earlier chapters. There are multiple forces involved in this process – including domestic elites, IFIs, foreign governments, and new economic actors thrown up in the course of conflict itself;[30] the interests of these groups do not always align, and they face considerable challenges in pushing forward their visions. Nonetheless, despite all these contingencies, there is a need to 'follow the money [in order to] uncover the power dynamics', as Mandy Turner (2017) has aptly put it – and within this unfolding process, the historically conditioned path of regional development posits the Gulf as a key driver of the contemporary moment.

The outcomes of these struggles will shape the region for years to come, not least for the ordinary people who live there. I have repeatedly stressed that the Gulf's role in making the region has acted to accentuate polarisation throughout *all* scales: between the Gulf and the rest of the

[29] For example, if the post-conflict political arrangements in Syria see a continued role for the Assad regime, it is likely that Iranian and Russian economic interests will also benefit from reconstruction – a trend foreshadowed in September 2017, when Iranian firms were granted multimillion-dollar contracts for the supply of power and electricity infrastructure following the months-long siege and aerial bombardment that devastated Aleppo through 2016 (AlAraby 2017).

[30] In this respect, Samer Abboud has detailed for the case of Syria how 'war economies take shape around processes of territorial fragmentation, sovereign retreat and protracted violence' (Abboud 2017, p. 92). He has described a whole series of 'micro-economies of violence' that involve acts such as 'looting, taxation, kidnapping, and aid theft and diversion [and that] are deeply intertwined in a specific supply chain that begins in Syria's borderlands and often ends in areas under siege' (Abboud 2017, p. 93). Employing such acts, armed groups (including from within the Syrian regime), have come to control checkpoints, transit corridors, and warehouses, profiting immensely from the supply of goods to besieged areas. Many Syrian business elites have also left the country to set up businesses in neighbouring countries; from there, they facilitate the other end of such supply chains – sourcing goods in countries like Turkey, which are then imported into Syria through border crossings managed by armed groups. This diverse collection of war profiteers will undoubtedly form part of whatever economic structures emerge in the reconstruction period.

Middle East, within the GCC itself, and inside individual national borders. It was precisely such juxtapositions of unevenness that underlay the protests of recent years, powerfully shaking the established patterns of political and economic power that acted to support these hierarchies. Nevertheless, despite the aspirations of those who took part in these struggles, the extreme polarisation of wealth and power across the region has not been fundamentally altered – in fact, it has dramatically worsened in the wake of war, conflict, and mass displacement. The current moment highlights one of the unresolved challenges of these revolts: an inability to fully confront the regional question in all its varied dimensions, most particularly the Gulf's leading role in producing and sustaining the profound inequalities of the regional scale. This scale remains an ever-present and potent reality, a prime determinant of social, political, and economic life in the Middle East – we can be certain that the last word has not been said on its future.

References

Aalbers, M. B. (2013). Neoliberalism is dead ... long live neoliberalism! *International Journal of Urban and Regional Research*, **37**(3), 1083–1090.

Abboud, S. (2017). Social change, network formation and Syria's war economies. *Middle East Policy*, **24**(1), 92–107.

Abdelaziz, M. (2016). Media Analysis of the Meeting between Prince Turki Al-Faisal and General Amidror. Washington Institute. www.washingtoninstitute.org/fikraforum/view/media-analysis-of-the-meeting-between-prince-turki-al-faisal-and-general-am.

Abdelmonem, D. (2011, March 7). Ongoing investigation: AUC board of trustees. *The Independent*, **2**(9), 3.

Abdel-Shahid, Shahira F. (2002). Privatization status and performance of privatized companies in Egypt. Working Paper No. 4. https://ssrn.com/abstract=312963.

Abu Dhabi Digital Government Gateway (ADDGG). (2017). Educational development in Abu Dhabi. www.abudhabi.ae.

Abul-Magd, Z. (2011, December 23). The army and the economy in Egypt. *Jadaliyya*. www.jadaliyya.com/pages/index/3732/the-army-and-the-economy-in-egypt.

Achcar, G. (2002). *Clash of Barbarisms: September 11 and the Making of the New World Disorder*. New York, NY: Monthly Review Press.

(2016). *Morbid Symptoms: Relapse in the Arab Uprising*. Stanford, CA: Stanford University Press.

Agility. (2014, 13 August). Forbes ranks Agility no. 65 of top 500 companies in Arab world. www.agility.net/EN/news/Pages/Forbes-Ranks-Agility-No.-65-of-Top-500-Companies-in-Arab-World.aspx.

Agriculture Development Fund (ADF). (n.d.). *laihat dawabit taqdim al-ttashilat al-aytmaniat wal-ttamwil al-maysir lil-mustathmirin al-ssaudiiyn fi atar mubadarat al-malik abd allah lilaistithmar al-zziraei fi al-kharij* [List of guidelines for credit facilities and concessional financing for Saudi Investors under the KAISAIA]. https://adf.gov.sa/Investor.aspx.

Agrimoney. (2013, March 28). Saudi extends foreign land spree with CFG takeover. www.agrimoney.com/news/saudi-extends-foreign-land-spree-with-cfg-takeover–5673.html.

Ahmed, A. (2017). Someone is using these leaked emails to embarrass Washington's most powerful ambassador. *Huffington Post*.

www.huffingtonpost.co.uk/entry/otaiba-ambassador-uae-leaked-emails_us_5932bf04e4b02478cb9bec1c.

Ahram Online. (2015, 28 June). Slums make up 40% of Egypt's urban areas: official. http://english.ahram.org.eg/NewsContent/3/12/133981/Business/Economy/Slums-make-up–of-Egypts-urban-areas-Official.aspx.

Ahronheim, A. (2017, 28 March). Israel pilots flying alongside pilots from the UAE in week-long Greek drill. *Jerusalem Post*. www.jpost.com/printarticle.aspx?id=485391.

Akhbar24. (2015, 30 July). *al-dakhli: tarhil 1.2 milyun makhalif wamukhalafa* [Interior Ministry: Deportation of 1.2 Million Violators]. https://akhbaar24.argaam.com/article/detail/227266/.

Al-Alami, F. (2012, 9 April). *istithmar ziraei kharijiun 'am makhzun ghidhayiyun dakhili?* [External agricultural investments or internal food supply?]. *Al Watan*. http://alwatan.com.sa/Articles/Detail.aspx?ArticleId=13368.

Al-Alas, O. (2017). *ashaab al-rada' al-abyad yuajihun safa'* [Doctors face Safa]. www.alraimedia.com/ar/article/local/2017/03/11/750941/nr/kuwait.

Al Arabiya. (2017, 6 November). Arab coalition affirms Saudi Arabia's right to respond to Iran's 'act of war'. https://english.alarabiya.net/en/features/2017/11/06/Arab-coalition-affirms-Saudi-Arabia-s-right-to-respond-to-Iran-s-act-of-war-.html.

AlAraby. (2016, 30 August). Reconstruction of war-torn Yemen 'could cost $15 billion'. www.alaraby.co.uk/english/society/2016/8/30/reconstruction-of-war-torn-yemen-could-cost-15-billion.

(2017, 13 September). Iran 'cashes in' on Syria intervention with Aleppo utilities contracts. www.alaraby.co.uk/english/news/2017/9/13/iran-cashes-in-on-syria-intervention-with-aleppo-contracts.

Al Attar, W. (2014). The Middle East as an emerging hub. Presentation at Platts Aluminium Symposium, 12–14 January. www.platts.com.

Albo, G. (2008). Neoliberalism and the Discontented. In L. Panitch and C. Leys, eds., *Socialist Register 2008: Global Flashpoints*. London: Merlin Press, pp. 354–362.

(2012). Contemporary Capitalism. In B. Fine and A. Saad-Filho, eds., *Elgar Companion to Marxist Economics*. London: Elgar, pp. 84–89.

Albo, G., Gindin, S., and Panitch, L. (2010). *In and Out of Crisis: The Global Financial Meltdown and Left Alternatives*. Oakland, CA: PM Press.

Al Dahra. (2013, 21 May). Loulis Mills and Al Dahra strategic alliance. Al Dahra holding news release. www.aldahra.com/en-us/media-center/news-releases/newsreleasedetail/id/4.

(n.d.). Al Dahra business model. www.aldahra.com/en-us/business-model.

Al-Jubeir, Adel bin Ahmed. (2016, 19 January). Can Iran change? *New York Times*.

Al Makahleh, Shehab and Iman Sherif. (2012, 12 July). UAE eyes overseas land to provide steady food supplies. *Gulf News*.

Almarai. (2015). Almarai annual report. www.almarai.com.

Al Masah Capital. (2015, December). GCC real estate sector. www.almasahcapital.com/.

Al-Masdar. (2012, 16 January). *Al-Tawqiya ala asharat itafaqiyat t'awan bayn tunis wa Qatar* [Ten cooperation agreements signed between Tunisia and Qatar]. https://ar.webmanagercenter.com/.

Alpen Capital. (2015a). GCC retail industry. www.alpencapital.com/.
(2015b, 28 April). GCC food industry. www.alpencapital.com/.
(2016a, May). GCC education industry report. www.alpencapital.com/industry-reports.html.
(2016b, February). GCC healthcare industry report. www.alpencapital.com/industry-reports.html.
Alpers, E. (2014). *The Indian Ocean in World History*. Oxford: Oxford University Press.
Al-Rasheed, M. (2010). *A History of Saudi Arabia*. Cambridge: Cambridge University Press.
Ambrose, J. (2016, 2 May). Can Saudi Aramco really be worth $2.5 trillion? *The Telegraph*. www.telegraph.co.uk/business/2016/05/01/saudi-aramco-how-do-you-put-a-price-tag-on-the-worlds-most-impor/.
Amel, M. (1986). *Fil-Dawla al-Tâ'ifiyya*. Beirut: Dâr al-Farabi.
Americana. (2012). Annual report. Kuwait. www.americana-group.com/.
(2014). Annual report. Kuwait. www.americana-group.com/.
Amwal Alghad. (2016, 10 April). Saudi Arabia's Savola: Egypt investments record $800 million. http://en.amwalalghad.com/investment-news/industry-trade/44998-saudi-arabias-savola-egypt-investments-record-800-million.html.
Anders, M. (2016, 14 March). What the refugee crisis means for investment in MENA. *Devex*. www.devex.com/news/what-the-refugee-crisis-means-for-investment-in-mena-87869.
Anderson, M. B. (2014). Class monopoly rent and the contemporary neoliberal city. *Geography Compass*, **8**(1), 13–24.
Anderson, R. (2017, 30 July). Illegal workers in Saudi face prison, SAR50,000 fine as crackdown begins. *Gulf News*. http://gulfbusiness.com/illegal-workers-saudi-face-prison-sar50000-fine-crackdown-begins/.
Angelo, H. and Hentschel, C. (2015). Interactions with infrastructure as windows into social worlds: a method for critical urban studies: introduction. *City*, **19**(2–3), 306–312.
Arab Gulf State Institute in Washington (AGSIW). (2017, 20 March). Gulf economic barometer.
Arab Organization for Agricultural Development (AOAD). (2015). *Arab Agricultural Statistics Yearbook*, vol. 35. League of Arab States: Khartoum, Sudan.
Arab Palestinian Investment Company (APIC). (2014, February). Information memorandum. www.pex.ps/PSEWebSite/NEWS/Corporate-Profile-English-APIC-12022014.pdf.
Arabian Business. (2016, 30 March). UAE's Green Valley plans $168m projects in Morocco, Bosnia. www.arabianbusiness.com/uae-s-green-valley-plans-168m-projects-in-morocco-bosnia-626749.html.
Argaam. (2015, 11 May). *taqrir khas: al-suwq al-saudi yashhad 'akthar min 100 istiqalat lilruwasa' al-tanfidhiayn wa'aeda' majalis al-iidarat khilal al 16 shahraan al-madia* [Special report: Saudi stock market sees more than 100 executive resignations in last 16 months]. www.argaam.com/ar/article/articledetail/id/377575.

Arrighi, G. (2009). *Adam Smith in Beijing: Lineages of the 21st Century*. London: Verso Books.

Awraq Investment. (2011). Jordanian banking sector brief. Awraq: Amman, Jordan.

Ayeb, H. (2012). Agricultural Policies in Tunisia, Egypt, and Morocco: Between Food Dependency and Social Marginalization. In *Reversing the Vicious Circle in North Africa's Political Economy, Confronting Rural, Urban, and Youth-Related Challenges*. Mediterranean Paper Series. Washington, DC: German Marshall Fund of the United States.

Balkan, N., Balkan, E., and Öncü, A., eds. (2015). *The Neoliberal Landscape and the Rise of Islamist Capital in Turkey*. New York, NY: Berghahn Books.

Bank Audi. (2015). Annual report 2015. www.bankaudigroup.com/group/annual-reports.

Barnard, A. (2017, 4 November). Saad Hariri quits as Lebanon prime minister, blaming Iran. *New York Times*. www.nytimes.com/2017/11/04/world/middleeast/saad-hariri-lebanon-iran.html.

Barthel, P.-A. (2010). Arab mega-projects: between the Dubai effect, global crisis, social mobilization and a sustainable shift. *Built Environment*, **36**, 133–145.

Barthel, P.-A. and Planel, S. (2010). Tanger-Med and Casa-Marina, prestige projects in Morocco: new capitalist frameworks and local context. *Built Environment*, **36**(2), 48–63.

Barthel, P.-A. and Vignal, L. (2014). Arab Mediterranean megaprojects after the 'Spring': business as usual or a new beginning? *Built Environment*, **40**(1), 52–71.

Bassens, D., Derudder, B., and Witlox, F. (2010). Searching for the Mecca of finance: Islamic financial services and the world city network. *Area*, **42**, 35.

Battat, M. L., Erekat, D. M., Lampietti, J. A., De Hartog, A. H., and Michaels, S. D. (2012). *The Grain Chain: Food Security and Managing Wheat Imports in Arab Countries*. Washington, DC: World Bank.

Baumann, H. (2017). *Citizen Hariri*. London: Hurst & Co.

Bayat, A. and Biekart, K. (2009). Cities of extremes. *Development and Change*, **40** (5), 815–825.

Bayliss, K. and Van Waeyenberge, E. (2017). Unpacking the public private partnership revival. *Journal of Development Studies*, **54**, 1–17.

Beer, Eliot. (2014, 15 June). AlMarai signs fodder port deal as Q1 profits rise 7%. *Food Navigator*. www.foodnavigator.com/Article/2014/06/16/Almarai-signs-fodder-port-deal-as-Q1-profits-rise-7.

(2015, 21 May). Al Ghurair to boost UAE food security. *Food Navigator*. www.foodnavigator.com/Article/2015/06/01/Al-Ghurair-to-boost-UAE-food-security.

(2016, 31 May). Siniora buys UAE's DMP, eyes GCC growth. *Food Navigator*. www.foodnavigator-asia.com/Article/2016/06/01/Siniora-buys-UAE-s-DMP-eyes-GCC-growth#.

Beinin, J. (2015). *Workers and Thieves: Labor Movements and Popular Uprisings in Tunisia and Egypt*. Stanford, CA: Stanford University Press.

Bellamy-Foster, J. (2010). The financialization of accumulation. *Monthly Review*, **62**(5), 1–17.

Bellamy Foster, J. and McChesney, R. W. (2012). The global stagnation and China. *Monthly Review*. http://monthlyreview.org/2012/02/01/the-global-stagnation-and-china#en49.

Bello, W. (2006). The rise of the relief-and-reconstruction complex. *Journal of International Affairs*, **59**(2), 281–296.

Ben Bouazza, B. (2012, 25 April). Qatar extends $1bn loan to cash-strapped Tunisia. *San Diego Tribune*. www.sandiegouniontribune.com/sdut-qatar-extends-1bn-loan-to-cash-strapped-tunisia-2012apr25-story.html.

Ben-Hamouche, M. (2011). Manama: The Metamorphosis of an Arab Gulf City. In Y. Elsheshtawy, ed., *The Evolving Arab City: Tradition, Modernity and Urban Development*. London: Routledge, pp. 184–217.

Benner, C., Berndt, C., Coe, N., and Engelen, E. (2011). Emerging themes in economic geography: outcomes of the economic geography 2010 workshop. *Economic Geography*, **87**, 111–126.

Bernstein, H. (2016). Agrarian political economy and modern world capitalism: the contributions of food regime analysis. *Journal of Peasant Studies*, **43**(3), 611–647.

Beyti. (2014, 30 April). Beyti to continue its marketing campaign for Tropicana juice in Egypt's governorate. http://beytiegypt.com/news-media/press-releases/press-release-2/.

Biedermann, F. (2009, 25 February). Amman reshapes itself for business. *Financial Times*. www.ft.com/intl/cms/s/0/1543e9d2-035d-11de-b405000077b07658.html#axzz44ALHTRVv.

Bishara, F. (2016, November). Ships passing in the night? Reflections on the Middle East in the Indian Ocean. *International Journal of Middle East Studies*, Roundtable on the Indian Ocean and the Mediterranean, **48**(4), 758–762.

Bitar, Z. (2013, 2 May). UAE moots the idea of agricultural free zones in Africa. *Gulf News*. http://gulfnews.com/business/economy/uae-moots-the-idea-of-agricultural-free-zones-in-africa-1.1178569.

BLOM. (2013, February). Egypt Securities. Talaat Mustafa Group.

Bloomberg. (2016, 25 February). McKinsey scores as Saudis call in consultants for economy reboot. www.bloomberg.com/news/articles/2016-02-25/mckinsey-scores-as-saudis-call-in-consultants-for-economy-reboot.

Bogaert, K. (2011). The problem of slums: shifting methods of neoliberal urban government in Morocco. *Development and Change*, **42**(3), 709–731.

(2013). Contextualising the Arab revolts: the politics behind three decades of neo-liberalism in the Arab world. *Middle East Critique*, 22(3), 213–234.

Bonizzi, B. (2014). Financialization in developing and emerging countries: a survey. *International Journal of Political Economy*, **42**(4), 83–107.

Borgmann, M. (2016, 9 May). Potentially game-changing Saudi Arabian government restructuring bolsters 9.5 GW renewable energy target by 2023. *Apricum*. www.apricum-group.com/saudi-arabia-announces-9-5-gw-renewable-energy-target-new-king-salman-renewable-energy-initiative/.

Boston Consulting Group (BCG). (2014). Global wealth 2014: riding a wave of growth. www.bcgperspectives.com.

(2017). Global wealth 2017: transforming the client experience.

Boyer, R. (2000). Is a finance-led growth regime a viable alternative to Fordism? A preliminary analysis. *Economy and Society*, **29**(1), 111–145.
Breisinger, C., Ecker, O., Al-Riffai, P., and Yu, B. (2012). *Beyond the Arab Awakening: Policies and Investments for Poverty Reduction and Food Security*. Washington, DC: International Food Policy Research Institute.
Brenner, N. (1999). Beyond state-centrism? Space, territoriality and geographical scale in globalization studies. *Theory and Society*, **28**, 39–78.
(2005). *New State Spaces: Urban Governance and the Rescaling of Statehood*. Oxford: Oxford University Press.
Brenner, N. and Schmid, C. (2015). Towards a new epistemology of the urban? *City*, **19**(2–3), 151–182.
Brenner, N. and Theodore, N., eds. (2002). *Spaces of Neoliberalism: Urban Restructuring in North America and Western Europe*. London: Blackwell.
Bromley, S. (1991). *American Hegemony and World Oil*. Cambridge: Polity Press.
Brown, C. (2008). *Inequality, Consumer Credit and the Saving Puzzle*. Cheltenham: Edward Elgar.
Bryan, R. (1987). The state and the internationalisation of capital: an approach to analysis. *Journal of Contemporary Asia*, **17**(3), 253–275.
Bsheer, R. (2017). W(h)ither Arabian Peninsula Studies? In Jens Hansen and Amal Ghazal, eds., *Handbook of Contemporary Middle East and North African History*. Oxford: Oxford University Press.
Buckley, M. and Hanieh, A. (2014). Diversification by urbanisation: tracing the property-finance nexus in Dubai and the Gulf. *International Journal of Urban and Regional Research*, **38**(1), 155–175.
Bundhun, R. (2011, 27 July). UAE investors urged to start developing farmland in Sudan. *The National*. www.thenational.ae/business/economy/uae-investors-urged-to-start-developing-farmland-in-sudan.
Bush, R. (2002). Land Reform and Counter-Revolution. In R. Bush, ed., *Counter Revolution in Egypt's Countryside: Land and Farmers in the Era of Economic Reform*. London: Zed Books.
(2004, May). Civil Society and the Uncivil State Land Tenure Reform in Egypt and the Crisis of Rural Livelihoods. Program Paper No. 9. United Nations Research Institute for Social Development.
(2016, December). Family farming in the Near East and North Africa. Working Paper No. 151. FAO (Food and Agriculture Organization of the United Nations).
Bush, R. and Martiniello, G. (2017). Food riots and protest: agrarian modernizations and structural crises. *World Development*, **91**, 193–207.
Business Times. (2015, 16 April). Saudi-backed group to control former Canadian Wheat Board. www.businesstimes.com.sg/energy-commodities/saudi-backed-group-to-control-former-canadian-wheat-board.
Business Year (TBY). (2014). The long haul. www.thebusinessyear.com/saudi-arabia-2014/the-long-haul/interview.
(2015). Food security: TBY talks to Mohammed Al Falasi, CEO of Jenaan Investment, on food security. www.thebusinessyear.com/uae-abu-dhabi-2015/food-security/column.
(2017). A greener future. www.thebusinessyear.com/saudi-arabia-2017/khalid-al-falih-minister-of-energy-industry-and-mineral-resources-saudi-arabia/qa.

Butter, D. (2015, 30 June). Revised interest in retail sector. *Middle East Economic Digest*. Supplement Egypt Construction Market Report, pp. 8–9.

Callinicos, A. (2009). *Imperialism and the Global Political Economy*. Cambridge: Polity.

Canakci, D. (1995, 11 October). Financial liberalization in the Middle East and North Africa: a case study of experiences in Egypt, Jordan and Tunisia. https://ssrn.com/abstract=1158173 or http://dx.doi.org/10.2139/ssrn.1158173.

Capital Business (CB). (n.d.). Restored confidence in the UAE real estate sector. http://cb-enterprise.com/main/details/real-estate/380.

Casey, S. (2015, 23 December). Saudi Arabia to take 20% stake in Brazil beef producer Minerva. *Bloomberg*. www.bloomberg.com/news/articles/2015-12-23/saudi-arabia-to-take-20-stake-in-brazil-beef-producer-minerva.

Cemnet. (n.d). The Global Cement Report – Online Database of Cement Plants. www.cemnet.com/global-cement-report/.

Central Bank of Egypt (CBE). (2017a). External Position of the Egyptian Economy. July/September 2016/2017.

(2017b). Financial and Monetary Sector – March 2017. *Monthly Statistical Bulletin*. www.cbe.org.eg/.

Central Bank of Jordan (CBJ). (2015). *Financial Stability Report*. Amman: Financial Stability Department, CBJ.

Chaaban, J. (2015, September 15). Mapping the control of Lebanese politicians over the banking sector. Presentation from Seminar at AUB IFI Auditorium.

Chang, D. (2016). From a global factory to continent of labour: labour and development in Asia. *Asia Labour Review*, **1**, 1–48.

Charbel, J. (2015, 15 March). Egyptian companies trapped in limbo by investment-friendly law. *Mada Masr*. www.madamasr.com/en/2015/03/15/feature/economy/egyptian-companies-trapped-in-limbo-by-investment-friendly-law/.

Chesnais, F. (2016). *Finance Capital Today: Corporations and Banks in the Lasting Global Slump*. Leiden: Brill.

Christophers, B. (2013). *Banking across Boundaries: Placing Finance in Capitalism*. Malden, MA: Wiley-Blackwell.

Cochrane, P. (2014, 22 December). Land of milk and money. *Executive Magazine*. www.executive-magazine.com/business-finance/business/dairy-land-of-milk-and-money.

Clapp, J. (2014). Financialization, distance, and global food politics. *Journal of Peasant Studies*, **41**(5), 797–814.

Coe, N., Lai, P., and Wójcik, D. (2014). Integrating finance into global production networks. *Regional Studies*, **48**(5), 761–777.

Construction Week Online (CW Online). (2015, 25 May). Saudi Arabia's $100bn KAEC could be ready by 2035. www.constructionweekonline.com/article-33784-saudi-arabias-100bn-kaec-could-be-ready-by-2035/.

Cooper, A. S. (2011). *The Oil Kings: How the U.S., Iran, and Saudi Arabia Changed the Balance of Power in the Middle East*. New York, NY: Simon and Schuster.

Cowen, D. (2014). *The Deadly Life of Logistics: Mapping Violence in the Global Trade*. Minneapolis, MN: University of Minnesota Press.

Cox, R. (1987). *Production, Power, and World Order: Social Forces in the Making of History*. New York, NY: Columbia University Press.

Cramer, C. (2006). *Civil War Is Not a Stupid Thing: Accounting for Violence in Developing Societies*. London: Hurst & Company.

Credit Suisse. (2016). *Global Wealth Databook November*. www.credit-suisse.com.

Crisp, W. (2015, 25 November). Electricity and energy ministry. *Middle East Economic Digest*. Supplement Egypt Projects.

Crotty, J. (2005). The Neoliberal Paradox: The Impact of Destructive Product Market Competition and Impatient Finance on Nonfinancial Corporations in the Neoliberal Era. In G. Epstein, ed., *Financialization and the World Economy*. Northampton, MA: Edward Elgar.

Crystal, J. (1995). *Oil and Politics in the Gulf: Rulers and Merchants in Kuwait and Qatar*. Glasgow: Cambridge University Press.

Cypher, J. (1989). The Debt Crisis as 'Opportunity': strategies to Revive US Hegemony. *Latin American Perspectives*, **16**(1), 52–78.

Daher, R. F. (2007). Reconceptualizing Tourism in the Middle East: Place, Heritage, Mobility and Competitiveness. In R. F. Daher, ed., *Tourism in the Middle East: Continuity, Change and Transformation*. Clevedon: Channel View Publications.

(2011). Discourses of Neoliberalism and Disparities in the City Landscape: Cranes, Craters, and an Exclusive Urbanity. In M. Ababsa and R. F. Daher, eds., *Cities, Urban Practices and Nation Building in Jordan*. Beirut: Presses de l'Ifpo, pp. 273–295.

Daniel, S. and Mittal, A. (2009). *The Great Land Grab: Rush for World's Farmland Threatens Food Security for the Poor*. Oakland, CA: Oakland Institute.

Dardot, P. and Laval, C. (2013). *The New Way of the World: On Neoliberal Society*. London: Verso.

Davies, K. (2013, January). China Investment Policy: An Update. OECD Working Papers on International Investment. OECD Publishing. http://dx.doi.org/10.1787/5k46911hmvbt-en.

Debruyne, P. (2013). Spatial Rearticulations of Statehood: Jordan's Geographies of Power under Globalization. PhD dissertation. University of Ghent.

Defense Security Cooperation Agency (DSCA). (2017, 1 November). Qatar – F-15QA Construction, Cybersecurity, and Force Protection Infrastructure. News release. www.dsca.mil.

Denis, E. (2012). The Commodification of the Ashwa'iyyat. In M. Ababsa, B. Dupret, and E. Denis, eds., *Popular Housing and Urban Land Tenure in the Middle East: Case Studies from Egypt, Syria, Jordan, Lebanon and Turkey*. Cairo: AUC Press, pp. 227–258.

Deutsche Bank. (2010, 15 July). Global Markets Research, Egypt: Real Estate.

(2012, 14 November). GCC financial markets long-term prospects for finance in the Gulf region. DB Research.

Dito, M. (2014). Kafala: Foundations of Migrant Exclusion in GCC Labour Markets. In A. Khalaf, O. AlShehabi, and A. Hanieh, eds., *Transit States: Labour, Migration and Citizenship in the Gulf*. London: Pluto Press, pp. 79–100.

Dixon, M. (2014). The land grab, finance capital, and food regime restructuring: the case of Egypt. *Review of African Political Economy*, **41**(140), 232–248.

Dos Santos, P. L. (2009). On the content of banking in contemporary capitalism. *Historical Materialism*, **17**, 180–213.

Dubai SME. (n.d.). Food and Beverages Manufacturing Report. Department of Economic Development. www.sme.ae/.

Duffield, M. (2014). *Global Governance and the New Wars: The Merging of Development and Security*. London: Zed Books.

Duménil, G. and Lévy, D. (2004). *Capital Resurgent: Roots of the Neoliberal Revolution*. Cambridge, MA: Harvard University Press.

EFG Hermes. (2016, September). Insights into the new reality. London MENA & Frontier Conference. files.efghermes.com.

Egypt Ministry of Finance (MoF). (2017). *al-muazanat al-amat lil-dawlat lil-sanat al-maliat 2017/2016* [Annual Budget 2016/2017]. www.mof.gov.eg/English/MofNews/WhatisNew/Pages/Budget20162017.aspx.

El-Batran, M. and Arandel, C. (1998). A shelter of their own: informal settlement expansion in Greater Cairo and government responses. *Environment and Urbanization*, **10**(1), 217–232.

Elsheshtway, Y. (2008a). The Great Divide: Struggling and Emerging Cities in the Arab world. In Y. Elsheshtawy, ed., *The Evolving Arab City: Tradition, Modernity, and Urban Development*. London: Routledge.

Elsheshtway, Y., ed. (2008b). *The Evolving Arab City: Tradition, Modernity and Urban Development*. London: Routledge.

Emaar. (2006). Emaar the Economic City IPO Prospectus. https://cma.org.sa.

Emirates NBD. (2015, 19 November). Macro Strategy.

Emirates 24/7. (2013, 20 October). Mohammed sets up higher committee for Dubai smart city. www.emirates247.com/news/mohammed-sets-up-higher-committee-for-dubai-smart-city-2013-10-20-1.524894.

Epstein, G., ed. (2005). *Financialization and the World Economy*. Cheltenham: Edward Elgar.

Etisalat. (2015). *Annual Report 2015*. Abu Dhabi: Etisalat Group.

(n.d.). Evolving the service provider architecture to unleash the potential of IoT. Etisalat White Paper. www.etisalat.com/en/system/docs/whitepapers/Etisalat-IoT.pdf.

European Bank for Reconstruction and Development (EBRD). (2012, 20 April). Deauville Partnership Finance Ministers' Meeting Communiqué. www.ebrd.com. Washington, DC: EBRD.

(2016). Jordan's Statement at the EBRD 2016 Annual Meeting and Business Forum London, 10–12 May. www.ebrd.com/documents/osg/am-jor-eng.pdf.

(2017). *Annual Report 2016*. London: EBRD.

European Investment Bank (EIB). (2011, May). *FEMIP Study on PPP Legal and Financial Frameworks in the Mediterranean Partner Countries*, vol. 1 (Luxembourg: EIB).

European Union (EU). (2013). European Union, trade in goods with GCC 6. http://trade.ec.europa.eu/doclib/html/111509.htm.

(2016). European Union, trade in goods with GCC 6. http://trade.ec.europa.eu/doclib/html/113482.htm.

EY Global. (2017, 27 July). Egypt enacts new investment law to promote foreign investments. EY Global Tax Alert Library.

Fahmy, N. (2015, 24 February). President approves 'terrorist entities' law. *Daily News Egypt*. https://dailynewsegypt.com/2015/02/24/president-approves-terrorist-entities-law/.

Fahy, M. (2017, 20 February). Bechtel lands contract to run key Saudi projects body. www.thenational.ae/business/property/bechtel-lands-contract-to-run-key-saudi-projects-body-1.76504.

Farazi, S., Feyen, E., and Rocha, R. (2011). Bank Ownership and Performance in the Middle East and North Africa Region. World Bank Policy Research Paper 5620. Washington, DC: World Bank.

Farrell, M. and Parasie, N. (2016, 9 June). Saudi Aramco IPO: the biggest fee event in Wall Street history. *Wall Street Journal*. www.wsj.com/articles/saudi-aramco-ipo-wall-streets-white-whale-1465464606.

Fassin, D. (2007). Humanitarianism: a nongovernmental government. *Nongovernmental Politics*, 149–160.

Fattah, H. (1997). *The Politics of Regional Trade in Iraq, Arabia, and the Gulf 1745–1900*. Albany, NY: State University of New York Press.

Ferziger, J. and Waldman, P. (2017, 2 February). How do Israel's tech firms do business in Saudi Arabia? Very quietly. *Bloomberg Business Week*. www.bloomberg.com/news/features/2017-02-02/how-do-israel-s-tech-firms-do-business-in-saudi-arabia-very-quietly.

Financial Times (FT). (2016, 1 March). The great land rush. FT investigations. https://ig.ft.com/sites/land-rush-investment/ethiopia/.

Fine, B. (2010). Neoliberalism as Financialisation. In A. Saad-Filho and G. Yalman, eds., *Economic Transitions to Neoliberalism in Middle-Income Countries*. New York, NY: Routledge, pp. 11–23.

Fine, B. and Saad-Filho, A. (2016). Thirteen things you need to know about neoliberalism. *Critical Sociology*, **43**(4–5), 685–706.

Food and Agriculture Organization of the United Nations (FAO). (2006, June). Food Security. Policy Brief, no. 2.

Food Security Information Network (FSIN). (2017, March). Global Report on Food Crises 2017. www.wfp.org.

Forbes. (2013). Top 500 companies in the Arab world 2013. www.forbesmiddleeast.com/en/list/top-500-companies-in-the-arab-world-2013/.

(2017). The world's biggest public companies. www.forbes.com/global2000/list/.

Foreman, C. (2017). Privatization comes of age. *MEED Business Review*, **2**(5), 16–18.

Foreman, C. and Rademeyer, E. (2017). GCC projects market records negative growth. *MEED Business Review*, **2**(2), 76–77.

French, S., Leyshon, A., and Wainwright, T. (2011). Financializing space, spacing financialization. *Progress in Human Geography*, **35**(6), 798–819.

Friedman, H. and McMichael, P. (1989). Agriculture and the state system: the rise and decline of national agricultures, 1870 to the present. *Sociologia Ruralis*, **29**, 93–117.

Froud, J., Haslam, C., Johal, S., and William, K. (2000). Shareholder value and financialization: consultancy promises, management moves. *Economy and Society*, **29**(1), 80–110.

Fuccaro, N. (2010). The making of Gulf ports before oil. *Liwa. Journal of the National Centre for Documentation and Research*, **2**(3), 19–32.

(2014). Rethinking the History of Port Cities in the Gulf. In L. Porter, ed., *The Persian Gulf in Modern Times: People, Ports, and History*. New York, NY: Palgrave-Macmillan.

Galal, E. (2016). Saleh Kamel: Investing in Islam. In D. della Ratta, N. Sakr, and J. Skovgaard-Petersen, eds., *Arab Media Moguls*. London: IB Taurus, pp. 81–97.

Gao, Y. (2012). *China as the Workshop of the World: An Analysis at the National and Industrial Level of China in the International Division of Labour*. London: Routledge.

Garcia-Kilroy, C. and Silva, A. C. (2011, March). Reforming Government Debt Markets in MENA. Policy Research Working Paper, No. 5611. Washington, DC: World Bank.

Gardner, A. (2010). *City of Strangers: Gulf Migration and the Indian Community of Bahrain*. Ithaca, NY: Cornell University Press.

Ghawi, S. (2015, 24 August). Jordan Vegetable Oil Industries suing traders, distributors to collect JD3.2m. *Jordan Times*. www.jordantimes.com/news/business/jordan-vegetable-oil-industries-suing-traders-distributors-collect-jd32m.

Gibson, H. (1989). *The Eurocurrency Markets, Domestic Financial Policy and the International Instability*. London: Macmillan.

Global Investment House. (2016a, 17 April). Mabanee, Global Research Initiation Report Equity – Kuwait Real Estate Sector.

(2016b, August). GCC Markets Performance.

Globes Business. (2015, 1 February). Elbit unit employee dies mysteriously in Saudi Arabia. www.globes.co.il/en/article-elbit-unit-employee-dies-mysteriously-in-saudi-arabia-1001005628.

Gobat, J. and Kostial, K. (2016, June). Syria's Conflict Economy. IMF Working Paper, Middle East and Central Asia Department.

GOLCER. (2014, June). Islamic Finance Bulletin. Gulf One Lancaster Centre for Economic Research.

Goswami, M. (2002). Rethinking the modular nation form: toward a sociohistorical conception of nationalism. *Comparative Studies in Society and History*, **44**(4), 770–799.

Gowan, P. (1999). *The Global Gamble: Washington's Faustian Bid for World Dominance*. London: Verso.

Grifferty, M. (2017, 5 June). Lift-off for GCC bonds and sukuk: the Middle East is now firmly on the global map of emerging market issuance centres. *The National*. www.thenational.ae/business/markets/lift-off-for-gcc-bonds-and-sukuk-1.27500.

Guardian. (2017, 2 August). Yemen: more than 1 million children at risk of cholera – charity. www.theguardian.com/world/2017/aug/02/yemen-more-than-one-million-children-at-risk-of-cholera-charity.

Gulf Finance House (GFH). (2016, October). *Sector Report: GCC Education*.

Gulf Petrochemicals and Chemicals Association (GPCA). (2015). *Annual Report*. www.gpca.org.ae/library/annual-reports/.

Haidar, M. (2011, 12 January). *qaribaan: al-rfe limajlis al-wuzara' bi-siaghat jadidat lil-aistratijiat al-ziraeiat 2020* [Council of Ministers Soon to Formulate New Agricultural Strategy 2020]. *Al Riyadh.* www.alriyadh.com/593971.

Hall, S. and Leyshon, A. (2013). Editorial: financialization, space and place. *Regional Studies*, **47**(6), 831–833.

Hanieh, A. (2011a). *Capitalism and Class in the Gulf Arab States*. New York, NY: Palgrave-Macmillan.

(2011b). The internationalisation of Gulf capital and Palestinian class formation. *Capital & Class*, **35**(1), 81–106.

(2013). *Lineages of Revolt: Issues of Contemporary Capitalism in the Middle East.* Chicago, IL: Haymarket Books.

(2015a). Capital, Labor, and State: Rethinking the Political Economy of Oil in the Gulf. In A. Ghazal and J. Hanssen, eds., *The Oxford Handbook of Contemporary Middle-Eastern and North African History.* www.oxfordhandbooks.com/view/10.1093/oxfordhb/9780199672530.001.0001/oxfordhb-9780199672530-e-3.

(2015b). Shifting priorities or business as usual? Continuity and change in the post-2011 IMF and World Bank engagement with Tunisia, Morocco and Egypt. *British Journal of Middle Eastern Studies*, **42**(1), 119–134.

(2016). Absent regions: spaces of financialisation in the Arab world. *Antipode*, **48**(5), 1228–1248.

Hardt, M. and Negri, A. (2000). *Empire*. Cambridge, MA: Harvard University Press.

Hart, G. (2016). Relational comparison revisited: Marxist postcolonial geographies in practice. *Progress in Human Geography*, **42**(3), pp. 1–24.

Harvey, D. (1974). Class-monopoly rent, finance capital and the urban revolution. *Regional Studies*, **8**(3), 239–255.

(1978). The urban process under capitalism: a framework for analysis. *International Journal of Urban and Regional Research*, **2**, 101–131.

(1999). *Limits to Capital*. London: Verso.

(2000). *Spaces of Hope*. Berkeley, CA: University of California Press.

(2005). *A Brief History of Neoliberalism*. Oxford: Oxford University Press.

Hassler, O. (2011). *Housing and Real Estate Finance in Middle East and North Africa Countries*. Washington, DC: World Bank.

Henderson, C. (2017). The Gulf Arab States and Egypt's Political Economy: Examining New Spaces of Food and Agriculture. PhD dissertation, SOAS, University of London.

Hopper, Matthew. (2015). *Slaves of One Master: Globalization and Slavery in Arabia in the Age of Empire*. New Haven, CT: Yale University Press.

Hourani, N. (2010). Transnational pathways and politico-economic power: globalisation and the Lebanese civil war. *Geopolitics*, **15**(2), 290–311.

(2014). Urbanism and neoliberal order: the development and redevelopment of Amman. *Journal of Urban Affairs*, **36**(Suppl. 2), 634–649.

Housing Bank for Trade and Finance. (2015). Annual Report. www.hbtf.com.

Howitt, R. (1993). 'A world in a grain of sand': towards a reconceptualization of geographical scale. *Australian Geographer*, **24**, 33–44.

Human Rights Watch (HRW). (2012, 28 August). Ethiopia: army commits torture, rape. www.hrw.org/news/2012/08/28/ethiopia-army-commits-torture-rape.

(2015, 10 May). *Detained, Beaten, Deported Saudi Abuses against Migrants during Mass Expulsions.* www.hrw.org/report/2015/05/10/detained-beaten-deported/saudi-abuses-against-migrants-during-mass-expulsions.

Huws, U. (2012). Crisis as Capitalist Opportunity: New Accumulation through Public Service Commodification. In Greg Albo, Leo Panitch, and Vivek Chibber, eds., *The Crisis and the Left: Socialist Register 2012.* London: Merlin Press, pp. 64–84.

Hvidt, M. (2009). The Dubai model: an outline of key development-process elements in Dubai. *International Journal of Middle East Studies*, **41**, 397–418.

Ijtehadi, Y. (2007, 5 May). Growing pains – private equity industry in MENA. *Arab News.* www.arabnews.com/node/298022.

International Monetary Fund (IMF). (2007). *Sovereign Wealth Funds and Reserve Assets: A Statistical Perspective.* Washington, DC: IMF.

(2014). *Article IV Consultation Staff Report: Egypt.* Washington, DC: IMF.

(2016a). *Government Finance Statistics.* Washington, DC: IMF. http://data.imf.org.

(2016b, October). *GCC Surveillance Note.* Washington, DC: IMF.

(2016c, October). *Regional Economic Update – Middle East and Central Asia.*

(2017a, May). *Regional Economic Update – Middle East and Central Asia.* Washington, DC: IMF.

(2017b, July). Article IV staff report – Jordan, table 3d. Washington, DC: IMF.

International Organisation of Migration (IOM). (2015). World Migration Report 2015 Urban Migration Trends in the Middle East and North Africa Region and the Challenge of Conflict-Induced Displacement.

Islamic Financial Services Board (ISFB). (2015). *Islamic Financial Services Industry: Stability Report 2015.* Kuala Lumpur: ISFB.

Ismail, S. (2013). Urban subalterns in the Arab revolutions: Cairo and Damascus in comparative perspective. *Comparative Studies in Society and History*, **55**(4), 865–894.

Issac, J. (2011, 13 May). Damac rejects Egyptian court verdict. *Khaleej Times.* www.khaleejtimes.com/business/local/damac-rejects-egyptian-8232-court-verdict.

Issawi, A. (2011, 19 September). *al-khaskhasa ... hikayat baye 'usul misr* [Privatisation ... The Story of Selling Egypt's Assets]. *Masress.* www.masress.com/akhersaa/3174.

Ivanonva, M. (2012). Marx, Minsky and the Great Recession. *Review of Radical Political Economics*, **45**(1), 59–75.

Jerusalem Post. (2017, 6 September). Netanyahu: cooperation with Arab world stronger than ever. www.jpost.com/Breaking-News/Netanyahu-Cooperation-with-Arab-world-stronger-today-than-ever-504369.

Jhanawi, K. (2017, 5 June). Qata' al-alaqat ma' Qatar [Cutting the relationship with Qatar]. *Al Sabah News.* www.assabahnews.tn/.

Jones, T. C. (2010). *Desert Kingdom: How Oil and Water Forged Modern Saudi Arabia.* Cambridge, MA: Harvard University Press.

(2012). America, oil and war in the Middle East. *Journal of American History*, **99**(1), 208–218.
Jordan Times. (2017, 8 April). Donors pledge around $40-billion aid to Syrian refugees' hosts. www.jordantimes.com/news/local/donors-pledge-around-40-billion-aid-syrian-refugees%E2%80%99-hosts.
Kamrava, M. (2009). Royal factionalism and political liberalization in Qatar. *Middle East Journal*, **63**(3), 401–420.
ed. (2016). *Gateways to the World: Port Cities in the Persian Gulf.* London: Hurst.
Kanna, A. (2009). Making cadres of the 'city–corporation': cultural and identity politics in neoliberal Dubai. *Review of Middle East Studies*, **43**(2), 207–218.
(2011). *Dubai: The City as Corporation.* Minneapolis, MN: University of Minnesota Press.
(2016). Gulf Urbanism: The Semantic Field of a Category Space. In M. Kamrava, ed., *Gateways to the World: Port Cities in the Persian Gulf.* London: Hurst.
Kerr, S. (2016, 10 June). Five goals of Saudi Arabia's ambitious transformation plans. *Financial Times.* www.ft.com/content/cbb86ed2-2e38-11e6-a18d-a96ab29e3c95.
(2017, 16 November). Saudi authorities offer freedom deals to princes and businessmen. *Financial Times.* www.ft.com/content/e888a676-caa9-11e7-ab18-7a9fb7d6163e.
Keshavarzian, A. (2016). From Port Cities to Cities without Ports. In M. Kamrava, ed., *Gateways to the World: Port Cities in the Persian Gulf.* London: Hurst.
Keulertz, M. and Woertz, E. (2015). States as Actors in International Agro-Investments. In C. Gironde and C. Golay, eds., *Large-Scale Land Acquisitions: Focus on South-East Asia*, International Development Policy Series No. 6. Geneva: Brill-Nijhoff, pp. 30–52.
Khalaf, A. (2014). The Politics of Migration. In A. Khalaf, O. AlShehabi, and A. Hanieh, eds., *Transit States: Labour, Migration and Citizenship in the Gulf.* London: Pluto Press, pp. 39–56.
Khalaf, A., AlShehabi, O., and Hanieh, A., eds. (2014). *Transit States: Labour, Migration and Citizenship in the Gulf.* London: Pluto Press.
Khaleej Times. (2013, 22 March). Al Dahra to set up distribution facility at Khalifa Port. www.khaleejtimes.com.
Khalili, L. (2017). The infrastructural power of the military: the geoeconomic role of the US Army Corps of Engineers in the Arabian Peninsula. *European Journal of International Relations*, 1–23. http://doi.org/10.1177/1354066117742955.
Kim, J. (2016, 6 April). Happy Saudi cows eat California alfalfa. *Marketplace.* www.marketplace.org/2016/03/28/world/happy-saudi-cows-eating california-alfalfa.
Kingdom of Saudi Arabia (KSA). (2016a). Vision 2030, Riyadh. http://vision2030.gov.sa/.
(2016b). National Transformation Program 2020, Riyadh. http://vision2030.gov.sa/.
Kinninmont, J. (2017, July). Vision 2030 and Saudi Arabia's Social Contract Austerity and Transformation. Research Paper, Chatham House, Middle East and North Africa Programme.

Kosik, K. (1976). *Dialectics of the Concrete: A Study on Problems of Man and World.* Dordrecht: D. Reidel.

Krippner, G. (2005). The financialization of the American economy. *Socio-Economic Review*, **3**, 173–208.

Kumar, S. (2016). Tunisia proposes $2 bln joint fund with Qatar. *The Peninsula.* http://economicme.com/news/tunisia-proposes-2-bln-joint-fund-with-qatar/.

Kuwait Life Sciences (KLSC). (2015). *Kuwait 2015 Health Mega-Projects Report.* www.klsc.com.kw/.

Langley, P. (2008). *The Everyday Life of Global Finance.* Oxford: Oxford University Press.

Lapavitsas, C. (2013). *Profiting without Producing: How Finance Exploits Us.* London: Verso.

Lefebvre, H. (1991 [1974]). *The Production of Space.* Malden, MA: Blackwell.

Leitner, H. and Miller, B. (2006). Scale and the limitations of ontological debate: a commentary on Marston, Jones and Woodward. *Transactions of the Institute of British Geographers*, **NS 32**, 116–125.

Lerman, E. and Teitelbaum, J. (2016, 17 April). Sailing through the straits: the meaning for Israel of restored Saudi sovereignty over Tiran and Sanafir Islands. BESA Center Perspectives Paper No. 340. https://besacenter.org/perspectives-papers/meaning-israel-restored-saudi-sovereignty-tiran-sanafir-islands/.

Linklaters. (2015, March). Kingdom of Morocco: a new law to promote public-private partnerships.

Lione, J. (2014). GCC region's schools. Faithful+Gould. www.fgould.com/middle-east/articles/gcc-regions-schools/.

Lizarralde, G. (2014). *The Invisible Houses: Rethinking and Designing Low-Cost Housing in Developing Countries.* New York, NY: Routledge.

Longva, A. N. (2000). Citizenship in the Gulf States: Conceptualization and Practice. In N. Butenschon, U. Davis, and M. Hassassian, eds., *Citizenship and the State in the Middle East: Approaches and Applications.* Syracuse, NY: Syracuse University Press, pp. xi–xvi.

Mahdi, Wa'el. (2010, 13 June). *Indunisia taftah al-bab li-aistithmarat saudiat 18 milyar rial baed tawaqufaha amayn* [Indonesia opens the door to 18 billion riyal in investments after two years]. *Al Watan.* www.alwatan.com.sa/Politics/News_Detail.aspx?ArticleID=6495.

Mahgoub, Y. (2008). Kuwait: Learning from a Globalized City. In Y. Elsheshtway, ed., *The Evolving Arab City: Tradition, Modernity and Urban Development.* London: Routledge.

Mahmood, H. (2013, September). Presentation by Houssam Mahmood, CEO of Al Dahra Agriculture. www.europeanforage.org.

Makdisi, S. (1997). Laying claim to Beirut: urban narrative and spatial identity in the age of Solidere. *Critical Inquiry*, **23**(3), 660–705.

Malek, C. (2014, 22 February). GCC's dependence on imported food to be highlighted at Dubai summit. *The National.* www.thenational.ae.

Mandel, E. (1975). The industrial cycle in late capitalism. *New Left Review*, **1** (90), 3–25.

Mango, T. (2014). The Impact of Real Estate Construction and Holding Companies: A Case Study of Beirut's Solidere and Amman's Abdali. PhD dissertation, University of Exeter.

Markaz. (2017, March). GCC Bonds and Sukuk Market Survey.

Marois, T. (2012). Finance, Finance Capital, and Financialisation. In. B. Fine and A. Saad Filho, eds., *The Elgar Companion to Marxist Economics*. Cheltenham: Edward Elgar, pp. 138–143.

Marot, B. (2012). The 'Old Rent' Law in Beirut: An Incentive or Disincentive for Gentrification? IFPO. https://ifpo.hypotheses.org/4376.

Marshall, S. and Stacher, J. (2012). Egypt's generals and transitional capital. *MERIP Middle East Report*, **42**(262).

Marston, S. A. (2000). The social construction of scale. *Progress in Human Geography*, **24**(2), 219–242.

Marx, K. (1973). *Grundrisse*. Harmondsworth: Penguin Books.

McBride, E. (2015, 4 November). The story behind Abraaj Group's stunning rise in global private equity. *Forbes*. www.forbes.com/sites/elizabethmacbride/2015/11/04/the-story-behind-abraajs-stunning-rise/#2537b71c20ac.

McDonald, David, A., ed. (2014). *Rethinking Corporatization and Public Services in the Global South*. London: Zed Books.

McFarlane, C. and Rutherford, J. (2008, June). Political infrastructures: governing and experiencing the fabric of the city. *International Journal of Urban and Regional Research*, **32**(2), 363–374.

McGann, J. (2008). Pushback against NGOs in Egypt. *International Journal of Not-for-Profit Law*, **10**(4), 29–42. www.icnl.org/research/journal/vol10iss4/special_3.htm.

McKinsey Global Institute (MGI). (2008, July). *The New Power Brokers: Gaining Clout in Turbulent Markets*.

McMichael, P. (2009). A food regime genealogy. *Journal of Peasant Studies*, **36** (1), 139–169.

(2012). The land grab and corporate food regime restructuring. *Journal of Peasant Studies*, **39**(3–4), 681–701.

(2016). Commentary: Food regime for thought. *Journal of Peasant Studies*, **43** (3), 648–670.

McNally, D. (2009). From financial crisis to world slump. *Historical Materialism*, **17**, 35–83.

MEED. (2015, 15 March). PPP agency develops pipeline of projects. www.meed.com/countries/egypt/ppp-agency-develops-pipeline-of-projects/3207302.article.

Meiksins Wood, E. (2003). *Empire of Capital*. New York, NY: Verso.

Melly, Paul. (2013). GCC Investors Eye African Farmland. *MEED Special Issue: Africa and the Middle East*, 20–21.

Melman, Y. (2008, 18 September). Should retired IDF officers do business in Arab states or not? *Haaretz*. www.haaretz.com/print-edition/features/should-retired-idf-officers-do-business-in-arab-states-or-not-1.254189.

MENAFN. (2015, 29 March). Almarai announces new investments, studies acquisition. www.farmlandgrab.org/post/print/24718.

MENA Private Equity Association (MENAPEA). (2015). 10th Annual MENA Private Equity and Venture Capital Report, 2015. www.menapea.com/.

Menoret, P. (2014). *Joyriding in Riyadh: Oil, Urbanism, and Road Revolt in Saudi Arabia*. Cambridge: Cambridge University Press.

Mezzadra, S. (2012, January). How many histories of labor? Towards a theory of postcolonial capitalism. *European Institute for Progressive Cultural Policies*. http://eipcp.net/transversal/0112/mezzadra/en.

Mitchell, T. (1991). The limits of the state: beyond statists approach and their critics. *American Political Science Review*, **85**(1), 77–96.

(2011). *Carbon Democracy: Political Power in the Age of Oil*. London: Verso.

Mohammed, I. (2017, 28 August). Expat remittances witness a drop in recent months. *Saudi Gazette*. http://saudigazette.com.sa/article/514038/SAUDI-ARABIA/Remittances.

Moody's Investors Service. (2017, 27 July). Sector Comment. Saudi Arabia's Local Sukuk Issuance Is Credit Positive for Islamic Banks. www.moodys.com/research/Saudi-Arabias-Local-Sukuk-Issuance-Is-Credit-Positive-for-Islamic–PBC_196653.

Moore, C. H. (1987). Prisoners' financial dilemmas: a consociational future for Lebanon? *American Political Science Review*, **81**(1), 201–218.

Muñoz-Martínez, H. and Marois, T. (2014). Capital fixity and mobility in response to the 2008–09 crisis: variegated neoliberalism in Mexico and Turkey. *Environment and Planning D: Society and Space*, 32(6), 1102–1119.

Nagraj, A. (2013, 9 April). Top 10 largest aluminium smelters in the world. *Gulf Business*. www.gulfbusiness.com.

National. (2017, 19 January). Sheikh Mohammed approves expansion of International Humanitarian City in Dubai. www.thenational.ae/uae/government/sheikh-mohammed-approves-expansion-of-international-humanitarian-city-in-dubai-1.9488.

National Bank of Kuwait (NBK). (2016). Consolidated Financial Statements 2016. www.nbk.com.

Nereim, V., Algethami, S., and Martin, M. (2017). Saudi Arabia's economic overhaul claims a victim. www.bloomberg.com/news/articles/2017-09-14/saudi-arabia-s-economic-overhaul-claims-a-victim.

Norfield, T. (2016). *The City*. London: Verso.

Novak, P. (2017). Placing borders in development. *Geopolitics*, **21**(3), 483–512.

Novelli, M. (2016). Public private partnerships in education in crisis and conflict affected contexts: a framing paper. Roundtable on Public Private Partnerships in Education in Crisis and Conflict Affected Contexts, Open Society Foundation, New York, 27–28 June.

Obeid, Abdullah. (2010). King Abdullah's Initiative for Saudi Agricultural Investment Abroad: A Way of Enhancing Saudi Food Security. Presentation from Expert Group Meeting on 'Achieving Food Security in Member Countries in Post-Crisis World', Islamic Development Bank, Jeddah, 2–3 May.

Office for the Coordination of Humanitarian Affairs (OCHA). (2016). United Nations. *Humanitarian Needs Overview Yemen 2017*.

(2017). *OCHA Humanitarian Response Plan*, Advance Executive Summary 2017.

Oguz, S. (2013). Turning the Crisis into Opportunity: Turkish State's Response to the 2008 Crisis. In Baris Karaagac, ed., *Accumulation, Crises, Struggles: Capital and Labour in Contemporary Capitalism*. Berlin: Lit Verlag.

Ollman, B. (2003). *Dance of the Dialectic: Steps in Marx's Method.* Urbana, IL: University of Illinois Press.

Omar, O. K. M. (2014). Impacts of agricultural policy on irrigation water demand: a case study of Saudi Arabia. *International Journal of Water Resources Development*, **30**(2), 282–292.

Ooredoo. (2015). Annual Report. http://ooredoo.com/en/investors/financial_information/annual-reports/.

(2016, 24 February). Ooredoo promotes 'internet of things' solutions with new service launches. *Cision PR News Wire*. www.prnewswire.com/news-releases/ooredoo-promotes-internet-of-things-solutions-with-new-service-launches-300225259.html.

Oosterlynck, S. and González, S. (2013). 'Don't waste a crisis': opening up the city for neoliberal experimentation. *International Journal of Urban and Regional Research*, **37**(3), 1075–1082.

Organisation for Economic Co-operation and Development (OECD). (2013). *State-Owned Enterprises in the Middle East and North Africa: Engines of Development and Competitiveness?* Paris: OECD Publishing.

(2016, 3 June). Jordan's statement from the London conference on Supporting Syria and the Region, 4 February 2016.

Ouda, Omar K. M. (2014). Impacts of agricultural policy on irrigation water demand: a case study of Saudi Arabia. *International Journal of Water Resources Development*, **30**(2), 282–292.

Oxford Business Group. (2014). *The Report: Egypt 2014.* www.oxfordbusinessgroup.com/egypt-2014.

Palley, T. I. (2002). Economic contradictions coming home to roost? Does the US economy face a long-term aggregate demand generation problem? *Journal of Post Keynesian Economics*, **25**, 9–32.

Palloix, C. (1977). Conceptualizing the internationalization of capital. *Review of Radical Political Economics*, **9**(2), 17–28.

Panitch, L. and Gindin, S. (2003). Global Capitalism and American Empire. In C. Leys and L. Panitch, eds., *Socialist Register 2004: The New Imperial Challenge*. London: Merlin Press, pp. 1–42.

(2012). *The Making of Global Capitalism: The Political Economy of American Empire*. London: Verso.

Panitch, L. and Konings, M., eds. (2008). *American Empire and the Political Economy of Global Finance*. London: Palgrave.

Parker, C. (2009). Tunnel-bypasses and minarets of capitalism: Amman as neoliberal assemblage. *Political Geography*, **28**, 110–120.

Parker, C. and Debruyne, P. (2011). Reassembling the Political Life of Community. Naturalizing Neoliberalism in Amman. In J. Künkel and M. Mayer, eds., *Neoliberal Urbanism and Its Contestations. Crossing Theoretical Boundaries*. New York, NY: Palgrave Macmillan, pp. 155–172.

Peck, J. (2001). Neoliberalizing states: thin policies/hard outcomes. *Progress in Human Geography*, **25**, 445–455.

Peck, J., Brenner, N., and Theodore, N. (2010). Postneoliberalism and its malcontents. *Antipode*, **41**(1), 94–116.

Peck, J., Theodore, N., and Brenner, N. (2013). Neoliberal urbanism redux? *International Journal of Urban and Regional Research*, **37**(3), 1091–1099.

Phillips, C. (2016). *The Battle for Syria: International Rivalry in the New Middle East*. New Haven, CT: Yale University Press.

Pike, A. and Pollard, J. (2010). Economic geographies of financialization. *Economic Geography*, **86**(1), 29–51.

Poulantzas, N. (1974). The internationalisation of capitalist relations and the nation-state. *Economy and Society*, **3**(2), 145–179.

Primack, D. (2016, 15 October). This company is trying to raise the world's largest private equity fund. *Fortune*. http://fortune.com/2016/10/15/private-equity-worlds-largest-softbank.

QNB. (2015). Al Ahli Annual Report 2015.

Ramos, S. (2010). *Dubai Amplified: The Engineering of a Port Geography*. Farnham, UK: Ashgate.

(2011). Dubai's Jebal Ali Port: Trade, Territory and Infrastructure. In Carola Hein, ed., *Port Cities: Dynamic Landscapes and Global Networks*. London: Routledge.

Reed, J. (2015, 7 October). Bank of Palestine has not only survived but remained profitable. *Financial Times*. www.ft.com/intl/cms/s/0/eec5a60c-50b1-11e5-b029-b9d50a74fd14.html#axzz44Ym0fnC3.

Reuters. (2011, 15 February). EBRD aims to complete Egypt inclusion study by spring.

(2016, 4 November). Tunisian PM sacks minister over criticism of Saudi Arabian Islam. *Reuters*. www.reuters.com/article/us-tunisia-saudi/tunisian-pm-sacks-minister-over-criticism-of-saudi-arabian-islam-idUSKBN12Z1QD.

(2017, 26 February). Bechtel wins contract to run Saudi project management office. www.reuters.com/article/saudi-projects-bechtel/bechtel-wins-contract-to-run-saudi-project-management-office-idUSL8N1G62AN.

Riyad Capital. (2015, 1 October). Saudi Arabian Cement, 3rd quarter 2015 overview. www.riyadcapital.com.

Roberts, M. (2016). *The Long Depression: Marxism and the Global Crisis of Capitalism*. Chicago, IL: Haymarket Books.

Robinson, W. (2002). Capitalist Globalization and the Transnationalization of the State. In M. Rupert and H. Smith, eds., *Historical Materialism and Globalization: Essays on Continuity and Change*. New York, NY: Routledge, pp. 210–229.

Roll, S. (2013). Egypt's Business Elite after Mubarak. A Powerful Player between Generals and Brotherhood. Stiftung Wissenschaft und Politik, Research Paper 8.

Roscoe, A. (2016, December). New hope for private players. *MEED Business Review*, **1**(11), 91.

Rossotto, C. M., Sekkat, K., and Varoudakis, A. (2005). Opening up telecommunications to competition and MENA integration in the world economy. *Journal of International Development*, **17**, 931–955.

Rouli, A. (2010, 21 September). *Thalatha tahadiyat tuajih al-mubadarat al-saudiat lilaistithmar al-ziraeii fi 21 dawlatan arabiatan wa'ajnabiatan* [Three challenges facing the Saudi Agricultural Investment Initiative in 21 Arab and foreign countries]. *Al Riyadh*. www.alriyadh.com/561305.

Rude, C. (2005). The Role of Financial Discipline in Imperial Strategy. In L. Panitch and C. Leys, eds., *Socialist Register 2005: The Empire Reloaded*, vol. 41, London: Merlin Press, pp. 82–107.

Sabry, S. (2010). How poverty is underestimated in Greater Cairo, Egypt. *Environment & Urbanization (IIED)*, **22**(2), 523–541.

Saeed, S (2016). Halwani Brothers targets exports worth EGP 150m by end of 2016. *Daily News Egypt*. https://dailynewsegypt.com/2016/10/14/559003/.

Sahoo, S. (2014, 9 September). Dubai International Humanitarian City sees growing demand as conflicts rage in the region. *The National*. www.thenational.ae/business/dubai-international-humanitarian-city-sees-growing-demand-as-conflicts-rage-in-the-region-1.240235.

(2016, 29 February). Agthia expands Saudi Arabia footprint with retail flour distribution deal. *The National*. www.thenational.ae/business/agthia-expands-saudi-arabia-footprint-with-retail-flour-distribution-deal-1.203312.

Saif, S. (2016, 5 September). When consultants reign. *Jacobin*. www.jacobinmag.com/2016/05/saudi-arabia-aramco-salman-mckinsey-privatization/.

Sakr, N. (2001). *Satellite Realms: Transnational Television, Globalization and the Middle East*. London: IB Taurus.

Salerno, T. (2011). Transnational Land Deals in Mindanao: Situating Ambivalent Farmer Responses in Local Politics. International Conference on Global Land Grabbing, 6–8 April.

Saoud, D. (2016, 28 August). UN official: rebuilding Arab war-torn countries a 'global public good'. *Arab Weekly*, issue 70.

Sathish, V. M. (2015, 22 May). UAE firm to give incentive to farmers abroad to enhance food security. *Emirates 24/7*. www.emirates247.com/business/corporate/uae-firm-to-give-incentive-to-farmers-abroad-to-enhance-food-security-2015-05-22-1.591515.

Saudi British Bank (SABB). (2016, May). Monthly Business Insight. www.sabb.com.

Saudi Gazette. (2016). Private sector to drive growth in education. http://saudigazette.com.sa/article/148862/Private-sector-to-drive-growth-in-education-sector-Al-Isa.

Saunders, A. (2015, February). The growing cement industry of the UAE. *Global Cement Magazine*, pp. 54–60.

Savola. (2015). Investor Presentation, Second Quarter 2015. www.savola.com.

Sayer, D. (1987). *The Violence of Abstraction: The Analytic Foundations of Historical Materialism*. Oxford: Basil Blackwell.

Schneider, M. (2008, December). *'We Are Hungry!' A Summary Report of Food Riots, Government Responses, and States of Democracy in 2008*. Ithaca, NY: Development Sociology, Cornell University. http://stuffedandstarved.org/drupal/files/We%20are%20Hungry%20%20A%20Summary%20Report%

20of%20Food%20Riots,%20Government%20Responses,%20andStates%20of%20Democracy%20in%202008.pdf.

Scott, A. (2015, 9 February). Al Ghurair adds to storage capacity with grain silos in Egypt. *The National*. www.thenational.ae/business/al-ghurair-adds-to-storage-capacity-with-grain-silos-in-egypt-1.29021.

Setser, B. and Ziemba, R. (2009, January). GCC Sovereign Funds: Reversal of Fortune. Washington, DC: Council on Foreign Relations Working Paper.

Setterfield, M. (2013). Wages, Demand and US Macroeconomic Travails: Diagnosis and Prognosis. In S. M. Fazzari, B. Z. Cynamon, and M. Setterfield, eds., *After the Great Recession: The Struggle for Economic Recovery and Growth*. Cambridge: Cambridge University Press, pp. 158–184.

Shaikh, A. (2016). *Capitalism: Competition, Conflict, Crises*. Oxford: Oxford University Press.

Shehabi, O. and Suroor, S. (2015). Unpacking 'accumulation by dispossession', 'fictitious commodification', and 'fictitious capital formation': tracing the dynamics of Bahrain's land reclamation. *Antipode*, **4**(1), 835–856.

Sims, D. (2010). *Understanding Cairo: The Logic of a City out of Control*. Cairo: University of Cairo Press.

Smaller, C. and Mann, H. (2009, May). A Thirst for Distant Lands Foreign Investment in Agricultural Land and Water. International Institute for Sustainable Development (IISD).

Smart Dubai. (2016, May). His highness Sheikh Mohammed Bin Rashid Al Maktoum adopts smart Dubai happiness agenda. www.smartdubai.ae/story060202.php.

Smith, N. (2003). Remaking Scale: Competition and Cooperation in Pre-National and Post-National Europe. In N. Brenner, B. Jessop, M. Jones, and G. MacLeod, eds., *State/Space: A Reader*. Marsden: Blackwell, pp. 227–238.

(2008). *Uneven Development: Nature, Capital, and the Production of Space*, 3rd edn. Athens, GA: University of Georgia Press.

Solomon, E. (2017, 5 June). The $1bn hostage deal that enraged Qatar's Gulf rivals. *Financial Times*. www.ft.com/content/dd033082-49e9-11e7-a3f4-c742b9791d43?mhq5j=e1.

Spiro, D. (1999). *The Hidden Hand of American Hegemony Petrodollar Recycling and International Markets*. Ithaca, NY: Cornell University Press.

Sri Lankan Bureau of Foreign Employment. (2015). Annual Statistical Report of Foreign Employment – 2015. www.slbfe.lk/page.php?LID=1&MID=213.

Staples, A. (2015). UAE's food security lies in Africa – Al Mansouri. *Gulf News*. http://gulfnews.com/business/economy/uae-s-food-security-lies-in-africa-al-mansouri-1.1621266.

State of Palestine (SOP). (2014, 23 February). *National Development Plan 2014–2016*.

Stetzel, D. (2015, 7 September). Egypt's sugar market eyes import tariff decision, price indications. *S&P Global Platts*. www.platts.com/latest-news/agriculture/london/egypts-sugar-market-eyes-import-tariff-decision-26201946.

Strategy&. (2015). GCC private banking study 2015: seizing the opportunities. www.strategyand.pwc.com/reports/gcc-private-banking-study-2015.

Sturm, M., Strasky, J., Adolf, P., and Peschel, D. (2008, July). The Gulf Cooperation Council Countries, Economic Structures, Recent Developments and Role in the Global Economy. European Central Bank, Occasional Paper Series, No. 92.

Subasat, T. (2016). *The Great Financial Meltdown Systemic, Conjunctural or Policy Created?* Cheltenham, UK: Edward Elgar.

Swyngedouw, E. (1997a). Excluding the Other: The Production of Scale and Scaled Politics. In R. Lee and J. Wills, eds., *Geographies of Economies.* London: Arnold, pp. 167–176.

(1997b). Neither Global nor Local: 'Glocalization' and the Politics of Scale. In K. Cox, ed., *Spaces of Globalization: Reasserting the Power of the Local.* New York, NY: Guilford Press, pp. 137–166.

(2004). Globalisation or 'glocalisation'? Networks, territories and rescaling. *Cambridge Review of International Affairs*, **17**(1), 25–48.

(2005). Governance innovation and the citizen: the Janus face of governance-beyond-the-state. *Urban Studies*, **42**(11), 1991–2006.

(2010). Rent and landed property. In B. Fine, A. Saad-Filho, and M. Boffo, eds., *The Elgar Companion to Marxist Economics.* London: Elgar, pp. 310–315.

Technical Education and Skills Development Authority (TESDA). (2017, 28 March). TESDA ready to assist displaced OFWS. Republic of the Philippines. https://tesdapampanga.wordpress.com/2017/03/28/tesda-ready-to-assist-displaced-ofws/.

Theodore, N., Peck, J., and Brenner, N. (2011). Neoliberal Urbanism: Cities and the Rule of Markets. In G. Bridge and S. Watson, eds., *The New Blackwell Companion to the City.* Marsden: Blackwell, pp. 15–25.

Theohary, Catherine A. (2015, 21 December). Conventional Arms Transfers to Developing Nations, 2007–2014. Congressional Research Service (CRS). https://fas.org/sgp/crs/weapons/R44320.pdf.

Thiollet, H. and Vignal, L. (2016). Transnationalising the Arabian Peninsula: local, regional and global dynamics. *Arabian Humanities* [Online]. http://cy.revues.org/3145.

Thompson, R. (2015). Al-Sisi's $200bn sales pitch. *Middle East Economic Digest*, **59**(11), 6–7.

Times of Israel (TOI). (2015, 5 June). In very rare public meet, Israeli, Saudi officials name Iran as common foe. www.timesofisrael.com/in-rare-meet-israeli-saudi-officials-name-iran-as-common-foe/.

(2016, 18 January). Israeli energy minister said to make secret visit to Abu Dhabi. www.timesofisrael.com/israeli-energy-minister-said-to-make-secret-visit-to-abu-dhabi/.

Tomich, D. (2016). *Slavery in the Circuit of Sugar: Martinique and the World-Economy, 1830–1848.* Albany, NY: State University of New York Press.

Tonkiss, F. (2014). *Cities by Design: The Social Life of Urban Form.* Hoboken, NJ: John Wiley & Sons.

Townsend, S. (2016, 9 April). The Gulf's sovereign dilemma. *Arabian Business.* www.arabianbusiness.com/the-gulf-s-sovereign-dilemma-627766.html#.V5HjBJP-yu4.

Turner, M. (2017, 29 August). Follow the money, uncover the power dynamics: understanding the political economy of violence. *Jadaliyya*. http://cities.jadaliyya.com/pages/index/27077/follow-the-money-uncover-the-power-dynamics_unders.

UAE Ministry of Foreign Affairs and International Cooperation (MOFAIC) (2016). United Arab Emirates Foreign Aid. December, Abu Dhabi.

Ulrichsen, K. C. (2014, September). *Qatar and the Arab Spring: Policy Drivers and Regional Implications*. Paper, Carnegie Endowment for International Peace. http://carnegieendowment.org/files/qatar_arab_spring.pdf.

(2016). *The Gulf States in International Political Economy*. Basingstoke: Palgrave Macmillan.

UNCTAD. (2016). *2016 World Investment Report*. Geneva: United Nations.

(2017). *2017 World Investment Report*. Geneva: United Nations.

United Nations Children's Fund (UNICEF). (2017, 26 July). Statement by UNICEF Executive Director, Anthony Lake, WFP Executive Director, David Beasley and WHO Director-General, Dr. Tedros Adhanom Ghebreyesus, following their joint visit to Yemen. www.unicef.org/media/media_98474.html.

United Nations High Commissioner for Refugees (UNHCR). (2015, 18 June). Worldwide displacement hits all-time high as war and persecution increase. www.unhcr.org/558193896.html.

United Nations Human Settlements Programme (UN-HABITAT). (2010). *State of African Cities 2010: Governance, Inequality and Urban Land Markets*. Nairobi: UN-Habitat.

(2011). *Tunisia Housing Profile*. Nairobi: UN-Habitat.

United Nations Office of the High Commissioner of Human Rights (UNHCHR). (2017, 5 September). Yemen: An 'entirely man-made catastrophe' – UN human rights report urges international investigation. Press release. Geneva. www.ohchr.org/.

United Nations (UN) Women. (2013, July). Gender-based violence and child protection among Syrian refugees in Jordan, with a focus on early marriage. Amman, Jordan. www.unwomen.org.

United States Agency for International Development (USAID). (2010, September). *Country Profile, Egypt, Property Rights and Resource Governance*. Washington, DC: USAID. http://usaidlandtenure.net/egypt.

United States Grain Council (USGC). (2015). USGC trade team builds Saudi Arabian confidence in U.S. corn. www.grains.org/news/success-stories/20150806/usgc-trade-team-builds-saudi-arabian-confidence-us-corn.

Valeri, M. (2009). *Oman: Politics and Society in the Qaboos State*. New York, NY: Oxford University Press.

(2015). The Ṣuḥār paradox: social and political mobilisations in the Sultanate of Oman since 2011. *Arabian Humanities*, **4**. http://journals.openedition.org/cy/2828.

Vignal, L. (2014). Dubai on Barada? The Making of 'Globalized Damascus' in Times of Urban Crisis. In S. Wippel, K. Bromber, C. Steiner, and B. Krawietz, eds., *Under Construction: Logics of Urbanism in the Gulf Region*. Farnham, UK: Ashgate, pp. 259–270.

(2016). *The Transnational Middle East: People, Places, Borders*. Abingdon, UK: Routledge.

Vitalis, R. (2007). *America's Kingdom: Mythmaking on the Saudi Oil Frontier*. Stanford, CA: Stanford University Press.

Walker, L. (2016, 20 April). As GCC tightens belt, Qatar shoppers spend $4,000 monthly on luxuries. *Doha News*. https://dohanews.co/as-gcc-tightens-belt-qatar-spends-4000-monthly-on-luxuries/.

Wealth-X. (2017). Billionaire Census 2017. www.wealthx.com.

Wiedmann, F. (2016). Real Estate Liberalization as Catalyst of Urban Transformation in the Persian Gulf. In M. Kamrava, ed., *Gateways to the World: Port Cities in the Persian Gulf*. London: Hurst.

Wikileaks. (2010). Saudi foreign agriculture investment plans: opportunities for increased trade, assistance, and US jobs. https://farmlandgrab.org/19160.

Windfuhr, M. and Jonsén, J. (2005). Food Sovereignty towards Democracy in Localized Food Systems. FIAN-International.

Wintour, P. (2017, 7 June). Russian hackers to blame for sparking Qatar crisis, FBI inquiry finds. *The Guardian*. www.theguardian.com/world/2017/jun/07/russian-hackers-qatar-crisis-fbi-inquiry-saudi-arabia-uae.

Woertz, E., Pradhan, S., Biberovic, N., and Jingzhon, C. (2008). *Potential for GCC Agri-Investments in Africa and Asia*. Dubai: Gulf Research Centre.

Wong, A. (2016, 31 May). The untold story behind Saudi Arabia's 41-Year U.S. debt secret. *Bloomberg*. www.bloomberg.com/news/features/2016-05-30/the-untold-story-behind-saudi-arabia-s-41-year-u-s-debt-secret.

World Aluminium. (n.d.). Primary aluminium production. International Aluminium Institute. www.world-aluminium.org/statistics/#data.

World Bank. (2002). *Jordan: Housing Finance and Urban Sector Reform Project*. Washington, DC: World Bank. http://documents.worldbank.org/curated/en/2002/10/2049156/jordan-housing-finance-urban-sector-reform-project.

(2003). *World Development Indicators*. Washington, DC: World Bank.

(2005). *MENA Region: The Macroeconomic and Sectoral Performance of Housing Supply Policies in Selected MENA Countries: A Comparative Analysis*. Washington, DC: World Bank.

(2008). *World Development Indicators*. Washington, DC: World Bank.

(2011). *Arab World Initiative for Financing Food Security Project*. Washington, DC: World Bank. http://documents.worldbank.org/curated/en/387951468299224201/Middle-East-and-North-Africa-Arab-World-Initiative-for-Financing-Food-Security-Project.

(2013, October). *Middle East and North Africa Regional Affordable Housing Project, Concept Note*. Washington, DC: World Bank Group. www.menatransitionfund.org/content/regional-affordable-housing-project-morocco-activities-wb-project-document.

(2015a, June). Tunisia Systematic Country Diagnostic (P151647).

(2015b). *Egypt, Arab Republic of: Mortgage Finance Project*. Washington, DC: World Bank Group. http://documents.worldbank.org/curated/en/2015/07/24746478/egypt-arab-republic-mortgage-finance-project.

(2016). *MENA Quarterly Economic Brief: The Economic Effects of War and Peace, January*. Washington, DC: World Bank.

(2017a, June). *Gulf Economic Monitor*, issue 1. Washington, DC: World Bank.
(2017b). *Migration and Remittances: Recent Developments and Outlook*. Migration and Development Brief, No. 27. Washington, DC: World Bank Group.
(2017c). *The Economics of Post-Conflict Reconstruction in MENA. MENA Economic Monitor, April*. Washington, DC: World Bank Group.
World Health Organization (WHO). (2016). Libya Humanitarian Response Plan 2016. www.who.int/hac/crises/lby/appeals/en/.
World Trade Organization (WTO). (2016, 7 April). Trade growth to remain subdued in 2016 as uncertainties weigh on global demand. Press release/ 768. www.wto.org/english/news_e/pres16_e/pr768_e.htm.
World Steel Association (WSA). (2016). *Steel Statistical Yearbook*. Brussels: WSA.
Zahlan, R. (1998). *The Making of the Modern Gulf States*. London: Ithaca Press.
Zain. (2016a). *Annual Report 2016*. www.zain.com/en/investor-relations/ financial-reports/.
(2016b, 24 February). Zain makes strategic investment in neXgen Group, forming a 'smart city' business unit. Press release. https://zain.com/en/press/ zain-makes-strategic-investment-in-nexgen-group-fo/.
Zhu, A. and Kotz, D. M. (2011). The dependence of China's economic growth on exports and investment. *Review of Radical Political Economics*, **43**(1), 9–32.
Ziadah, R. (2017). Constructing a logistics space: perspectives from the Gulf Cooperation Council. *Environment and Planning D: Society and Space* (forthcoming).

Index

Abboud, Samer, 268
Abdul Aziz bin Fahd, Prince, 229
Abdulkadir Al Muhaidib and Sons Group (Saudi), 85
Abdullah bin Abdulaziz al Saud, King, 260
Abdullah bin Ali Al Thani, Sheikh, 248
Abdullatif & Mohammad Al Fozan Co., 85
Abraaj Capital (UAE), 122, 142–143, 194
Abu Dhabi Commercial Bank, 197
Abu Dhabi Food Control Authority (ADFCA), 126
Abu Dhabi Fund for Development (ADFD), 165, 267
Abu Dhabi Investment Authority (ADIA), 38–39, 126
Abu Dhabi Investment Council, 38
Abu Dhabi Islamic Bank, 189, 197
Abu Dhabi National Energy Co., 223
Abu Dhabi National Oil Co. (ADNOC), 71, 212, 214
Abu Dhabi Securities Exchange, 100
Adeptio (Saudi), 140
Africa Middle East Resources (AMER), 86
Aggad Group (Saudi), 159–160
Aggad, Omar, 160
Aggad, Tarek, 159
Agility (Kuwait), 125, 182, 228, 264
agribusiness, Gulf, 26, 112–119, 124, 126–127, 129–130, 143, 145
  companies, 26, 112, 115, 128, 132–133, 144
agro-commodity circuits, 112–123, 129–130, 133, 140, 142, 144
Agthia Group (UAE), 126–127, 129
Ahli United Bank, 189
Airbus, 60
Al Abbar, Mohammed, 86, 140
Al Ahli Bank (Kuwait), 189
Al Alfi, Moataz, 141
Al Araimi, Salim Saeed Hamad Al Fannah, 85
Al Bahar Group (Kuwait), 103
Al Baraka Bank, 189
Al Baraka Banking Group (Bahrain), 63, 191
Al Baraka Banking Group (Saudi), 191
Al Busaidi dynasty (Oman), 22
Al Dahra (UAE), 124–127, 133, 139, 182
Al Falih, Khalid bin Abdulaziz, 211–212, 216
Al Fulaij Group (Kuwait), 103
Al Futtaim Group (UAE), 85, 110, 155
Al Ghafran clan (Qatar), 248
Al Ghanim Group (Kuwait), 71, 98
Al Ghosaibi Group (Saudi), 69
Al Ghurair Group (UAE), 64, 103, 110, 112, 126–127, 139
Al Habtoor Group (UAE), 216
Al Hashim, Safa, 227
Al Hilal Bank (UAE), 197
Al Hobayeb family (Saudi), 190
Al Homaizi family (Kuwait), 190
Al Homaizi, Suad, 190
Al Issa family (Saudi), 69
Al Jomaih family (Saudi), 88
Al Khabeer Capital (Saudi), 216
Al Khaleej Sugar, 126
Al Khalifa dynasty (Bahrain), 21–22, 246, 248
Al Kharafi Group (Kuwait), 64, 71, 88, 98, 103, 110, 112, 140, 142, 154
Al Maktoum family (UAE), 21
Al Marai Group (Saudi), 116, 123, 127–128, 138, 140, 143, 210, 219
Al Masira Investments, 190
Al Masri, Sabih, 158–159, 190
Al Muhaidib Group (Saudi), 103
Al Nahyan family (UAE), 21
Al Naimi, Ali, 211
Al Obaid, Abdullah, 120
Al Oula Real Estate Dev't Holding Co. (Saudi), 85
Al Rajhi Bank, 103, 189

Al Rajhi Group (Saudi), 64, 103, 110, 112, 116, 118, 122, 127, 139, 191, 203, 216
Al Rasheed, Madawi, 19
Al Sabah family (Kuwait), 21, 190
Al Safi (Saudi), 143
Al Sager Group (Kuwait), 103
Al Saghyir family (Saudi), 89
Al Saher, Kathem, 169
Al Saud dynasty (Saudi), 19–20, 86, 229
Al Shathry, Khaled, 69
Al Shaya Group (Kuwait), 64, 99, 110
Al Shirawi, Hesham, 121
Al Tayer Group (UAE), 98
Al Thani dynasty (Qatar), 20–21, 101, 110, 248
Al Thani, Jassim bin Mohammed, 20
Al Thani, Tamin bin Hamad, 20, 247
Al Waleed bin Talal, Prince, 47, 141, 229
Al Wathba Production and Distribution Complex, 127
ALBA (Bahrain), 72
Aldar Properties, 101
Algeria
  financial markets, 177–179, 187
  PWT projects, 162
  telecom business, 165, 168
Ali Reza Group (Saudi), 69, 86
Alibaba (China), 205
Alitalia (Italy), 47
Americana Group (Kuwait), 140–141
Amlak Finance (UAE), 85
Arab Monetary Fund, 184, 196
Arab Palestinian Investment Co., 143
Arab Radio and Television (ART), 63
Arab uprisings (2011-), 4, 22–23, 28, 162–164, 183, 240–242, 244, 247, 252, 255, 262
Arabi Group (Kuwait), 228
Arabian Industrial Fibers Co. (AIFC), 69
Arabtec Construction (UAE), 154
ARASCO (Saudi), 128
Arjomand Group (UAE), 85
Asia Global Technology (AGT) (Switzerland), 253
ASTRA Group (Saudi), 143, 158
Aujan Coca-Cola Beverages Co. (Saudi), 143

Babtain Group (Kuwait), 71
Bahrain Petroleum Co. (BAPCO), 71
Bahri Dry Bulk (BDB) (Saudi), 128
Bamatraf, Hatem, 171
Bank Dhofar (Oman), 197
Bank of International Settlements (BIS), 43, 46
Bank of Sharjah, 189
Bank Sohar (Oman), 197
banks, Gulf, 102–109, *See also* individual banks
Bar, Shmuel, 254
Barclays (UK), 1, 39, 47
Barwa Bank (Qatar), 197
Barwa Real Estate, 86
Baskin Robbins, 141
Bassens, D., 177
Batelco (Bahrain), 86, 89
Bayat, A., 146
Bechtel engineering (US), 160, 207, 221
Bernstein, Henry, 115
Beyti (Egypt), 138
Biekart, K., 146
bin Fahad, Rashid Mohammed, 118
Bin Laden family (Saudi), 86, 156
Bin Laden Group (Saudi), 219–220
Bin Laden, Bakr, 229
bin Saeed Al Mansouri, Sultan, 121
bin Suhaim Al Thani, Sultan, 248
Bisco Misr, 142
Bishara, Azmi, 249
Blackstone Group, 1
Blair, Tony, 211
Body Shop, The, 99
Bogaert, Konrad, 152
bonds, Gulf, 102, 175, 193, 195, 202, 218–220
Boston Consulting Group (BCG), 39, 207, 233
Boubyan Petrochemicals, 216
Brazil
  agribusiness, 123
  Foreign Direct Investment (FDI), 51
  imports, 52, 54
  mergers and acquisitions (M&A), 51
Brenner, N., 147
BRICS, 4, 49, 51
British Airways, 2, 47
Bsheer, Rosie, 7
built environment, 27, 32, 54, 66, 73–82, 85–86, 90, 111, 147–151, 154, 156–158, 170–171, 183, 198
Bunge, 123, 142
Burgan Bank, 189
Burger King, 139
Bush, Ray, 134

Camden Market, 2
Campaign Against the Arms Trade, 60
Canadian Wheat Board (CWB), 123
Canary Wharf, 2, 47
capital accumulation, Gulf, 7, 9, 12, 20, 24–28, 32, 54, 62, 64, 67, 70, 82, 103, 111–112, 135, 147–148, 161, 174, 201, 214, 230, 234–235, 248

Capital City Partners, 86
capitalism, 7–14, 33, 61, 101, 113, 142, 174, 185
Arab capitalism, 3, 190
Egyptian capitalism, 16, 198
global capitalism, 2, 4, 6, 16, 25, 30–32, 34, 43, 52, 61–62, 240
Gulf capitalism, 6, 25–28, 39, 52, 62, 69, 86, 109, 114, 118, 145, 147, 170, 172–173, 200, 228, 240, 245
neoliberal capitalism, 8–9, 31
Carrefour franchise, 99, 142–143, 155
CEPSA (Spain), 47
Chaaban, Jad, 191
Challenger fund, 39
Cheesecake Factory, The, 99
China, 2, 29–30, 36–37, 41–42, 54, 56, 61, 199
exports, 54
financial surpluses, 35, 51, 61
Foreign Direct Investment (FDI), 29, 51
imports, 29–30, 52, 59
mergers and acquisitions (M&A), 51
Chinese and Japanese (C&J) holdings, 42
Citigroup, 47
City of London, 34, 43–47
class formation, Gulf, 7, 11, 15, 32, 52, 54, 64, 70, 76, 81, 89, 109, 111, 143, 172, 174, 177, 236
Clean Energy Strategy (UAE), 217
Colgate-Palmolive, 98
colonialism, 5, 16, 19
British colonialism, 5, 19, 21, 102
French colonialism, 17, 102
commercial services, Gulf, 55–58, 215
conflicts within Gulf, 246–251
and Qatar, 246–251
construction business, 54, 58, 62, 70, 151, 156, 160, 220–221, 223, 229
construction companies, 65, 77, 81–82, 155, 161, 172, 221
construction projects, 46, 73, 77, 81, 85
infrastructure construction, 46, 73
Costa Coffee, 141
Council for Economic and Development Affairs (CEDA) (Saudi), 203, 210
Credit Suisse, 1, 47
cross-border capital flow, 2–3, 10, 21, 25, 31, 33, 36, 48–49, 51, 89, 150

Dae-oup Chang, 29
Daimler, 47
Dallah Al Baraka Group (Saudi), 63, 70, 86, 103
DAMAC Properties (UAE), 154, 219
Danah Al-Safat (Kuwait), 143
Danone, 142–143
Dardari, Abdullah, 237
Deauville Partnership, 255
Debenhams, 99
Deloitte, 207
Depression (1929-32), 36
Deutsche Bank, 1, 47
Disney-Jawa Enterprises, 86
Dos Santos, P., 175
Dow Chemicals (US), 68, 71
du telecom (UAE), 86–88, 110
Dubai Aluminium (Dubal), 72
Dubai Financial Market (DFM), 85, 100
Dubai Healthcare City, 216
Dubai Hills Estate, 82
Dubai Holding Commercial Operations Group, 88
Dubai International Capital, 47
Dubai World, 47

Eagle Hills, 86
Economic Zones World (UAE), 121
Egypt, 134–143, 156–158
Abdul Fattah Sisi, 139, 249, 260
Agrarian Reform Law, 134
agribusiness, 136, 139–140, 142
agro-commodities, 135
Al Burouj, 152
Anwar Sadat, 134
BNP-Paribas, 189
Cairo Amman Bank (CAB), 190
Cairo Poultry Co. (CPC), 140
Central Bank of Egypt (CBE), 249, 260
conflicts, 239, 241, 249, 262
construction projects, 151, 154
Dream Farms, 152
Egyptian Canning Co. (ECC), 140
Egyptian Mortgage Refinance Co. (EMRC), 184
Egyptian Starch and Glucose Co. (ESGC), 135, 140–141
exports, 130–131, 140–141
Farm Frites Egypt, 141
financial markets, 177, 179–180, 183, 185, 187, 189, 192, 261
Future Generation Foundation (FGF), 141
Gamal Mubarak, 141
Gen. Abdul Fattah Sisi, 261
Golden Pyramids Plaza Co., 157
Hosni Mubarak, 134–135, 139, 141, 155–156, 164, 171, 241, 249, 256, 259–260, 262
Hussain Al Sajwani, 155
imports, 133

Egypt (cont.)
  Law 96, 134
  Marissi, 152
  Mivida, 152
  Mohammed Morsi, 249, 260–261
  National Democratic Party, 141
  National Société Générale Bank (NSGB), 189
  Nile River Bus, 164
  Orascom Construction (OC), 161
  Piraeus Bank, 189
  privatisation, 141, 164
  Public-Private Partnerships (PPPs), 164
  PWT projects, 162, 165
  QNB-AlAhli, 192
  Rashidi El-Mizan, 139
  real estate companies, 157
  retail business, 142
  Rooya Group, 156
  Sheikh Yusuf al-Qaradawi, 249
  Sixth of October Development and Investment Co. (SODIC), 156
  support from Gulf, 260
  Talaat Moustafa family, 156
  Talaat Mustafa Group (TMG), 156
  telecom business, 165, 168
  The Arab Contractors, 161
  Toshka project, 139
  Uptown Cairo, 152
  Zuheir Garranah, 155
Emaar (UAE), 82–86, 101, 154
Emaar Malls, 85
Emaar Middle East, 85
Emaar the Economic City (EEC), 85–86
Emirates Airline, 246
Emirates Aluminium (Emal), 72
Emirates Global Aluminium, 72, 214
Emirates International Telecommunications (EITC), 88
Emirates-NBD, 189
employment/unemployment, 209, 220, 222–225, 229
  women, 224
  youth, 225
Emrill Services (UAE), 85
Equate Petrochemical Co. (Kuwait), 71
Eships, 125
Eshki, Anwar, 253
Estée Lauder, 99
Etihad Airways (UAE), 47, 246
Etihad Rail (UAE), 223
Etisalat (UAE), 86–89, 101, 165–171, 219
Etisalat Misr (UAE), 171
Eurobonds (Oman), 218
Euromarkets, 33–34, 43–44
European Bank for Reconstruction and Development (EBRD), 163, 256–259, 265
European Union (EU), 52, 56, 164, 262
  exports, 54
  Foreign Direct Inverstment (FDI), 48
  imports, 52
  mergers and acquisitions (M&A), 49

Fahd, King, 63
Falcon Eye (UAE), 253
financial crisis (2008-09), global, 36–38, 42, 45, 47, 52, 100, 109, 182, 199–200, 233, 235
financial markets, global, 31, 42, 205, 219
financial markets, Gulf, 61, 64, 66, 85, 100–109, 174–177, 180, 182, 186, 188–189, 192, 195–196, 218–220
financial surpluses, Gulf, 1, 7, 25, 31–33, 35–43, 45–46, 49, 52, 58, 61–62, 67, 82, 100, 153, 207
financial system, global, 42–43, 46, 51, 61, 176
financialisation, 27, 36, 61, 174–186, 194–198, 219
  definition of, 174
  indicators of, 178, 181
  of the non-financial, 175, 181–182, 214, 219
First Abu Dhabi Bank, 197
First Gulf Bank (UAE), 197
fiscal measures, new, 225–228
FlyDubai, 246
food exports, Gulf, 133
food imports, Gulf, 130–133
food security, 27, 115–123, 125–130, 139, 144
Foot Locker, 99
Foreign Direct Investment (FDI), 3, 29, 32, 47–52, 111, 120, 159, 186, 260
French, S., 176
Friedmann, Harriet, 115
Fuccaro, Nelida, 5
Fujairah Strategic Grain Terminal, 127

G3 Global Grain Group, 123
Galfar Engineering & Contracting Co. (Oman), 85
Genero Capital (UAE), 160
Ghadeer, 143
Ghandour, Fadi, 194
Ghurair family (UAE), 86, 126
Glencore, 2, 47
global financial system, 34
Global Pension Fund (Norway), 38
Godiva chocolatier, 63

Grain Silos Organisation (GSO) (Saudi), 129
Great Recession. *See* financial crisis (2008-09), global
Green Valley Group Real Estate (UAE), 155
greenfield investments, 48–49
Gulf Air, 246
Gulf Finance House (Bahrain), 197, 216

H&M, 99
Halwani Brothers (Saudi), 139
Hamad bin Jassim Al Thani, Sheikh, 39
Hamas, 247, 249
Hamed bin Zayed Al Nahyan, Sheikh, 125
Hardees, 141
Harrods, 2
Hart, Gillian, 17
Harvey Nichols, 99
Harvey, David, 147, 172
Hassad Foods (Qatar), 120
Henderson, Christian, 141
Hezbollah, 243, 245
Hokair Group (Saudi), 99, 154
humanitarian issues, 239–240, 263–266
Humpty Dumpty (Abu Dhabi), 109
hydrocarbon industry. *See* oil and gas industry

Ibn Saud, 19–20, 202
  Hussa Sudairi, 20
  Sudairi Seven, 20
Independent Water and Power Projects (IWPPs), 215
India
  exports, 55
  imports, 52, 54, 59
  mergers and acquisitions (M&A), 51
  remittances, 222, 235
Industrial Property Authority (MODON) (Saudi), 211
Internally Displaced Persons (IDPs), 238–239
International Bank of Qatar (IBQ), 197
international banking system, 31, 34, 43, 46, 51
international financial institutions (IFIs), 240, 255–260, 262, 268
International Humanitarian City (IHC) (UAE), 264
International Labour Organization (ILO), 81
International Monetary Fund (IMF), 37–38, 177, 200, 208, 220, 255–256, 260–261
International Renewable Energy Agency (IRENA) (UAE), 217, 252
internationalisation
  of agribusiness, 115–119, 123, 129, 133
  of agro-firms, 26
  of capital, 10, 26, 46, 61–62, 109–112, 120, 127, 129, 133–140, 142–143, 147–148, 153–156, 159, 165, 171, 186–193, 195, 234
  of construction business, 81
  of production, 34, 36, 126
  of real estate business, 157
  of telecom business, 89
Internet of Things (IoT), 170–171
Investcorp Bank (Bahrain), 160
Iran, 244, 247
  conflicts, 59, 238, 240, 243, 247, 252
  exports, 29
  Iraq-Iran War, 243
Iraq, 143, 238, 243
  Asiacell, 169
  conflicts, 238–239, 244, 247
  exports, 29
  financial markets, 187–188
  imports, 133
  invasion of, 247
  Iraq-Iran War, 243
  Korek Telecom, 182
  Prime Minister Haider al Abadi, 247
  reconstruction of, 266–267
  telecom business, 165–169
Islamic finance (IF), 219
Islamic Development Bank (Saudi), 165, 265, 267
Islamic finance (IF), 177, 188, 195–198
  banks, 197, 219
  bonds (*sukuk*), 195, 202, 218–219
  Islamic bonds (*sukuk*), 219
  Islamic debt issuance, 219
  Islamic Financial Services Board, 188, 195, *See also* individual banks
Israel, 192, 233, 240–241, 246, 251–255
  and Bahrain, 254
  Dore Gold, 253
  and Egypt, 253
  Elbit Systems, 254
  Intuview, 254
  Iron Dome, 254
  Logic Industries, 253
  Prime Minister Benyamin Netanyahu, 254
  and Saudi Arabia, 253
  and UAE, 252–253
  Yaakov Amidor, 237

Japan, 37, 41–42, 52
  financial surpluses, 35, 51, 61
  imports, 52, 54
  mergers and acquisitions (M&A), 49
Jawa, Ahmed Bin Jamal Bin Hassan, 86
Jebel Ali Free Zone, 127

Jebel Ali Port, 3, 161, 264
Jenaan Investment Co. (UAE), 126–127
Jones,Toby, 60, 115, 119
Jordan, 151–152, 262, 264–265
  Abdali Project, 152
  agribusiness, 143
  Amman Development Corridor, 165
  Amman Stock Exchange, 184
  Arab Bank, 190
  Arab Potash Co., 182
  Aramex, 194
  Central Bank of Jordan, 183
  conflicts, 239
  construction projects, 151, 154
  exports, 130–131
  financial markets, 177, 179–180, 184, 187–188, 190
  Housing and Urban Development (HUDC), 151
  Housing Bank for Trade and Finance (HBTF), 192, 198
  imports, 131, 133, 141
  Jordan Islamic Bank (JIB), 191
  Marsa Zayed Project, 152
  Mortgage Refinance Co. (JMRC), 184
  privatisation, 167
  Public-Private Partnerships (PPPs), 164
  PWT projects, 162, 164
  real estate companies, 157
  Saraya Aqaba, 154
  telecom business, 165–169
JP Morgan Chase (US), 211, 219
  International Council, 211

Kamel, Saleh Abdullah, 63–64, 70, 191, 229
  Al-Suq (The Market), 63
Kanna, Ahmed, 6, 209
Kellogg's, 142
KFC, 141
Khalifah bin Hamad Al Thani, Sheikh, 248
Khalili, Laleh, 162
King Abdullah Economic City, 85
King Abdullah Initiative for Saudi Agricultural Investment Abroad (KAISAIA), 120–121
King Salman Energy Initiative (Saudi), 216
Kingdom Group (Saudi), 139, 141, 154, 216
Kissinger, Henry, 211
Kochavi, Mati, 253
Kollsman Inc. (US), 254
Kosik, Karel, 16–17, 64
Kuwait Finance House, 216
Kuwait Fund for Arab Economic Development (KFAED), 165, 267
Kuwait Health Assurance Co. (KHAC), 228
Kuwait Investment Authority, 38, 47
Kuwait Oil Co. (KOC), 68
Kuwait Projects Co. (KIPCO), 228
Kuwait Projects Holding Co., 219

land grab, 26, 119–123
Lapavitsas, C., 175
Lebanon
  agribusiness, 143
  Audi family, 190
  Bank Audi, 189–193
  Bankmed, 190
  Central Bank of Lebanon, 192
  conflicts, 158, 239, 244
  construction projects, 151, 154
  Credit Libanais, 198
  Eurobonds, 193
  exports, 130–131
  Fahd Hariri, 190
  financial markets, 177, 179–180, 184, 188, 191
  FRH Investment Holding, 190
  Hariri family, 160, 190, 192, 229, 245
  imports, 133
  Lebanese Civil War, 243
  Marwan Ghandour, 192
  Prime Minister Sa'ad Hariri, 190, 229, 245
  privatisation, 168
  PWT projects, 162, 165
  Rafic Hariri, 160, 228
  Raymond Audi, 192
  real estate business, 160
  Saradar Group, 190
  Solidere, 152, 160
  telecom business, 168
Lefebvre, Henri, 12, 15
Libya, 246
  conflicts, 236, 239, 242
  financial markets, 178–179, 187
  PWT projects, 162
  reconstruction of, 237, 266–267
  telecom business, 168
London Stock Exchange, 2, 47
London Stock Exchange Group, 47
Lootah Group (UAE), 85
Loulis Mills (Greece), 125
Lulu Group International (UAE), 99
Lulu Hypermarkets, 99, 142

MA Kharafi & Sons (Kuwait), 193
Ma'aden Aluminium (Saudi), 72
Mabanee Development Co. (Kuwait), 99

Madinah Airport, 202–204
Majid Al Futtaim Group (UAE), 98–99, 142–143, 154, 219
Makhlouf, Mouayed, 265
manufacturing activities, 65, 71, *See also* petrochemical industry
  aluminium production, 65, 71–73
  cement production, 72–73
  steel production, 72–73
Marshall, S., 142
Marston, S.A., 13
Marx, Karl, 9, 198, 201
Masayoshi Son, 1
Mashreq Bank (UAE), 103
Masraf Al Rayan (Qatar), 197
Mass Food Group, 142
McKinsey & Co., 2, 206, 208
McKinsey Global Institute, 33, 38
McLaren Group, 47
McMichael, Philip, 114
McNally, David, 4
Mecca Metro (Saudi), 204
MENA Transition Fund, 184
mergers and acquisitions (M&A), 2–3, 49–52, 111, 186, 197, 216
Mezzadra, Sandro, 23
migrant labour, 23–24, 27, 81, 201, 221–224, 235, 265
  deportation of, 221–223, 229, 235
  remittances, 222, 235
military hardware, importation of, 32, 58–61
millionaire households, 39, 234
Minister of State for Happiness (UAE), 87
Ministry of Economy and Planning (MEP) (Saudi), 207
Ministry of Energy, Industry and Mineral Resources (MEIMR) (Saudi), 211
Mirow, Thomas, 259
Mitchell, Timothy, 33, 58, 118
Mobily (Saudi), 86, 88
Mohammed bin Abdulaziz, Prince, 202
Mohammed bin Nayef, Crown Prince, 203
Mohammed Bin Rashid Al Maktoum, Sheikh, 85, 87–88, 161, 167
Mohammed bin Salman al-Saud (MBS), Crown Prince, 1, 203, 205, 210–211, 229, 234, 243
Mohammed Bin Saud Al Kabeer Al Saud, Sultan, 127
Mohammed bin Zayed bin Sultan Al Nahyan, Crown Prince, 243
Mohammed Hussein Al Amoudi, Sheikh, 122
Morocco, 130, 143, 170
  CIH Bank, 196
  construction projects, 151, 154
  exports, 130–131
  financial markets, 177, 179–180, 184, 186–187
  Green Valley Project, 155
  Maroc Telecom, 167, 169
  privatisation, 164, 167
  Public-Private Partnerships (PPPs), 154, 164
  PWT projects, 162
  real estate companies, 157
  telecom business, 165–170
Mossack Fonseca law firm, 40
Mothercare, 99
Motorola, 160
Mumtalakat, 48
Muslim Brotherhood (MB), 247–249

National Bank of Abu Dhabi, 197
National Bank of Kuwait (NBK), 103, 189
National Bank of Ras Al-Khaimah (UAE), 223
National Commercial Bank (Saudi), 189, 216
National Project Management Organization (NPMO) (Saudi), 207, 221
National Transformation Program (NTP) 2020 (Saudi), 204, 206–207, 212, 223
neoliberalism, 9–10, 111–112, 134, 146, 149–151, 163, 171, 175, 209, 240, 251, 263, 265
  neoliberal globalisation, 11, 35, 46, 62
  urban effect, 27, 146–150, 153–154
Nestle, 142–143
neXgen advisory firm, 170
Nixon Administration (US), 34
Norfield, Tony, 43–45
North America, 52, 56
  financial markets, 186
  Foreign Direct Investment (FDI), 48
  imports, 52
  mergers and acquisitions (M&A), 49

offshore financial centres, 21, 34, 39–43, 46, 50, 103, 178, 234
  Cayman Islands, 34, 41–42, 60
oil and gas industry, 22, 65, 68, 72, 159
  exports, 3, 29–30, 41, 43, 67, 71
  reserves, 2, 21–22
  resources, 68, 199
  revenues, 22, 30, 36, 118, 189, 199–201, 262
Ojjeh, Mansour, 48

Olayan Group (Saudi), 47, 98, 103, 110, 129, 139, 154
Oldendorff Group (Germany), 125
Oliver Wyman & Co., 207
Ollman, Bertell, 15
Oman Oil Co. (OOC), 71
Omatel (Oman), 86
Ooredoo (Qatar), 86, 89, 166–171, 219
Ooredoo Oman, 86
Orange (France), 167, 169
Otaiba, Yusef, 247

P&O, 2, 47
Palestine, 158–160
  Abdali Project, 160
  Al Shawa family, 193
  Amar Real Estate, 158
  Bank of Palestine, 193, 198
  Bashar al Masri, 159, 184
  capital accumulation, 254
  conflicts, 158
  Consolidated Contractors Co. (CCC), 160
  EDGO, 159
  financial markets, 188
  Khoury family, 184, 190
  Masri family, 158, 160, 168, 184, 190
  Massar International, 158–159
  Mohammed Mustafa, 159
  Munib Masri, 158
  Palestine Development and Investment Corp. (PADICO), 158, 167, 190
  Palestine Investment Fund (PIF), 159–160
  Palestine Liberation Organisation (PLO), 252
  Palestine Mortgage & Housing Corp. (PMHC), 184
  Palestine Mortgage and Housing Corp. (PMHC), 158
  Palestine Real Estate and Investment Co. (PRICO), 158, 190
  Palestinian Authority, 158
  PALTEL, 190
  privatisation, 167
  Rawabi City, 152, 159
  real estate companies, 157–158
  refugees, 254
  Samer Khoury, 160
  Sovereign Wealth Fund, 159
  telecom business, 165–169, 190
  Wataniya (National), 169
Palloix, Christian, 10
Panama Papers, 40
Panda Retail Co., 99, 142
Peck, Jamie, 14
Pepsi-Cola, 138, 143
Petrochemical Industries Co. (Kuwait), 71
petrochemical industry, 30, 68, 70, 72
  companies, 68, 70–71, 88, 110
  exports, 30, 68
  manufacturing, 68, 70–71, 73
petrodollar recycling, 34, 58, 60, 102
Pizza Hut, 141
power, water and transport (PWT), 27, 148, 162–164
  infrastructure, 165, 171
  projects, 162, 164
PricewaterhouseCoopers LLP, 207
Prince Mohammed bin Abdulaziz International Airport. *See* Madinah Airport
private equity (PE) business, 1, 38, 101–103, 109, 122, 138, 140, 160, 193–194
privatisation, 9, 129, 164–165, 178, 213–214, 217, 220, 223, 256
  of agro-food sector, 128–129, 134–135
  of banks, 184, 188, 261
  of education, 215–216
  Egypt, 164, 262
  Jordan, 167, 265
  Kuwait, 212
  of land, 149, 151, 155
  of medical services, 216, 227
  Morocco, 164, 167
  Oman, 212
  Palestine, 167
  of PWT, 163–164, 171, 211, 227
  Saudi Arabia, 202–206, 212
  of telecom, 165
  Tunisia, 167
Public Institution for Social Security (Kuwait), 103
Public Investment Fund (PIF) (Saudi), 38, 69, 140, 159, 206, 212
Public-Private Partnerships (PPPs), 163–164, 203–205, 214–218, 220, 223, 227, 259, 261, 266
  Jordan, 265
  legislation, 215, 256
  Morocco, 154
  Oman, 212

Qaboos, Sultan, 22
QATALUM, 72
Qatar Air, 47
Qatar International Islamic Bank (QIIB), 195
Qatar Investment Authority, 38–39, 47

Qatar National Bank (QNB), 189, 192, 197–198
Qatar National Food Security Programme (QFNSP), 120
Qatar Petroleum, 71, 223
Qatar Rail, 223
Qatar Stock Exchange (QSE), 101
Qatari Diar, 82, 86, 154, 159

Ramos, Stephan, 161
real estate business, 27, 150, 156
  companies, 82, 85, 88, 148, 156–157, 170
  development, 65, 77, 81–86, 99, 110, 152–156
refugees, 77, 238, 263–266, *See also* Internally Displaced Persons (IDPs)
Rentier State, 67
retail business, 66, 70, 89–100
  companies, 91
Rice, Condoleezza, 211
RSH retail, 86
Rum Agricultural Co., 143
Russia
  exports, 59
  imports, 52, 54
  mergers and acquisitions (M&A), 51

Sainsbury's, 2
Salam Bank (Bahrain), 86
Saline Water Conversion Corp. (Saudi), 205
Salman bin Abdulaziz Al Saud, King, 202, 210, 229, 243
Salman's Royal Decrees, 211
Saudi Agriculture and Livestock Company (SALIC), 120, 122
Saudi Arabia Monetary Authority, 38
Saudi Aramco, 68, 205–206, 211–212, 254
Saudi Basic Industries Corp. (SABIC), 68–71
Saudi British Bank, 103, 160
Saudi Electricity Co., 205, 211
Saudi Fund for Development (SFD), 165, 267
Saudi Grains Organisation (SGO), 205
Saudi Industrial Development Fund (SIDF), 211
Saudi Landbridge, 204
Saudi Oger, 160, 203, 220, 228–229
Saudi Postal Authority, 205
Saudi Railway, 204
Saudi Star conglomerate, 122
Saudi Telecom, 86, 89
Saudi-UAE axis, 24, 81, 117, 233, 236, 240, 243, 247–248, 251–252, 254
Savola Group (Saudi), 99, 112, 116, 127, 138, 140, 142
Sayer, Derek, 15
Schmid, C., 147
Sharbatly, Abdulrahman, 157
Shard, the, 2
Shi'a Muslims, 22, 243–244
SHUAA Capital, 197
Siemens, 160
Siniora Food Industries, 116
SIPRI Arms and Military Expenditure Programme, 59
Smart City concept, 87, 89, 170, 253
Smart City concept (Dubai), 87–88
  Dubai Design District, 88
  Higher Committee for Smart Cities, 87
  Smart Dubai Platform, 87
SoftBank Vision Fund (SVF), 1–2, 170
Sohar Aluminium Co. (Oman), 72
Sovereign Wealth Funds (SWFs), 31–32, 38–40, 47, 82, 110, 140, 206
Stacher, J., 142
Starbucks, 99
Starling Group, 86
Sultan Qaboos Medical City (Oman), 216
Sunni Muslims, 22, 243
Supporting Syria & the Region Conference (2016), 264
SWF Institute, 38
Syria, 238, 268
  Bashar Al Assad, 243, 245, 268
  conflicts, 4, 131, 236, 239, 242, 244
  exports, 130
  financial markets, 178–179, 187–188
  PWT projects, 162
  reconstruction of, 237, 266–267
  refugees, 263–266
  telecom business, 165

Taanayel Les Fermes, 143
Tadawul (Saudi), 100
Taliban, 249
TAV (Turkey), 202
Tecom, 88, 110
Teeba, 143
telecom business, 7, 65, 86–89, 110, 165–171
  companies, 86–89, 149, 166
  infrastructure, 165, 171
  networks, 148, 162, 171–172
  privatisation of, 167
TGI Friday's, 141
Tomich, Dale, 16–17, 64
Tradewinds Corp., 86

transportation business, 56, 58, 62
infrastructure, 62, 150, 204, 220
Travelodge Hotels, 47
Tristar (UAE), 125
Trucial States, 5
Tunisia, 130, 143, 151, 249–251
and Qatar, 250
and Saudi Arabia, 250
Ben Ali, 241–242, 249, 256
conflicts, 239, 249
construction projects, 151, 154
Ennahda party, 249–250
exports, 130–131
financial markets, 177, 179–180, 183–184, 187–188
Leila Trabelsi, 242
Mohamed Sakher El Materi, 242, 250
Moncef Marzouki, 250
National Housing and Savings Fund (CNEL), 151
Nidaa Tounes party, 250
Pres. Beji Caid Essebi, 144
privatisation, 167
Public-Private Partnerships (PPPs), 164
PWT projects, 162
real estate companies, 157
Salem Abd El Jalil, 250
telecom business, 165–169
Tunis Financial Harbour, 152
Tunisia Economic City, 250
Tunisian Central Bank, 250, 262
Tunisie Telecom, 88, 167, 169
Turki al Faisal, Prince, 253
Turner, Mandy, 268
Twitter, 2, 47

Ulrichsen, Kristian Coates, 39
Ultra-High Net Worth (UHNW) individuals, 233
Unilever, 98
Union National Bank (UAE), 197
United Kingdom (UK), 42, 60, *See also* City of London
banks, 31, 43–44, 46
David Cameron, 265
exports, 59–60
financial markets, 35, 41, 43, 46
mergers and acquisitions (M&A), 2
United Nations High Commissioner for Refugees (UNHCR), 264
United States (US), 8, 34, 46, 51, 61, 240–241, 247, 252
balance of payments, 51
banks, 34, 36, 43
Barack Obama, 244
debt, 31, 34, 40, 51
exports, 54, 59–60
financial markets, 35, 46
Foundation for the Defense of Democracies (FDD), 247
military, 162
Pres. Donald Trump, 244, 247, 251–252
Rex Tillerson, 251
Robert. Gates, 247
Treasury International Capital (TIC), 40, 42
Treasury securities, 34, 36, 40, 42, 47
US Shale Gas, 71
USAID, 184

Valeri, Marc, 22
Vision 2030 (Saudi), 203–204, 206–208, 216, 223, 227
Viva Bahrain, 86
Vivendi (France), 167
Vodafone Qatar, 86, 89
Volkswagen, 2, 47

Wahhabism, 19–20, 243, 250
Wataniya Telecom (Kuwait), 86
Weberian assumptions, 15, 67
Wessal Capital, 154
World Bank, 35, 129, 145, 151–152, 164–165, 168, 184, 196, 200, 208, 255, 262, 265–266
International Finance Corp., 265

Yemen, 145, 238, 244
Abd Rabbuh Mansour Hadi, 244, 246
Ali Abdullah Saleh, 242, 244
Ansar Allah, 244
conflicts, 4, 59, 230, 236, 239, 242, 244, 246
exports, 130–131
financial markets, 187
Houthis, 244, 246
imports, 131, 133
reconstruction of, 237, 266–267

Zain (Kuwait), 86, 88–89, 168, 170–171
Ziadah, Rafeef, 263